Criminal Inves
Law and Practice,
Second Edition

MW00489774

Criminal Investigation

Law and Practice, Second Edition

Michael F. Brown

Butterworth–Heinemann

Boston   Oxford   Johannesburg   Melbourne   New Delhi   Singapore

Copyright © 2001 by Butterworth–Heinemann
℞ A member of the Reed Elsevier group
All rights reserved.

No part of this publication may be reproduced, stored in a retrieval
system, or transmitted in any form or by any means, electronic,
mechanical, photocopying, recording, or otherwise, without the prior
written permission of the publisher.

 Recognizing the importance of preserving what has been written,
Butterworth–Heinemann prints its books on acid-free paper whenever
possible.

Butterworth–Heinemann supports the efforts of American
Forests and the Global ReLeaf program in its campaign for
the betterment of trees, forests, and our environment.

Library of Congress Cataloging-in-Publication Data

Brown, Michael F., 1949–
    Criminal investigation : law and practice / Michael F. Brown.—2nd ed.
      p. cm.
    Includes bibliographical references and index.
    ISBN 0-7506-7352-4 (alk. Paper)
    1. Criminal investigation—Handbooks, manuals, etc.   I. Title

  HV8073.B688   2001
  363.25—dc21   00-051933

British Library Cataloguing-in-Publication Data
A catalogue record for this book is available from the British Library.

The publisher offers special discounts on bulk orders of this book.
For information, please contact:

Manager of Special Sales
Butterworth–Heinemann
225 Wildwood Avenue
Woburn, MA 01801–2041
Tel: 781-904-2500
Fax: 781-904-2620

For information on all Butterworth–Heinemann publications available,
contact our World Wide Web home page at: http://www.bh.com

10 9 8 7 6 5 4 3 2 1

Printed in the United States of America

Contents

Preface

Crime is a major concern for many people. Indeed, for some it is *the* major concern in their lives. Every day people are forced to change how they live because they were a victim of a crime or are fearful of becoming a victim. Police administrators, academicians, politicians, and private citizens are seeking ways to make life safer and, therefore, more enjoyable. One means to make life safer is to remove criminal offenders from the streets and place them in confinement for some period of time. That is one of the major roles of criminal investigators. These individuals use a wide variety of techniques to identify, arrest, and subsequently assist in the prosecution of offenders and thus to make the streets safer.

Criminal Investigation: Law and Practice, Second Edition, has been written to provide future law enforcement officers with a basic understanding of the investigative process. It merges two areas that are crucial to the successful completion of an investigation: the law, both criminal and procedural, and criminal investigative techniques. Rarely do practicing investigators have an attorney available for consultation at every key point in an investigation. It is therefore incumbent on the investigator to have a working knowledge of both the law and the techniques of criminal investigation. A number of years ago, an experienced homicide detective advised me to weigh every action taken in an investigation against how it would appear in court before a judge and jury. *Criminal Investigation* is designed to keep the student mindful of the importance of both the criminal and procedural law and the investigative technique. It is also written to provide the student investigator with the information needed to complete an investigation that can result in a successful prosecution.

The book is divided into fourteen chapters. The first eight chapters are configured in order to help the student investigator walk through the steps of a fairly complex investigation. The remaining six chapters provide specific information on the investigation of particular types of crimes, such as assaults, homicides, sex offenses, and drugs.

Criminal justice, law enforcement, and criminal investigation are dynamic areas. New knowledge is being developed in both the behavioral and natural sciences every day. This information increases the possibility of successful identification and prosecution of those who commit crime. It is hoped that *Criminal Investigation* will provide future investigators with the knowledge and insight that will allow them to become competent professionals in this very demanding field.

Acknowledgments

Many friends and colleagues have played a role in the completion of *Criminal Investigation: Law And Practice*. There are several whom I would like to acknowledge for their help and support. Mr. H. Morley Swingle, Cape Girardeau County Prosecuting Attorney, provided the examples used to illustrate key points and offered insights into how the police and prosecutors can work to achieve successful prosecutions. Dr. Paul Keys, Dean of the College of Health and Human Services at Southeast Missouri State, provided encouragement to make the time needed to complete the book. Numerous police officers and investigators provided insights into the subtleties of the investigative process, including Jim Lummus and Mike Braun. I want to thank Mr. Tom Beardslee for his advice on the intelligence section in Chapter 3 and Jennifer Packard, Assistant Editor, of Butterworth–Heinemann for her help and advice. I would also like to thank Jennifer Plumley, Production Editor of Butterworth–Heinemann for her meticulous review of this edition. Finally, I wish to thank my wife, Kathleen, who, even after 28 years, continues o encourage me to undertake new challenges.

Michael F. Brown, Ph.D.

1. Introduction to Criminal Investigation

"We must not judge the means," said Dupin, "by this shell of an examination. The . . . police so much extolled for acumen, are cunning, but no more. There is no method in their proceedings, beyond the method of the moment."

C. August Dupin, *The Murders in the Rue Morgue*, Edgar Allan Poe

No area of law enforcement is more misunderstood and shrouded in myth than criminal investigation. It has only been within the last 25 or 30 years that law enforcement administrators and academics have begun to question the conventional wisdom associated with criminal investigations.

In 1975, the Rand Corporation published *The Criminal Investigation Process* (Greenwood and Petersilia, 1975). In this study, researchers questioned the value of follow-up investigations. While the study was criticized for methodological errors, it did bring a number of common investigative practices under scrutiny. Some of the more widely discussed conclusions in the Rand study were as follows:

How cases were solved: The single most important determinant of whether or not the case will be solved is the information the victim supplies to the officer who responds immediately. If information that uniquely identifies the perpetrator is not presented at the time the crime is reported, the perpetrator, by and large, will not be subsequently identified.

Investigative effectiveness: Differences in investigative training, staffing, work loads, and procedures appear to have no appreciable effect on crime, arrest, or clearance rates.

Collecting physical evidence: Most police departments collect more physical evidence than can be productively processed. Our analysis shows that allocating more resources to increase the processing capabilities of the department can lead to more identifications than other investigative actions.

Investigative thoroughness: In relatively few departments, investigators consistently and thoroughly document the key evidentiary facts that reasonably ensure the prosecutor can obtain a conviction of the most serious applicable charges.

In *Solving Crimes: The Investigation of Burglary and Robbery*, published in 1987, John Eck again examined the criminal investigation process. As the result of a two-year study of robbery and burglary conducted in three jurisdictions—DeKalb County, Georgia; St. Petersburg, Florida; and Wichita, Kansas—Eck drew conclusions that differed substantially from those reached earlier by the Rand researchers.

Specifically, the Rand authors concluded that patrol officers solve most cases that can be solved and that follow-up investigations should be limited to only the most serious crimes. In contrast, Eck concluded that preliminary and follow-up investigations were complimentary. He felt emphasizing one aspect of investigation over the other would reduce the overall effectiveness of investigation. Eck offered two explanations for these different findings.

First, he noted that the Rand study examined only cases cleared by arrest, while he examined the total process of investigation, in which cases cleared by arrest is only one element. By examining the total process of conducting an investigation, it was possible to determine how various techniques had an impact on the outcome. Eck also suggested that, as a result of the Rand study findings, law enforcement administrators had placed emphasis on patrol officers conducting preliminary investigations and on case screening. Eck felt these factors had resulted in an overall improvement in the manner in which investigations are conducted.

Eck made a number of recommendations for improving the investigative process. Perhaps the most innovative recommendation was the creation of a triage system of criminal case screening. In this system, cases are screened into one of three categories: those that can be solved, those that have been solved, and those that may be solved with a reasonable amount of effort. Under the triage system, investigative supervisors and managers are required to make an objective determination of the presence of solvability factors prior to committing any resources to an investigation. Triage screening is linked to the concept of targeting career and persistent criminals. In this way, scarce investigative resources are employed more efficiently, based on data rather than subjective feelings.

Eck suggested that police officers, both patrol officers and detectives, make greater use of informants. This suggestion was linked to the recommendation that departmental policies be developed to control and manage informants.

Eck and others have sought to bring increased objectivity to criminal investigations. A good example is the frank recognition that the practice of re-interviewing witnesses is often a public relations device, undertaken to appease angry victims of crime, and a practice that, ironically, may lead to strained relations because of frequent, time consuming, and unproductive contacts with police.

Despite these inconsistent findings, some patterns or themes can be identified. First, both patrol officers and detectives play a significant role in the investigative process. Second, traditional investigative techniques, such as neighborhood canvassing, and the use of informants continue to be useful for solving cases. Third, physical evidence, if used correctly, is valuable in supporting other evidence. Finally, sound management practices can improve investigative efficiency.

Criminal investigation is a series of complex tasks that require years to master. The purpose of this book is to examine those tasks and to explain how they can be used effectively to solve criminal cases.

Criminal Investigation Defined

Criminal investigation is the process of legally gathering evidence of a crime that has been or is being committed. The criticism leveled against the Paris police by Poe's fictional detective Dupin in "Murders in the Rue Morgue" quoted at the beginning of this chapter may have been an accurate description of the approach to investigation taken by the police 150 years ago, but no longer reflects how criminal investigations are conducted. Today criminal investigation has become one of the most complex areas of law enforcement, requiring highly trained professionals with the required skills and experience to build a case that may be successfully prosecuted.

Every day, highly trained criminal investigators solve crimes using a variety of techniques. The usefulness of these different techniques depends on the type of crime and the knowledge and experience of the investigator. It is the obligation of every professional investigator to be completely familiar with all of the tools available and to use those techniques to the fullest extent possible in a democracy.

Goals of Criminal Investigation

The ultimate goal of any criminal investigation is to determine, to the extent possible, the truth about how a crime occurred. Criminal investigators, as police officers, hold enormous power. The Anglo-American legal system does not require absolute proof of a defendant's guilt but rather that the defendant's guilt be proven beyond a reasonable doubt. Despite the numerous safeguards built into the system, it is possible that an innocent person could be convicted and punished for a crime he or she did not commit. It is the investigator's responsibility to ensure that miscarriages of justice do not occur. O.W. Wilson, one of the major police reformers of this century, wrote of the need to investigate serious crimes, to recover stolen property, and to assist in the prosecution of cases (Wilson, 1977). These are important goals, but the investigator should remain mindful that the basic task is to determine the truth. Determining the truth is often a difficult task. Even in the most thorough investigations, some questions will always remain unanswered. Faulty or biased recollections of witnesses, coupled with the lack of physical evidence, will prevent the investigator from recreating an event exactly as it occurred. Under the American system of justice, we believe it is preferable to let the guilty go free than to deprive an innocent person of freedom. The defense need only plant a reasonable doubt in the minds of the jurors to obtain an acquittal. This sometimes creates a conflict for society and the investigator. Innocent people have been convicted of crimes they did not commit. Conversely, poorly planned and conducted investigations have resulted in acquittals where convictions based on the facts were possible. A commitment to finding the truth should be what guides professional criminal investigators.

CASE STUDY

In 1994, the American public was once again horrified by the commission of what appeared to be another senseless act of violence. In this case, Susan Smith, a young mother of two little boys in South Carolina reported that an unidentified bandit had stolen her car from her at gunpoint. In the course of stealing her car, the bandit had abducted her two sons, Michael, 3 years old, and Alexander, 14 months old. The boys were in the back seat of the car. Her report launched a massive investigation that resulted in hundreds of tips being provided from all around the United States.

Yet, as the search proceeded, investigators close to the case began to have doubts about Mrs. Smith's story. The details of her story did not fit and inconsistencies became more apparent as the investigation continued. In the days after the initial report, investigators began to suspect that Mrs. Smith could be guilty of the unthinkable crime of murdering her own children.

Investigators then conducted two investigations. In the public investigation they searched for the boys and their alleged kidnapper. In the second, secret, investigation they focused on Susan Smith. At the time these investigations were underway, detectives could not be sure which, if either, approaches would be successful. Ultimately, after meticulous examination of the evidence, an investigator was able to obtain a confession from Susan Smith by confronting her with the evidence.

In this classic investigation, detectives conducted a professional investigation while protecting the rights of the accused and responded to intense media pressure for a story. The investigation resulted in the conviction for the crime of first-degree murder. They had found the truth.

Criminal Investigation and Criminal Law

Criminal investigation is distinguished from other types of investigation in that the investigators focus on crime, or what appears to be crime. Paul Tappen's comprehensive definition of crime provides a point to begin an analysis of the criminal investigative process and the investigator's role in that process:

> Crime is an intentional act or omission in violation of criminal law (statutory or case law) committed without defense or justification, and sanctioned by the state as a felony or misdemeanor. (Tappen, 1960, p. 10)

Crime Is an Intentional Act or Omission

To convict for the commission of a crime, the state must prove that the defendant intended to perform an illegal act or intentionally failed to perform some legally required duty. Every crime consists of two parts: the *mens rea* and the *actus reus*. *Mens rea*, the intent to commit a crime, is defined as:

> A guilty mind; a guilty or wrongful purpose; a criminal intent. Guilty knowledge or willfulness. (*Black's Law Dictionary*, 1983, p. 510)

The investigator must find evidence for the jury to determine if the defendant was acting freely and knew that his or her actions were likely to have certain predictable consequences. The investigator must gather evidence that demonstrates a person was acting intentionally. One means to do this is to ask the person what he or she was thinking at the time the act occurred, but this approach has obvious shortcomings. First, the suspect in a criminal case is not likely to admit his or her guilt and accept responsibility for a crime. Second, the Miranda warning requires that suspects in custody who are being interrogated about involvement in a crime be told that they have the right to refuse to answer any questions asked of them by the police. This right, found in the Fifth Amendment to the Constitution, protects the individual against self-incrimination. Unless suspects voluntarily choose to talk to the police, the privilege against self-incrimination prevents the police from presenting any questions to the suspect. How, then, can the state prove that the person charged with a crime acted intentionally?

The only reliable means by which an investigator can show that a defendant was acting under the required *mens rea* is to gather facts the jury can use to infer or conclude that the defendant knew what he or she was doing. From the beginning of a case, investigators must look for physical and testimonial evidence that shows what the defendant's state of mind was at the time the act occurred.

CASE STUDY

An 18-year-old woman entered a large department store. She walked to the women's clothing section and removed three swimming suits from a rack. She then walked to a dressing room, where she remained for approximately 10 minutes. She left the dressing room and returned two of the suits to the rack. After she returned the items, she walked toward the front door of the store. As she was walking toward the door, a security guard looked into the dressing room and saw that the third swimming suit was not there. The officer never lost sight of the woman, and after she walked past the cash registers she was detained by the security officer and taken to an office. At that point, a search of her purse revealed the third swimming suit. In most states the crime of stealing is defined as:

A taking and a carrying away of the personal property of another with the intent to steal.

One of the key tasks for an investigator is to show that the *defendant intended to steal or permanently deprive the owner of his/her property*. In a case such as this, the investigator will demonstrate the intent to steal by carefully documenting the actions of the defendant and the security guard. Testimony that the defendant removed the swimming suit from the rack, took it to a dressing room, and then concealed it in her purse before walking past the cash registers reflects her intent to steal. This evidence would be enough to convince a jury of the defendant's intent to permanently deprive the owner of his or her property.

Actus Reus or Intentional Act

Actus reus literally means the "guilty act." It refers to a wrongful deed taken in furtherance of the criminal intent of the guilty mind. Under the American system of jurisprudence, a person may not be punished for his or her thoughts. In a committed crime, a person must actually perform some act that is defined as illegal or must fail to perform some legally required duty. For example, a bank teller may think about supplementing his income from a cash drawer but until money is actually taken and used by the teller for some illegal purpose, no crime has been committed. Similarly, a crime may be committed when someone fails or refuses to perform a legally required duty, such as failing to file an income tax return or failing to provide a decent level of care for her children.

In Violation of Statutory or Case Law

Professional peace officers are obligated to know the statutory criminal law that provides the basis of their authority. Statutory law is created by various elected legislative bodies, such as the United States Congress, state legislatures, and city governments. *Statutory laws* consist of a *corpus delicti* or elements that make up specific crimes. Police must not only be familiar with the elements of these better known crimes, they must also be familiar with all statutory law. Police must also know how these laws have been interpreted in the courts. Court interpretation of substantive criminal law is known as case law. *Case law* provides clarification and adds meaning to the elements of a particular substantive criminal law. For example, *robbery* is defined as forcible stealing. A pickpocket who removes a man's wallet from his back pocket has committed the crime of stealing, theft, or larceny, depending on the name given to the offense in that jurisdiction. Similarly, a purse snatch would be stealing. If, however, the intended victim refuses to give up the purse without a struggle, the act becomes robbery since force is used to obtain the victim's property.

Defenses

Committed Without Defense of Justification

Under the Anglo-American legal system, persons may not be held accountable for their actions if it can be shown that the defendant was acting under a specific recognized defense. Defense is defined as:

> That which is offered and alleged by the party proceeded against in an action or suit, as a reason in law or fact why the plaintiff should not recover or establish what he seeks. (*Black's Law Dictionary*, 1983, p. 218)

The better-known defenses in criminal cases are:

· Infancy
· Insanity
· Involuntary intoxication
· Entrapment
· Self-defense

Infancy

Under most legal systems, persons under a certain age are considered too young to possess the mental capacity to form the criminal intent or *mens rea* (*infancy*). Under common law, children under the age of seven were presumed to lack the mental capacity to form the required criminal intent. If children under the age of seven committed crimes, they were not subject to criminal prosecution. Today, the age of infancy varies from state to state. For example, in some states if the child is between seven and 14, the prosecution may offer evidence that the youthful defendant they knew that he was violating the law. The modern trend seems to be for states to lower the age at which children can be prosecuted as adults. It is important to remember that children who commit crimes will likely come to the attention of the juvenile court for treatment or care. While they may not be prosecuted, they will receive attention.

Insanity

In order to be held accountable for what she has been accused of, the defendant must be shown to have been acting under his or her own free will. If some other factor, such as a mental disorder, affects the defendant's ability to exercise free will, the defense may argue that the defendant is not guilty by reason of *insanity*. In the United States, there are currently different tests of insanity, the most common of which is the M'Naughten Rule, or the right versus wrong test. Under this test of insanity, the defendant is considered to be insane for purposes of prosecution if "the party accused was laboring under such a defect of reason, from disease of the mind, as to not know the nature and quality of the act he was doing; or, if he did know it, that he did not know that what he was doing was wrong" (M'Naughten's Case, 8 Eng. Rep. 718). Under the right versus wrong test, the state must prove that the defendant knew what he or she was doing was wrong. It is the investigator's job to gather evidence that reflects on the defendant's state of mind at the time the act occurred. Attempts by defendants to escape, to destroy evidence, or to otherwise try to conceal their identities would demonstrate that the defendant was sane for purposes of prosecution. This evidence indicates that the defendant was trying to avoid the punishment associated with the commission of a crime, which in turn demonstrates the ability to distinguish between right and wrong.

CASE STUDY

A young man entered a multistory hotel and proceeded to the top floor, where he entered a room that was open. The maid, who was cleaning the room, asked if he was the guest staying the room. He replied that he was, and shortly afterward the maid completed her tasks and left. At that point the man assembled two rifles that he had concealed in a large box. He walked to the balcony, where he loaded the weapons and proceeded to shoot nine people on the streets below. Three of his victims were fatally wounded. He was arrested immediately and charged with numerous felonies, including first-degree murder. His defense was insanity, that is, that he did not know the difference between right and wrong. At the trial, several items of evidence were offered to prove he knew what the consequences of his actions would be. One of the most damaging pieces of evidence was a statement made to police officers shortly after he was arrested—that he loaded his own ammunition before the shooting and that he had loaded the ammunition "extra hot so it would reach farther." This statement was offered to show that he knew what he was doing and was therefore responsible for his actions.

In recent years other types of defenses have been offered, most of which are modifications of the insanity defense. These new, and generally unsuccessful, defenses include the delayed stress syndrome, the battered wife or "burning bed defense," premenstrual syndrome, and the spurned wife defense. All these defenses are predicated on the idea that defendants were unable to control their actions because of some form of extreme trauma or stress.

Involuntary Intoxication

Generally voluntary intoxication is not recognized as a defense against criminal liability. In some limited situations, however, involuntary intoxication may be accepted as a defense. The defense here is akin to duress.

CASE STUDY

In *Burrows v. State* an 18-year-old boy was hitchhiking across Arizona. He was picked up by a man who had been drinking heavily. The driver threatened the boy if he did not drink with him. The boy was forced to drink both beer and whiskey. At some point, Burrows became incoherent and killed the driver. The jury was allowed to hear evidence of the fact that the boy was forced to drink against his will and therefore was not responsible for his actions (Burrows v. State, 38 Ariz. 99, 297 P. 1029 [1931]). Where involuntary intoxication is offered as a defense, the jury may consider it as a factor in determining the degree to which the defendant may or may not be responsible for the act. It must be remembered that this defense applies only when it can be shown that the defendant was coerced or tricked into consuming the intoxicant.

Entrapment

The *entrapment* defense is based on the idea that a person cannot be lured into the commission of a crime by police and then be prosecuted for it. The entrapment defense is not found in the Constitution. It is rather assumed to be based in the belief that legislatures do not support the practice of allowing police to cause an innocent person to commit a crime he or she would not normally be predisposed to commit. Two basic tests of entrapment exist—the subjective and the objective. Under the subjective test for entrapment, the prosecution must prove that the defendant was predisposed to commit the crime. This may be done by the police creating an opportunity to commit a crime but not making a situation in which an innocent party would do something he or she would not normally do. Under the objective test, the defendant will attempt to prove that the conduct of the police went well beyond merely creating an opportunity to commit a crime. In the subjective test, the focus of the trial is on the defendant's state of mind (Sorrells v. U.S. 287 U.S. 435 [1932]). In the objective test, the focus is on the conduct of the police. Under current case law, the subjective test is most widely used in the United States (Sherman v. U.S. 356 U.S. 369 [1958]).

In 1992, in the case of *Jacobson v. U.S.*, the Supreme Court revisited the entrapment defense. In this case, the defendant had been arrested and convicted of receiving child pornography. Jacobson, a Nebraska farmer, had been identified as someone who might have an interest in child pornography from a mailing list obtained from a bookstore that distributed pornographic materials. The defendant had purchased magazines from the bookstore prior to the time when receiving and possessing such items had been defined as a crime under either federal or Nebraska law. Over a period of approximately two and a half years, a postal inspector sent mail to Jacobson, from five fictitious organizations, exploring his willingness to obtain child pornography and thereby break the law. Jacobson ordered two magazines containing photographs of nude preteen and teenage boys. Postal inspectors arrested him after a controlled delivery of the magazines. A subsequent search of his residence did not reveal any additional pornography or materials, other than the items sent by the postal inspector.

The Supreme Court held that, as matter of law, the prosecution had failed to demonstrate that Jacobson had the predisposition to commit the crime. The Court stated that to overcome an entrapment defense, the prosecution must prove beyond a reasonable doubt that the defendant was already disposed to commit the crime before being approached by law enforcement officers.

Self-Defense

Self-defense is based on the right of every person to defend himself or herself against death or injury. A person may claim self-defense if three conditions are met. First, persons must believe that the assailant intends to assault them; second, the defensive force used to defend oneself cannot be unreasonable when compared with the harm it is intended to prevent; and finally, the threatened party must believe that use of defensive force is unavoidable. Self-defense may involve both nondeadly and deadly force.

CASE STUDY

Witnesses reported a man breaking through the front door of their house only to collapse and die on the front room floor. The witnesses knew that the man had lived two doors away. Police went to the dead man's house, where they found the man's wife. She was interviewed about the death and the events leading up to it. She related that he had come home drunk, as he often did, and had threatened her. At some point he picked up a small semiautomatic handgun and threatened her with it. She then retrieved a larger caliber revolver and shot him in self-defense. An examination of the scene indicated that the man had dived through a window at the back of the house in an apparent attempt to escape from her. An examination of the body revealed an entrance wound made by a large caliber weapon under the man's ribs on the right side of his body. An exit wound was located on the upper-right shoulder of his torso. This evidence indicated that the man was running away and was actually in the air going through the window at the time he was shot. The physical evidence in this case made self-defense questionable. Follow-up investigations did reveal that the woman had reported a number of assaults in the past committed by the man. In the end, the case was disposed of by a negotiated guilty plea to voluntary manslaughter. This plea was probably appropriate, given the facts of the case.

Anticipating the Defense

As an investigation progresses, investigators and prosecutors should anticipate what defenses may be raised by the defense and be prepared to respond. Although neither the investigator nor the prosecutor can know the defense's strategy beforehand, training and experience can provide some insights into how the defense may present its case. In any situation, the state must be prepared to respond to whatever defense is offered. A story is told that Abraham Lincoln, while practicing law, accepted the case of young man who was charged with the murder of his parents. Legend has it that when Lincoln realized that he could do little for his client, he asked for leniency because the young man was an orphan.

Sanctioned by the State

A crime is considered to be a wrong against the state and is prosecuted in the name of the state. An act is considered a crime, however, only after a duly elected legislative body has passed a law proscribing a particular behavior. Certain acts, while harmful or disruptive to society, may not be crimes. For example, the taking of a child from one spouse by another spouse before a court has awarded custody following a divorce action is certainly disruptive. However, until custody has been awarded, no crime such as kidnapping or unlawful restraint has occurred. Unless a crime in actually committed against a child or the other spouse, police cannot act because no crime has been committed.

As a Felony or Misdemeanor

Crimes are classified into two general categories: felonies and misdemeanors. A *felony* is a crime punishable by more than one year of incarceration or imprisonment in a state or federal penitentiary. A *misdemeanor* is a crime punishable by less than a year of incarceration or imprisonment in a county or city jail. The better-known felonies are aggravated assault, burglary, rape, sodomy, murder, manslaughter, and kidnapping. Common misdemeanors are petty larceny, simple assault, and disturbing the peace.

The Investigative Process

The tools available to an investigator have increased in number and sophistication. For example, DNA fingerprinting and the cognitive interview have made the task of trying to uncover the truth more successful. Yet, despite advances in technology, the fundamentals of criminal investigation remain the same. O'Hara has written that the criminal investigation is based on the three I's:

· Information
· Instrumentation
· Interviewing

Information

Criminal investigation, indeed, the entire process of enforcing the law, is information based. No police officer is any better than his or her information. We live in an information-based society; it is now literally possible to track a person from cradle to grave in the United States. It is the responsibility of the investigator to know how to find and use all legitimate sources of information available.

Instrumentation

Instrumentation, or *forensic science*, is a second major tool available to the investigator. Forensic scientists have developed an impressive array of techniques to help in the solution of crimes. Serology, the study of blood; dactylography, the study of fingerprints and ballistics; and the study of firearms and projectiles have proven invaluable in the identification and conviction of criminals. Recent breakthroughs in the study of deoxyribonucleic acid, DNA analysis, is the most exciting advance in forensic science in recent memory. Additional breakthroughs will undoubtedly continue to enhance the ability of an investigator to solve crimes.

Interviewing

Interviewing victims and witnesses of a crime is the final "I" of investigation. The skillful use of interviewing techniques by a trained investigator encourages persons with knowledge of a crime to provide that information to the police. Supreme Court decisions in the 1960s caused prosecutors to rely more heavily on physical evidence because of difficulties in getting confessions admitted as evidence. Ironically, restrictions placed on interviewers by the Miranda decision in 1966 forced police to look at interviewing techniques used in the past, and in time caused them to develop new, more effective techniques of interviewing witnesses and victims.

Criminal Procedure and the Investigator

The law of arrest, search, and seizure is another tool available to the investigator. Police officers sometimes view the law, particularly the law of criminal procedure, as a barrier to the successful investigation of a crime. This attitude is much like that of a foot soldier as he looks at the sea. To the soldier, a body of water is an obstacle between him and where he needs to be. A sailor, on the other hand, looks at the sea as a road, an avenue, to take him where he wants to go. While the law, particularly criminal procedural law and the rules of evidence, do restrict the actions of the investigator, they also provide guidance on what investigative techniques are acceptable in a democratic society. Once the investigator has mastered criminal law, criminal procedure, and the rules of evidence, she can sail the legal sea as well as prosecutors, defense attorneys, and judges.

Types of Investigations

Reactive Investigations

Reactive investigations begin after a crime has been reported to the police. Reactive investigations are of three types: "walk through," the "whodunit" and the "where are they" investigations (Sanders, 1977).

Walk-Through Investigations

Walk-through investigations involve a suspect already known to the police, and in many cases the suspect is in custody. In these cases the investigator must carefully sift through and evaluate available information to find evidence that will link a perpetrator to that specific crime. The important factor in cases of this type is to adhere to all legal requirements in order to ensure a successful prosecution or to increase the chances for a plea bargain that is acceptable to both the state and the victim.

Whodunit Investigations

Whodunit investigations occur in cases where no suspect has been immediately identified. The effectiveness of whodunit investigations has come under scrutiny in the last fifteen years. Greenwood and Petersilia (1975) analyzed the investigative sections of several large police departments. They concluded that the bulk of the investigator's time was spent gathering and processing information. One of the most controversial conclusions related to how cases were solved:

> The single-most important determinant of whether or not a case will be solved is the information the victim supplies to the immediately responding patrol officer. If information

that uniquely identifies the perpetrator is not presented at the time the crime is reported, the perpetrator, by and large, will not subsequently be identified. (Greenwood and Petersilia, 1975)

More recently, Eck challenged these findings, suggesting that both patrol officers and follow-up investigations play a role in the solution of cases (Eck, 1983).

Where-Are-They Investigations

Where-are-they investigations are usually referred to as fugitive investigations. In these cases a suspect has been identified, and it is the investigator's task to locate him. Fugitive investigations are discussed in Chapter 13.

Reactive investigations usually begin with a uniformed patrol officer responding to a report of a crime. At this point, the job of gathering evidence begins. Once the preliminary investigation, including processing of physical evidence, is complete, a follow-up investigation, usually by a detective, is begun. The primary focus of this book is on the three types of reactive investigations—the walk through, the whodunit, and the where are they.

Proactive Investigations

In the nineteenth and early twentieth centuries, detectives concentrated on particular suspects (Richardson, 1970; Lane, 1967; Byrnes, 1980). Detectives identified an active suspect and set about building a case on that person by obtaining witness testimony, obtaining confessions from suspects, and/or staking out a location and actually catching the suspect in the act.

By the 1930s, investigators began to concentrate less on particular criminals and more on specific crimes. The shift away from focusing on suspects came about basically because of the increased use of physical evidence. Investigators came to view the process of collecting physical evidence as the most critical part of the investigation. The emphasis on specific crimes was further supported by a tendency of investigators to restrict their interviews to victims and witnesses to the crime without much concern for detailed neighborhood canvasses (Eck, 1983, p. 13).

In the last few years, investigators have begun to shift the focus from crimes that have already occurred to monitoring criminals who are part of an ongoing pattern of crimes, such as selling stolen property or drug trafficking. These are *proactive investigations*. Proactive investigations are conducted in order to gain evidence leading to convictions against participants in some type of continuing criminal activity. The most common type of proactive investigation used today is the undercover or covert drug investigation. The use of proactive investigative techniques has been and will continue to be controversial (Marx, 1988). Unlike reactive investigations, in which the police respond to reports of crimes that have already taken place, in proactive investigations police initiate investigations against suspected criminals. Proactive investigations require the use of investigative techniques that come under close scrutiny in a democracy. These techniques include electronic surveillance, grants of immunity from prosecution to participants in the crime, and informants. Law enforcement administrators must develop policies that provide direction to investigators in all these crucial areas before undertaking these types of investigations. Proactive investigative techniques are discussed in Chapter 12 on drug investigations.

Ethics and Criminal Investigation

A series of disclosures about the conduct of individual officers and groups of officers have shocked the police and the public for the last several years. The Rodney King beating, and more recently, disclosures about the Los Angeles Police Department's Community Resources Against Street Hoodlums (CRASH), serve for some as the proof that law enforcement officers routinely abuse their authority for whatever purpose that suits them. Others felt that the police are justified in using whatever means are available to them to accomplish the goal of protecting the public.

At the same time that the public is demanding that restraints be placed on government and its agents, it is also demanding to know everything about certain events. The apparently insatiable appetite for information about high-profile cases indicates that no detail is too small for scrutiny, at least in some cases. The extent to which law enforcement officers break the law or bend the rules will never be known, but it seems safe to say that officers have gone beyond acceptable limits. The practical question, however, is how do the many responsible, hard-working law enforcement officers know when their behaviors are unethical? In the pages to follow, we will review some of the more common ethical issues faced by law enforcement officers in the performance of an investigation.

During the course of an investigation law enforcement officers will be faced with a number of ethical questions. How officers answer those questions, how they feel about themselves, how victims go about repairing their lives, and even how the suspect views the justice system may have an impact on the prosecution of the case. Some of these issues are:

· The use of deception in conducting interrogations and interviews
· The use of deception in locating and apprehending witnesses or fugitives
· The use of criminal informants
· Dealing with issues of search and seizure

Marx, in his work on covert investigations, set forth some principles, which, although directed at providing guidance in defining the ethical issues involved in covert investigations, can be adapted to criminal investigation in general.

Ethical Arguments for Using Deception in a Criminal Investigation

Citizens grant the government the right to use means they individually forsake. Crimes are prosecuted in the name of the state. Private citizens are no longer able to punish others who have wronged them. The power to apprehend and punish the wrongdoer now belongs to the agents of social control, the police, courts, and corrections. The argument is that in order to protect the public, it is right for the police to trick a criminal into making a confession or lure the criminal to a location where he can be apprehended.

Deception is ethical when its targets are persons who have freely chosen to commit the crime, which may result in the police using the deceptive practices. The Anglo-American justice system is based on the belief that individuals who commit crimes choose to do so. That is, they exercise their free will and after weighing consequences will voluntarily act against the law. A discussion of the limits of free will is beyond the scope of this book, but is essential to understand that for the legal system to function, there must be support for belief that individuals opt to engage in crime. Since persons choose to violate the law, it can be argued that the state has the right to apprehend and punish them for the acts they voluntarily commit in order to protect public safety.

Deception is ethical when used for a good and important end. This argument for the use of deception requires the goals of the justice system be reviewed. At the simplest level the argument can be made that the public needs to be protected from persons who would commit violent and predatory crimes. Similarly, people want to be protected against persons who would steal or damage their property. Consensus about the value of some criminal laws tends to erode when people discuss drug violations, public order crimes, and nuisance offenses, but most people would agree that the protection of the public against people who commit crimes is an important end.

Deception is ethical when there is reasonable suspicion or probable cause to believe that a criminal act has been or will be carried out. The police cannot simply start an investigation of someone without a reason. The time and resources needed to complete even a rudimentary investigation prevent the indiscriminate use of investigative power. Therefore, before the police begin an investigation, they must have at least a reasonable suspicion to believe that a crime has been or is being committed. Reasonable suspicion is a legal concept, which holds that there must be some articulate facts to support the belief that a crime occurred. A mere "hunch" will not justify opening an investigation of someone. Thus, the investigator is being the law to determine if an investigation should be initiated.

Deception is acceptable when there is reasonable suspicion or probable cause to believe that a particular person committed the crime. Just as an investigation should not be opened without reasonable suspicion, an investigation of a person or of a group should not be undertaken without a reasonable suspicion that a specific person or group was involved. The consequences of an investigation for a person or group can be profound. The police may ask embarrassing or irritating questions. They may talk to friends and neighbors; they may request that the person submit to examinations or tests, which can be intrusive. For these reasons the police should have at least a reasonable suspicion that someone is involved in a crime.

When citizens use questionable (criminal) means, the police are justified in using equivalent means. The victims of a crime may feel the consequences of that event for the remainder of their lives. In some extreme cases they may never fully recover. It is argued, therefore, that if persons who choose to engage in acts disrupt someone's life, then the police are justified in taking additional measures to protect the public. They are, as the old cliché goes, fighting fire with fire.

Special Risks Justify Special Precautions

Law enforcement is generally perceived as a dangerous occupation. While the accuracy of that perception has been debated there can be no question that law enforcement officers are killed and injured on the job. The argument made here is that if society makes certain behaviors a violation of law then those persons who are charged with the enforcement of those laws must be given the means to accomplish the goal of bringing offenders before the court for prosecution. These techniques include the use of special, sometimes risky and marginal techniques involving deception to reach that goal.

Accomplishing a Good or Important End

Deception Is Acceptable When Used to Accomplish a Goal and/or Good End

The issue here is what the goals of criminal investigation are and how criminal investigators reach those goals. Law enforcement in a democratic society has a number of goals, including the detection and apprehension of criminal offenders, and assisting the courts in the prosecution of those offenders. The primary goal is the protection of life and property, which is certainly laudable. Does this good end, however, allow the law enforcement officer the freedom to employ any effective technique to achieve that goal? In other words do the ends justify the means? The answer is clearly no. The excesses committed by the members of the Los Angeles Police Department Community Resources Against Street Hoodlums (CRASH) team have demonstrated that the goal of public safety must be balanced against the harm done to civil liberties (Chua-Eoan, Cohen 2000). The end, however laudable it may be, does not always justify the means. In the final analysis, the decision on what to do will be a continuous process of balancing two or more equally valid ends.

Deception Is Acceptable When Used to Obtain a Conviction

The goal of an investigation is to determine the truth to the best extent possible, given the facts. The use of investigative resources to silence political opponents is one of the most sensitive issues in any democracy. The current investigation of the Branch Davidian compound fire of April 19, 1993, reflects the public's concern about how and why government power and resources were used to resolve the issue. Investigations should be conducted with the expectation that the case will ultimately be presented in court. In some cases, it may be necessary to conduct investigations in order to obtain background on a case or obtain intelligence information about a crime, but again these investigations are to be conducted with the intention of prosecuting the perpetrator.

Deception is ethical when its use makes an investigation less intrusive and less coercive than other investigative techniques. The American people are very protective of their personal freedoms. The United States was founded on the belief that all persons have certain inalienable rights, which include the right to privacy and the right to be left alone. Technology has made it possible for people, including government agents, to intrude into the most private places often with the result that no significant criminal activity is detected. The argument is that by using deceptive techniques, police can identify and investigate only those persons who are truly involved in crime and are able to avoid getting into areas that are secret and private.

Deception is ethical when it is undertaken with the expectation that its use will eventually be made public and judged in court. Although similar to the purpose of an investigation to obtain a conviction, deception differs in that by going to court through the process of conducting a speedy and public trial, the public will have the opportunity to see and learn what really happened. The public is suspicious of the government and its agents. People want to know how the police go about protecting them from criminal activity. At the same time, the public has an insatiable appetite for the sensational, often sordid, details of some spectacular crimes. Several significant issues get coverage as a trial begins. The government's obligation to protect its citizens, the public's right to know what is going on, and the defendant's right to a fair trial often collide at the trial. The expectation is that a capable judge can mediate the conflicts and preserve the integrity of the system, as Judge Richard Maitch did in the Oklahoma City bombing trial of Timothy McVeigh.

Deception is ethical when persons of upright character in accountable organizations use it. When an organization is given the responsibility and authority to perform certain tasks, members of that organization must expect to be held accountable for the use of that power. By nature, many criminal investigations must be conducted in secret. Persons who know they are under investigation and who possess the means to abscond cannot be expected to wait to be arrested. Similarly, criminals can destroy evidence, threaten witnesses, and develop plausible explanations to explain away their behavior. Despite the need for secrecy, investigators must conduct the investigations with the expectation that their conduct will be reviewed in open court. At that time, their character and veracity will come under review. In those cases where members of law enforcement agencies have not maintained the highest standards as defined by the law and by agency policies and procedures, those persons and those who supervise them must be held accountable. The events at Ruby Ridge, Idaho, and Waco, Texas, demonstrate the concerns that the public has regarding the use of police power in this country.

Arguments Against the Use of Deception

While many of the arguments presented above are compelling, the use of deception by law enforcement officers is equally compelling. It can be argued that the goal of protecting the public may not justify the use of any technique to obtain a conviction. The arguments presented below are not in order.

Truth Telling Is Moral, Lying Is Immoral

Telling the truth is at the heart of any relationship. Parties to a relationship must be able to believe what they are being told by someone else. It may seem that lying to a suspect in an interrogation is appropriate in order to establish the truth, but the long-term consequences of lying may have profound consequences for the justice system. For example, the primary goal of the criminal justice system is to protect lives and property. One way to do that is to arrest and convict persons who break the law. Persons who are convicted may be incarcerated, and while they are locked up they will have only a limited ability to prey on the public. While they are locked up, the public has some degree of protection. Ultimately, however, most people who are locked up will eventually return to society. If they harbor a grudge for a perceived injustice administered by the justice system they are less likely to abide by society's rules. If, however, they believe they were told the truth throughout the process, they are more likely to see the system as being fair. Thus, representatives of the government can ultimately benefit from telling the truth to criminals.

The Government Should Not Make Deals With Criminals

The American system of justice requires that the defendant's guilt be proven by "proof beyond a reasonable doubt." Even with such a high standard of proof, it is never possible to know exactly what happened in an event. Given the secretive nature of most crimes, it is incumbent on investigators and prosecutors to use a variety of types and forms of evidence, including people who are involved in crime. In some types of cases—drug conspiracies, organized crime, and crimes where only participants really know what happened—investigators may request leniency for offenders, and prosecutors may grant it in return for the cooperation of a key participant. Without this kind of cooperation, prosecutors may well find that they cannot convict the guilty. Persons opposed to these kinds of deals argue that participating in this process taints government and its agents. Government agents should neither participate in the commission of a crime, nor should they break the law to enforce it.

In some extreme cases, government agents have allowed criminals to continue to engage in crimes as long as the criminal continues to serve as an informant or provide some other type of service, which the police or prosecutor find valuable. In some cases police have engaged in illegal activity such as burglary or illegal wiretapping in order to obtain evidence. Again, the argument simply states that, as representatives of the criminal justice system, police should not engage in activities that detract from the image of the system as a symbol of fairness and honesty.

Through its actions, the government should reduce, not encourage crime. The government should not create an intention to commit a crime that is impossible to carry out. Entrapment—as a defense to a crime—has not proven to be a particularly effective tactic. The person seeking to take advantage of the entrapment defense must tell his story on the witness stand before a judge and probably a jury. He must admit that he did in fact commit the act as charged. He must tell the story with the hope that the judge or jury will consider the conduct of the police so egregious that he will be found not guilty.

The Government Should Not Tempt the Weak

In the case of *Sherman v. United States*, limits of the system were again tested. In this case, a government informant named Kalchinian met Sherman, the defendant, at a doctor's office where both were being treated for drug addiction. The two met again repeatedly at the doctor's office or at the pharmacy where they were getting their prescriptions filled. During these meetings, the two began to engage in conversations and to discuss their shared experiences as they tried to overcome their addictions. Eventually, Kalchinian asked Sherman if he knew of a good source of illegal drugs. He asked Sherman to supply him with a source because he was not responding to treatment. Sherman tried to avoid the issue. After receiving a number of requests made while Kalchinian complained of suffering due to lack of drugs, Sherman finally acquiesced. Several times after that he obtained drugs that he shared with Kalchinian. Sherman told the informant that the drugs cost $25 and that Kalchinian owed him $15. Thus, the informant shouldered the larger share of the cost of the drugs plus he paid for the taxi and other incidental expenses related to the transaction. After several such transactions, the informant told an agent of the Bureau of Narcotics that he had another drug seller for them. On three occasions during November 1951, drug agents observed Sherman give drugs to Kalchinian in return for money supplied by the government.

At his trial, Sherman claimed that the informant and the agents had entrapped him. He claimed the informer had convinced an otherwise unwilling person to commit a crime he was not predisposed to commit. The Supreme Court stated, "It is patently clear the petitioner (Sherman) was induced by Kalchinian. The informer himself testified that believing petitioner to be undergoing a cure for narcotics addictions, he nonetheless sought to persuade petitioner to obtain for him a source of narcotics..." The government cannot disown Kalchinian and insists that he is not responsible for his actions. Although he was not being paid, Kalchinian was an active government informer who had recently been the instigator of at least two other prosecutions (Sherman, 1958, p.374).

It can be argued that Sherman was not totally without blame in this situation. He was, however, making some effort to end his drug addiction. Government influence prevented, or at least delayed, that end.

Do Not Harm the Innocent

As government agents conduct investigations, they will inevitably come in contact with persons who have knowledge of crimes but were not participants themselves in the actual crime. Most states have laws that require that individuals who know of a crime must report that information to the authorities. Those laws are often vague, not widely known to the public and rarely prosecuted. The police in their efforts to find the truth may be tempted to bring extreme pressure on such otherwise innocent persons in order to obtain information. The practice of jailing persons who refuse to testify before a grand jury suggests an extreme degree of coercion brought to bear on an individual. Intense forms of interviewing can also be more pressures than is justified to find the truth.

Respect the Sanctity of Intimate Relations

The argument here is that government agents should not be able to go into areas where people expect to be left alone. With the increased availability of electronic surveillance equipment, it is more and more likely that these devices will be used to invade those spaces.

Respect the Sanctity of Private Places

In an increasingly crowded world, it is becoming more and more difficult for individuals to find privacy and the opportunity to be left alone. Investigations, both overt and covert, will result in intrusions into someone's most private places. Searching a person's home or asking prying questions will inevitably lead to areas that any person would wish to keep from outsiders. Many would argue that the government and its agents should not be allowed to intrude into these places.

Respect the Freedom of Expression and Action

The ability to express one's opinion, however unpopular it may be, is at the heart of a democracy. Presumably, if someone is willing to subject himself to the court of public opinion after taking an unpopular stand then he should be allowed to do so. In truth, most people in and out of government take a dim view of positions that conflict with their own. The police, as agents of government, have the ability to use their resources to investigate individuals and groups who espouse what appear to be marginal or extreme points of view. Few people are able to withstand the threat of having the might and majesty of government focused on them. They will succumb to the chilling effect of government scrutiny to keep their opinions to themselves, possibly to the detriment of the greater society by not raising valid questions about how or why government performs their activities. One of the most difficult questions facing governments is when to use its resources to prevent someone from taking an unpopular position.

The government should not be allowed to do by stealth what it is not permitted to do openly. The Fourth Amendment states in part that the right of the people to be secure in their houses, papers and shall not be violated. That has been interpreted to mean that government agents may not enter an area where someone has a reasonable expectation of privacy without first obtaining prior judicial approval in the form of a search warrant or by obtaining the permission of the person whose expectation of privacy is at issue. In other cases, a government agent, such as an undercover police officer or confidential informant who befriends a criminal, can gain entry to that person's home by stealth. By claiming they are someone else, they trick criminals into actually inviting them into the most private aspects of their lives. It can then be argued that before being allowed to engage in covert investigations or being allowed to use informants, the police should first obtain a search warrant.

In their book, Blanchard and Peel offer a quick checklist or test that working law enforcement officers can use when faced with an ethical issue. They suggest that anyone making a decision should ask three questions: (1) How will this make me feel about myself? (2) What will this look like in the news? and (3) How will my family feel about this?

If the answer to any of these questions causes the investigator to pause, then they should give their actions more thought.

Periodically the officer must do a self-assessment of some core values, which all officers should possess. First and foremost, peace officers must obey the law. Certainly the law places restrictions on the police. Those laws were created to limit the power of government and its agents. The preservation of personal freedoms is more important than arresting and prosecuting every law violator. That is a hard concept for some investigators to accept, but it is the price of living in a democracy.

In the end, law enforcement officers will always face a variety of ethical issues every day as they perform their duties. They will always be pulled by a number of forces including the need to function within the concepts upon which a democracy is based and the need to protect the public. Both of these obligations are part of the oath they agree to when they are sworn in as law enforcement officers. The discussion and the test provided above may serve to guide them as they conduct an investigation.

Conclusion

Criminal investigation is a complex and fascinating component of law enforcement. Investigators must master the techniques that will enable them to reach the ultimate goal in any investigation—to find the truth. Criminal law, both substantive and procedural, forms the basis of the criminal investigator's ability to act. In order to secure a conviction for the commission of a crime, the state must prove that the defendant intended to perform an illegal act or intentionally failed to perform some legally required duty. It is the responsibility of the criminal investigator to gather evidence on the apparent commission of a crime as well as evidence to show that a suspect intended to commit a crime. Above all, the criminal investigator must adhere to the legal requirements placed on law enforcement in a democratic society. To do this, the investigator must know and understand criminal law, the law of criminal procedure, and the rules of evidence. These are legal requirements, which are discussed in Chapter 2.

References

Black's Law Dictionary, 5th ed. St. Paul, MN: West Publishing, 1983.

Blanchard, Kenneth and Peale, Norman Vincent. *The Power of Ethical Management*, New York, Fawcett Crest Books, 1988.

Burrows v. State, 38 Ariz. 99, 297, P. 1029 (1931).

Byrnes, Thomas. *Professional Criminal in America*. Reprinted in 1980 as *Rogues Gallery: 247 Professional Criminal in 19th Century America*, New York: Chelsea House.

Chua-Eoan, Howard. "Black and Blue." *Time Magazine*, March 6, 2000, Vol. 155, No. 9, p. 24.

Cohen, Adam. "Gansta Cops." *Time Magazine*, March 6, 2000, Vol. 155, No. 9, p. 30.

Eck, John. *Solving Crimes: The Investigation of Robbery and Burglary*. Washington, DC: Police Executive Research Forum, 1983.

Eck, John. *Problem Solving: Problem Oriented Policing in Newport News*. Washington, DC: Police Executive Research Forum, 1987.

Goldstein, Herman. *Problem Oriented Policing*. New York: McGraw Hill, 1990.

Greenwood, Peter and Petersilia, Joan. *The Criminal Investigative Process: Summary and Policy Implication*. Santa Monica, CA: Rand Corporation, 1975.

Jacobson v. United States, 503 U.S. 540, 112 S. Ct. 1535, 118 L. Ed. 2d 174 (1992).

Lane, Roger. *Policing the City: Boston, 1822–1908*. Cambridge, MA: Harvard University Press, 1967.

Manning, Peter. "Community Policing." *American Journal of Police* 3(3):205–227, 1984.

Marx, Gary. *Police Undercover Work: Ethical Deception or Deceptive Ethics? Police Ethics: Hard Choices in Law Enforcement*, ed. Heffernan, William and Stroup, Timothy, New York: John Jay Press 1985.

Marx, Gary T. *Undercover Police Surveillance in America. Berkeley*, CA: University of California Press, 1988.

O'Hara, Charles E. and O'Hara, Gregory L. *Fundamentals of Criminal Investigation*, 5th ed. Springfield, IL: Charles C. Thomas, 1980.

Perkins, Rollin M. and Boyce, Ronald N. *Criminal Law*, Mineola, NY: The Foundation Press, 1982.

Poe, Edgar Allan. "The Murders in the Rue Morgue." *Graham's Magazine*, 1841.

Richardson, James. *New York Police: Colonial Times to 1901*. New York: Oxford University Press, 1970.

Sanders, William. *Detective Work*. New York: Free Press, 1977.

Sherman v. United States, 356 U.S. 369, 78 S.Ct. 819 (1958).

Skolnick, Gerome and Bayley, David H. *The New Blue Line: Police Innovation in Six American Cities*. New York: The Free Press, 1986.

Sorrells v. U.S., 287 U.S. 435 (1932).

Tappen, Paul. *Crime, Justice and Correction*. New York: McGraw-Hill, 1960.

Wilson, James Q. and Kelling, George. "Broken Windows: The Police and Neighborhood Safety." *Atlantic Monthly* 249(3):29-38, 1982.

Wilson, James Q. *The Investigators*. New York: Basic Books, 1978.

Wilson, O.W. and McClaren, Roy C. *Police Administration*, 4th ed. New York: McGraw-Hill, 1977.

2. The Investigator and the Law

It is of the highest importance in the art of detection to be able to recognize out of a number of facts which are incidental and which vital. Otherwise your energy and attention must be dissipated instead of concentrated.

Sherlock Holmes, *The Adventure of the Reigate Squire*, Sir Arthur Conan Doyle

Law provides the basis for every police officer's actions. Without a complete understanding of criminal law, criminal procedure, and the rules of evidence, an investigator cannot hope to be successful in building a criminal case. Throughout history, humankind has sought mechanisms to ensure that its members conduct themselves in a manner that is acceptable to most of its members. These mechanisms are given a number of names, including norms, mores, and folkways. Most of these codes of conduct are taught to children and, over time, become part of the individual's unconscious behavior. When internal mechanisms of social control fail or appear to fail, cultures elevate proscription of the behavior to the status of law. It becomes an act defined and made punishable by law. Police investigators must know all the laws that exist in a jurisdiction and be prepared to use them as the basis for investigations and subsequent prosecutions.

CASE STUDY

A patrol officer was sent to an emergency room to take an accident report. Upon arriving, the officer was directed to a young woman who was wearing a large wig, a tightly fitting, low-cut top, and a tight, short skirt. Her attire reminded the officer that she was a prostitute working for a well-known local procurer. She had a large gash, approximately 6 inches long, on the left side of her face near her ear. She stated that she had fallen and struck a railing on the porch of her residence. The officer noted the implausibility of the story and suggested that she had been attacked by the procurer. She broke into tears and admitted that the officer was correct. He then encouraged her to use this event as reason to break from her association with the man and to tell the officer of the man's illegal activities. She then informed the officer that the person in question had a stolen television set in his living room. The officer used this and other information to obtain a search warrant. The house was searched, the TV was found, and the man was arrested for possession of stolen property.

Investigators should be prepared to use any criminal law available to arrest and subsequently prosecute criminal offenders.

Criminal Procedure, Arrest, Search, and Seizure

Criminal procedural law, particularly the laws of arrest, search, and seizure, are the tools of the investigative craft that are used by an investigator on a daily basis. An understanding of the laws of arrest, search, and seizure begins with an appreciation of the different levels of proof and the types of action that may legally be taken with regard to each of them. The levels of proof that a police officer must commonly work with are listed in Table 2.1.

Proof

The levels of proof at each extreme of the continuum—no proof and absolute proof—are not usually a concern for the investigators as they work their cases. An understanding of the other five levels of proof—suspicion, reasonable suspicion, probable cause, preponderance of evidence, and proof beyond a reasonable doubt—is, however, central to the investigator's ability to investigate a crime and to enforce the law. They must therefore be examined in detail.

Suspicion

Suspicion is more than no proof but is not enough evidence to justify any type of governmental intrusion into any area where someone has an expectation of privacy. Unsubstantiated information from informants or anonymous phone calls and an investigator's "hunch" fall into this category. Suspicion may justify opening a case or at least delving into the facts more deeply. This type of evidence requires the investigator to seek corroboration of the information by checking records and/or by interviewing other individuals to determine if follow-up investigation is justified.

CASE STUDY

A patrolman received information in the form of an anonymous phone call made to the police station that a man with a history of burglary convictions had committed a residential burglary on the officer's beat. The patrolman examined the report of the preliminary investigation conducted by another patrolman to familiarize himself with

Table 2.1   Levels of proof and the actions that may be taken on each

Level of Proof	Action
No proof	No action may be taken.
Suspicion	The investigator may begin an investigation.
Reasonable suspicion	Conduct an investigative detention (stop and frisk).
Probable cause	Arrest and/or search.
Preponderance of evidence	The amount of evidence needed to support a verdict in a civil lawsuit.
Proof beyond a reasonable doubt	The amount of evidence needed to prove a defendant's guilt in a criminal case.
Absolute proof	No other explanation for the event exists.

the facts of the case. He also obtained the suspect's photograph. The officer decided to talk to the man identified in the phone call at his home. When the man answered the door, he was wearing an item of jewelry closely matching the description of an item taken in the burglary. The officer felt he had probable cause to arrest the suspect. The man was arrested and later confessed to the burglary.

Reasonable Suspicion

The courts have recognized a level of proof between suspicion and probable cause—reasonable suspicion. *Reasonable suspicion* is that amount of evidence needed to justify an investigative detention, or as it was called in the past, the "stop and frisk." The police officer who conducts an investigative detention must be able to justify his actions by showing "specific and articulate facts which, taken together with rational inferences from those facts, reasonably warrant that intrusion" (Terry v. Ohio, 392 U.S. 1 [1968]).

Reasonable suspicion may be established through an officer's own observations or hearsay evidence (Adams v. Williams, 407 U.S. 143 [1972]). When seeking to establish reasonable suspicion, the officer will use the totality of circumstance in determining if an investigative detention is legal (U.S. v. Cortez, 449 U.S. 411 [1981]). When a police officer receives information, either through his own senses or from some other source, which leads him to believe that criminal activity is occurring, or is about to occur, then the officer can briefly detain the individual. That detention can last until the officer has determined that no crimes are occurring or until probable cause develops, at which time the officer can arrest the detainee. The facts in *United States v. Cortez* provide an excellent example of how reasonable suspicion is established and how it may develop into probable cause.

United States v. Cortez

U.S. Border Patrol agents in Arizona had observed several sets of footprints in an isolated area near the Mexican border. This area was known to officers as a location heavily trafficked by aliens illegally entering the United States. Agents estimated from the numbers of tracks that approximately eight to 20 persons had walked north from the border to an east-west highway, and then turned east until they reached milepost 122, where they stopped. A distinctive "V" or chevron-shaped shoe print was found several times at the scene. The person leaving the shoe print became known as "Chevron" by the agents. The agents concluded a pattern could be identified from the facts they had gathered. The aliens were apparently coming across at night, near the weekend, and because the tracks turned east, the pickup vehicle was probably also coming from the east. They further concluded that the truck had to be large enough to accommodate a large group of aliens and would turn back east after the pickup. Finally, they concluded that a group traveling on foot would arrive at the pick up site between 2 and 6 a.m. Agents conducted a surveillance approximately 27 miles east of milepost 122 and observed a pickup truck with a camper shell traveling west. The vehicle returned almost an hour and half later, driving east. The border patrol agents stopped the truck to conduct an immigration check. One of the agents noticed that the passenger in the truck was wearing a pair of shoes that matched the "chevron" shoe print. The agents looked in the camper shell and found six illegal aliens. The driver and passenger were arrested and convicted of transporting illegal aliens. The Supreme Court later upheld their conviction. In the opinion the Court approved the actions of the officers as follows:

> We see here the kind of police work often suggested by judges and scholars as examples of appropriate and reasonable means of law enforcement. Here, fact on fact and clue on clue afforded a basis for the deductions and inferences that brought officers to focus on "chevron." (United States v. Cortez at 419 [1981]).

An aggressive investigative detention can be an effective tool for the detection of crime when used by a knowledgeable law enforcement officer. To be truly effective, however, the officer must be able to establish probable cause in order to arrest a suspect or to conduct a search.

Probable Cause

The Fourth Amendment to the United States Constitution states:

> The right of the people to be secure in their persons, houses, papers, and effects, against unreasonable searches and seizures, shall not be violated, and no Warrants shall issue, but upon probable cause, supported by oath or affirmation, and particularly describing the place to be searched and persons or things to be seized.

Every phrase of the Fourth Amendment has been extensively examined, particularly over the last quarter century. The probable cause requirement has been a major concern of law enforcement officers. Probable cause is the minimum amount of evidence necessary to justify an arrest of a person or the search of a particular location. The classic definition of probable cause appeared in *Carrol v. United States*:

> Probable cause exists where the facts and circumstances within the knowledge of the arresting officers and of which they had reasonably trustworthy information are sufficient in themselves to warrant a man of reasonable caution in believing that an offense has been committed or is being committed or that property could be found in a particular place or on a particular person. (Carrol v. United States, 267 U.S. 132 [1925])

Establishing Probable Cause

Police officers may establish probable cause through a variety of techniques. An officer may establish probable cause through his own observations. This may be done by observing a theft or an assault committed in his presence, or by smelling the odor of burning marijuana coming from a vehicle during a car stop.

More often, probable cause is established through the use of hearsay or secondhand information provided to the officer from any number of sources. Hearsay information is often provided by a third party. Sources of information are usually referred to as *informants*, although the term has now fallen into disfavor among law enforcement professionals. More recently, terms such as *cooperating individual* or *contributor* have gained popularity among law enforcement officers because of the stigma attached to the words *informant* and *informer*.

Using the Cooperating Individual's Information

If the cooperating individual who provides information will allow the officer to use his name in an affidavit for a warrant, judges are less likely to question the appropriateness of issuing a warrant. The practice of using hearsay information is more likely to become an issue when law enforcement officers rely on unnamed or "confidential informants."

The Sixth Amendment states that the accused in any criminal case has the right to confront his accusers. The practice of using unnamed or secret informants conflicts with that guarantee. Further, the practice of using anonymous informants conflicts with the public's sense of fairness. It seems wrong to rely on evidence provided by unnamed individuals who may be involved in acts that are more serious than those of the person being prosecuted.

The use of hearsay information provided by confidential informants had been a concern for a number of years, but the issue was directly confronted in *Aguilar v. Texas* in 1964. In that case, two Houston narcotics detectives obtained a search warrant based on an affidavit that stated:

> Affiants have received reliable information from a credible person and do believe that heroin, marijuana, barbiturates, and other narcotics and narcotics paraphernalia are being kept at the above-described premises for the purpose of sale and use contrary to the provisions of the law. (Aguilar v. Texas, 378 U.S., 108, 84 S.Ct. 1509 [1964])

The U.S. Supreme Court found the affidavit to be inadequate and held that a magistrate must find probable cause for himself and not rely on the "mere conclusions" of the officers. *Aguilar v. Texas* resulted in the creation of what became known as the *two-pronged test* for establishing probable cause using hearsay evidence. The two-pronged test required, first, that a police officer wishing to use a cooperating individual's information establish the credibility of the informant and, second, that the officer demonstrate that the informant's information was believable.

The first prong of the test is usually satisfied in one of three ways. First, an informant's reliability can be shown by documenting that he made statements that could lead to criminal prosecution. This procedure is based on the assumption that rational people do not confess to crimes that they did not commit. This technique is particularly useful when using an informant for the first time.

A second method for establishing a cooperating individual's reliability is to demonstrate that the source has been used on different occasions and has established a "track record." Once a track record has been established, the person preparing an affidavit for a warrant could demonstrate an informant's reliability by including statements to the effect that the informant has "provided accurate information in the past that has led to X arrests and X convictions." This technique is preferred in that a specified number of arrests and convictions provides a more concrete standard by which a judge can evaluate a source's reliability.

A third, less desirable, technique to show a source's reliability is to simply state that the informant has provided accurate information in the past without listing any number of arrest convictions. This technique is less desirable because the judge has less evidence upon which to make a decision to issue a warrant.

The second prong of *Aguilar*, establishing the reliability of an informant's information, is most commonly satisfied by stating the informant had direct knowledge of the facts listed in the affidavit. For example, the source may say that evidence of a crime was seen at a particular location or that the source heard the suspect make incriminating statements.

Corroborating Information

In *Spinelli v. U.S.*, the Supreme Court continued to emphasize the need to demonstrate an informant's reliability. Although the Court overturned the defendant's conviction for racketeering, the technique of using corroboration was established. Under this concept, the court suggested that other reliable facts, when combined in sufficient number, might be adequate to justify a finding of probable cause by a magistrate. Thus, traditional investigative techniques, such as surveillance and record checks, could support the issuance of arrest or search warrants (Spinelli v. United States, 89 S.Ct. 584 [1969]).

In 1983, the Supreme Court handed down *Illinois v. Gates*, a decision that has had a profound impact on the use of hearsay information and informants for establishing probable cause. In *Gates*, the Court ruled that the standard to be used in determining if probable cause exists should be the "totality of the circumstances test." On May 3, 1978, the Bloomingdale, Illinois, Police Department received the following anonymous letter:

> This letter is to inform you that you have a couple in your town who strictly make their living on selling drugs. They are Sue and Lance Gates; they live on Greenway, off Bloomingdale Road in the condominiums. Most of their buys are done in Florida. Sue, his wife, drives their car to Florida where she leaves it to be loaded up with drugs, then Lance flies back after she drops the car off in Florida. May 3, she is driving down there again and Lance will be flying down in a few days to drive it back. At the time Lance drives the car back he has the truck loaded with over $100,000 in drugs. Presently, they have over $100,000 worth of drugs in their basement.
>
> They brag about the fact they never have to work and make their entire living on pushers.
>
> I guarantee if you watch them carefully you will make a big catch. They are friends with some big drug dealers, who visit their house often.
>
> Lance Susan Gates
> Greenway
> In Condominiums

After receiving the letter, a detective obtained the defendant's address and subsequently learned that Lance Gates had made a reservation for a May 5 flight to Florida. The detective made arrangements for a DEA surveillance of Gates on the flight. Gates made the flight and stayed overnight in Florida in a motel room registered in Susan Gates' name. The following morning Gates, along with an unidentified woman, began driving north in a car with license plates registered to Lance Gates. Investigators obtained a search warrant for the condominium and the car, which was served when the Gates arrived at the condominium. Marijuana was found in both the auto and the residence.

In *Gates* the Supreme Court eliminated the absolute requirement of the first prong of the *Aguilar* two-pronged test, that of establishing the credibility of the informant. At no point in the letter did the informant identify himself or otherwise provide information as to his credibility, at least from the perspective of *Aguilar*. The judge inferred the informant's credibility from the detailed information provided in the letter. The Court felt that information in the letter, after it had been corroborated by investigators, was adequate to establish probable cause. The *Gates* Court held:

> [T]here was a probability that writer of the anonymous letter had obtained his entire story either from the Gateses or someone they trusted. And corroboration of major portions of the letter's predictions provide just this possibility. (Illinois v. Gates, 103 S.Ct. at 2336 [1983])

The Supreme Court described the *Aguilar* test as "hyper technical" and called for a "commonsense" approach to be used by judges in determining the existence of probable cause. *Gates* did not negate *Aguilar* completely, however. Including the informant's name in the affidavit or using key phrases, such as "confidential source has provided accurate information in the past that has led to X arrests and X convictions," or including statements that are against the informant's penal interests are still effective means of establishing probable cause. Thus, while *Aguilar* is no longer the controlling case on the hearsay method of establishing probable cause, some of the techniques it gave rise to are still of use to an officer when presenting information to a judge.

Totality of Circumstances Test

Under the totality of circumstances test, judges are given considerable discretion in determining if a search warrant should be issued. *Gates*, however, did not give the issuing judge unrestricted discretion to determine probable cause. In *Gates*, the Court wrote "an affidavit must provide the issuing judge with a substantial basis for determining the existence of probable cause" (103 S.Ct at 2332). In addition, the Court required that "sufficient information must be presented to the judge to allow that official to determine probable cause; his action cannot be a mere ratification of the conclusions of others. In order to ensure that such an abdication of the judge's duty does not occur, courts must continue to conscientiously review the sufficiency of affidavits on which warrants are issued" (103 S.Ct. at 2333).

Preponderance of Evidence

Black's Law Dictionary defines preponderance of evidence as follows:

> Evidence which is of greater weight or more convincing than the evidence which is offered in opposition to it: that is, evidence which as a whole shows that the fact sought to be proved is more probable than not. (*Black's Law Dictionary*, 1983, p. 616)

A preponderance of evidence may be thought of in terms of the scales of justice. Each fact carries some weight with a jury and the side that offers more facts or evidence than the opposition will win or "preponder" by offering more facts than the opposing side. A preponderance of evidence is seldom of immediate concern to an investigator, except on suppression hearings. For example, in a suppression hearing the defendant may move, or request that, an item of evidence be suppressed or excluded from use in the proceeding because it was obtained illegally by the police. The illegal conduct of the police must be proven by a preponderance of evidence (Lego v. Twomey, 404 U.S. 477 [1972]).

Proof Beyond a Reasonable Doubt

Proof beyond a reasonable doubt is the standard against which the evidence in a criminal trial is weighed. As an experienced homicide investigator once told a young patrolman, "Before you do something, think about what it will look like in court." This admonition to the patrolman serves to remind all law enforcement officers of the reason criminal investigations are conducted, to determine the truth, to the extent possible, and, when appropriate, to prosecute and convict the guilty parties.

Like *reasonable suspicion* and *probable cause*, *proof beyond a reasonable doubt* cannot be precisely defined. It is the investigator's task to provide the prosecutor with as much evidence as is legally available in order to demonstrate the defendant's guilt at trial. Proof beyond a reasonable doubt is defined as follows:

> [S]uch proof as precludes every reasonable hypothesis except that which it tends to support and which is wholly consistent with defendant's guilt and inconsistent with any other rational conclusion. Such is the required standard of proof in criminal cases. (*Black's Law Dictionary*, 1983, p. 635)

In the trial of Harvard Professor Webster for the murder of Dr. Parkman, Chief Justice Shaw penned the most eloquent definition of reasonable doubt:

> It is that state of the case, which, after the entire comparison and consideration of all the evidence, leaves the minds of the jurors in that condition that they cannot say they feel an abiding conviction, to a moral certainty, of the truth of the charge.

In 1970, the Supreme Court held that the Fourteenth Amendment to the Constitution required that a criminal defendant's guilt be proven beyond a reasonable doubt in both adult trials and juvenile adjudicatory hearings (In re Winship, 397 U.S. 358 [1970]).

In a 1994 case, *Sandoval v. California*, the Supreme Court provided some guidance as to what constitutes proof beyond a reasonable doubt. Judge Lance Ito referred to the *Sandoval* opinion in the O.J. Simpson case. In a concurring opinion in *Sandoval*, Justice Ruth Bader Ginsburg offered the following ideas based on jury instructions given in federal criminal trials:

> The Federal Judicial Center has proposed a definition of reasonable doubt that is clear, straightforward, and accurate. That instruction reads:
> "The government has the burden of proving the defendant guilty beyond a reasonable doubt. Some of you may have served as jurors in civil cases, where you were told that it is only necessary to prove that a fact is more likely true than not true. In criminal cases, the government's proof must be more powerful than that. It must be beyond a reasonable doubt.
> "Proof beyond a reasonable doubt is proof that leaves you firmly convinced of the defendant's guilt. There are very few things in this world that we know with absolute certainty, and in criminal cases the law does not require proof that overcomes every possible doubt. If, based on your consideration of the evidence, you are firmly con-

vinced that the defendant is guilty of the crime charged, you must find him guilty. If on the other hand, you think there is a real possibility that he is not guilty, you must give him the benefit of the doubt and find him not guilty." (Sandoval v. California, CRL 2232 [1994])

An understanding of the levels of proof is essential for a criminal investigator to perform her job. Equally important, however, is an understanding of the role of arrest and search warrants in the investigative process.

The Warrant Requirement

The Supreme Court has long indicated a preference for search warrants, holding that searches conducted without such prior judicial authority are *prima facia* illegal. In *Katz v. U.S.* the Court stated:

> [The] Constitution requires that the deliberate, impartial judgment of a judicial officer be interposed between the citizen and the police . . . and searches conducted outside the judicial process, without prior approval by judge or magistrate, are per se unreasonable under the Fourth Amendment—subject to a few specifically established and well defined exceptions. (Katz v. United States, 389 U.S. 347 [1967] at 357)

Investigators must become familiar with the process of obtaining both search and arrest warrants. Examples of warrants appear on the following pages. They each include an application for a search warrant, the affidavit for a search warrant, a copy of the warrant, and the return of the warrant, in which the officers conducting the search report what they recovered to the judge who signed the warrant.

The Court has demonstrated its strong support for the warrant requirement by creating the "good faith" exception to the exclusionary rule. In the *United States v. Leon* and a companion case, *Massachusetts v. Shepard*, the Court ruled that the exclusionary rule need not be applied to evidence obtained by law enforcement officers who acted in good faith on a search warrant properly issued by a magistrate but later determined to be defective. Thus, today almost any item of evidence an officer recovers in a search is admissible as long as he is acting pursuant to a search warrant issued by a neutral magistrate.

In yet another drug case, the Court had to decide if a visitor in another person's house has an expectation of privacy under the Fourth Amendment. In *Minnesota v. Carter*, 119 S.Ct. 469 (1998) the Court was faced with the following factual situation. An informant advised a police officer that while walking past an apartment window he had observed people putting white powder into bags. The officer then walked past the same window and saw the same type of activity— people putting white powder into bags for several minutes. The officer notified police headquarters and returned to the scene while a search warrant was being prepared. When two men left the apartment in an automobile they were stopped by the police. When the car door was opened, officers saw a black zippered pouch and a handgun. The occupants of the auto were arrested and the car was searched. The search revealed pagers, a scale and 47 grams of cocaine in plastic sandwich bags. The officers returned to the apartment and arrested the female occupant. A woman was later found to be the leaseholder of the apartment, and the two men were visiting. A search warrant was served, and cocaine residue from the kitchen table and plastic bags was recovered.

The subsequent investigation revealed that the woman was the renter, and that the men lived in Chicago and had traveled to Minnesota for the purpose of dividing the cocaine. They had not been in the apartment before and had been there only about two and a half hours on that day. The two men appealed their convictions on the grounds that the actions of the police, looking through the window into the apartment, violated the Fourth Amendment prohibition against unreasonable searches and seizures. They based most of their argument on the earlier case of *Minnesota v. Olson*, 495 U.S. 91 in which the Court held that an overnight guest had a sufficient expectation of privacy in a host's dwelling to claim Fourth Amendment protection.

In this case, the Supreme Court held that the issue was not whether a search had occurred, rather that a search, which may have occurred did not violate the defendant's rights. They cited three reasons for arriving at this conclusion: (1) The defendants were not overnight guests, (2) they were there to conduct what amounted to a business transaction, and (3) they were only in the apartment for a few hours. The Court noted that an overnight guest could claim the protection of the Fourth Amendment while someone who is merely present with the consent of the householder may not. The Court went on to point out that by dividing up the cocaine at that location the apartment had become a commercial premise with a corresponding lessened expectation of privacy. The Court seems to be saying that the men had been there to engage in drug transactions. Thus, officers should continue to look to *Olson* for guidance in such cases.

Exceptions to the Search Warrant Requirement

Search is defined as a governmental intrusion into an area where a person has a reasonable expectation of privacy. If no government official is involved in a search or if police go into an area where the person has no recognized expectation of privacy, then by definition no search has occurred.

Searches conducted without a search warrant are illegal unless they fall within certain clearly defined exceptions:

- Search incident to arrest
- Investigative detention
- Vehicle exception search
- Plain view seizure
- Inventory or impound search
- Consent searches
- Open fields
- Abandonment

Search Incident to Arrest

When a law enforcement officer makes a custodial arrest, he has the authority to search the person arrested and the area under his immediate control. It is important to remember, however, that the authority to search incident to arrest is often limited by state statutes with regard to strip searches and body cavity searches. The difficulty in defining the extent of the search incident will be in determining what constitutes the area under the arrestee's immediate control. The answer lies in the "wingspan" rule. The Supreme Court has ruled that police may search an

IN THE CIRCUIT COURT OF SOUTH COUNTY, MISSOURI

STATE OF MISSOURI

CASE NO.____

COUNTY OF SOUTH

APPLICATION FOR SEARCH WARRANT

James Smith, Prosecuting Attorney for the County of South, State of Missouri, being duly sworn, deposes and states that evidence of the commission of the crime of assault is presently located in an upstairs apartment located at 220 N. Park, City of Southville, State of Missouri, which is described as the only upstairs apartment in the house located at 220 N. Park in Southville, State of Missouri, a house that has red brick on the bottom and white stucco on top, with the entrance to the upstairs apartment being reached by going up stairs that are on the outside of the building on the east side of the building. The evidence to be searched for includes a switchblade knife, a pistol holder, a .38 caliber ammunition round, blood smears that would indicate a violent struggle had occurred in the apartment within the last few days in which a woman was beaten, kicked, cut with a knife, and forced to look down the barrel of the gun.

Basis of the affiant's information and belief is contained in the attached affidavit of Patrolman Rodney W. Baker, of facts concerning the said matter, and said affidavit is attached hereto and incorporated herein by reference and is submitted herewith as basis which this Court may find existence of probable cause for the issuance of said warrant.

WHEREFORE, complainant prays that a search warrant be issues as provided by law.

OFFICE OF THE PROSECUTING ATTORNEY

By:_____
James Smith #12345

Subscribed and sworn to before me this ___day of ____, 19____.

_____
CIRCUIT COURT JUDGE

TIME:_____

Figure 2.1   Application for search warrant (example 1)

IN THE CIRCUIT COURT OF SOUTH COUNTY, MISSOURI

STATE OF MISSOURI

SS. CASE NO._____

COUNTY OF SOUTH

AFFIDAVIT

I, Rodney F. Becker, upon my oath state to he court as follows:

1. I am a police officer with the Southville Police Department. I have been a police officer for four years and two months.

2. On September 3, 1991, I interviewed Brandy Barnes, age 21, of Southville. Brandy told me that this morning at 7:30 a.m. a badly beaten white female came to Brandy's home and knocked on the door. The white female identified herself as Jennifer Doe and said that her boyfriend had beaten her. Doe said the beating had started on Thursday night and had continued until Saturday morning, and that she had snuck out while he was asleep. Doe was still bleeding from her wounds. She said her boyfriend had thrown knives at her feet, had said he would kill her, and made her look down a gun barrel, had hit her on her ears so many times that she had dried blood in her ear, and had stomped on her knee. Doe told Brandy she had come to Brandy's apartment because a friend of Doe's used to live there and Doe thought the friend still did. Brandy took Doe to the hospital.

3. Patrolman Judy Green talked briefly with Doe at Northwest Hospital today and Doe told Green that her boyfriend had pointed a small gun at her and that he had beat her up. I spoke today with Jennifer Doe's mother, Janice Doe, who told me that Jennifer's boyfriend is George Jones, approximately 32 years old, who lives in the first block of Broadway on Park Street in Southville, Missouri, and that it is the first house south of a white brick apartment. I drove by that location and found it to be 220 N. Park, City of Southville, County of South, State of Missouri. The upstairs apartment is reached by going up the stairs on the outside of the building on the east side of the building. The building is red brick on the bottom and white stucco on the top. Her mother said he drove a black Trans Am. When I drove by that location at approximately 1:10 p.m., the black Trans Am was parked outside. Its license plate number was ABC 123. I ran that through the computer and it checked to a George R. Jones of Johnston City, Missouri.

4. A check of George R. Jones' criminal record shows me that he has a felony forgery conviction from West County from January 9, 1987. His date of birth is May 16, 1955. He is a white male, 5'10", 180 pounds.

5. Mrs. Doe told me that she believed Jones had beat her daughter about a month ago because her daughter had bruises on her head, neck, and shoulder at that time.

6. She said her daughter had been dating him since back in the spring, and that she had been living with him off and on during the summer months.

Figure 2.2   Affidavit (example 1)

AFFIDAVIT (Con't.)

7. I saw Jennifer Doe at Northwest Hospital. She has numerous cuts on her breasts, neck, legs, and stomach. An X had been cut on her lower abdomen. She had a severe bruise on her left knee. She had a severe black eye on her left eye. Her right eye was also bruised. She had cuts on her back. She had a stab wound on the top of her right foot. She had four cuts on her scalp. She had severe bruising on both legs and both arms and on her back. One of the nurses treating her indicated to me that Jennifer may have broken bones on the left side of her face and in her left hand. The nurse also indicated that there was a vaginal tear and swelling in her genital area, and that Jennifer had told the medical personnel that Jones had kicked her in the genital area.

8. Brandy told me that Doe had said the beating had happened at Doe's boyfriend's apartment.

9. After obtaining a warrant for Jones' arrest, I went, with other officers, to Jones' apartment described at the top of the building. Captain Burn went up the stairs and knocked on the door. Nobody answered. He tried the doorknob and found it was unlocked. We went in and found Jones in bed. We arrested him.

10. Captain Burn told him he was under arrest while he was in bed. At the same time he was telling him he was under arrest, Captain Burn pulled down the covers on the bed. We saw a switchblade knife on the bed next to Jones. He would not consent to a search of the house. We left the knife in the bed.

11. While we were in the house we saw in plain view a .38 caliber round of ammunition on a knee-high chest of drawers near the bed. Brad German saw in plain view a pistol-holster on the floor at the east side of the bed. Blood was smeared on the door frame leading into the bedroom. Blood was splattered on the floor of the living room and on papers on the floor in the living room. There were also blood stains on the sheets. Brad German says he noticed what appears to be a human skull on a lamp table on the north wall of the living room. A can of black powder labeled as gun powder was on the floor beside the bed.

12. Photographs of the front and back of the apartment to be searched are marked Exhibits A and B respectively and are attached hereto and incorporated herein by reference.

I have read this Affidavit and the facts contained herein are true to the best of my knowledge.

_____
Rodney F. Becker

Subscribed and sworn to before me this __ day of ___, 19__

_____
Circuit Court Judge

TIME:_____

Figure 2.2   Affidavit (example 1) *Continued*

IN THE CIRCUIT COURT OF SOUTH COUNTY, MISSOURI

STATE OF MISSOURI

SS. CASE NO._____

COUNTY OF CAPE GIRARDEAU

SEARCH WARRANT

THE STATE OF MISSOURI TO ANY PEACE OFFICER IN THE STATE OF MISSOURI:

WHEREAS, an application for a search warrant in writing, duly verified by oath, has been filed with the undersigned Judge of this Court, stating upon information and belief that evidence of the commission of the crime of assault is located in an upstairs apartment of a house located at 220 N. Park, City of Southville, County of South, State of Missouri. Which is described as the only upstairs apartment of the house located at 220 N. Park, a house with red brick on he bottom and white stucco on top, with the entrance to the upstairs apartment being reached by going up stairs that are on the outside of the building on the east side of the building. The evidence to be searched for includes a switchblade knife, a pistol holster, a .38 caliber ammunition round, blood smears or splattering pools, a gun, and any other evidence that would indicate that a violent struggle had occurred in that apartment within the last few days in which a woman was beaten, kicked, cut with a knife, and forced to look down the barrel of a gun.

WHEREAS, the Judge of this Court from the sworn allegations of said complaint and from supporting written affidavit filed therewith has found that there is probable cause to believe the allegations of the complaint to be true and probable cause for the issuance of a search warrant herein.

NOW, THEREFORE, these are to command you that you search the said dwelling above described within ten days after the issuance of this warrant by day and night, and take with you, if need be, the power of your County or City, and, if said above-described property or any part thereof be found on said property by you, that you seize the same and take same into your possession, making a complete and accurate inventory of the property so taken by you in the presence of the person from whose possession the same is taken, if that be possible, and giving to such person a receipt for such property, together with a copy of this warrant, or, if no person be found in possession of said property, leaving said receipt and said copy upon the premises searched, and that you thereafter return the property so taken and seized by you, together with a duly verified copy of the inventory thereof, and with your return this warrant to this Court to be dealt with in accordance with the law.

Witness my hand and the seal of this Court on this ____day of ___, 19___

_____
CIRCUIT COURT JUDGE

TIME:_____

Figure 2.3   Search warrant (example 1)

IN THE CIRCUIT COURT OF SOUTH COUNTY, MISSOURI

STATE OF MISSOURI

COUNTY OF CAPE GIRARDEAU

RETURN AND INVENTORY

I, _____, being a peace officer within and for the aforementioned County, to_wit: _____. Do hereby make return to the above and within warrant as follows: that on the ___day of ___, 19__, and within ten days after issuance of said warrant, I went to the location and premises described therein, and that upon said premises I discovered the following personal property described in the warrant which I then and there took into my possession:

_____

_____

that I made this inventory in the presence of the person from whose possession I took said property (that there was no person present from whose possession said property was taken); that I delivered to such person a receipt for the property taken, together with a copy of this warrant (that, there being no person in possession of said property present on said premises, I left a copy of this warrant with a receipt for the property taken, in a conspicuous place on said premises); that I have placed said property so taken in the possession of this court.

_____

Subscribed and sworn to before me this ____day of _____, 19___

_____
Clerk, Magistrate Court

RETURN AND INVENTORY CONTINUATION   PAGE____of____

_____
_____
_____
_____
_____
_____
_____
_____
_____
_____
_____
_____
_____

_____
Officer

(Attached additional sheets as necessary)

Figure 2.4   Return and inventory (example 1)

IN THE CIRCUIT COURT OF CAPE GIRARDEAU COUNTY, MISSOURI

STATE OF MISSOURI

SS. CASE NO._____

COUNTY OF CAPE GIRARDEAU

APPLICATION FOR SEARCH WARRANT

James Smith, Prosecuting Attorney of the South, State of Missouri, being duly sworn, deposes and states upon information and belief that a quantity of stolen property consisting of a PSE compound bow and quiver, Easton arrows, a Winchester Model 97 12 gauge shotgun, hip quiver and belt, Mallard Tone Duck call, 2 Duck Commander calls, 3 Olt goose calls, one pair of Gortex gloves, one Gortex gloves, one Gortex hunting coat, and two pairs of Jersey gloves, and a quantity of marijuana, and drug paraphernalia consisting of a bong and a bowl, are presently located in a small house at 20 E. Oak Street, reached by driving toward the river on Oak Street, turning left at the bridge and then making a quick right, with the house being the second house on the left, all in the City of Southville, County of South, State of Missouri.

Basis of affiant's information and belief is contained in the attached affidavit of witness of facts concerning the said matter of Robert E. Lee, Jr., and said affidavit is attached hereto and incorporated herein by reference and is submitted herewith as basis upon which this Court may find existence of a probable cause for the issuance of said warrant.

WHEREFORE, complaint prays that a search warrant be issued as provided by law.

OFFICE OF THE PROSECUTING ATTORNEY

BY:_____
Prosecuting Attorney #12345
County of South
Courthouse Park
Southville, MO 54321
(314) 651-2000

Subscribed and sworn to before me this ____day of ___, 19__.

_____
CIRCUIT COURT JUDGE

TIME:____

Figure 2.5   Application for search warrant (example 2)

IN THE CIRCUIT COURT OF SOUTH COUNTY, MISSOURI

STATE OF MISSOURI

                                                    SS. CASE NO._____

COUNTY OF SOUTH

AFFIDAVIT

I, Robert E. Lee, Jr., being duly sworn, depose and state the following:

1. I am a Police Officer with the City of Southville Police Department, Southville, Missouri, and have been so for fifteen and a half years.

2. I am currently the Assistant Narcotics Investigator for the Southville Police Department and have attended the Basic Narcotic Investigation Course and Clandestine Lab Course offered by the Drug Enforcement Administration.

3. On December 19, 1996, at approximately 11:15 a.m., I received an anonymous phone call from a person who sounded on the telephone to be a white male. The caller requested to remain anonymous and offered information pertaining to stolen guns and property and drug paraphernalia.

4. The caller stated that on approximately December 11, 1996, he was at a residence in Southville, Missouri, and had seen a quantity of marijuana, a "bong" and a "bowl". He also saw two stolen shotguns. One of the shotguns is described as a 12 gauge. Both are single shot models. The directions to the house are as follows: As you go toward the river on Oak Street, turn left at the bridge and then make a quick right. The house is a small one, the second house on the left.

5. The caller stated that the occupants of the residence smoke marijuana "all the time" and, have liquor and beer in the residence. The people who live there are under twenty-one.

6. The caller said the stolen property observed at the residence were two stolen guns, a compound bow and arrows, several "goose calls", radar detectors, and car stereos.

7. The caller says the people living at he residence are Greg Harty, Bryant Kamp, and Christy Roll.

8. On December 19, 1996, I was in contact with the Board of Probation and Parole in Southville. A representative there said that Harty is a white male, born July 14, 1969, 6'0", 130 lbs, brown hair and blue eyes, last known address 20 E. Oak Street, Southville, Missouri. He is still on probation and the address should still be good. Their records show that he has a roommate named Bryant Kamp.

Figure 2.6   Affidavit (example 2)

AFFIDAVIT (Con't.)

9. On December 19, 1996, I was notified by Detective Ken Money that he is investigating a theft at 2801 Blue Road, Lot 57, in Southville, Missouri, that occurred on December 11, 1996, where PSE compound bow nd quiver, easton arrows, Winchester Model 97 12 gauge shotgun, hip quiver and belt, Mallard Time Duck call, 2 Duck Commander duck calls, 3 Olt goose calls, one pair of Gortex gloves, one Gortex hunting coat, and two pair of Jersey gloves, were stolen. .

10. The caller said he personally saw the bow and arrows, goose calls, and shotgun at Harty's residence and that two males named Kent Bryant and John Smith, who were at the house, said they had stolen them.

11. Detective Keith Brown went to the outside of the house today and took a photograph of it. The photograph is marked Exhibit A and is attached hereto and incorporated herein by reference. It is described as a small house at 20 E. Oak Street, a small brick-fronted house with awnings over the front windows, reached by driving toward the river on Oak Street, turning left at the bridge and them making a quick right, with the house being the second house on the left, all in the City of Southville, County of South, State of Missouri

12. The caller, also, said that Greg Harty is a dealer in stolen property, mainly stolen radar detectors and stereos.

13. Based on my experience and training in working drug cases I found this anonymous information to be credible and believable.

14. I have read this Affidavit and the facts contained herein are true to the best of my knowledge.

_____
Robert E. Lee, Jr.

Subscribed and sworn to before me this __ day of ___, 19__.

_____
Circuit Court Judge

TIME:____

Figure 2.6   Affidavit (example 2) _Continued_

IN THE CIRCUIT COURT OF SOUTH COUNTY, MISSOURI

STATE OF MISSOURI

SS. CASE NO._____

COUNTY OF SOUTH

SEARCH WARRANT

THE STATE OF MISSOURI TO ANY PEACE OFFICER IN THE STATE OF MISSOURI:

WHEREAS, as application for a search warrant in writing, duly verified by oath, has been filed with the undersigned Judge of this Court, stating upon information and belief that a quantity of stolen property consisting of a PSE compound bow and quiver, Easton arrows, Winchester Model 97 12 gauge shotgun, hip quiver and belt, Mallard Tone Duck call, 2 Duck commander duck calls, 3 Olt goose calls, one pair of Gortex gloves, one Gortex hunting coat and two pairs of Jersey gloves, and a quantity of marijuana, and drug paraphernalia consisting of a bong and a bowl, are presently located in a small house at 20 E. Oak Street, reached by driving toward the river on Oak Street, turning left at the bridge and then making a quick right, with the house being the second house on the left, all in the City of Southville, County of South, State of Missouri.

WHEREAS, the Judge of this Court from the sworn allegations of said complaint and from supporting written affidavit filed therewith has found that there is probable cause to believe the allegations of the complaint to be true and probable cause for the issuance of a search warrant herein.

NOW, THEREFORE, these are to command you that you search the said house above described within ten days after the issuance of this warrant by day and night, and take with you, if need by, the power of your County or City, and, if said above-described property or any part thereof be found on said property by you, that you seize the same and take into your possession, making a complete and accurate inventory so taken by you in the presence of the person from whose possession the same is taken, if that be possible, and giving to such person a receipt for such property, together with a copy of this warrant, or, if no person be found in possession of said property, leaving said receipt and said copy upon the premises searched, and that you thereafter return the property so taken and seized by you, together with a duly verified copy of the inventory thereof, and with your return to this warrant to this Court to be dealt with in accordance with the law.

Witness my hand and the seal of this Court on this __day of _____, 19__.

_____
CIRCUIT COURT JUDGE

TIME:_____

Figure 2.7   Search warrant (example 2)

IN THE CIRCUIT COURT OF SOUTH COUNTY, MISSOURI

STATE OF MISSOURI

COUNTY OF SOUTH

RETURN AND INVENTORY

I, _____, being a peace officer within and for the aforesaid County, to-wit: _____, do hereby make return to the above and within warrant as follows: that on the ___ day of _____, 19 __, and within ten days after issuance of said warrant, I want to the location and premises described therein, and that upon said premises I discovered the following personal property described in the warrant which I then and there took into my possession:_____

_____

that I made this inventory in the presence of the person from whose possession I took said property; that I delivered to such person a receipt for the property taken, together with a copy of this warrant; that I have placed said property so taken in the possession of this court.

_____

Subscribed and sworn to before me this ___ day of _____, 19__.

_____
Circuit Judge

RETURN AND INVENTORY CONTINUATION   Page ___of____

_____
_____
_____
_____
_____
_____
_____
_____
_____
_____
_____
_____
_____
_____

_____
Officer

(Attach additional sheets as necessary)

Figure 2.8   Return and inventory (example 2)

area in which the arrested person could reach in order to obtain a weapon, gain the means to escape, or destroy evidence (Chimel v. California [1969]). If the person is arrested from a vehicle, the officer may search the entire passenger compartment of the vehicle (New York v. Belton [1981]).

Investigative Detention

Investigative detention is often referred to as "stop and frisk." The *investigative detention* is based on the authority of peace officers to stop and briefly detain persons when the officer has a reasonable suspicion that the person is then or is about to commit a crime. Any investigative detention should be documented by officers to provide investigative leads at a later time.

Vehicle Searches

The authority to conduct a warrantless search of a motor vehicle is one of the oldest yet most misunderstood exceptions to the warrant requirement. In *Carrol v. United States*, 267 U.S. (1925), the Court held that peace officers may search a vehicle if three factors are present. First, the officer must have probable cause to believe that evidence of a crime or contraband is concealed somewhere in the vehicle. Second, the vehicle must be in a place where it is lawfully accessible to the police, such as on a city street. Finally, the scope of the search must be restricted to areas where the item searched for could be hidden. For example, police could not search for a stolen engine in a glove compartment. In 1983, the Supreme Court revitalized the vehicle exception in *United States v. Ross*, 456 U.S. 798 (1982). Recreational vehicles are subject to the vehicle exception as long as they are mobile and are in an area accessible to the police.

In *Wyoming v. Houghton*, 119 S.Ct. 1297 (1999), the Court held that when an officer has probable cause to search a vehicle, the officer may search objects belonging to a passenger in the vehicle as long as the item the officer is looking for could reasonably be found in a passenger's belongings. *Houghton* clears up some of the confusion that has surrounded the search of vehicle occupants. In this case, Sandra Houghton was a passenger in a vehicle stopped by the Wyoming Highway Patrol. During the stop, the officer saw a hypodermic syringe in the driver's shirt pocket. The officer asked why the driver had a syringe. The driver responded, stating that he used it to take drugs. Houghton was then asked, at which time she responded with a false answer and denied having any identification. The passengers were then removed from the car, and the officer began searching for contraband. One officer found Houghton's purse and removed her wallet and some identification. He continued to search her purse and found a syringe containing methamphetamine and related drug paraphernalia. She was arrested for possession of a controlled substance. The Wyoming Supreme Court reversed her conviction and the State of Wyoming appealed. The U.S. Supreme Court reversed the Wyoming Supreme Court and held that when probable cause exists to search a vehicle, that it may extend to the entire vehicle including the belongings that are capable of concealing the object of the search. The Court stated that passengers, like a driver, had a lesser expectation of privacy in the vehicle.

In *Maryland v. Dyson*, the Court once again dealt with the warrantless search of a vehicle. The Court has ruled that a warrantless search of a vehicle is permitted when officers have probable cause that a motor vehicle contains evidence or contraband, even in the absence of exigent circumstances. In this case, a Maryland sheriff's deputy received a tip from a reliable informant that an alleged drug dealer was traveling to New York to purchase drugs and would be returning to Maryland. The informant provided the deputy with a vehicle description including the make, color and license plate number and the fact that the vehicle was a rental. The deputy followed up on this tip and found that the license number, DDY 787, provided by the informant belonged to a red Toyota Corolla and had been rented to the alleged drug dealer. When the alleged drug dealer, Kevin Dyson, returned in the rental as predicted by the informant, deputies stopped and searched the car. The search revealed 23 grams of crack cocaine found in a duffel bag in the trunk. Dyson was convicted of conspiracy to possess cocaine with the intent to distribute.

Dyson appealed his conviction on the grounds that the trial court had erred in denying his motions to suppress the cocaine on the alternate grounds that deputies lacked probable cause to search the vehicle in the first place. He further argued that if probable cause existed, the warrantless search was unreasonable because there was sufficient time after the deputy had received the tip to obtain a warrant and that no exigent circumstances existed.

The Supreme Court ruled that although the Fourth Amendment generally requires an officer to obtain a warrant before conducting a search, the Court had held almost 75 years ago that there is a vehicle exception to the warrant requirement. The Court went on to say that the automobile exception does not require exigent circumstances to justify the search without a warrant. Thus, in *Maryland v. Dyson*, the Supreme Court maintained the vehicle exception to the search warrant requirement. Officers will continue to follow the guidelines established in *Carroll v. United States* and *United States v. Ross*.

Plain View Seizures

Plain view seizure means police can seize anything immediately recognized as evidence if it is in plain view and if three clearly defined criteria are met. First, the officer must be prepared to prove that he was lawfully in the place where the observations were made. Second, he must observe something that he knows to be subject to seizure. In most cases, this will be contraband, such as an illegal firearm or some type of drug. Finally, the item must be readily observable. The requirement that the item be in the open is the reason why this act is referred to as a *seizure* not a *search*. If the officer had to look for the item, then it is a search and cannot be justified as a plain view seizure (Coolidge v. New Hampshire, 403 U.S. 443 [1974]; Texas v. Brown, 460 U.S. 730 [1983]).

Minnesota v. Dickerson and the "Plain Feel" Doctrine

In 1993, the Supreme Court expanded an investigating officer's powers to conduct a search in what has come to be called the *plain feel doctrine*. In *Minnesota v. Dickerson*, 61 LW 4545 (1993), the Court held that under certain circumstances police officers may seize any drugs they find while conducting a pat down of an individual for weapons, as long as they stay within the guidelines established in *Terry v. Ohio*, 392 U.S. 1 (1968). Justice White wrote, "if a police officer lawfully pats down a suspect's outer clothing and feels an object whose contour or mass makes its identity immediately apparent, there has been no invasion of the suspect's privacy beyond that already authorized by the officer's search for weapons, if the object is contraband, its warrantless seizure would be justified." Thus, a police officer who conducts an investigative detention and who has reasonable suspicion to believe that the suspect may be armed can, as always, pat down or frisk the person to find weapons. If, while conducting a frisk, he feels what his training and experience indicates—that the person is in possession of something the officer believes is drugs, such as a plastic bags of marijuana or crack cocaine—the officer may seize the drugs under the plain feel doctrine.

Inventory or Impound Searches

Law enforcement officers are often required to take possession of motor vehicles or other types of property to protect the interests of both the department and the officer, and of the owner of the vehicle or property. When police impound a vehicle, they assume the role of *involuntary bailee*, meaning that they have a limited obligation to see that the vehicle be moved to a location where it will be secure. Once the vehicle is impounded, police must inventory its contents to determine the presence of valuables or dangerous items. If, while conducting the inventory, police find contraband, the item may be seized and the owner prosecuted for possessing it (South Dakota v. Opperman, 428 U.S. 364 [1976]).

Inventory searches are valid if:

1. The officer is legally in possession of the vehicle, such as impounding an illegally parked car
2. The officer is acting pursuant to a standard department operational procedure
3. The search is restricted to areas where valuables or dangerous items might be concealed

However, this means that officers can search the passenger compartment, the trunk, and the glove box, including containers in those areas (Colorado v. Bertine, 479 U.S. 564 [1987]).

Consent Searches

Police officers may ask permission to search a building, vehicle, or container. In a consent search, the officer is asking the person to waive his or her Fourth Amendment right to refuse the search (Bumper v. North Carolina, 391 U.S. [1968]). The search will be considered valid if the person giving consent does so voluntarily and has lawful control of the item or area to be searched. The person giving consent may limit the scope of the search and may withdraw consent at any time. When requesting consent to search, peace officers are not required to inform the person that he or she may refuse to give consent (Scheckloth v.

Bustamonte, 412 U.S. 218 [1973]). Similarly, officers are not required to obtain a written waiver of rights form, although either of these would be helpful in proving that consent was given voluntarily.

Open Fields

The open fields doctrine states that open areas outside the "curtilage" of a structure are not protected by the Fourth Amendment prohibition against unreasonable searches and seizures (Oliver v. United States, 466 U.S. 170 [1984]. *Curtilage* is the ground and buildings that are for the exclusive use of the person living there, including residential yards, fenced areas, garages, and outbuildings close to the house. Law enforcement officers may go into areas that are outside the curtilage in order to look for evidence of a crime.

Abandonment

A person has no expectation of privacy with regard to property or items that have been abandoned. *Abandonment* means giving up something without limitation as to any particular person or purpose. Thus, if someone checks out of a motel room and leaves behind incriminating evidence, police can seize it for use against the defendant in a criminal case.

The Criminal Trial and the Rules of Evidence

The criminal trial is the capstone of the American judicial system. Even though a relatively small number of cases actually come to trial, the trial is the standard by which evidence both for and against the defendant is measured. The prosecuting attorney's professional judgment about the strengths or weaknesses of a case will determine whether it will go to trial, be plea bargained, or be dismissed.

In a trial, evidence is presented to prove the defendant's guilt or innocence. The rules of evidence govern the actions of the trial court judges when they determine if a piece of evidence should be admitted.

The criminal investigator must have a good working knowledge of the rules of evidence in order to be effective, both in and out of the courtroom. The more detailed and complete the investigator's knowledge of these rules is, the better able he or she will be to judge the strength of a case and to assist the prosecutor in preparing the case for court.

Trier of Fact

In a criminal trial, someone must determine what the facts of the case are and then make a decision about the defendant's guilt or innocence. Under the American system of justice, defendants in a criminal case have a right to have their case heard before a jury of their peers. This normally means that a person can have the facts of his or her case determined by a group of 12 men and women who have no opinions about their guilt or innocence before the trial begins. This process is referred to as the *trial by jury*, and the jurors are known as the *trier of fact*. The jurors hear the evidence and reach a verdict based on the evidence presented to them.

In some cases, the defendant may wish to waive the right to a jury trial and have a judge serve as the trier of fact. This type of proceeding is a *bench trial*. In a bench trial, the judge serves as both the administrator of the trial and the trier of fact. The decision about which type of trial the defendant should have is made by the defendant with the advice of an attorney.

Evidence and Proof

Evidence is the means by which facts are proven in a lawsuit. *Proof* is the end product of the evidence presented to the trier of fact. *Black's* defines *proof* this way:

> The effect of evidence; the establishment of a fact by evidence. Any fact or circumstance which leads the mind to the affirmative or negative of any proposition. The conviction or persuasion of the mind of a judge or jury, by the exhibition of evidence, of the reality of a fact alleged. (*Black's Law Dictionary*, 1983, p. 635)

When adequate evidence has been presented to a jury, then a fact has been proven. In most cases, no single piece of evidence will be adequate to prove a fact. The investigator's task is to gather evidence to build a case, much like a bricklayer building a wall, brick by brick. When the evidence is presented at trial, the jury is charged with the responsibility of deciding what the facts of the case are and of rendering a verdict based solely on those facts.

Presumptions

A *presumption* is a rule of law that enables the party, in whose favor the presumption operates, to take the case to the jury without even presenting evidence of that fact. A presumption of law is not evidence, and it should not be thought of by the trier of fact as evidence.

Presumption of Innocence

The *presumption of innocence* is most often associated with a criminal trial. *Black's Law Dictionary* defines the *presumption of innocence* as follows:

> A hallowed principle of criminal law to the effect that the government has the burden of proving every element of a crime beyond a reasonable doubt and that the defendant has no burden to prove his innocence. (*Black's Law Dictionary*, 1983, p. 618)

The presumption of innocence requires that the prosecution prove the defendant's guilt beyond a reasonable doubt. This means that if, after hearing all the evidence, the jury remains unconvinced about the defendant's guilt, they must find him not guilty.

Presumptions are of two types: conclusive and rebuttable. Juries are required to follow presumptions when weighing the evidence in a criminal case. There are few *conclusive* or irrebuttable presumptions. For example, there is a presumption that a child under the age of seven years lacks the mental ability to formulate the mental intent to commit a crime. Most presumptions are rebuttable, such as the presumption of innocence, the presumption that the defendant was sane at the time a crime was committed, or that a person who has not been heard from in seven years is dead. A presumption is *rebuttable* if it can be disproved by evidence offered to the contrary.

Inferences

Inferences are sometimes referred to as *presumptions of fact* and are similar to presumptions. They differ, however, in that juries are freer to accept or reject inferences based on their perceptions of the facts. For example, a rape victim might identify a defendant as her attacker from the witness stand. This identification would give rise to an inference that the defendant is guilty of the crime. The jury may, however, feel equally free to reject the inference based on the witness's recitation of the facts.

Weight of Evidence

Once the evidence is before a jury, jurors have an obligation to determine how believable it is or how much weight they wish to give an item of evidence. Subject to the rules of law already described, juries are given great latitude in determining how much weight should be given to evidence. Date rape trials present a particularly difficult example of how juries are called upon to weigh evidence. In cases of this sort, the outcome will hinge on how much the jury believes the victim's testimony in relationship to that of the defendant. As the old saying goes, "it's her word against his," and the jury must decide who is telling the truth.

Burden of Proof

The prosecution's *burden of proof* in a criminal case is to demonstrate the defendant's guilt beyond a reasonable doubt. This is the highest level of proof required in the American judicial system. The Supreme Court stated the importance of this high legal standard in the case of *In Re Winship*:

> The requirement of proof beyond a reasonable doubt has a vital role in our criminal procedure for cogent reasons. The accused during a criminal prosecution has at stake interests of immense importance, both because of the possibility that he may lose his liberty upon conviction and because of the certainty that he would be stigmatized by the conviction.
>
> Moreover, use of the reasonable doubt standard is indispensable to command the respect and confidence of the community in applications of the criminal law. It is critical that the moral force of the law not be diluted by a standard of proof that leaves people in doubt whether innocent men are being condemned. (In Re Winship, 397 U.S. at 363, 364, 90 S.Ct. at 1972)

In every criminal case, the defendant is presumed to be innocent. It is the state's obligation to prove the defendant's guilt; this is the prosecution's burden of proof. The burden of proof in a criminal case never shifts from the prosecution. If, after hearing all the evidence, the jury has a reasonable doubt as to the defendant's guilt, that is, the jurors are not convinced beyond a moral certainty that the accused is in fact guilty as charged, the jury must return a verdict of not guilty. The word *reasonable* plays a major role in this process. The law does not require that the defendant's guilt be determined by absolute proof, requiring the exclusion of every possible explanation for what occurred. If the jury has no *reasonable* explanation why they doubt the defendant's guilt, they must find for the state. Juries can occasionally be manipulated, but on the whole they work remarkably well as fact finders.

Forms and Types of Evidence

Evidence is classified by form and type. The forms of evidence are as follows:

- Real evidence
- Documentary evidence
- Testimonial evidence
- Judicial notice

Real Evidence

Real evidence is often referred to as physical evidence and consists of tangible objects that the jury can see. Common types of real evidence are guns and other weapons used in crimes, money, and/or clothing worn by a suspect.

Documentary Evidence

Documentary evidence is sometimes referred to as "writings" and is similar to real evidence. Documentary evidence examples include checks, ransom notes, robbery notes, and suicide notes.

Testimonial Evidence

Testimonial evidence is oral testimony provided by witnesses to a crime. This testimony may be given on the witness stand or be taken by deposition.

Judicial Notice

Judicial notice is evidence of facts that are common knowledge. By taking judicial notice of facts that are known to them and the public, the trial judge can speed up the trial by avoiding the tedious process of proving an accepted fact. Trial court judges generally take judicial notice of well-known geographic facts, the meaning of certain words such as grass for marijuana, or the sex of a witness.

Evidence may also be classified by type. The types of evidence are as follows:

- Direct evidence
- Circumstantial evidence
- Cumulative evidence
- Corroborative evidence

Direct Evidence

Direct evidence is evidence that directly proves a fact in issue. Eyewitness testimony, in which a victim positively identifies someone as the person who committed a crime, is direct evidence.

Circumstantial Evidence

Circumstantial evidence indirectly proves a fact in issue. It is evidence from which the trier of fact can infer facts in a case. Most of the evidence located by investigators is circumstantial and, when combined with other evidence, will be adequate to prove the defendant's guilt beyond a reasonable doubt. Fingerprints found at a crime scene are circumstantial evidence. They may prove that the suspect was at the scene but not that he committed the crime. The location of the prints can lead to inferences that the suspect is guilty. For example, if the prints are found at a location to which the defendant would not usually have access, then the jury could reasonably infer that the defendant was at that location and is very possibly guilty of the crime.

Cumulative Evidence

Cumulative evidence is additional evidence on issues that have already been proven by direct or circumstantial evidence. As such, trial judges may not allow it in as evidence unless the proponent of the evidence is able to offer some reason why it should be admitted. For example, if several persons observe the same event, only one or two good witnesses are needed to prove that the event, in fact, occurred.

Corroborative Evidence

Corroborative evidence is offered to support other direct or circumstantial evidence by showing reliability of sources. For example, if a witness claims to have been at a certain place, phone, gas, or motel receipts showing that the person was there tend to corroborate or support what the witness says.

Admissibility

Not every item of evidence developed in an investigation may be presented to a jury. The trial court judge must first determine that the evidence is admissible. The rule of *admissibility* is that basically all items of evidence are admissible as long as they are both *relevant* and *material*, subject to certain other restrictions. For example, grisly photographs might be both relevant and material, but might still be excluded by a trial court judge because the graphic violence might upset jurors, thereby prejudicing them against the defendant.

Relevancy

To be admissible, evidence must be relevant, that is, it must have some probative value. The item of evidence must tend to prove the proposition for which it is offered. The trial judge must determine if the evidence offered tends logically to prove a fact.

Materiality

To be admissible, evidence must not only be relevant, but also material; that is, the evidence must relate to the central issue of the proceeding. Again, the trial judge will be required to determine if the evidence is related to the issue. Materiality and relevancy have been merged into the single concept of *admissibility*. For example, the testimony of a witness that a person closely matching the defendant was seen running from the scene of robbery is offered at trial. The evidence is both relevant, in that it tends to prove that the defendant was in the area, and material, in that it relates to the central issue in the trial and proves that the defendant had the opportunity to commit the robbery. Conversely, a defendant's previous conviction for shoplifting would be inadmissible in his trial for armed robbery. The fact that he has a stealing conviction does not prove that he committed a robbery, and therefore it is irrelevant. It is also immaterial because the issue in this trial is whether he committed robbery not stealing. The trial judge would rule the evidence inadmissible.

Witness Competency

All potential witnesses are competent to testify in a legal proceeding if they meet three requirements:

1. The prospective witness must understand the significance of the oath, that is, he or she must understand the obligation to tell the truth.
2. The prospective witness must be able to communicate to the trier of fact. This may be done by his or her own means or, in some cases, through an interpreter.
3. Finally, the prospective witness must have some knowledge and recall about the matter he or she is called upon to testify about.

Witness competency most often becomes an issue at trial where the witness is very young or is mentally handicapped. If the issue of competency arises, the trial judge will determine if the witness meets the requirements to be a competent witness. At one time, atheists were deemed incompetent to testify because it was assumed they could lie with impunity because of their lack of religious faith. Because the oath a witness takes places a legal, rather than religious, obligation on the witness, this is not normally a concern today.

In all cases in which witnesses are interviewed, the investigator should note the person's mental ability and communication skills in order to advise the prosecutor about the strengths of each witness, especially if the witness is particularly crucial to the case.

CASE STUDY

A 15-year-old girl with an IQ of approximately 80 was invited by a 20-year-old neighbor boy to accompany him to a nearby park to feed the squirrels. Once there, he beat and raped her. She found her way home, and her parents called the police. She was taken to a hospital, where the doctors determined that there was abundant physical evidence of a violent sexual assault. The suspect was arrested. Clearly, the victim had knowledge of matter upon which she would be called upon to testify. The question was whether she would understand the importance of the oath and be able to communicate to the jury. With careful preparation on the part of the prosecutor, the victim was able to testify and the rapist was convicted.

Competence of Evidence

As illustrated earlier, the term *competency* is most often used in relationship to the competency of witnesses. Competency is also used in relation to evidence. Evidence must not only be relevant and material, it must also be competent. *Competency* in this sense refers to the reliability of evidence. The source of the evidence must be reliable. For example, in many rural jurisdictions county coroners are often morticians who have no training in medicine, law, or death investigation. The coroner would not be competent to offer an opinion on the cause of a homicide victim's death.

Privilege

Investigators may be unable to use some evidence because of evidentiary privileges. Legal *privileges* are rules of law that prevent the use of some evidence that would otherwise be admissible. The purpose of evidentiary privileges is to protect relationships by preventing the court from compelling the parties to the relationship from testifying against the each other. Under the law, the maintenance of certain relationships is considered to be more important than any benefit to the state that might be derived from forcing parties to a relationship to testify against others in that relationship. The best known of the privileges is the attorney-client privilege.

Attorney-Client Privilege

Communications that occur between a person seeking legal advice and a licensed attorney are privileged. The attorney cannot be compelled to testify as to the content of those communications. The purpose of this privilege is to ensure the flow of truthful information between attorneys and their clients so that the attorney can prepare the best case for the client.

Marital Privilege

The communications between married spouses is usually privileged. The communications that occur during a marriage are privileged, and the privilege extends after the marriage to communications that occurred during the time the couple was legally married. The privilege has some limitations, however. It does not extend to crimes committed by one spouse against the other spouse, or to children resulting from the marriage. Thus, an abusive spouse cannot prevent their partner from testifying against them by invoking this privilege.

Law Enforcement Officer-Informant Privilege

In some states, the communications between a law enforcement officer and a confidential informant are privileged. In those states where the privilege exists, officers may claim privilege if they are called upon to disclose the identity of a confidential informant.

In recent years, journalists have claimed the existence of a First Amendment privilege covering communications between a journalist and a source. This privilege has not been recognized by the courts, and if a judge orders a journalist to divulge his source, he can be jailed for contempt of court if he refuses to do so.

Character Evidence

During the course of an investigation, police will obtain a great deal of information about victims and suspects in a crime. While this evidence may be of use for providing background on the parties, it is usually inadmissible. Character evidence, that is, evidence of a person's character or character traits, is not admissible to prove that the behavior occurred on a particular occasion. As with most rules of law, there are exceptions. Character evidence may be offered when it relates to an element of a crime, a claim, or an element of a defense. When this occurs, the trial judge will rule that character is "in issue" and allow it to be entered into evidence. For example, in one case, a mother was charged with involuntary manslaughter for allowing her children to ride with her intoxicated husband. In this case, evidence of the character trait or tendency of the husband to drive while intoxicated was essential to prove the charge of involuntary manslaughter against her. Of course, when character evidence is offered by one party, the opposing party may offer character evidence to rebut it.

Evidence of Past Crimes, Wrongs, or Acts

More importantly for the prosecution is the use of evidence of other crimes, wrongs, or acts by the suspect or victim. The general rule is that evidence of past crimes, wrongs, and acts is inadmissible to prove the character of a person or that the person acted in a particular way. Evidence of past misconduct may be admissible, however, to prove motive, opportunity, intent, preparation, planning, knowledge, identity, or absence of mistake or action.

CASE STUDY

A badly injured baby was brought to a hospital by her parents. She died shortly after arrival. The baby's father had been caring for her that day. Doctors discovered signs of previous serious recent injuries on the victim's body. Evidence of these injuries was admitted at the murder trial of the father to establish the battered child syndrome, even though nothing tied the injuries to him. Jurors were instructed that they could consider the evidence for only three very specific purposes:

1. To impeach the wife's testimony that she was afraid of her husband
2. To establish the battered child syndrome
3. To show the *intent* on the part of the defendant to commit the crime (Estelle v. Mcguire, 50 Cr.L. 2012 [1991])

Obviously, this is a very subtle distinction for the trier of fact to make, but it is possible and is admissible for those reasons. Investigators should make every effort to uncover evidence that reflects on the past crimes and misconduct of the defendant and to make this evidence known to the prosecutor, who may then be able to use it at trial.

Hearsay Evidence

Courts have long recognized the dangers of using second-hand information as evidence. After a story has been told and retold several times, it may have been altered to such an extent that it is no longer believable. As the rules of evidence evolved, the tendency of trial court judges has been to exclude evidence provided by second-hand sources. Second-hand information is known as *hearsay evidence*, derived from the words *heard say*. In other words, *hearsay* is statements or testimony in court that are based on what a witness heard someone else say. The court's reluctance to allow hearsay to be offered as evidence is based on the belief that such evidence is frequently untrustworthy and unreliable.

The Sixth Amendment also guarantees the defendant in a criminal case the right to confront his accusers. Since hearsay is repeated by someone other than the original speaker, the defendant is denied the opportunity to cross examine the declarer on the witness stand. For these reasons, hearsay was not allowed in as evidence for several centuries. McCormick defines *hearsay* as:

> a statement, other than one made by the declarant while testifying at the trial or hearing, offered in evidence to prove the truth of the matter asserted. (Cleary, 1984, p. 729)

A *statement* refers to something the person said or to some assertive conduct by the declarer somewhere other than in court. It must have been made by someone other than the person who is currently repeating it on the witness stand. Finally, the statement is only hearsay if it is offered to prove a matter asserted in the statement. For example, a witness tells a police officer that a friend was spending a great deal more money than he normally would. The man goes on to state that his friend said that he took the money in a robbery of a liquor store the night before. If the state attempted to use this statement as evidence, the defense would object to its use as hearsay. It is clearly a statement, it was made by someone other than the witness who was then testifying on the stand, and it is being offered to the trier of fact as proof that the defendant did, in fact, commit the robbery he is charged with. Because the evidence is hearsay, it is inadmissible unless it falls under one of several recognized exceptions to the hearsay rule. It is the trial attorney's responsibility to determine if an exception to the hearsay rule exists under which the statement could be entered in as evidence.

CASE STUDY

An auto manufacturing plant was located in a large midwestern city. Law enforcement agencies developed evidence of extensive drug use and sales among employees at the plant. An undercover police officer was placed in the plant on an assembly line for approximately six months, during which he assembled information for several cases of selling and distribution of drugs. Shortly after the covert phase of the investigation was ended, the officer was killed in an automobile accident. None of the cases he had investigated could be prosecuted because they would have been based primarily on hearsay evidence, his reports. The reports were statements that could only have been read into the record by someone other than the officer who had prepared them. Because they would be offered to prove the matter asserted, that certain defendant's sold or distributed drugs, they were hearsay and were inadmissible. It was necessary to dismiss all the cases the officer had put together during that time.

Exceptions to the Hearsay Rule

Despite concerns about the potential harm to one party or another that might result from the trier of fact hearing an item of hearsay, jurists concluded that under certain circumstances hearsay could be both relevant and material in judicial proceedings. In order to make it possible to permit the use of hearsay evidence, a number of exceptions to the hearsay rule have been recognized. Although there is no single theory to explain the exceptions to the hearsay rule, they all have, in the words of Wigmore, "circumstantial guarantees of trustworthiness." In general, the exceptions to the rule are based on two principles:

1. That there is something about the circumstances under which the statement was made that supplies some evidence of the reliability of the hearsay
2. The person to whom to the hearsay is attributed is unavailable for cross-examination

Dying Declarations

One of the best known and most widely discussed of the exceptions is the *dying declaration*. The dying declaration is the statement by someone, usually deceased, and therefore beyond the subpoena power of the court about the cause and circumstances of that person's death. The reasons for the exception are (1) the indicia of reliability is provided by the assumption that a person would not lie at the moment of death and (2) the person who made the declaration is now dead and therefore beyond the subpoena power of the court. In most states, the person who made the statement must have died, although in some states juries may be allowed to decide if a person believed he or she was dying, and then later recovered. When taking a dying declaration, investigators must keep several points in mind:

1. They must establish that the person making the statement is aware that death is imminent.
2. They must document what the person says orally (ideally in writing, on audiotape, or on videotape).
3. They must maintain the chain of custody of this evidence, as is appropriate with any critical evidence.

Confessions

A *confession* is a statement admitting or acknowledging all the facts necessary for conviction of the crime at issue (Cleary, 1984, p. 362). The goal of any interrogation is to obtain the truth about a criminal event, and if the truth is that the suspect being questioned committed that crime, then the interrogator's goal is to obtain a confession. Although a confession is hearsay, it falls under one of the recognized exceptions to the hearsay rule. It must be remembered, however, that the hearsay rule is only one aspect of the process of getting a confession before a jury. The state must be prepared to prove that all of the defendant's Fourth, Fifth, and Sixth Amendment rights were fully protected by the investigating officers. More will be said about these in Chapter 7 on interrogation.

Admissions

Investigators are much more likely to obtain admissions about a suspect's involvement in a crime than they are to obtain a confession. Investigators sometimes think of an admission as a partial acceptance of guilt. In a limited sense it is, but under the rules of evidence, the term *admission* is given a much broader meaning and one that the investigator should be familiar with. An *admission* is a statement or conduct made out of court by someone who is involved in the case, and a statement or action that is inconsistent with the position he or she is currently taking or defending at trial. Anything the defendant did that is inconsistent with the actions of an innocent person could be an admission.

In *People v. Stanton*, the Supreme Court of Illinois distinguished between an admission and a confession as follows:

> There is a distinction between a statement, which is only an admission, and one that constitutes a confession of guilt of the crime charged. A confession is a voluntary acknowledgment of guilt after the perpetration of an offense, and it does not embrace mere statements or declarations of independent facts from which guilt may be inferred, while an admission is any statement or conduct from which guilt of the crime may be inferred but guilt does not necessarily follow. (People v. Stanton, 158 N.E. 2d 47 [1959])

As with a confession, before admission can be entered into evidence, the proponent of the statement must demonstrate that the admission was made voluntarily.

Res Gestae Exception

Res gestae is Latin for "things done," that is, acts that occur as part of some larger event. The most common type of hearsay encountered under this exception is the spontaneous or excited utterance, declaration, or act. If a witness overhears someone make an excited or spontaneous statement after a shocking or unusual event, the statement may be offered to prove the truth of the matter asserted in the statement.

Conclusion

This chapter has been devoted to an examination of the law that guides the actions of every professional American law enforcement officer. In recent decisions, the Supreme Court has demonstrated a willingness to trust the judgment of better-educated and better-trained officers. The Court has given police officers the legal tools needed to perform their tasks of protecting lives and property of the citizens in their community. This is a great responsibility, but it is one that must be accepted by law enforcement officers in a free society. The remainder of this text is based on a merger of legal requirements and investigative techniques that are the tools of the investigative craft.

An investigator must approach any investigation from the perspective that every case he or she works may go to trial. The rules of evidence provide the guidance to investigators when evaluating any piece of evidence, whether it is physical, testimonial, circumstantial, or direct. Armed with a knowledge of criminal procedure and rules of evidence, the investigator begins to consider how to manage a criminal case. Our discussion now turns to one of the most important aspects of criminal investigation, how the investigator can manage the limited human and technical resources available.

References

Acevedo v. California, 111 S.Ct. (1982).

Adams v. Williams, 407 U.S. 143 (1972).

Aguilar v. Texas, 378 U.S. 108 (1964).

Black's Law Dictionary, 5th ed. St. Paul, Minnesota: West Publishing, 1983.

Bumper v. North Carolina, 391 U.S. 543 (1968).

Carroll v. United States, 267 U.S. 132 (1925).

Chimel v. California, 395 U.S. 752 (1969).

Cleary, Edward W., et al. *McCormick on Evidence*. St. Paul, Minnesota: West Publishing, 1984.

Colorado v. Bertine, 479 U.S. 564 (1987).

Coolidge v. New Hampshire, 403 U.S. 443 (1974).

Commonwealth v. Webster, 59 Mass. (5 Cush.) 295,320 (1850).

Estelle v. McGuire, 50 Cr.L. 2012 (1991).

Illinois v. Gates, 103 S.Ct. 2317 (1983).

Imwinkelried, Edward J., et al. *Criminal Evidence*. St. Paul, Minnesota: West Publishing, 1979.

In Re Winship, 397 U.S. at 363, 364, 90 S.Ct. 1972.

Katz v. United States, 389 U.S. 347 (1967).

Lego v. Twomey, 404 U.S. 477 (1972).

Maryland v. Dyson, 119 S.Ct. 2013 (1999).

Minnesota v. Dickerson, 61 LW 4545 (1993).

New York v. Belton, 453 U.S. 454 (1981).

Oliver v. United States, 466 U.S. 170 (1984).

People v. Stanton, 158 N.E. 2d 47 (1959).

Schneckloth v. Bustamonte, 412 U.S. 218 (1973).

South Dakota v. Opperman, 428 U.S. 364 (1976).

Spinelli v. United States, 393 U.S. 410 (1969).

Terry v. Ohio, 392 U.S. 1 (1968).

Texas v. Brown, 460 U.S. 730 (1983).

United States v. Cortez, 449 U.S. 411 (1981).

United States v. Ross, 456 U.S. 798 (1982).

Wigmore, Evidence, 1422 Chadbourn rev. 1974.

Wyoming v. Houghton, 119 S.Ct. 1297 (1999).

3. Managing Criminal Investigations and the Intelligence Function

At least I have got a grip of the essential facts of the case. I shall enumerate them to you, for nothing clears up a case so much as stating it to another person, and I can hardly expect your cooperation if I do not show you the position from which we start.

Sherlock Holmes, The Adventure of Silver Blaze, Sir Arthur Conan Doyle

Management and Supervision of Criminal Investigators

Sound management practices can improve the investigation process. Good management begins when the police become involved in a case. Upon arriving at the crime scene, the officer must first assist the victims or provide aid to any injured parties. Once this is done, the next step is to determine what crime, if any, has been committed.

At this point, the supervisor must determine if the investigative process should be initiated. This sounds like an obvious activity, but officers sometimes go through the routine without considering why it should be done. Supervisors must ensure that the scene is secured, that witnesses are separated and interviewed, and that the neighborhood is canvassed. The pressure to get officers back into service to answer other calls can result in the inconsistent use of these necessary investigative techniques. Supervisors must ensure that necessary investigative procedures are followed.

One of the most difficult decisions to be made by the field supervisor is whether to call an evidence technician to the scene. Generally, a technician should be called in the following situations:

Where a suspect has been arrested at or near the scene, and there is a likelihood that evidence can be found at the scene that will link the suspect to the crime.

When a suspect has been identified, but not arrested, and physical evidence can be used to support the identification.

When other leads are likely to be fruitful in identifying a suspect.

When the crime committed had a distinctive *modus operandi* (M.O.), indicating that it is part of a pattern. (Eck, 1983)

Under any circumstances, supervisors at the scene will be expected to exercise judgment when determining what steps should be taken next in the investigation.

Once the preliminary investigation is complete, the facts must be summarized in a report. The supervisor must ensure that the patrol officer has identified and reported any solvability factors present. Solvability factors were first used extensively by the Rochester, New York Police Department in the early 1970s. *Solvability factors* are a checklist of items of evidence that both patrol officers and supervisors can use to ensure the preliminary investigation is complete. The most common solvability factors are identified by obtaining answers to the following questions:

- Was there a witness to the crime?
- Can a suspect be named?
- Can a suspect be located?
- Can a suspect be described?
- Can a suspect be identified?
- Can a suspect vehicle be identified?
- Is the stolen property traceable?
- Is there a significant M.O. present?
- Is there significant physical evidence present?
- Has an evidence technician been called?
- Is the evidence technician's report positive?
- Is there a significant reason to believe that the crime may be solved with a reasonable amount of investigative effort?
- Was there a definite limited opportunity for anyone except the suspect to commit the crime?

After reviewing the patrol officer's report, the investigative supervisor must determine if the case should receive any additional attention. Several forms have been developed to assist the supervisor in determining if follow-up is appropriate. These forms are self-explanatory and relatively easy to use. Supervisors are expected to exercise professional judgment based on experience and training to determine if follow-up investigation will be worth the effort. Figure 3.1 is applicable to general investigations, while the forms in Figures 3.2 and 3.3 relate to burglary and robbery, respectively.

Case screening is a "scart," a combination of science and art. In science, outcomes are predictable. In art, the results are uncertain until the product is complete. When determining if additional time and energy should be committed to an investigation, supervisors must use their experience and judgment to determine if follow-up is needed. The absence of solvability factors in a brutal crime will make an investigator's job more difficult, but the nature of such a crime requires that every effort be made to bring the case to a successful conclusion.

Assigning Cases

Typically, investigations are conducted by individual investigators or by a pair of detectives who are assigned specific cases by a supervisor. This system has the

A. Gravity of Offense
    a. Felony = 4 points
    b. Misdemeanor = 3 points
    c. Victimless crime = 2 points
    d. Violations/status offense = 1 point

B. Probability of Solution. Whether there are:
    a. Suspects
    b. Witnesses
    c. Physical evidence
    d. Undeveloped leads
    (Score one point for each factor present)

C. Urgency for Action
    a. Danger to others = 4 points
    b. Immediate action required = 3 points
    c. Impact on the victim = 2 points
    d. Pattern/frequency = 1 point

D. Supervisory Judgement
    a. Department policy
    b. Totality of circumstances
    c. Investigators case load
    (Score one point for each factor present)

Scoring and Application of Priority System:

Priority	Points	Report Investigative Process Within
A	16-22	1-5 days
B	10-16	15 days
C	4-10	30 days
D	Less than 4	Suspended (form letter to victim)

Figure 3.1   Priority rating factors

advantages of accountability and the creation of a sense of responsibility for the case on the part of the officer. Under a system of assigning cases to individuals, the performance of specific investigators is somewhat easier to evaluate. Conversely, there are disadvantages to this system. When an investigator is off-duty, no progress can be made on a case, and under this system, there are no incentives for investigators to work together. Investigators tend to be competitive, and under the system of assigning cases on an individual basis, they are evaluated on the "big case" or "good arrest," not on whether they contributed to the solution of a crime.

This system of assigning cases to individuals or partners makes it more difficult to take advantage of each investigator's interviewing or warrant-drafting skills. Finally, supervisors are at a disadvantage when trying to determine if additional resources should be committed to an investigation. They are relying on information given to them by the case officer to enable them to make that determination.

Instructions:

1. Circle the weighting factor for each information element that is present in the incident report.
2. Add the circled factors.
3. If the sum is less than or equal to 10, suspend the case. Otherwise follow up the case.

Information Element   *Weighting Factor*

Estimated time lapse between crime
and the initial investigation:
     Less than 1 hour 5.0
     1 to 12 hours...1.0
     12 to 24 hours...0.3
     More than 24 hours...0.0

Witness's report of offense...7.0
On-view report of offense...1.0
Usable fingerprints 7.0
Suspect information developed - description or name..................9.0
Vehicle description 0.1
Other 0.0

*Total Score:*_____

Figure 3.2   Burglary case disposition decision rule

The Investigative Team

Assigning cases to teams of investigators may be a more effective approach to conducting investigations. The team approach to investigations has been successful in the investigation of major cases, in which the seriousness of the crime is enough to cause individuals to work together (Brown, 1976). The concept has also been successful in more routine kinds of investigations (Lacasse, 1986).

A team approach to managing investigations offers a means by which supervisors can become more involved in the process and that puts them in a better position to make decisions about resource allocations and personnel assignments. The supervisor begins by examining the report completed after the preliminary investigation for solvability factors and, along with team investigators, determines what leads should be followed up. The case is then discussed with all investigators present so that each is fully informed of what needs to be done in the case. This information should be recorded on a lead sheet, which is then assigned to an investigator. The team approach enables the supervisor to monitor the case and makes it possible to continue an investigation on a timely basis.

Under this system, investigators can be assigned leads on a 24-hour basis. Progress will not end at the completion of an investigator's shift. A team assignment of cases allows supervisors to take advantage of each investigator's skills in interviewing or in drafting arrest and search warrants.

This system also causes investigators to work more closely with each other, thereby making it possible to learn from each other. Team management also

---

<u>Instructions:</u>

1. Circle the weighting factor for each information element that is present in the incident report.
2. Add the circled factors.
3. If the sum is less than 10, suspend the case. Otherwise follow up the case.
4. Weighting factors do not accumulate; i.e., if both the auto license and color are given, the total is 3.0, not 4.8.

Information Element	Weighting Factor
Suspect named	10*
Suspect known	10*
Suspect previously seen	10*
Evidence technician used	10
Places suspect frequented named	10*
Each physical evidence item matched	6.1
Vehicle registration	
Query information available	1.5
Vehicle stolen	3.0
Useful information returned	4.5
Vehicle registered to suspect	6.0
Offender movement description	
On foot	0.0
Vehicle (not car)	0.6
Car	1.2
Car color given	1.8
Car description given	2.4
Car license given	3.0
Weapon used	1.6

Total Score:_____

* These values as calculated actually exceed the threshold of 10. The values provided here are conceptually simpler and make no difference in the classification of groups.

Figure 3.3 Robbery investigation decision mode

facilitates exchanges of information among investigators. Criminal investigation is an information-based activity. Without information, an investigator gropes for answers. In those departments in which investigators handle cases individually, the tendency is to hoard information. The reason for this is simple: investigators are rewarded as individuals for "big cases" and "good arrests." The supervisor's job is to build a team in which investigators share information to solve crimes that result in the team being rewarded as a group.

Leadership

Implementing a team approach to managing investigations requires leadership and commitment on the part of supervisors. It is a change that is often met with skepticism. Investigators are experienced police officers who, in the words of Arthur Niederhoffer, "have gotten out of the bag" and are no longer working in uniform. They are accustomed to setting their own schedule and making decisions about what should be done in "their" cases. It is the responsibility of the investigative supervisor to bring all available resources to bear on the goal of detecting criminals and bringing them to justice. The investigative supervisor plays a major role in the ongoing process of bringing increased rationality to managing criminal investigations.

Managing the Intelligence Function

Information is the lifeblood of law enforcement. Without information, the police are powerless to perform their tasks of protecting the lives and property in the community. As the world becomes increasingly complex, police administrators and planners are finding it more and more necessary to collate seemingly unrelated bits of information into some kind of understandable whole so that they can use their already strained resources as effectively as possible.

The need for accurate and timely information about ongoing criminal activity has led to the creation of criminal intelligence units to gather, analyze, and disseminate information in support of operational units within the law enforcement agency. These units are given the responsibility of providing administrators with accurate information about crime, particularly organized crime, in the community. The intelligence function, however, does not fall into the traditional reactive investigative format common to most law enforcement agencies. Individuals are entitled to live their lives free from governmental intrusions. At the same time, increased crime in most jurisdictions makes it necessary to gather, analyze, and use information to protect the public.

Tactical and Strategic Intelligence

Intelligence information may be placed in two general categories: tactical and strategic. Tactical intelligence is information that directly supports an immediate law enforcement objective. It is information that relates to some present activity and must be made available to operational personnel on a timely basis. A tip from a reliable informant that a shipment of cocaine will arrive at a specific time and place is tactical intelligence. Informants, patrol officers, and investigators are the primary users of tactical intelligence.

Strategic intelligence is information that relates to larger issues and may be used by decision makers to make projections about future law enforcement needs. Decision makers may also use strategic intelligence as a basis for agency policy. Strategic intelligence is essential to monitor the activities of any organized criminal activities that present a threat to the safety of the community.

Agency Cooperation and Coordination

Historically, law enforcement agencies are very proprietary and guarded about their intelligence information, as they should be. The reluctance to share information, however, often obstructs and limits the necessary cooperation between all types of public and private agencies that deliver law enforcement and policing services.

Information sharing comes in many forms. The American police system is among the most decentralized and fragmented in the world, consisting of federal, state and local agencies. Regardless of size, all of these agencies need two basic types of information on a daily basis. The first, not the topic here, but worth mentioning, is timely information concerning policy, changes in law, and practice, including innovative ways to address problems and issues.

This type of information is usually gained through organizations like the International Association of Chiefs of Police, National Sheriff's Association, or a myriad of other organizations that collect, digest, and disseminate this policy-type information to its membership. Or, an administrator will seek out an agency or individual demonstrating a level of expertise in a particular area, and seek council from them. And this information for the most part is freely given.

However, the second type of information is intelligence. Intelligence information is not normally disseminated freely, for good reason. It is typically about individuals, whom have rights protected by state and federal guidelines. Not only that, but it is often speculative information about individuals, obtained through surveillance or informants, and they may not yet have committed a crime, or at least a new crime. This information must be protected for the rights of the individuals, the integrity of the investigation, and for the safety of the sources. It is for this reason that criminal intelligence functions in the various agencies should have similar goals, methods, and guidelines.

There must be a strong foundation for cooperation between police agencies. The sharing and coordination of data and intelligence with other police forces or relevant government agencies is critical. In our area, this is not so much because organized crime and its activities are national and international in scope, but it because the criminal community has become increasingly mobile and is committing crimes in more than one jurisdiction. In many cases, these are the same faces we see over and over; when they become known in one jurisdiction, they move to a neighboring jurisdiction, and are able to commit crimes undetected until they become known to that jurisdiction. They may also commit crimes in multiple jurisdictions simultaneously. We are constantly re-inventing the wheel and forced to react to criminal activity with the same people, or their family members and associates, because we do not share information. At the operational level, the need for inter-agency cooperation is already recognized in the large number of formal and informal joint task force operations. But there is some bias against task forces operated by certain agencies, or who have reputation for not responding to information provided them and are a one-way information highway, with no information returning to contributing agencies.

There should be ways to allow all intelligence units within and among police forces to work together most effectively, to avoid turf dispute and unnecessary duplication of effort. An overall sense of informal or formal cooperation between intelligence units among different police agencies must be present. A forum needs to be provided at a neutral site, where information can be collected, analyzed, and disseminated back to contributors in a meaningful and timely manner. The relevant agencies should be brought together on a periodic but regular basis to share, exchange, discuss, and record their intelligence, ideas, insights, strategies, and for training in new and innovative methods in intelligence collection and analysis.

Some proponents say there should be a national structure that institutionalizes and facilitates the uniform collection, analysis, and dissemination of intelligence information. And that it must have a mandate among all police intelligence units and be viewed as the competent centralized institution with which to share raw data and intelligence. Proponents also state that such a national structure should be accompanied by national standards that ensure that there is a uniformity in all aspects of the criminal intelligence function, from collection, to analysis, to dissemination. The political reality is that such a nationally orchestrated system is highly unlikely. To be sure, there are national indexes such as the National Crime Information Center (NCIC) and the DEA's National Drug Pointer Index (NDPIX) system that provide a wealth of information, and will lead local officers to others having dealings with certain individuals. But, a national intelligence system is hardly in place, and in fact would likely be hard to sell to an American population deeply concerned about the protection of privacy.

There has been some attempt at this through The Regional Information Sharing Systems Projects (R.I.S.S.), and there has not been a public objection, but that is probably because the project is extremely low profile, and is not known to the general public. They have no investigative function, and provide money, equipment, and analysis for member agencies.

National Law Enforcement Telecommunication System

At another level, there is a great need for the coordination of information between all agencies. This not only includes public police forces, but also private policing, government regulatory bodies, and private sector firms. The need for a greater coordination and cooperation among all these different agencies lies in the reality that organized criminal activities transcend the responsibility of police and the criminal justice system. As such, an intelligence system in particular must include information from a diverse range of sources in many different agencies in both the public and private sector. While it is agreed that a nationally acceptable standard should be adopted for intelligence functions, success would seem to depend on the implementation of such functions at a local or at most regional level.

The use of criminal intelligence still remains largely misunderstood and under-utilized. Many intelligence programs in the United States have been abandoned and nearly all have failed to reach their potential. This criticism, leveled by noted authors on the subject, stemmed from the fact that intelligence is seldom more than an accumulation of often irrelevant data that serves only marginally useful purposes.

Nonetheless, criminal intelligence is gaining recognition as a vital cog in crime enforcement. The commitment to this function, the advancement in the use of criminal intelligence, and the advent and utilization of sophisticated computer technology has furthered this police function. The key to the establishment of an effective regional intelligence network is training of an initial cadre of intelligence officers and analysts. These officers could then return to their respective agencies, and establish a recognizable intelligence function, even if it is just one officer with the responsibility to collect suspect and crime information. A logical additional dimension of that training would be to have a designated local center for collection of data from the individual departments, for analysis and dissemination back to the agency and/or to the rest of the region at the contributing agency's request. It would also be a database that could be queried from contributing agencies for information about individuals they are investigating. Again, this is essentially what the R.I.S.S. projects are designed to do, but with the added advantages of a comprehensive and recurring training function, and a local approach and point of contact.

Link Analysis Software

With the increased use of computers comes the collateral benefit of the ability to manage large amounts of information from a variety of sources and produce an intelligence product based on the needs of the customer.

Link analysis software, while initially expensive, can save hours, days, and months of tedious analysis by linking key elements of a case to produce a clearer picture of relationships between people, places, events, vehicles, telephone conversations, bank accounts, and organizations. The initial data entry is a time-consuming part of the process, but once entered, the data can produce countless scenarios and combinations in the form of charts and graphs for analysts to consider.

To the smaller departments, this means fewer analysts can produce more intelligence products in a shorter time. There is also the possibility for a group of smaller departments to coop the software, enter their own data, and produce their own link analysis. This kind of sharing could translate into cooperation between agencies.

Analysis of Intelligence Information

Raw intelligence information is of little value for tactical or strategic use until it is analyzed. Analysts should be trained to identify relationships between seemingly unrelated bits of information. The analysts will be looking for patterns or networks of continuing criminal activity, such as drug trafficking, prostitution, or gambling.

Protecting Intelligence Information

Intelligence information should be made available to users on a "need to know basis." Law enforcement managers must be sensitive to the consequences of allowing unauthorized personnel access to classified information. In one midwestern police department, employees were routinely hired as secretaries without undergoing a background investigation. As a result, it was discovered that a young woman who had been working in the detective section had been stealing information from allegedly secure files at the request of her boyfriend, who was a local drug dealer. All intelligence activities should be governed by policies that have been prepared prior to gathering any intelligence information.

The Criminal Intelligence Unit

Most law enforcement agencies have the legitimate need to maintain criminal intelligence files. Before a unit is created, however, agency administrators must be clear on what the unit's goals are and how those goals may be achieved within the limits set by the law.

Goals for the Intelligence Unit

No law enforcement agency should begin to gather information about an individual or group until the purpose of the intelligence process has been clearly defined. The International Association of Chiefs of Police (IACP) has suggested the following goals and programs for an intelligence unit:

1. Reduction of organized crime in the community
2. Reduction of the opportunities for organized crime to infiltrate the community, including businesses
3. Establishment of a program to deter organized crime in the community

The IACP further recommends the following programs for the intelligence unit:

1. Establish an early detection system to identify attempts by organized crime to infiltrate the community
2. Develop and initiate innovative investigative techniques in criminal intelligence investigations
3. Strengthen interagency coordination of investigations
4. Provide public awareness of organized crime problems in the community
5. Detect and reduce the opportunity for corruption in governmental operations
6. Provide advanced training for criminal intelligence personnel (Law Enforcement Policy on the Management of Criminal Intelligence, IACP, 1985)

Once the need for an intelligence unit has been defined and its goals have been established, personnel assigned to that duty can begin the process of gathering and analyzing intelligence information. A flowchart of the intelligence-gathering process appears in Figure 3.4.

Gathering Raw Information

There are three primary sources of raw information. These are undercover police officers, informants, and surveillance. Undercover police officers are the best source of information about criminal activity. This is true in intelligence work for the same reasons it is true in covert investigations. Undercover investigators are trained police officers who have an understanding of the intricacies of the criminal justice system. They understand how information will be used to monitor and ultimately prosecute criminals. The information obtained by undercover officers will be determined by how deeply they can penetrate a criminal organization. As a result, intelligence officers must develop other sources of information closer to the criminal activity; that source is the criminal informant.

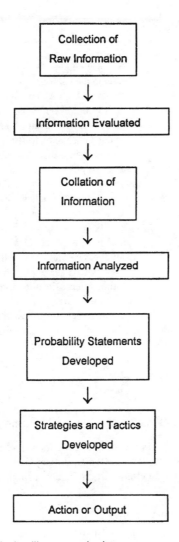

Figure 3.4   Flowchart of the intelligence-gathering process

Criminal Informants

The motives that drive an informant to talk are discussed in Chapter 5. It is advisable to review informant motivation and to remain alert to the need to determine why the informant is cooperating with law enforcement. An informant's photograph and fingerprints should be kept on file along with information on an informant's record of cases. Investigators should maintain an informant's reliability assessment.

Assessing an informant's reliability is a difficult and somewhat subjective process. The assessment will be based on corroboration of the information provided by the informant. A sample evaluation scale appears in Table 3.1.

Table 3.1   Sample evaluation scale

Index Value	Summary Phrase	Definition
A	Completely reliable	Refers to the source who is undoubted in authenticity, trustworthiness, and competency. Information in the past has proven reliable in all instances.
B	Usually reliable	Refers to a source about whom there may be some doubt about authenticity, trustworthiness, or competency. However, information obtained from this source in the past has proven reliable in the majority of instances.
C	Fairly reliable	Refers to a source about whom there are usually some doubts about its authenticity, trustworthiness, or competency. Information obtained from this source in the past has proven reliable in a moderate number of cases.
D	Not usually reliable	Refers to a source about whom there is doubt as to authenticity and trustworthiness. Information from this source has not proven reliable in the past, although occasionally reports have been valid.
E	Unreliable	Refers to a source about whom there is serious doubt about authenticity, trustworthiness, and competency.
F	Reliability has not been determined	Refers to a source whose reliability has not been determined by investigation or experience.

Analysis of Information

Analysis of raw information is a demanding job. Dintino notes:

> Intelligence is the end product of a complex process, sometimes physical and always intellectual. The end product is most often an informed judgment; it may simply be a thoughtful description of a state of affairs; it can be a single factors best guessed. (Dintino, 1983, p. 9)

The analysis process is very similar to the hypothetical-deductive process used by academics. The process begins with the collection of information from the sources already discussed. Once the information has been gathered, it must be evaluated for its reliability and accuracy. The information must next be collated to determine any linkages between the various bits and pieces of information available at that time. The information is then analyzed. From this analysis, analysts may be able to form probability statements with regard to the existence of ongoing criminal activities in the community. From deductions made by the criminal intelligence units, administrators make decisions about future strategies and tactics to be employed by their agency. In theory, if a problem has been accurately identified and the correct strategy developed, the criminal activity under scrutiny should decline in prevalence.

Guidelines for Intelligence Files

The main objective of a criminal intelligence file system is to provide law enforcement agencies with a sound database that meets the needs of law enforcement in its efforts to protect the public and to suppress criminal operations.

POLICE DEPARTMENT
Intelligence Report

CONFIDENTIAL   Page 1 of ___

Number: _____ - _____   Distributed: _____
                #   Yr   Mo   Dy   Yr

Area(s): _____

Subject: _____

Date of Information:_____   Evaluation: _____ _____
                    Mo   Dy   Yr   Source   Content
                                                       Reliability Validity

Source: _____

        _____

        _____

Place and Date Acquired: _____   _____
                             Place   Date

Collection Authority: _____
                         Cite specific guideline authority

Intelligence Officer: _____   _____
                           Name   Date

Intelligence Information
_____

_____

_____

_____

_____

a:\intellig.rpt

Figure 3.5   Sample intelligence form

Intelligence files are an analyst's most important single resource. It is through
the systematic collation and comparison of raw data that finished intelligence is
produced. In fact, intelligence more often refers more to the way in which information is organized and used than to the content of that information. For these
reasons, proper use of files by analysts assumes particular importance.

When beginning a new project or when responding to requests for a specific assessment, the analyst should examine the relevant files for information on the subject before collecting new data. A search through the related indices and data files may provide enough information on a suspect person or on a particular illicit operation to fulfill a tactical requirement. At a minimum, a thorough examination of data currently on hand will help direct further collection efforts.

Another important use of central intelligence files is to follow-up on new information presented in field reports or derived from other sources. Upon receipt of new information, the analyst will often consult central files to help place the new information in context. Using such follow-up activities, an analyst may recognize patterns of activity in a particular suspect or may connect a previously unfamiliar criminal or racket with known activities documented in the intelligence files.

Much of intelligence analysis is concerned with establishing relationships among seemingly diverse pieces of information in general, and among seemingly diverse individuals and activities in particular. Efficient intelligence files are structured, not only to accommodate such relationships, but also to simulate them by cross-referencing people, places, and actions.

There are several approaches to organizing an intelligence filing system. Selecting the best one depends on the needs of the unit. In some very small units, the file system consists solely of jacket files, in which all reports on a specific individual are filed in that individual's personal folder. This traditional approach poses severe limitations to rapid retrieval of information, because specific raw data are not indexed, and retrieval must rely heavily on the memory of file room personnel. It does not provide a way to determine quickly the extent of information that may be accumulating on criminal activity by geographic area or at a specific location, or by category or subcategory. Thus, it cannot provide an analyst with classes of information necessary to establish links or to assess patterns or trends in criminal activity.

This method can be improved by establishing a master name file in which all reports pertaining to an individual are indexed on a file card that contains the person's name, the report number, data, and types of activity. The report itself can then be filed according to the file system in the individual's jacket file, in an intelligence case file, or serially by report number. The name-index card allows for rapid retrieval of a specific report, wherever it is filed, by querying the master name file and identifying the report by number or name. The card also provides a quick summary of the criminal activity related to the individual.

A criminal intelligence file consists of stored information on the activities and associations of individuals and groups known or suspected to be involved in criminal acts or in threatening, planning, organizing, or financing criminal acts. More specifically, this stored information relates to:

1. Individuals who:
   a. Are currently involved in or suspected of being involved in the planning, organizing, financing, or commission of criminal activities; or who are suspected of having threatened, attempted, planned, or performed criminal acts; or
   b. Have an established association with known or suspected crime figures.

2. Organizations and businesses that:
   a. Are currently involved in or suspected of being involved in the planning, organizing, financing, or commission of criminal activities; or that have threatened, attempted, planned, or performed criminal acts; or
   b. Are operated, controlled, financed, infiltrated, or illegally used by crime figures.

File Content

Material stored in the criminal intelligence file should be restricted to documents of criminal intelligence, and related information from the public record and media sources. Information not meeting the agency's criteria for file input should be excluded from storage in the criminal intelligence file. Examples of excluded material are religious, political, or sexual information that does not relate to criminal conduct and associations with individuals that may not be of a criminal nature. It is recommended that public record information and media information be retained in file systems separate from criminal intelligence. Separation of criminal intelligence from other files better protects both the confidentiality of the intelligence file and the individual's right to privacy.

Indexing

The file must provide multiple paths for querying the stored information. This can be done by indexing all items of relevant information to the subject or functional category. Normally, this is accomplished by using index cards on which the desired amount of information is recorded concisely, with references made to the basic document. While indexing in this manner takes more clerical time, the cost is more than offset by an improvement in analyst efficiency. A normal set of card indices would include name, aliases, address, telephone numbers, and auto licenses. Suggestions of further information to be included on each type of index card follow:

1. **Name index.** This should include, in addition to the individual's name, the aliases used and the birth date. The intelligence report is then indexed onto the name card by recording the date, report number, and the criminal activity or the code for the criminal activity. A new card can be made out each time a report is received, or successive reports on the same individual can be recorded on the card. An accumulation of reports on an individual may indicate that an important new criminal figure is emerging.

2. **Alias index.** This card should relate aliases and nicknames to the names of known criminals who are called by such nicknames and aliases. Often an informer knows an individual only by a nickname. Indexing in this manner may initially help to identify a known criminal in a new area. Alias cards can also be filed alphabetically in the name index, eliminating the need to check more than one file.

3. **Address index.** An address index should include address, district (or area of jurisdiction), and type of premises (residence, bar, restaurant, pool hall). Each

report should be indexed on the address card as it is on the name card, so that reports of activity at a specific address can be quickly retrieved. The accumulation of entries for a specific address may indicate a new focus for criminal meetings that demands further investigation.

4. Telephone number index. The telephone index file should be restricted to those numbers having useful information. For example, reports of who uses a particular phone, and whether it is a home, bar, or public phone, can be helpful. They suggest relationships as to what type of activity is going on or being planned. Information on telephone numbers is available from the telephone company.

5. Auto license index. An auto license file is useful where a state has not computerized its license records or a unit is otherwise unable to access a state-wide computerized system directly. Even with a computerized system, an index system may be useful to keep track of persons other than the registered owner who use a car. A card index is also important when out-of-state cars become involved in criminal activity in the jurisdiction.

Two other useful indices are a biographic form and a location index. A *biographic form* is based on the belief that it is necessary to gather all information possible in one place concerning major known or alleged criminals in the jurisdiction. This is of great assistance to the analyst in responding to requests for information on such persons. The usefulness of the approach is greatly enhanced if the form is kept up-to-date and has an index attached to it, recording the base documents from which the biographic data are derived.

A *location index* offers a place to abstract a brief note concerning all reported crimes (or at least those categories of criminal activities of interest to the intelligence analyst) occurring either at a specific location or in a selected geographic area. This index can be useful in discovering associations among criminals who engage in different types of crimes, for example, narcotics and fencing, or fraud and "shylocking." It is the law enforcement agency that categorizes crime and observes jurisdictional boundaries, not the criminal.

In these major indices—biography and location—each report should contain a brief abstract of important points. If done correctly, the need for retrieving the basic report would be reduced or eliminated. The abstract should include names of known or alleged criminals, together with a concise statement of their reported activities, and where and when they occurred. Often this is enough for the analyst to link persons and locations, or criminal activities and persons. By photocopying the forms as new information is added, the analyst can have updated information on assigned areas of crime at all times. These data can be referred to as the analyst reviews the daily flow of new information. Hence, much clerical and reading time can be saved.

Basic Report Filing

An important decision with respect to the filing system is how and where to file basic reports. Often the basic report, once indexed, is filed in a jacket file of the most important person mentioned or in a criminal activity file that is central to the report. Some agencies have a system in which intelligence case numbers are given to certain major criminals, types of criminal activity, and areas, and the basic documents are filed accordingly after being indexed. In either of these cases, if the report refers to more than one person or type of criminal activity, each must be recorded on its own index card and cross-referenced to the jacket where it is filed.

The recommended approach is to file all reports in series once they are indexed. Analysts and clerks can rely on cross-index files and abstracts for searches.

File Criteria

Information to be retained in a criminal intelligence file should meet file criteria designed by the agency. These criteria should outline the parameters of the agency's criminal interests (crime categories) and provide specifics for determining whether subjects involved in these crime categories are suitable for file inclusion.

File input criteria will vary somewhat among agencies because of differences in size, functions, staffing, geographical location, and crime problems. The following file input criteria are suggested as a model for a criminal intelligence file system. The categories listed in the model are not exhaustive and will vary according to the needs of the individual agency.

A. *Permanent File:* Information pertaining to an identifiable subject that meets the file criteria established by the agency is justified for retention in a permanent criminal intelligence file.

1. Information that relates that an individual, organization, business, or gang has been involved, is involved, or is suspected of being involved in one or more of the following criminal activities:

   · Narcotics trafficking
   · Unlawful gambling
   · Loan sharking
   · Extortion
   · Vice and pornography
   · Infiltration of legitimate business for illegitimate purposes
   · Stolen securities
   · Bribery
   · Major fencing activities
   · Major crime, including homicide, burglary, auto theft, kidnapping, destruction of property, robbery, forgery, and arson
   · Manufacture, use, or possession of explosive devices for purposes of fraud, intimidation, or political motivation
   · Threats to public officials and private citizens

2. In addition to falling within the confines of one or more of the abovementioned criminal activities, the subject to be entered into the permanent file

should be identifiable, distinguished by a unique identifying characteristic, for example, date of birth, criminal identification number, and driver's license number. Identification at the time of file input is necessary to distinguish the subject from any similar in the file or any others that may be entered at a later time.

B. *Temporary File:* Information that initially does not meet the criteria for permanent file storage but yet may have enough potential validity for the agency to want to retain it, should be kept in a "temporary" file. It is recommended that retention of information in a temporary file not exceed a one-year period unless a compelling reason exists to extend this time period. During this period efforts should be made to identify the subject or to validate the information so that it may be transferred to the permanent file at the end of the one-year period, and if a compelling reason for its retention is not evident, the information should be removed and destroyed. An individual, organization, business, or gang may be given temporary file status in the following cases:

1. Subject is unidentifiable: The subject, although suspected to be engaged in criminal activities, has no physical descriptors, identification numbers, or distinguishing characteristics available.
2. Involvement is questionable: The subject's involvement in criminal activities is questionable; however, based on one or both of the following reasons, it would be beneficial to the agency to retain a record of the subject for a limited period of time during which the information can be validated.
   a. Possible criminal association: Individual or organization, although not currently reported to be criminally active, associates with a known criminal and appears to be aiding or abetting illegal activities.
   b. Criminal history: Individual or organization, although not currently reported to be criminally active, has a history of criminal conduct, and the circumstances currently being reported, that is, a new position or ownership in a business, affords an opportunity to again become criminally active.
3. Reliability/validity unknown: The reliability of the information source and/or the validity of the information content cannot be determined at the time of receipt; however, the information appears to be significant and merits temporary storage while verification attempts are made.

Privacy Considerations

The file system must anticipate problems raised by statutes directed toward protecting personal privacy. It is no longer possible to enter all information on individuals into intelligence files automatically as it is received. Each item must be subjected to the test of relevancy and to its legality under appropriate state and national laws. There is little problem during an active case in which searches have been carried out with warrants. What is touchy is the decision on allegations for which the source is not known or has not been totally accurate in the past, or where there is no criminal record on the subject.

Sensitivity and Reliability of Information

The need to mark information to indicate its sensitivity and reliability is often overlooked in intelligence information handling. The sensitivity of information relates both to its source and its content. For example, information that could only have come from a source close to the inner circle of a criminal group would be sensitive because, should any group member learn that the police had this information, the informant could be identified. Similarly, if information concerning expected criminal activity were discovered, it could "blow" the eventual enforcement action against this group of criminals. Thus, a single report can be sensitive in terms of source and substance.

In order to protect sensitive information, the intelligence analyst must have a means for indicating the degree of sensitivity of the information. The material can be marked with a numerical or letter code that can be associated with the report as a whole or parts thereof. Determining sensitivity is usually the responsibility of the person or agency forwarding the information to the unit. However, in certain circumstances, the unit classified information because of its awareness of other information.

Defining degrees of sensitivity is sometimes difficult because all information that enters the intelligence system is considered confidential. Thus, ordinarily, information in the intelligence system is classified either as "confidential" or as "sensitive," meaning it must be controlled by the supervisor and not circulated though normal channels. This confidential classification is necessary to protect the integrity of the system, as well as the privacy of the persons to whom the information relates. Hence, information in the intelligence system must be circulated only to those with a right to see such material (e.g., a law enforcement officer) and a need to know (working on a case for which the data are relevant). To classify information above confidential, that is, as sensitive, should mean that the originator believes access to the information should be restricted. Thus, it cannot be processed in the normal manner and entered into the general intelligence file but must be kept initially in a secure file to which access is limited to those receiving express permission by the supervisor.

Reliability of information poses a similar problem. The bulk of material the intelligence unit receives consists of allegations, most of which may at least initially be unverified. There may be doubt as to the accuracy of the source, or information already in the files may dispute the new information. The subject of the information (either a person or activity) may be new, and further investigation may be required. Therefore, it is imperative that the originating source indicates the reliability of the information on the report. In some cases, the analyst may give the information a second classification as to its reliability that is based on knowledge of other related material in the files.

An understanding of the reliability of information is also essential to protect the privacy of individuals. The intelligence unit must be wary of circulating information, the validity of which is in doubt. But if the material must be circulated, the intelligence unit must state its reservations clearly on the report. An example of the need for care in handling such material is an allegation received about criminal acts of politicians or civil servants. Such reports must be treated with special care because such allegations may have been made for political reasons.

Information Evaluation

Information retained in the criminal intelligence file should be evaluated for source reliability and content validity prior to filing. Most of the information an intelligence unit receives consists of allegations or information that is initially unverified. Evaluating the information's source and content at the time of receipt indicates to future users the information's worth and usefulness, and is essential in protecting the individual's right of privacy. Circulating information that may not have been evaluated or for which the source reliability is poor or the content validity is doubtful is detrimental to the agency's operations and violates the individual's right of privacy. To ensure uniformity within the intelligence community, it is strongly recommended that stored information be evaluated according to the schedule set forth in Table 3.1.

Information Classification

Information retained in the criminal intelligence file should be classified to indicate the degree to which it should be kept confidential in order to protect sources, investigations, and the individual's right of privacy. Classification also dictates the internal approval process that must be completed prior to dissemination of the information to personnel outside the agency. Classification of information should be the responsibility of a carefully selected and specifically designated individual in the intelligence unit.

The status of criminal intelligence is subject to continual change. It is important that information be reclassified to the appropriate security level as its sensitivity increases or decreases.

Classification systems may differ among agencies as to the number of levels of security and levels of release authorization. In establishing a classification system, agencies should define types of information falling under each level of security and the level of authority required for dissemination approval.

In order to ensure conformity within the intelligence community, it is recommended that stored information be classified according to a system similar to that set forth in Table 3.2.

Informant Source

In a number of situations, agencies may elect to identify information sources for items stored in their criminal intelligence files. Accordingly, each law enforcement agency should establish criteria that indicate when source identification is appropriate. In addition, the value of information stored in a criminal intelligence file is often directly related to the source of such information. Some factors to consider in determining whether source identification is warranted include:

- The nature of the information reported
- The potential need to refer to the source's identity for further investigative or prosecutorial activity
- The reliability of the source

Table 3.2   Information classification system

Security Class	Dissemination Criteria	Release Authority	Examples
Class I Confidential	Restricted to law enforcement intelligence personnel having a specific need-to-know and right-to-know	Intelligence unit commander	1. Information pertaining to law enforcement cases currently under investigation 2. Corruption (police or other government officials) 3. Informant identification information
Class II Sensitive	Restricted to law enforcement intelligence personnel having a specific need-to-know and right-to-know	Intelligence unit supervisor	1. Criminal intelligence reports that refer to organized crime or terrorism 2. Publications obtained through intelligence unit channels that are not deemed to be confidential
Class III Restricted	Restricted to law enforcement intelligence personnel having a specific need-to-know and right-to-know	Intelligence unit personnel	1. Reports that at an earlier date were classified confidential or sensitive, and for which the need for high security no longer exists 2. Nonsensitive reports published by local law enforcement agencies

Where source identification is warranted, it should reflect the name of the agency and the individual providing the information. In those cases where identifying the source by name is not practical for internal security reasons, a code number could be used. A listing of coded sources of information can then be retained by the intelligence unit supervisor. In addition to identifying the source, it may be appropriate in a particular case to describe how the source obtained the information, for example, a reliable police informant, "head" or "a reliable law enforcement source of _____ Police Department saw" a particular event at a particular time.

In many cases, there is no need to indicate the source of the stored information. However, each item of information should be individually judged against established criteria to determine whether or not source identification is appropriate.

Information Quality Control

Information to be stored in the criminal intelligence file should undergo a review for compliance with established file input guidelines and agency police prior to being filed. This quality control requirement should be the responsibility of a carefully selected and specifically designated individual in the intelligence unit.

The quality control reviewer is responsible for seeing that all information entered into the criminal intelligence file conforms with the agency's file criteria and has been properly evaluated and classified. Review of file input will ensure the agency is maintaining the quality of criminal intelligence file necessary for meeting established guidelines.

File Dissemination

In order to protect the right of privacy of individuals contained in the criminal intelligence file and to maintain the confidentiality of the sources and the file itself, agencies should adopt sound procedures for disseminating stored information. Section 703 B of the California Administrative Code, Chapter I, Title 11, limits dissemination of criminal history record information to criminal justice agencies, and only to those with a specific need-to-know as well as a right-to-know. These terms that can be applied to intelligence information access are defined as follows:

Need-to-know: Requested information is pertinent and necessary to the requesting agency for initiating, furthering, or completing an investigation.

Right-to-know: Requesting agency has official capacity and statutory authority to gain access to the information being requested. The classification and evaluation assigned the information are, in part, dissemination controls. They denote who may receive the information as well as the internal approval level(s) required for release of the information.

The integrity of the criminal intelligence file can be maintained only by strict adherence to proper dissemination guidelines. Abuses in the operation of the system due to failure to comply with dissemination guidelines may result in the violation of an individual's right of privacy and may endanger the confidentiality of the file itself.

To eliminate unauthorized use and abuses of the system, a department may wish to use a dissemination control form that can be maintained with each stored document. This control form records the date of the request, the name of the agency and individual requesting the information, the need-to-know, the information provided, and the name of the employee handling the request. Depending upon the needs of the agency, the control form may also be designed to record other items useful to the agency in the management of its operations.

File Purge

Information stored in the criminal intelligence file should be periodically reviewed and purged to ensure that the file is current, accurate, and relevant to the needs and objectives of the agency, and to safeguard the individual's right of privacy as guaranteed under federal and state laws. Law enforcement agencies have an obligation to keep stored information on individuals current and accurate. Review of criminal intelligence should be done on a continual basis as agency personnel use the material in carrying out day-to-day activities. In this manner, information that appears to be no longer useful or cannot be validated can be immediately purged from the file and destroyed.

To ensure that the review and purge of the file are done systematically, agencies should develop purge criteria and time schedules. Operational procedures of the purge, as well as the manner of destruction, for purged materials should be established.

A. *Purge Criteria.* General considerations that may be applied to the review and purging of information stored in the criminal intelligence file are as follows:

1. Utility
   · How often is the information used?
   · For what purpose is the information being used?
   · Who uses the information?

2. Timeliness and appropriateness
   · Is the information outdated?
   · Is the information relevant to the needs and objectives of the agency?
   · Is the information relevant to the purpose for which it was collected and stored?
   · Is the information available from other sources?
   · Is this non-intelligence information that should be stored elsewhere?
   · Is the security classification assigned the information still appropriate?

3. Accuracy and completeness
   · Is the information still valid?
   · Is the information adequate for identification purposes?
   · Can the validity of the data be determined through investigative techniques?

B. *Purge Time Schedule.* Review of the criminal intelligence file for purging purposes can vary from once each year to once every seven years. Local agencies should develop a schedule best suited to their needs.

C. *Manner of Destruction.* Material purged from the criminal intelligence file should be destroyed under the supervision of members of the intelligence unit and in accordance with applicable state and local regulations.

File Security

The criminal intelligence file should be located in a secured area with file access restricted to authorized personnel. Physical security of the criminal intelligence file is imperative to maintain the confidentiality of the information stored in the file and to ensure the protection of the individual's right to privacy.

Allocating Investigative Resources Using the Criminal Act Continuum

Investigative managers are tasked with the responsibility for allocating limited resources as effectively and efficiently as possible. The criminal act continuum provides a model in which supervisors can use available information to allocate resources in a manner that impacts most directly on the crime problem at hand (Willmer, 1970; Unsinger, 1977; and Kuykendall, 1982). The criminal act continuum is based on the idea that criminals "emit signals" as they contemplate or commit crimes. As the crime proceeds, it is possible to intervene at various points to prevent the act or apprehend the criminal.

Concept and Planning Phase

In the concept phase, the criminal or criminals form the idea of a crime. At this stage, the investigator can do little because persons cannot be prosecuted for their thoughts. In the planning stage, the criminal(s) take steps toward committing a crime. For example, a robber may acquire a weapon and look for suitable targets, or a drug dealer may make contact with a source of supply for the drugs he plans to sell.

Act, Escape, and Fugitive Phase

The *act* is the actual commission of a crime. The crime any last only a few seconds, as in a robbery or assault; several hours, as in a burglary; or it may go on for an indefinite period, as in some types of drug trafficking. At this point the suspect may be apprehended, but it is more than likely that he will not be. If the suspect is not apprehended, he will enter the escape phase of the continuum and become a fugitive.

Disposal and Repeat Cycle

In some crimes, such as burglary, stealing, or robbery, the criminal will need to dispose of the fruits of the crime in some way. In the disposal phase, the criminal may sell or barter the property, thus becoming vulnerable to detection. The criminal offender may also form a new criminal concept and repeat the entire process with another crime. Research on repeat offenders suggests that career criminals are likely to continue to be involved in crime until they are apprehended.

Intervention Points

If investigators can determine what phase of the criminal act continuum the criminal is in, it is possible to select specific strategies to detect and arrest the offender. This process relies on determining the relationship between five basic investigative techniques, the information sources available to the investigator, and the stage the crime is in.

Investigative Techniques and the Continuum

The five basic investigative techniques are interviewing, scientific analysis, role playing, pattern analysis, and monitoring. Interviewing is the staple of investigative work, the process of getting victims of crime and witnesses of crime to provide information to the police. Scientific analysis is the process of gathering and analyzing physical evidence. Role playing refers to assuming another identity as part of a covert or undercover operation. Pattern analysis refers to the analysis of crime to determine if an event is part of a larger pattern of offenses, such as burglary, robbery, sex offenses, or homicide. Monitoring refers to keeping a suspect under surveillance by any means, including physical or electronic surveillance. Various sources of information may be available to investigators at different stages on the continuum.

To use the continuum, the investigative supervisor will determine approximately what phase of the continuum the act is in and then determine what, if any, sources of information might be available to help detect and arrest the criminal. The criminal act continuum is not a cure-all for the investigative manager, but it does provide a format in which to systematically approach the issue of resource allocation in an investigation.

References

Blanchard, Kenneth and Peale, Norman Vincent. "The Power of Ethical Management," New York, Fawcett Crest Books, 1988.

Brown, Lee P. "Team Policing: Management of Criminal Investigation." *The Police Chief* (September): 65–67, 1976.

Cawley, Donald F. et al. *Managing Criminal Investigations Manual*. Washington, DC: U.S. Department of Justice, Law Enforcement Assistance Administration, 1976.

Dintino, Justin J. and Martens, Frederick T. *Police Intelligence Systems in Crime Control*. Springfield, IL: Charles C. Thomas, 1983.

Eck, John E. *Managing Case Assignments: The Burglary Investigation Decision Model Replication*. Washington, DC: Police Executive Research Forum, 1979.

Eck, John E. *Solving Crimes: The Investigation of Robbery and Burglary*. Washington, DC: Police Executive Research Forum, 1983.

Greenwood, Peter W., Petersilia, Joan, and Chaiken, Jan. *The Criminal Investigation Process*. Lexington, MA: D.C. Health, 1977.

Intelligence and Investigative Records. Washington, DC: U.S. Department of Justice, U.S. Government Printing Office, 1985.

Kuykendall, Jack. "The Criminal Investigative Process: Toward a Conceptual Framework." Journal of Criminal Justice 10:131–145, 1976.

Law Enforcement Policy on the Management of Criminal Intelligence. Gaithersburg, MD: International Association of Chiefs of Police, 1985.

Lacasse, Terry C. "An Alternative Approach to Investigations." *FBI Law Enforcement Bulletin* 55(10): 9–12, 1986.

Morris, Jack. *Police Informant Management: A Guide for the Use of Contributors*. Orangevale, CA: Palmer Enterprises, 1983.

Morris, Jack. *Police Intelligence Files: An Introduction to the Use of Confidential Police Files*. Orangevale, CA: Palmer Enterprises, 1983.

Pilant, Lois. "Spotlight on ... Computerizing Criminal Investigation." *The Police Chief* 40(1): 28–41.

Source Debriefing Guide. Washington, DC: Office of Intelligence, Drug Enforcement Administration, United States Department of Justice.

Unsinger, Peter. "Utilizing the Entire Criminal Continuum to Deter and Detect Crime." *Crime Prevention Review* 4:8–12, 1977.

Willmer, M. *Criminal and Information Theory.* Edinburgh: University of Edinburgh Press, 1970.

4. Collection and Preservation of Evidence

I have no data yet. It is a capital mistake to theorize before one has data. Insensibly one begins to twist facts to suit theories, instead of the theories to suit the facts.

Sherlock Holmes, *A Scandal in Bohemia*, Sir Arthur Conan Doyle

Evidence is defined as:

Any species of proof, or probative matter, legally presented at the trial of an issue, by the act of parties and through the medium of witnesses, records documents, exhibits, concrete objects, etc., for the purpose of inducing in the minds of the court or jury as to their contention. (*Black's Law Dictionary*, 1983, p. 287)

Physical evidence is typically the most convincing evidence in a criminal case. Physical or forensic evidence establishes its own basis of reliability. It does not rely on the sometime faulty recollections or the biased perspectives of witnesses.

Courts have long demonstrated a preference for physical evidence over other forms of evidence. For example, the *corpus delicti* rule in the law of homicide states that no criminal conviction can be based solely upon the defendant's out of court confession without some other evidence to establish the *corpus delicti* of the homicide (Perkins, 1982, p. 142).

In a series of cases in the 1960s, beginning with *Escobedo v. Illinois* and *Miranda v. Arizona*, the Supreme Court placed restrictions on the use of confessions in criminal trials. These restrictions resulted from the questionable practices used by law enforcement officers to obtain statements and confessions from suspects. Restrictions on the use of confessions forced police and prosecutors to concentrate more on the use of physical evidence to build cases. Today the availability of significant physical evidence will often be a major factor in a prosecutor's decision to file charges. Prosecutors will often be reluctant to file in cases where there is little or no physical evidence to support testimonial evidence or witness identifications.

Uses of Physical Evidence

Physical evidence can be of use in determining that a crime has been committed. The following case study illustrates this point.

CASE STUDY

In a small town in central Kansas, an older couple perished in an apparently accidental fire in their home. Shortly after the funeral, the couple's only son and sole beneficiary of their life insurance attempted to cash in his parent's policy. He became upset when told that he would receive the check in several weeks. His actions made local law enforcement officers suspicious. Investigators obtained a search warrant to exhume the bodies for a careful post mortem examination. The autopsy revealed that both persons had died of gunshot wounds to the chest prior to the fire. If the investigators and coroner been more cautious in their initial investigation, physical evidence of the crime would have been discovered. Had it not been for the greed of the killer, a crime would have gone undetected.

Physical evidence may be valuable in linking a specific suspect to a crime. Physical evidence may also provide leads to a specific suspect.

CASE STUDY

In this case the suspect attempted to steal a pickup truck. He was able to get the truck started and began driving away in the dark with the lights off to avoid attracting attention. As the driver accelerated, the truck struck a tree. On impact he was thrown against the steering wheel, causing a laceration to his forehead and, more importantly for identification later, his glasses were thrown to the floorboard of the truck. The glasses were taken to an ophthalmologist to determine the prescription. The doctor not only determined that the prescription was unique but also noted that the frames were also unusual. It was possible to trace the glasses from the prescription. A suspect was later convicted, in large part due to the glasses and the match on the blood type.

In order to understand how evidence can link a suspect to a crime, it is important to understand the distinction between class and individual characteristics of evidence.

Individual and Class Characteristics

Evidence can be evaluated by the extent to which it can be used to link a suspect to a crime. Physical evidence is separated into two general categories: evidence with individual characteristics and evidence with class characteristics.

Evidence that has individual characteristics can be used to identify a specific suspect and link that suspect to a particular crime. Some of the better-known examples of individual evidence are fingerprints, palm prints, and footprints.

Class characteristics are common to a group or class of objects. Common examples of evidence with class characteristics are fibers and other items that can be placed in a general category, such as oil found at a crime scene that leaked from the crankcase of an engine and soil transferred to or from a crime scene. At this time DNA evidence is still described as evidence with class characteristics with decisions about identity being based on statistical probability. It may well be possible to make positive identifications based on DNA or other types of blood or genetic evidence in the not to distant future.

CASE STUDY

The nude body of a middle-aged female was found in a ditch alongside a gravel road. Near the body, on the road, investigators saw a small puddle of motor oil, which was recovered and placed in a plastic bag. While processing the crime scene, investigators saw an old car similar to one belonging to a local young man who had a history of violence and sexual deviance begin to turn onto the road where the victim's body had been located. The driver of the car saw the investigators and stopped, turned around, and left rapidly in the direction he had come. Investigators later seized the car and requested that oil from the crankcase be compared with the oil recovered at the location where the body was found. The oil matched, but chemists were unable to testify with certainty the oil on the road came from that car. Clearly, however, this was a compelling piece of physical evidence. The driver was later convicted of murder based in part on the physical evidence in the form of the motor oil.

In many cases it will not be readily apparent whether a piece of evidence has class or individual characteristics. Only laboratory analysis can answer that question. An investigator should process each item of evidence as if it had individual characteristics.

Procedure at the Crime Scene

Upon receiving a call, an officer must proceed to the scene as quickly and safely as possible. Once at the crime scene, the officer must gain control of the situation and the scene, and prevent further violence or destruction of evidence. If a potential for more violence exists, it may be necessary for the officer to alter the crime scene by picking up a weapon or removing a weapon from someone present. If anyone at the scene has been injured, the officer should render first aid or arrange for medical assistance.

Upon gaining control of the area, the officer must take immediate steps to identify and protect the crime scene. This will be done to prevent the scene from being altered, which will reduce the possibility of accurately reconstructing the circumstances of the crime. Before beginning to search for evidence, the investigator should take the time to look at the scene. An officer's initial observations and impressions at a crime scene may not be supported by facts revealed as the investigation progresses.

For example, when investigators first entered the scene of the homicide depicted in Figure 4.1, they felt they might be dealing with a sexually motivated crime, or at least one in which the sexual deviance played some part. The investigation revealed that the killer had stabbed the victim after both had consumed several beers at the victim's home. The assailant had stabbed the victim after an argument. After stabbing the victim, the killer decided to take the victim's wallet. He discovered that the victim's blood had soaked into his trousers. The killer began pulling the victim's pants cuffs in order to pull his pants, and therefore the wallet, away from the bloody area without bloodying his own hands. In the course of pulling the victim's pants, the killer pulled the victim's ankles and dragged him across the floor. By the time he completed this process of getting the wallet, the victim's body was in the position in which it was found. The killer simply left the victim there. Sex, as such, had not been the primary motive for this crime. It was primarily a drunken dispute that resulted in a death.

Indoor Crime Scenes

In an indoor crime scene it is possible for the officer to prevent unauthorized personnel from entering the scene by posting officers at the doors. It is also necessary to keep a written and photographic log of all persons who enter the scene.

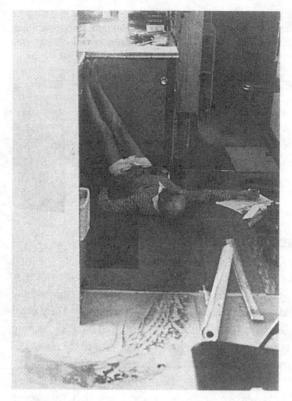

Figure 4.1   A crime scene may not always be what it first appears to be

The department should institute a policy that requires all persons who enter the scene to write a report stating their reasons for being there. This practice reduces unnecessary traffic through the crime scene.

Outdoor Crime Scenes

With an outdoor crime scene, the officer will have to contend with the weather as well as curiosity seekers. Most law enforcement agencies are equipped with plastic tape or rope that can be used to cordon off an area. In the event of rain or other foul weather, it may be necessary to cover an item of particular importance to protect it from the elements. For example, an investigator may need to cover tire tracks with a cardboard box to prevent them from being washed away. In some cases it may be necessary to make a note of where an object was and to pick it up to prevent its destruction.

Search Warrants

In some cases, investigators may need to obtain a search warrant before gathering any physical evidence. In *Mincey v. Arizona*, the Supreme Court ruled that there is no "murder scene" exception to the search warrant requirement. *Mincey* resulted from a four-day warrantless search of an apartment in which an undercover police officer had been killed in a drug raid. In response to the defense's motion to suppress, the state argued that the Supreme Court should recognize a "murder-scene" exception to the search warrant requirement. The Court stated:

The Fourth Amendment proscribes all unreasonable searches and seizures, and it is a cardinal principle that "searches conducted outside the judicial process, without prior approval by judge or magistrate, are per se unreasonable under the Fourth Amendment—subject only to a few specifically established and well delineated exceptions" . . . The Arizona Supreme Court did not hold that the search of the petitioner's apartment fell within any of the exceptions to the warrant requirement previously recognized by this Court, but rather that the search of a homicide scene should be recognized as an additional exception. The Court stated, "We decline to hold that the seriousness of the offense under investigation itself creates exigent circumstances of the kind that under the Fourth Amendment justify a warrantless search." (Mincey v. Arizona, 437 U.S. 436 [1978])

Thus, in cases in which the crime has occurred in an area where the defendant may have an expectation of privacy, the warrant requirement still applies (Mincey v. Arizona, 437 U.S. 385 [1978]). This situation can arise quite often in domestic violence or arson cases. For example, if a husband assaults his wife in their home, the investigator must be certain about the legal authority upon which the search for evidence should proceed. If the victim is conscious, she may give consent. If consent cannot be obtained, the officer should obtain a search warrant before processing evidence. The investigator should provide for the security of the scene to prevent the destruction of evidence while a warrant is obtained.

Securing a Building While a Search Warrant Is Being Obtained

When investigators are faced with a situation in which they may need a search warrant before they enter a structure and begin to gather evidence, they may have a legitimate concern that someone may enter the scene and destroy or move evidence. In these situations, the police have the authority to secure the scene until a search warrant is obtained. In *Segura v. United States* the Supreme Court held that

> The home is secured in Fourth Amendment, not primarily because of the occupant's possessor interests in the premises, but because of their privacy interests in the activities that take place within . . . A seizure affects only possessor interests, not privacy interests. Therefore, the heightened protection per se accord privacy interests is simply not implicated where a seizure of premises, not a search, is at issue. (Segura v. United States, 468 U.S. 796 at 810 [1984])

Therefore, police can secure a scene and prevent anyone from entering the area. The Court went on to note in its opinion that the scene can be protected by placing an officer within the structure or by placing a perimeter around it after the area has been inspected to determine if anyone is in the scene. Indeed, good investigative procedure requires determining that the scene is completely secure, both internally and externally.

Chain of Custody

Rules of evidence require that any evidence be presented to a jury in substantially the same condition it was found. This obliges the officer collecting evidence to establish the *chain of custody*. An officer collecting an item of evidence is responsible for it and should keep it in her possession until it can be placed in an evidence locker or safe. Most law enforcement agencies have standard chain of custody forms available to officers to ensure complete documentation for each item of evidence. An example of a chain of custody form appears in Figure 4.2.

REGIONAL CRIME LAB

EVIDENCE CHAIN OF CUSTODY   Agency Case No.____

Lab Case No. _____

Crime:_____

Date:_____

Location:_____

Specimen:_____

_____

Dept. Submitting:_____

Victim:_____

Suspect:_____

_____

_____

IN CUSTODY OF	TIME	PLACE	DATE
From:_____	_____	_____	_____
To:_____	_____	_____	_____
From:_____	_____	_____	_____
To:_____	_____	_____	_____
From:_____	_____	_____	_____
To:_____	_____	_____	_____
From:_____	_____	_____	_____
To:_____	_____	_____	_____
From:_____	_____	_____	_____
To:_____	_____	_____	_____

ANALYSIS REQUESTED: *(PLEASE EXPLAIN)*

_____

_____

_____

_____

Figure 4.2   Chain of custody form

Crime Scene Search

Investigators must search every crime scene to recover any physical evidence that might be there. The selection of a search pattern will depend on whether the scene is indoor or outdoor, and the nature of the area to be searched.

Indoor Search Patterns

Widening-Circle Search

When using the widening-circle search pattern, the searcher starts in the center of the area and works out to the perimeter as illustrated in Figure 4.3. The searcher may repeat the search process by starting at the perimeter of the area and working back toward the center. The search technique can be enhanced by having a second officer follow to double-check the first searcher's observations.

Zone Search

In a zone search, the area to be searched is divided into separate zones, and one officer is then assigned to search a particular zone using an appropriate pattern. After each zone has been searched, the searching officers can change zones and search again (Figure 4.4). This technique can be very effective in searching a house, in which each room can be thought of as a zone.

Outside Search Patterns

Outdoor searches may be more difficult to conduct because it is often difficult to determine which areas are part of the crime scene and which are not. A murder that occurred in a midwestern state illustrates this point.

CASE STUDY

While on a date, a young couple had an argument that ended with the young man strangling his date. He then drove into the countryside, where he dragged her body into a freshly plowed field and buried it in a shallow grave. He then returned home. The victim's parents called the police when their daughter did not return home at the expected

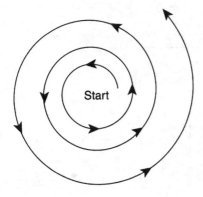

Figure 4.3   Widening-circle search pattern

time. The boy was contacted by the police and immediately admitted killing the girl. He agreed to help the officers find the body. The problem was that the crime had occurred in the dark and plowed fields look alike. In addition, the boy had become completely lost trying to find a place to hide the body. The suspect could not locate the field or recognize any landmarks. An aerial search did locate the body approximately 150 feet from an unpaved road. The entire area had to be secured to protect the scene because it appeared that the suspect could have taken two or more routes into or out of the burial site.

Zone Search

A zone search outdoors requires that the area to be searched be identified and divided into zones or sectors, which are then searched by individual officers. After a zone has been searched, the officers may exchange areas to double-check the previous search. (See Figure 4.4)

Strip Search

Areas to be searched may be divided into strips and systematically searched. The searcher begins by dividing the area to be searched into stripes or lanes at one end and then walks, or in some cases crawls, through the scene, looking for any possible items of evidence. A strip search pattern is illustrated in Figure 4.5.

Grid Search

A grid search is really an extension of the strip search. The difference is that the searcher goes back over the same area from a different direction, as illustrated in Figure 4.6.

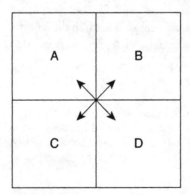

Figure 4.4   Zone search

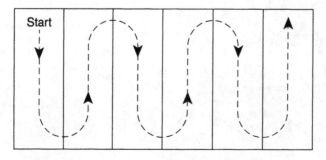

Figure 4.5   Strip crime-scene search pattern

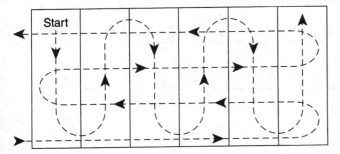

Figure 4.6   Grid crime-scene search pattern

Point-to-Point Search

A point-to-point search is much like the tale of Hansel and Gretel. Occasionally a criminal may leave a trail to his location. In one case, a thief stole a bag of small change. He was unaware that the bag had a hole in it, and he dropped change along the path back to his apartment, which was nearby. A criminal may leave a trail of blood after cutting herself or leave footprints in the snow or dirt that can be followed. In these cases, the officer must act quickly to prevent the loss or destruction of evidence. (See Figure 4.7)

Crime Scene Photography

It is essential that the trier of fact have a clear understanding of what a crime scene looks like. Photographs provide one of the best means by which to provide them with the necessary information. The purpose of crime scene photography is to provide the jury with a clear idea of what happened at the scene. Crime

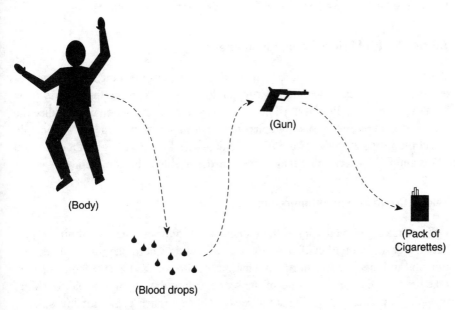

Figure 4.7   Point-to-point search

```
┌─────────────────────────────────────────────────────────────┐
│                                                             │
│   PHOTOGRAPHER_____      │
│                                                             │
│   DATE_____ / _____ / _____  ROLL #_____       │
│                                                             │
│                                                             │
│   LOCATION_____      │
│                                                             │
│   CASE FILE_____      │
│                                                             │
│   AGENCY_____      │
│                                                             │
└─────────────────────────────────────────────────────────────┘
```

Figure 4.8   Photographer's plaque

scene photographs need not be aesthetically pleasing, but they must provide a clear and accurate visual representation of where the crime took place.

When taking photographs, the investigator should begin each role of film with a photograph of a plaque that identifies the scene, as illustrated in Figure 4.8. The plaque should have a place for the case number, the time and date the photos were taken, and the photographer's name.

The photographer should also keep a log of all pictures taken. The photographic log (Figure 4.9) can be valuable when determining the sequence in which the pictures were taken, as well as in establishing a record of the photos taken.

Admissibility of Crime Scene Photographs

In order to be admissible, crime scene photographs must meet the requirements of any other item of evidence. Initially the photos must be relevant, that is, they must tend to prove a fact. Photos must not cause a sympathetic reaction or prejudice the jury. For example, grisly photographs, while relevant, may upset a jury and unduly affect the jury's attitude toward the defendant. Trial judges are given a great deal of discretion in determining if an item of evidence should be admitted.

Taking Crime Scene Photographs

Officers taking photographs at the scene have a continuing responsibility to prevent the destruction of evidence. Investigators will want to begin their investigation and will need information on what has occurred. Evidence technicians may take the investigators on a tour of the scene, cautioning them to avoid touching, dropping, or leaving anything at the scene. This approach allows the investigator to actually view the scene, which provides them with a clearer idea of what hap-

PHOTOGRAPHIC LOG

PAGE___OF___

LOCATION_____

DATE_____

CASE IDENTIFIER_____

PREPARER/ASSISTANTS_____

CAMERA_____

TYPE OF FILM AND RATING_____

REMARKS_____

Photo#	Description Of Photographic Subject	Camera Settings And Lens Type	Distance	Use Of Scale	Sketch (If Applicable)

Figure 4.9   Photographic log

pened there. It also creates the potential for loss or damage of evidence. A second, and preferred, method of informing investigators about a crime scene is to take several photographs with quick-developing film. These photos provide investigators with the needed information without their having to actually enter the scene and risk the loss of evidence. These pictures can be taken by a single photographer, thus protecting the scene from unnecessary intrusions.

Before taking pictures, the evidence officer should develop a plan for photographing the scene. The simplest plan is to go from the general to the specific in showing how the crime occurred. The photographer should begin by taking photos that will be used to orient the jury. This can be done by taking aerial photographs or by taking several shots of the scene from different points of the compass. Care should be taken to get pictures of addresses and other identifying information. Essentially, the photographer takes photos to illustrate the *corpus delicti* or body of the crime.

Ideally, at the scene of a major crime scene, two investigators should be assigned to take pictures. This helps to ensure that an adequate number of pictures are taken. It also ensures that the scene is completely covered.

All items of evidence must be photographed before being moved. Again, it is advisable to take two pictures of each important item, being sure to fill the frame with the image of the item, and thus ensuring that adequate enlargements can be produced from the resulting negative or slide. One picture is taken to illustrate how the item appears, and the second is taken with a ruler beside it to indicate the relative size of the object. Pictures are usually taken at eye level because this is the usual manner in which a person views an object. Pictures of specific items of evidence are taken at a 90-degree angle to the object to provide a precise photographic representation of the object. (Figure 4.10)

Color and Black-and-White Photography

Crime scene photography should normally be done in color because this is how people actually view the world. Occasionally a trial judge may restrict the use of color photos of particularly gruesome or emotional subjects. Black-and-white prints may be made from color negatives if the need arises; however, these prints may lack contrast.

Figure 4.10   Photograph taken at a 90-degree angle with a ruler in the frame to show scale

Selection of a Camera and Lenses

There are many cameras that may be used for crime scene photography. In the past, the 4 × 5 Speed Graphic was widely used by evidence technicians. The speed graphic is large and cumbersome, but it has the advantage of producing a large cut-film negative. The large negative produces in a very clear print. More recently, agencies have adopted the 35mm camera because it is portable and inexpensive to use. With a modest amount of training, officers can become quite proficient in using a 35mm camera for crime scene photography.

Under normal circumstances, a 50mm lens will provide good all-around service. Investigators should also have 70mm to 210mm lens and a 28mm wide-angle lens available for more specialized photography, such as close-up or wide-angle photographs. It is advisable to almost always (except where glass is in the picture) use a flash. Most 35mm cameras have a flash attachment that may be joined to the body of the camera using a device called a hot shoe. When using flash photography, the shutter speed should be set at 1/60 of a second, the speed at which most photographers can hold a camera steady and thus produce a clear picture. However, when possible, a tripod should be used for stability to prevent blurred pictures produced by movement of the photographer, especially when attempting to take photographs at shutter speeds of less than 1/30 of a second. The increased availability of inexpensive 35mm cameras makes it possible for most police departments to put a camera in every patrol car. While these cameras are not as versatile as more expensive models, they work reasonably well in most situations and are quite durable.

Videotaping Crime Scenes

The availability of inexpensive portable video cameras has provided an additional means to record a crime scene. Video may provide a more complete record of a crime scene than photography by allowing one to film the entire scene. The investigator doing the taping should follow the same steps as taken when photographing a scene. Taping should begin outside the scene and then proceed to illustrate each important aspect of the crime. Attention should be given to showing each element of the *corpus delicti* of the crime. The video camera should not be turned off until the scene has been completely recorded in order to counter the defense argument that investigators altered the tape or intentionally avoided taping evidence that might be detrimental to the state's case. Generally, a videotape should be made of serious crimes of violence and crimes resulting in loss and/or damage of property of great economic value.

Some prosecutors and evidence technicians have questioned the value of videotaping a crime scene because tapes may not add a great deal to the jury's understanding of how the crime occurred and because the use of videotape may actually slow the legal proceedings against the defendant. While filming, investigators should be careful not to say anything that is not relevant to the process of gathering evidence at the scene. Videotape is subject to discovery, that is, the defense has the right to see and hear the tape before a trial. The defense will also insist on acquiring a transcript of the audio portion of the videotape. As with any evidence, the trial judge has the authority to excise any film that is inflammatory, and it should be expected the defense would object to any footage that is gruesome. If, in the judgment of the prosecutor and the investigator, videotapes may aid the jury in determining the truth, it may be worthwhile to record the scene with this in mind. But it should be remembered that defense attorneys will delay a trial by requesting time to review the tape, thus making the trial more expensive and time consuming than if the tape had not be made.

Crime Scene Sketching

As with crime scene photographs, the purpose of crime scene sketches is to aid the jury in their attempt to understand how a crime occurred. Photographs are a valuable aid to the prosecution, but they are two-dimensional and may not show a relationship between objects. In addition, key items of evidence may not be sufficiently distinct in a photo, and thus it may lose some of its impact on the jury. Crime scene sketches are the simplest yet most effective means to illustrate the relationship of significant items of evidence to each other.

Crime scene sketches are of two types, rough and finished. Rough sketches are made by investigators at the scene. They need not be drawn to scale but must include accurate measurements. Graph paper is useful when drawing rough sketches.

A finished sketch should be drawn to scale and should include the following information:

- Title of the sketch
- Date and time the crime occurred
- North represented by an arrow
- Outline of the crime scene
- Doors, windows, and other relevant items
- Legend
- Scale
- Identification of the officer who prepared the sketch

Preparing the Sketch

When preparing a diagram of the scene, it is important to remember the purpose of the sketch is to aid the trier of fact to understand how the crime occurred. An effort should be made to eliminate extraneous items. The person preparing the sketch should determine what is essential to aid the jury's understanding.

Measurements

All measurements should be made from permanent fixed objects, such as buildings, telephone poles, or trees. Indoor measurements should be made from specific points, such as corners or doors. When measuring an object so that it can later be returned to its original position, it is necessary to take measurements from two positions to two points on the item. For example, when measuring the location of a gun, measurements should be made from the butt *and* from the muzzle of the weapon. All measurements should be double-checked and verified before completing the sketch and submitting it as evidence. Objects on the sketch should be marked and recorded on the legend.

Types of Crime Scene Sketches

Floor Plan   The floor plan sketch (Figure 4.11) is basically a drawing of the major items found at the scene. It may be useful to prepare one sketch of the outline of the scene and then to make a number of photocopies of the original. The investigator sketching the scene can then add items to the photocopies as needed. It may also be helpful to make sketches on clear acetate overlays, on which additional relevant items are added.

Exploded or Cross-Projection Sketch   The cross-projection sketch (Figure 4.12) is an extension of the floor plan sketching technique, with the walls of the

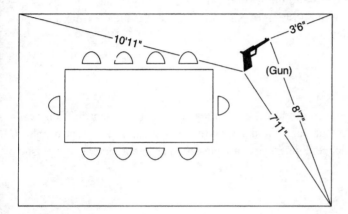

Figure 4.11   Floor plan sketch

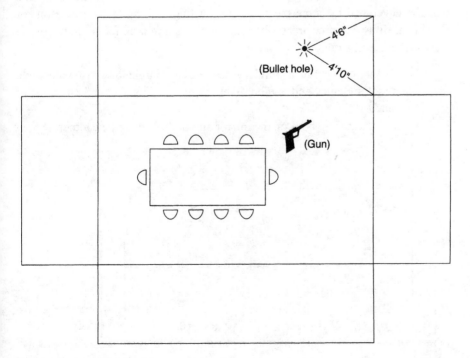

Figure 4.12   Cross-projection sketch

crime scene included in the diagram. The cross-projection sketch is drawn from an angle that resembles looking down at a shoebox, in which the walls of the crime scene are analogous the sides of the shoebox. The sides of the box may then be cut and laid flat so that the jury can see the relationship of objects to each other. This type of sketch is particularly useful for showing important evidence, such as bloodstains and bullet holes.

Midline Sketch　Crime scene sketches often become cluttered with too many lines and items. One way to avoid this is to use a midline sketching system (Figure 4.13) in which the investigator preparing the sketch divides the area to be sketched into two or four equal parts, similar to a zone search. A steel tape is then stretched through the room or subdivided parts of the room. The investigator can then measure the position of particular items of evidence from appropriate points on the tape measure.

Fingerprints

Fingerprints are perhaps the best-known means of positive identification available to law enforcement. Jurors understand the concept and give great weight to fingerprints as evidence. Fingerprints are classified as latent, patent, and plastic.

Latent Fingerprints

Latent prints are the most commonly found fingerprints, but they are also the most easily destroyed. Latent prints are not generally visible to the naked eye and must be developed by some means, either dusting or fuming. The investigator should carefully examine areas where latent prints might be found. Some of the places where prints might be found are:

- The point of entry at a burglary scene (The burglar is most vulnerable when making entry and is more likely to make a mistake while nervous or distracted.)
- Medicine cabinets, both on the mirror and on bottles in the cabinet
- Refrigerator

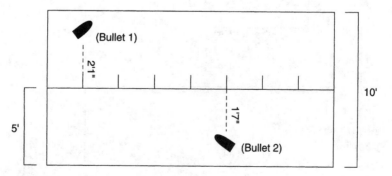

Figure 4.13　Midline sketch technique

· Other items that might have been touched as a suspect moves through the scene

Searching for Prints on a Vehicle

There are a number of places on a vehicle where fingerprints might be found:

- · On or near the door handle
- · On the rear-view mirror
- · On the dashboard
- · On the steering wheel
- · On the outside mirror
- · On the windows

Recovering Latent Fingerprints

Dusting   The oldest and most common technique for developing latent finger-prints is dusting. Dusting involves spreading fine graphite powder over a hard, smooth surface using a brush. The investigator gently spreads the powder over the object being examined. It is important to avoid the temptation to make "one more" stroke with the brush, hoping to make the print clearer. Powders come in a number of different colors to increase the contrast in the developed print from which the object is recovered. Excess powder should be gently blown from the surface. Fingerprint tape is placed over the developed print, taking care not to allow air bubbles to form under the tape. The tape with the print is then lifted and transferred to a 3×5 inch card.

Iodine Fuming   This technique uses fumes that result from heating iodine crystals. The fumes are absorbed into porous surfaces, such as paper, and produce a brownish fingerprint. The print will remain fixed as long as the oils deposited on the surface remain. In time, however, the print fades and should therefore be photographed as soon as possible. Iodine fuming has been used for a number of years and has, to a large extent, been replaced by the ninhydrin chemical technique.

Ninhydrin Chemical   In the ninhydrin technique, ninhydrin is applied to an object by spraying, brushing on, or even immersing the object in the chemical, resulting in bonding of the ninhydrin to amino acids deposited on the object. The ninhydrin chemical is applied after the object's surface has been heated using an external source of heat, such as a hair dryer. The developed prints tend to be purple or reddish in color. Care should be taken when using this technique because ninhydrin will dissolve most inks.

Cyanoacrylate (Super Glue Fuming)   Within the last several years, "super glue" or "crazy glue" fuming has increased the investigator's ability to recover latent fingerprints from surfaces that were thought to be inaccessible to fingerprinting. This recovery technique involves the use of fumes from drying cyanoacrylate that adhere to a latent fingerprint and usually produce a gray or white print. The crazy glue technique is particularly useful in developing fingerprints on plastic, such as bags of marijuana or other drug containers. The technique is also useful in recovering fingerprints from glass, glassine packages, lead-based glossy paper, leather, and metal objects, including firearms.

This detection process begins with placing three or four drops of cyanoacrylate glue in a container of aluminum foil, which is then placed in a pan of water inside a larger container, such as a fish tank or some other glass or plastic container that can be sealed with glass or plexiglass. The item to be fumed is placed in the container, which is then sealed. Obviously, the item to be fumed should be positioned in such a way that the maximum number of surfaces are exposed. The process of fuming takes approximately two to 24 hours to complete and may be accelerated by adding a heat source, such as a light bulb under a metal can, inside the container. The object being fumed should be watched to monitor for the emergence of any prints.

Patent Prints

Patent fingerprints are visible to the unaided eye and are usually left in material such as blood, dust, grease, or dirt. When collecting patent prints, the investigator should photograph the print, including a scale reference, and then transport the object upon which the print was found to the laboratory, where the print can be examined under controlled conditions.

Plastic Prints

Plastic prints are left in a soft substance, such as wet paint or putty. Plastic prints are fairly durable but should be collected as soon as possible and transported to the laboratory in the same manner as patent prints.

Photographing Fingerprints

Before any attempt is made to recover a fingerprint, it should be photographed. There are a number of fingerprint cameras on the market today. However, a less expensive option is to attach a special lens to a regular 35mm camera, place the lens over the fingerprint, and then make the photograph.

Firearms Evidence

Firearms are one of the most commonly encountered items of evidence at homicide or assault scenes. No firearm should ever be moved or altered in any way until it has been photographed and measured in place.

Safety must be the overriding consideration when dealing with firearms. For this reason, every investigator should possess a working knowledge of firearms. The investigator must make several observations before moving the weapon, including whether the hammer on the weapon is cocked or whether the bolt is back, the position of the safety, and the position of any spent or live ammunition.

Once all measurements and observations have been made, the weapon may be picked up. Care should be taken to avoid destroying any evidence, including fingerprints and blood on the firearm. The firearm should be picked up by its trigger guard or by a rough surface, such as the checkered part of the grips on a gun, to avoid destroying fingerprints. Safety can also be increased by carefully unloading any live ammunition that might be in the weapon, if possible.

When unloading the weapon, the investigator should make note of the position of any live or spent rounds in the cylinder of a revolver or in the magazine of a semiautomatic pistol. The make, model, caliber, serial number, and any unique information about the gun should also be recorded.

Interior and Exterior Terminal Ballistics

Firearms analysis often involves interior and exterior ballistics. *Interior ballistics* refers to the functioning of various firearms through the firing cycle of the weapon. *Exterior ballistics* refers to the study of a projectile in flight from its point of origin to its termination.

One of the first tasks facing an investigator in a case involving a shooting is to determine if a specific firearm fired the bullets or cartridge cases recovered at the crime scene. This determination is made based on knowledge of the interior functioning of a firearm. In a revolver, for example, the firing pin may leave a unique impression on the primer. Semiautomatic pistols may leave firing pin impressions as well as extractor marks on ejected shell cases.

Striations on Projectiles

The interior of a rifled barrel often consists of lands and groves that twist to either the right or the left, depending on the make of the weapon. Lands and grooves are designed to cause a projectile to rotate as it is pushed down the barrel by the propellant, much like the spiral a quarterback puts on a forward pass of a football. As the bullet is forced down the barrel, tiny microscopic scratches, called *striations*, are left on it by the lands and grooves. These striations are unique to each weapon and are the means by which a particular gun can be identified.

Bore and Caliber

Bore refers to the diameter of the interior of the barrel. In a rifled barrel, bore is the distance measured between the opposing lands or ridges. The bore is the caliber of the weapon. For example, a .38 caliber projectile is 38 one-hundredths of an inch in diameter, and a 9mm bullet is 9mm in diameter. Some of the more common handgun calibers are .22, .32, .357, .44, 9mm, 10mm, and the .45.

Shotguns are usually smoothbore weapons, that is, their barrels do not have lands and grooves. Thus, shots or slugs (a single projectile) fired from a shotgun will not usually have striations. Spent shot shells may be of value in identifying a weapon by breach-face impressions. Shells may have distinctive marks made by a firing pin on the primer or by an extractor on the extractor groove. Shot shell cartridge cases should be photographed and measured in place and then transported to an evidence locker. Shotgun calibers are measured in gauges. The *gauge* is determined by theoretically dividing a pound of pure lead in a set number of equal parts and rolling those parts into a perfect sphere; the diameter of the sphere is then measured. Thus, a 12 gauge is a pound of lead divided into 12 parts, a 16 gauge is a pound divided into 16 parts, and so on. The exception to this rule is the 410 shotgun, with a bore that measures 410 one-thousandths of an inch in diameter.

Recovering Spent Projectiles

When recovering spent cartridges and projectiles, care should be taken to avoid making new scratches on the items, as it is the scratches that will be examined by the firearms expert and used for making his determinations. Spent cartridges may be picked up by placing a soft object down the mouth of the case or by using plastic forceps. Investigators should never attempt to remove an embedded spent bullet with a knife or other sharp object, as these are likely to scratch the object.

Marking Firearms Evidence

Spent cartridges should be marked on the inside of the mouth of the cartridge, wrapped in soft tissue, and the packaged in a clear plastic bag. They must be handled with extreme care when being marked because bullets are made from soft metals, such as lead and copper, and it is thus very easy to inadvertently place new scratches over existing striations. Spent projectiles should be marked on the base of the bullet. A spent bullet can contain impressions from an object that it struck, such as the weave of cloth, hair, or fibers. Modern projectiles often break into tiny fragments on impact. When it is impossible to mark small fragments, they should be isolated and placed in cotton or tissue in a pillbox. The box should then be marked with the appropriate information.

Firearms should be marked in a place that will not mar the weapon nor alter an area that may be of evidentiary value. Long guns should be marked on the stock, and handguns should be marked under the grips.

Drugfire

Drugfire is an automated, database-driven, multimedia firearms evidence imaging system developed by the Federal Bureau of Investigation (FBI). The name *Drugfire* reflects the belief that firearms evidence is associated with street crime, which in turn is often associated with drug sales and use. The system was designed to increase the effectiveness of firearms examiners by making it possible to maintain, share, and search data files on unsolved cases that have firearms evidence. Drugfire is not envisioned to be a centrally located database maintained by the FBI; rather, it is a national network of firearms laboratories, clustered by state or region, that exchange information with other Drugfire clusters.

Drugfire has been used to link firearms evidence to unrelated firearms cases through "cold searches" of firearms evidence. As noted earlier, during the firing cycle microscopic marks are left on cartridge cases and bullets. These marks are unique to the weapon that fired them and can be compared with test specimens. Using this technology, Drugfire has been developed as a means to store, share, and search cartridge and bullet imagery. At this time, however, Drugfire is focused on cartridge case imagery rather than bullet imagery. This is presently a more cost-effective use of resources, because cartridge cases are not as likely to be damaged as projectiles and are therefore more easily compared. Eventually images of highly characteristic bullet striations will be stored in the Drugfire database for comparison and use.

Drugfire will not replace firearms examiners. After a preliminary match has been made through Drugfire, a forensic firearms examiner makes a microscopic comparison and identification to verify the match. By using traditional, court-accepted comparison microscope techniques, it is possible to avoid issues of admissibility that might arise at trial. Drugfire has increased the solution of several types of crimes by:

- Collecting and sharing forensic firearms data imagery
- Providing rapid, comprehensive searching of local and regional firearms evidence files
- Overcoming jurisdictional and logistical constraints by performing remote electronic comparisons of digital images
- Linking unsolved shootings to other incidents and/or confiscated firearms
- Extending the capabilities and expanding the crime-solving role of forensic laboratories
- Using firearms evidence to link repeat offenders to crimes, and to expedite their identification and apprehension (Sibert, 1994)

In the 1990s, forensic ballistics became much more useful to the criminal investigator. The federal government funded two automated computer based systems, the Bureau of Alcohol Tobacco and Firearms' (BATF) Integrated Ballistics Identification System (IBIS) and the FBI's Drugfire system. Both programs provided new sources of information for the investigator on firearms evidence. Unfortunately the two systems were not interoperable, that is, they could not "speak" to each other. In 1997, the BATF and the FBI agreed to work to solve the problem. The BATF will have overall responsibility for system sites, and the FBI will establish and maintain a secure high-speed communications network. The result of these changes should be a single, integrated network capable of identifying both bullets and shell casings found at any violent crime scene where a firearm was used. This program will be known as the National Integrated Ballistics Information Network (NIBIN).

Gunshot Residue Test

When the primer in a cartridge case is detonated, tiny particles of barium lead copper and antimony, called *gunshot residue*, are deposited on the hand of the person holding the weapon. Residue will remain on the shooter's hands for about six hours, or until the person washes his or her hands or in some other way causes the residue to be removed. Thus gunshot residue should be recovered as quickly as possible.

Kits for recovering gunshot residue are produced commercially, although many regional crime laboratories prepare kits for local departments. Most kits consist of cotton swabs on plastic rods, with the swab on one end of the rod removed. Wooden rods can cause chemical reactions and alter the results, and thus should not be used. The removal of one end of the swab is necessary to prevent confusion regarding different samples.

After the sample has been taken, it should be placed in a marked plastic tube. Glass tubes should be avoided because glass can interfere with the test. A minimum of six swabs should be taken and clearly labeled as follows: left back, left palm, right back, right palm, control, and cartridge. The swab is then dipped in a solution of 5 percent nitric acid and the relevant area of the shooter's hand is swabbed. A variation of this technique involves spraying the solution on the suspected area and then swabbing it with a dry applicator. Gunshot residue analysis should be performed for all cases in which a firearm was discharged, such as alleged assaults and suicides.

Tool Marks

Tool marks are the impressions or striations made by an object that comes in contact with a surface. They are often associated with forced entry, such as burglary and auto theft. If the suspected tool is recovered, it should be packaged in tissue or cotton to prevent it from being damaged. The tool should be examined to determine if it contains trace or transfer evidence from the scene. Tool marks are commonly found at the point of entry or where an object was forced open.

The mark should be photographed and measured before attempting to recover it. If the owner is willing, the impression should be removed and taken to a lab. If this is not possible, the impression should be cast using commercial casting materials.

Biological Evidence

Blood Evidence

Blood is commonly found at scenes of violent crimes, such as homicides, assaults, and rape. Blood may appear in several forms, including spray, pools, drops, or smears. Bloodstains may not always be readily apparent. For example, dried blood may be black, brown, gray, blue, or green. If the investigator suspects that a stain may be blood, she should transport the object or a sample to the laboratory for analysis.

Investigator Safety

If an investigator will be handling any kind of blood or other biological evidence, it is advisable to wear disposable rubber gloves. In fact, evidence technicians or investigators charged with the collection of evidence should make it a practice to wear gloves when processing any evidence. Because chlorine bleach solution will kill the Acquired Immunodeficiency Syndrome (AIDS) virus, it is important to use it to clean all equipment that may have come into contact with blood or other body fluids. It is also advisable to spray shoes and other items of clothing with an aerosol disinfectant to kill the AIDS virus.

Acquired Immunodeficiency Syndrome (AIDS)

What Is HIV Infection and AIDS? *Acquired Immunodeficiency Syndrome (AIDS)* is a fatal disease that breaks down the body's immune system. It destroys the body's ability to fight infection and illness. AIDS is the disease caused by the *Human Immunodeficiency Virus (HIV)*. A virus is a small organism that can cause disease. Most individuals infected with HIV do not currently have AIDS, but most, if not all, of them will develop the disease. No one will develop AIDS unless he or she has been infected with HIV. By preventing HIV infection, we can prevent AIDS. AIDS can affect anyone, which makes the disease a problem for all of us.

According to the U.S. Department of Health and Human Services, approximately 1 in every 250 Americans is infected with HIV. Each year, between 40,000 and 80,000 Americans become infected with HIV.

HIV infection weakens the body's natural ability to fight diseases. As the immune system fails, a person infected with HIV may develop a variety of life-threatening illnesses, such as:

· Extreme weight loss
· Severe pneumonia
· Forms of cancer
· Extensive damage to the nervous system

Illnesses that Signal the Onset of AIDS   The AIDS virus affects individuals differently. The time between infection and the onset of symptoms varies. After a person is infected, antibodies to the virus appear in the blood. *Antibodies* are substances the body makes to fight an infection. Most HIV-infected individuals will test positive for AIDS when these antibodies are detected in their blood. HIV-infected individuals may not show signs of illness for many years so that an infected person can appear completely healthy. In some people, symptoms of illness may develop within one or two years, while others may stay healthy for as long as 10 or more years.

How Is HIV Infection Transmitted?   Transmission of HIV is closely linked to activities that allow direct insertion of the virus into the blood. Blood is the most important source of HIV. HIV is transmitted when blood or body fluids from someone who is HIV-positive enters another person's bloodstream. HIV is most commonly transmitted via four body fluids:

1. Blood
2. Semen
3. Vaginal secretions
4. Breast milk (in rare instances)

Activities that are known to transmit HIV include engaging in unprotected sex—vaginal, anal, or oral—with an infected person or sharing needles or syringes with someone infected with HIV. Women infected with HIV can pass the virus to their infants during pregnancy or birth. In some cases, HIV can be passed on during breast-feeding. Some individuals have become infected from blood transfusions, especially prior to 1985, when careful screening and laboratory testing of the U.S. blood supply began.

HIV is not spread through casual contact and is not transmitted through air, food, or water. HIV is not a food-borne illness, nor can it be transmitted in the workplace through casual contact, such as sneezing, coughing, or sweating, or from tears, clothing, telephones, breathing the same air, sharing eating utensils, or using the same rest room facilities.

Humans will not get AIDS from a mosquito or other insect bites. HIV does not live in a mosquito and is not transmitted through a mosquito's salivary glands, like other diseases, such as malaria or yellow fever. When an insect bites a person, it does not inject its own blood or a previous victim's blood into the new victim—it injects saliva. HIV lives for only a short time inside an insect and HIV does not reproduce; therefore, it cannot survive in insects.

There has never been a confirmed case of HIV being transmitted by kissing. HIV has been found in the saliva and tears of AIDS patients in only minute quantities. It is important to understand that finding a small amount of HIV in a body fluid does not mean that HIV can be transmitted by that body fluid. HIV has not been recovered from sweat, and contact with sweat has never been shown to result in transmission of HIV. Although HIV has been transmitted between family members in a household setting, this type of transmission is rare. These transmissions are believed to have resulted from contact between the skin or mucous membranes and infected blood.

Law Enforcement Considerations   Law enforcement officers may face the risk of exposure to blood during the conduct of their duties. At a crime scene or during the processing of suspects, it is possible to encounter blood-contaminated hypodermic needles or weapons, or to be called upon to assist with body removal. Exposure may also occur during a search of prisoners, their cells, or while subduing violent and combative individuals. Officers may encounter a range of assaultive and disruptive behaviors that may potentially result in exposure to blood or to other body fluids containing blood. Behaviors of particular concern are:

· Biting
· Attack resulting in blood exposure
· Attacks with sharp objects

Such behaviors may occur in a range of law enforcement situations, including arrest, routine interrogations, domestic disputes, and lockup operations. Hand-to-hand combat may result in bleeding and may involve a greater risk of blood-to-blood exposure.

When blood is present and/or a suspect or an inmate is combative or threatens officers, gloves should be put on as soon as conditions permit. An extra change of clothing should be available at all times in case of blood contamination of an officer's clothing.

Investigators should be concerned about infection with HIV through administration of cardiopulmonary resuscitation (CPR). While there have been no documented cases of HIV transmission through this mechanism, the possibility of contracting other infectious diseases exists. Protective masks and one-way airways should be used. Hands and other body parts should be washed immediately after contact with blood or other body fluids. When washing facilities are not available, waterless antiseptic hand cleanser should be used. Any blood spills should be cleaned using an Environmental Protection Agency (EPA)-approved germicide, or a 1 to 1,000 parts solution of household chlorine bleach may be used.

Plastic bags should be used for removal of contaminated items. Shoes and boots should be covered with disposable shoe coverings. These items should be included in the evidence kit.

Postexposure Management   Investigators who have any blood-to-blood exposure with a person who is HIV positive should be tested immediately. Symptoms to be noted are an illness with a sudden fever within approximately 12 weeks after exposure. Individuals who have been exposed to the AIDS virus should be retested 6 weeks, 12 weeks, and 6 months after the first test.

Universal Precautions   Bluntly stated, a person who has AIDS will die from complications resulting from the disease. Investigators cannot be too careful when dealing with persons or evidence that might contaminate with HIV or other blood-borne pathogens.

Recovering Blood Evidence

Bloodstains or suspected bloodstains should be photographed and measured. Whenever possible, the suspected stain should be taken to the lab, where it can be examined under controlled conditions. If it cannot be moved, it should be carefully recovered. If the stain is on a hard surface, it can be scraped off with a sharp instrument, such as a razor blade or disposable scalpel. The stain should be scraped onto a piece of clean white paper. The paper should be folded, placed in an envelope, and sealed. A control sample of the unstained surface should be sent to the lab in a separate container. If the stain cannot be scraped off, the investigator may moisten a piece of clean cotton and soak up as much of the stain as possible. The cloth should be air dried, placed in a paper bag, and then sent to the lab with the proper identification and a control sample.

Blood evidence should *never* be placed in a plastic bag and sealed. This could cause the blood to putrefy and make it impossible to work with and identify.

Fluid blood may be collected after it has been photographed. The blood should be soaked up with clean cotton, such as a sterile bandage or swab, allowed to air dry, and then transported to the lab in a paper bag. The bag should be properly marked. Fluid blood may also be recovered with a clean medicine dropper, placed in a clean vial, and sealed. The sample should be refrigerated but not frozen, and no anticoagulant should be placed in the sample. The vial should be transported to the laboratory immediately.

If the blood is on an item of clothing, care should be taken not to change the position of the clothing if the item is part of a crime. White paper should be placed between the folds of clothing, and the item should be allowed to air dry. The clothing should be placed in a clean dry box and taken to the lab.

DNA (Deoxyribonucleic Acid)

Until recently serologists were unable to identify a specific individual by his or her blood type. It is not yet possible to testify with absolute certainty that blood came from a particular person. It is possible, however, to testify that the statistical probability that blood or other biological evidence came from more than a very small number of people is so small as to be almost a total impossibility.

British scientists made one of the most significant breakthroughs in forensic science of this century in developing DNA profiling. *DNA profiling* has made it possible to come close to positively identifying a person from whole blood, semen, hair roots, skin tissues and organs, bone and bone marrow, and dental pulp. DNA is found in the chromosomes of nucleated cells and is the genetic coding that determines each person's individual characteristics. "Human cells contain within them all of the information needed to produce a complete human body. The human blueprint is carried in discrete packets of information known as chromosomes, and the material of which they are made is called DNA" (Kelly et al., 1987, p. 106). A human has 46 chromosomes, 23 of which come from the mother and 23 from the father. With the exception of identical twins, no two persons have exactly the same DNA. Eventually DNA analysis may serve as a means for positively identifying an individual. It can even be removed from nucleated cells that are several years old.

The total DNA in a cell is approximately 3 feet in length. The DNA molecule resembles a twisted ladder and is called a *double helix*. The double helix is made up of two strands consisting of four chemicals: adenine, thymine, guanine, and cytosine. Adenine always bonds with thymine, and guanine always bonds with cytosine to form the base pairs AT and GC. How these pairs are repeated is unique to each individual. These pairs are repeated millions of times in every human cell. Pairs are repeated in an exact order and may be counted. The profile created by counting these repeated base pairs forms the basis of a positive DNA identification.

Other Physical Evidence

Hairs and Fibers

Hairs and fibers are referred to as *exchange evidence*, that is, an exchange has occurred between a suspect and a victim, or between the suspect and an object, such as a head and a baseball cap. Hair generally has class characteristics, although if the hair follicles have been recovered it may be possible to identify a person from their DNA with statistical certainty. Hair analysis may reveal information about a person's race, the part of the body it was taken from, and how it was removed.

Recovering Hair and Fiber Evidence

The crime scene should be carefully searched, and hairs and fibers should be recovered with plastic tweezers. Each individual sample should then be placed in a separate clean, crush-proof container, such as a plastic vial or pillbox. Care should be taken not to fold or crush a sample.

It may be desirable to vacuum areas of a crime scene in order to ensure that all hairs and fibers are recovered. It is important to use clean filter bags on each area vacuumed and to note where each bag was used. This is necessary so that the investigator can later testify that evidence came from a particular location.

It is necessary to obtain comparison samples from suspects or from persons known to have been at the crime scene. The investigator may be required to obtain a court order or search warrant to obtain samples from reluctant subjects. The area around the subject should be combed to remove loose hairs and then approximately 20 hairs should pulled, not cut, from different parts of the body. Each hair should be packaged separately and marked appropriately.

Casting Footprints

In the past, casting footprints has been a tedious and often futile endeavor. Improved casting materials have made the process significantly less cumbersome. As with any impression, a footprint should be photographed and measured before any effort is made to recover it. Photographs should be made using indirect lighting, and the camera used should be suspended from a tripod.

Casts are made using dental stone, the material used by dentists to make impressions for dentures. Investigators should include these materials in their evidence collection kit. Two pounds of dental stone are mixed with 12 ounces of water in a plastic bowl. For this reason, 2 pounds of dental stone should always be pre-measured and kept in a plastic bag for use as needed at a crime scene. When using dental stone, it is not necessary to build a mold around the impression, as is the case with plaster of paris. Generally, 2 pounds of dental stone can cover approximately 2 feet of a tire impression. The dental stone is poured into the impression using a spatula to slow the rate at which the material enters the impression. The cast should be allowed to cure for approximately 30 minutes and should not be cleaned until it is transported to the laboratory.

It is also possible to recover impressions in snow or ice using dental stone. The investigator first prepares the impression by spraying it with a commercially prepared snow print wax. After the impression is treated, the dental stone is poured into the impression, using the same technique as used for any other impression. The impression should be allowed to set for at least one hour.

Soil

Soil is most useful for comparing material found at a crime scene with that recovered from a suspect's clothing, shoes, or car. The investigator should obtain three tablespoons of soil from all areas where the suspect has been or is thought to have been. Clean instruments, such as plastic spoons, should be used to avoid contamination. The samples should be placed in a clean pillbox or container, sealed and appropriately labeled for identification. A sketch of the location where the sample was recovered should be submitted with every sample.

Paint

Paint evidence is most often associated with hit-and-run or other motor vehicle accidents and burglary, although transfer evidence of this type can be associated with any crime. Paint may be recovered by taping a packet made from clean white paper into the surface near the stain and scraping the suspected stain into the packet with a clean instrument, such as a plastic scalpel, to avoid contamination. Avoid using metal instruments because they may transfer metallic elements to the sample. The packet should be folded and placed in an envelope along with the scraping blade and sealed. Control samples should be taken from areas near the suspected stain. The investigator should not attempt to recover paint from within a tool mark because this will alter the impression made by the tool. The entire area, including the paint stain, should be removed and submitted as evidence.

Glass

Glass can be very valuable as evidence because of its physical characteristics and methods of manufacture. It is also possible to match glass fragments. Glass may be compared by thickness, color, grain, density, refractive index, and light dispersion. Glass may be described as *standard*, which means it was recovered from a known source, and *questioned*, which indicates it was recovered from a suspect. Samples of glass should be taken from different locations. Surfaces of glass should be marked to note whether they faced in or out. The glass itself should be packaged in a strong cardboard box to ensure that the glass is not damaged further. Examination of glass will reveal the direction a projectile was traveling and perhaps the sequence in which a number of projectiles were fired.

Underwater Search and Recovery

Criminals have often prevented the recovery of evidence by simply throwing an object into a body of water. Lack of resources and imagination has caused investigators to assume that evidence under water cannot be recovered. With improvements in SCUBA (Self-Contained Underwater Breathing Apparatus) technology, the ability to recover evidence has increased enormously. Many law enforcement agencies have created dive teams to perform a number of tasks, including underwater search and recovery.

Planning for a dive team should begin by determining what the capabilities of the team should be. There are substantial differences in trying to find and recover a firearm, a body, and an automobile. In most cases, the dive team should restrict its operations to attempts to recover standard types of evidence, such as weapons, vehicles, and bodies in fresh water. More complex undertakings in contaminated water should be left to professional divers.

Dive Team Organization

A dive team should consist of four members: a team leader, a primary diver, a safety diver, and a line tender. In addition, if enough people are available, someone should be designated as the recorder. The recorder will be responsible for keeping a log of all the events in the investigation and dive operation as they occur. The team leader should be an experienced scuba diver as well as an experienced criminal investigator and supervisor. The team leader is responsible for planning and coordinating the operation and must ensure that a rescue diver is in the water, ready to assist the primary diver at all times. The line tender is responsible for the safety of the primary diver and for maintaining the integrity of the search by ensuring that the entire area is searched.

Planning the Dive

When planning an underwater operation, the safety of all members of the dive team is always the overriding consideration for the team leader. Many of the same techniques are used in an underwater investigation as in land-based investigations. The team leader begins by ensuring that the scene is secure, if this has not already been done. Witnesses are then interviewed to determine where the object to be located might be. It is important to narrow down these possible locations to reduce the amount of time spent on the underwater search effort. Once the approximate location of the item has been established, the location is marked with a weighted line placed by a diver. The scene is then photographed, measured, and sketched.

After gathering the available information, the team leader develops an operational plan and discusses it with the team members. The pre-dive meeting should include:

1. A description of the item to be located
2. How the item will be handled if found
3. What search patterns will be used
4. Discussion of all hazards that might be encountered, including obstructions, currents, visibility, and trot lines

The primary diver, that is, the person actually searching for the object, must be mentally and physically prepared to make the dive. Running search patterns in cold, zero-visibility water over uneven bottoms cluttered with debris is hard, often dangerous work. Normally a diver will have a rope attached to one wrist, with the arm to which the rope is attached extended from the body at a 90-degree angle. The diver determines what search pattern is most appropriate and begins the search by dropping straight to the bottom of the body of water to be searched. Once on the bottom, the diver pauses for a few seconds to compose himself and to assess the situation. He then places the forearm of his free arm on the bottom and begins to move it slowing back and forth on the bottom, being sure to cover each part of the area to be searched. The primary diver advances slowly over the bottom, making sure that he covers the entire area.

The primary diver is responsible for collecting the evidence once it is found. The same principles of evidence collection apply underwater as on land. Evidence should be photographed and measured in place if possible. The location of the items is marked with a float, although the float should not be tied directly to the item unless it so large that it will not float. The diver who recovers the evidence begins the chain of custody. Great care should be taken when recovering an item, as it is possible that fingerprints in grease or paint might be recovered. Clothing found should be placed on a clean white sheet and air dried. Clothing should never be wrung out. All items should be marked appropriately. A firearm or other metal object should be placed in an airtight container, along with the liquid and sediment in which it was found.

Conclusions

Physical evidence may have a tremendous influence on the outcome of criminal trial. Investigators must remain alert to recover any type of evidence that might lead to the identification of a suspect or link a suspect to a crime. While the evidence is being processed, the investigator must remember the purpose of gathering evidence is to prove the truth about a suspect's guilt or innocence.

References

Black's Law Dictionary, 5th ed. St. Paul, MN: West Publishing, 1983.

Damore, Michael. "DNA Fingerprinting: What Every Criminal Lawyer Should Know." *Criminal Law Bulletin* 27 (2): 114–33, 1991.

Escobedo v. Illinois, 378 U.S. 748 (1964).

Federal Bureau of Investigation. *Handbook of Forensic Sciences.* Washington, DC: U.S. Government Printing Office, 1995.

Federal Bureau of Investigation. *Uniform Crime Reports, Crime in the United States.* Washington DC: U.S. Government Printing Office, 1989.

Fiatal, Robert A. "DNA Testing and the Frye Standard." *FBI Law Enforcement Bulletin* 59 (6): 26–31, 1990.

Fox, Richard H. and Cunningham, Carl L. *Crime Scene Search and Physical Evidence Handbook.* United States Department of Justice, Law Enforcement Assistance Administration, National Institute of Law Enforcement and Criminal Justice. Washington, DC: U.S. Government Printing Office, 1985.

Hicks, John W. "DNA Profiling: A Tool for Law Enforcement." *FBI Law Enforcement Bulletin* 57 (8): 1–5, 1988.

Kelly, K.F., Rankin, J.J., and Wink, R.C. "Method and Application of DNA Fingerprinting: A Guide for the Nonscientist." *The Criminal Law Review* 2 (87): 105–110, 1987.

Mincey v. Arizona, 437 U.S. 385 (1978).

Miranda v. Arizona, 384 U.S. 436 (1966).

Moenssens, Andre, Inbau, Fred E., and Starrs, James E. *Scientific Evidence in Criminal Cases,* 3rd ed. Mineola, NY: Foundation Press, 1986.

Perkins, Rollin M. and Boyce, Ronald N. *Criminal Law.* Mineola, NY: Foundation Press, 1982.

Purcell, Noreen, Winfree, L. Thomas, Jr., and Mays, G. Larry. "DNA (Deoxyribonucleic Acid) Evidence and Criminal Trials: An Exploratory Survey of Factors Associated with the Use of 'Genetic Fingerprinting' in Felony Cases." *Journal of Criminal Justice* 22 (2): 145–157, 1994.

Segura v. United States, 468 U.S. 796 at 810 (1984).

Sibert, Robert W. "Drugfire: Revolutionizing Forensic Firearms Identification and Providing the Foundation for a National Firearms Identification Network." *Crime Laboratory Digest* 21 (4): 63–67, 1994.

Svensson, Arne, Wendal, Otto, and Fisher, Barry A.J. *Techniques of Crime Scene Investigation,* 3rd ed. New York: Elsevier, 1981.

Wambaugh, Joseph. *The Blooding.* New York: William Morrow, 1989.

5. Investigative Leads

You know my methods in such cases, Watson, I put myself in the man's place, and having first gauged his intelligence, I try to imagine how I should myself have proceeded under the same circumstances.

Sherlock Holmes, *The Adventure of the Musgrave Ritual*, Sir Arthur Conan Doyle

After recovering and processing physical evidence at the crime scene, the investigator will need to determine what direction the next phase of the investigation should take. In many cases, leads will be developed while the physical evidence is gathered or during the subsequent interviews that are part of a neighborhood canvass. Leads may become apparent as the preliminary investigation progresses, but the investigator must remember that no single approach will be useful in every case. Generally leads fall under the acronym MOM:

Method: How was the crime committed?

Opportunity: Who had a chance to commit the crime?

Motive: Who had a reason to commit the crime?

Almost without exception, leads developed by an investigator will fall into one of these three categories. The emphasis on a lead will vary with the crime. For example, motive may be particularly important in a murder or assault investigation, while opportunity or method may be more important in a larceny or burglary case. The acronym MOM provides a starting point for investigators to organize their thoughts.

Solvability Factors

Investigators need to be aware of the presence of solvability factors, as discussed in Chapter 3. *Solvability factors* are items of evidence, either testimonial or physical, that individually or in combination with other factors may lead to the identification of a suspect. By answering as many of these questions as possible, the investigator may determine if a case justifies additional investigative effort. The presence of one or more solvability factors will usually be adequate to warrant follow-up by a detective. Questions that require patrol officers to determine if solvability factors can be identified are often included in report forms used to complete preliminary investigations.

Modus Operandi

Modus operandi, or method of operation (M.O.), may be thought of as the criminal's signature. *Modus operandi* is the means by which a criminal commits a particular type of crime. Therefore, if perpetrators go undetected for a period of time, it may be possible to identify them based on their *modus operandi* because they are likely to follow a pattern. It is essential that patrol officers complete a thorough preliminary investigation in order to gather all the facts about how the crime occurred. Some of the more common crimes in which a pattern may be detected are as follows:

· Burglary
· Robbery
· Stealing
· Rape and other sex offenses
· Arson
· Auto theft
· Murder

While investigating certain crimes, the investigator must attempt to determine as precisely as possible how a crime occurred. Many departments have developed checklists, such as that in Figure 5.1, that are used by patrolmen in a preliminary investigation to ensure that detailed information is collected on the suspect's *modus operandi.*

Victim's Background

In assaults, homicides, sexual assaults, and burglary cases, it is often useful to review the victim's actions in the hours and days prior to the crime. The investigator should always be sensitive to the feelings of the victim. As investigators begin probing into a victim's actions, the victim may become angry or defensive, and may begin to feel that he or she is under investigation. The investigator may wish to begin the interview of a victim by explaining why it is necessary to ask these questions and how the information gained may be of value in developing leads for a follow-up investigation. The investigator should try to reconstruct the victim's actions prior to the crime, and should begin by asking the victim if he or she knows who committed the crime or if the victim suspects anyone. Experience shows that many crimes are solved by information provided to the first officer arriving on the scene. This fact was noted in the Rand Corporation study of the criminal investigation process but is often overlooked by experienced investigators and investigative supervisors.

Knowledge

Knowledge can be used as a lead in several ways. In most cases the investigator must ask, "who had the knowledge needed to commit this crime?" Did the crime require specific knowledge or information possessed by a small number of individuals?

RAPE - ATTEMPT RAPE A

LOCATION OF COMPLAINANT (01) (12 HRS. PRIOR TO OFFENSE)
1. BAR
2. PARTY
3. PLACE OF ENTERTAINMENT (MOVIE, ETC.)
4. RESIDENCE (OWN, OTHER)
5. SCHOOL
6. SPORTING EVENT
7. PARK/RECREATION FAC.
9. OTHER
10. N.A.

SOLICITED, OFFERED (02) (PRIOR TO OFFENSE)
1. FOOD, DRINK, CANDY
2. RIDE
3. ASSISTANCE, INFO.
4. MONEY
5. DRUGS
6. OTHER
7. N.A.

TELEPHONE (03)
1. PULLED/CUT CORD
2. USED CORD TO TIE COMP.
3. CALLED COMP. (BEFORE, AFT.)
4. OTHER
5. N.A.

CHARACTERISTICS OF SUSPECT (04)
1. UNUSUAL ODOR/BODY ODOR, SHELLFISH, etc.)
2. ABNORMAL GENITALS
3. EJACULATED
4. UNABLE TO ACHIEVE ERECTION
5. USED COMP'S NAME
6. KNOWN (PH. FAMILIAR NAME)
7. OTHER
7. N.A.

SUSPECT'S ACTIONS (05)
1. RIPPED/CUT CLOTHING
2. TOOK COMP'S CLOTHING
3. USED LUBRICANT
4. RAPED MORE THAN ONCE
5. UNNATURAL SEX ACTS
6. OTHER
7. N.A.

FORCE (06)
1. BOUND COMPLAINANT
2. BIT COMPLAINANT
3. HIT COMPLAINANT
4. SHOT COMPLAINANT
5. COVERED COMP'S FACE
6. CHOKED COMPLAINANT
7. CUT, STABBED COMPLAINANT
8. OTHER
9. N.A.

COMPLAINANT WAS (07)
1. ELDERLY
2. MENTALLY RETARDED
3. INTOXICATED
4. PHYSICALLY HANDICAPPED
5. JUVENILE
6. N.A.

(64) ROBBERY M.O.

SUSPECT'S ACTIONS (01)
1. ASSAULTED COMP.
2. BOUND COMP.
3. USED NOTE
4. DEMANDED JEWELRY
5. ASKED FOR CIGARETTES/MERCHANDISE
6. SHOPLIFT, THEFT INVOLVEC
7. PURSE SNATCH
8. PROSTITUTION INVOLVED
9. USED LOOKOUT
10. APOLOGETIC
11. MADE GESTURES
12. SEX ACTS INVOLVED
13. USED STOLEN VEHICLE
14. SHOTS FIRED
15. OTHER
16. N.A.

SOLICTED/OFFERED (02)
1. AID FOR VEHICLE
2. RIDE
3. CIGARETTE/LIGHT
4. USE PHONE
5. INFORMATION
6. MONEY
7. SEX
8. CON GAME
9. DRUGS
10. OTHER
11. N.A.

FORCED COMP. TO: (03)
1. LIE DOWN
2. OPEN SAFE
3. ENTER REST ROOM
4. REAR OF BLDG.
5. ENTER VEH. TRUNK
6. DISROBE
7. PLACE PROPERTY IN SACK
8. OTHER
9. N.A.

COMPLAINANT WAS (04)
1. OPENING/CLOSING BUSINESS
2. MENTALLY/PHYSICALLY HANDICAPPED
3. FEMALE
4. ALONE
5. INTOXICATED
6. ELDERLY
7. ELDERLY
8. JUVENILE
9. N.A.

(65) ATTEMPT BURGLARY M.O.   BURGLAR

POINT OF ENTRY (01)
□ FRONT □ REAR □ SIDE
1. DOOR
2. WINDOW
3. SLIDING GLASS
4. DUCT/VENT
5. ADJ. BLDG.
6. ROOF/FLOOR
7. WALL
8. OPEN GARAGE
9. OVERHEAD DOOR
10. OTHER/UNK.

POINT OF EXIT (02)
□ FRONT □ REAR □ SIDE
1. DOOR
2. WINDOW
3. SLIDING GLASS
4. DUCT/VENT
5. ADJ. BLDG.
6. ROOF/FLOOR
7. WALL
8. OPEN GARAGE
9. OVERHEAD DOOR
10. OTHER/UNK

METHOD OF BREAKING (03)
1. KEY
2. SMASH GLASS, GAIN MERCHANDISE
3. BROKE/CUT GLASS, GAIN ENTRY
4. PRIED/JIMMIED
5. REMOVED
6. CHOPPED/SMASHED
7. REMOVE A/C FAN
8. BROKE/REMOVED DOOR PANEL
9. CUT/BROKE LOCK
10. UNLOCKED/NO FORCE
11. HID IN BLDG.
12. REMOVED WINDOW PANE
13. OTHER/UNK.

INSTRUMENT USED (04)
1. KEY
2. PRYING TOOL
3. SAW/DRILL
4. BOLT CUTTER
5. CHOPPING TOOL
6. HAMMER
7. BRICK/ROCK
8. CHAIN, LOCKS/V. GRIPS
9. TAPE
10. VEHICLE
11. BODILY FORCE
12. INCENDIARY DEV.
13. OTHER/UNK.

ALARM (05)
TYPE SYSTEM
1. LOCAL
2. CENTRAL STA.
3. PROPRIETARY
4. POLICE
5. AUTO DIALER
TYPE PROTECTION
6. BELL, SIREN
7. SILENT
8. AUDIO
9. MOTION
10. POINT
11. PERIMETER

BURGLARY ELEMENTS (06)
1. ALARM INOPERATIVE
2. BURGLARIZED DURING PAST 12 MOS.
3. ADMITTED STRANGER OR TRADESMAN DURING PAST 7 DAYS (RES. BURG. ONLY)
4. TELEPHONE SURVEY, UNUSUAL CALLS, HANGUPS, WRONG NO., PAST 7 DAYS (RES. BURG. ONLY)
5. HOUSE VACANT/UNDER CONST.
6. SAFE BREAK/ATTEMPT METHOD _____
7. OTHER
8. N.A.

SUSPECT'S ACTIONS (07)
1. MALICIOUS DESTRUCTION
2. REMOVED PRINTS
3. USED TOOLS FOUND AT SCENE
4. BURGLARY NOT COMPLETED
5. ATE/DRANK ON PREMISES
6. TURNED LIGHTS ON-OFF
7. DEFEATED LATER
8. BROKE INTO COIN-OP.
9. MACHINE, KNEW LOC. OF HIDDEN CASH
10. DEFEATED, ATTEMPTED DEFEAT OF ALARM
11. TRIPPED ALARM, RETURNED LATER
12. OTHER
13. N.A.

COMPLAINANT WAS: (08)
1. PRESENT
2. ABSENT (AD IN PAPER)
3. AT FUNERAL
4. AT WEDDING
5. AT CHURCH
6. AT WORK
7. AT SCHOOL
8. MOVING
9. OUT OF TOWN
10. SHOPPING
11. SPORTING EVENT
12. PLACE OF ENTERTAINMENT (MOVIE, ETC.)
13. OTHER
14. UNK.

FORM 76-2 S/N 117-0101

Page ____ of ____

Figure 5.1 Sample *modus operandi* checklist. Similar checks can be developed to aid patrol officers in the investigation of stealing, assaults, or murder.

CASE STUDY

A convenience store chain followed a practice of having one of the managers of each of its 14 stores make the rounds of every store every eight hours to pick up the receipts from the previous shift. At approximately 6 a.m., as the manager was making the last pickup on a bitterly cold New Year's morning, a masked robber relieved him of the cash receipts from New Year's Eve. The cash amounted to about $50,000, all in used, small-denomination bills. The investigation focused on present and past employees, including managers, because they were the group most likely to know how the pickup schedule worked. The robber ultimately proved to be a clerk who had resigned shortly after the robbery. He had called attention to himself by suddenly showing a dramatic increase in his spending, living beyond what would be expected of an unemployed convenience store clerk.

Benefit

The investigator should determine who would be better off because this crime was committed. Benefit may provide leads in crimes such as murder, larceny, and arson. Common examples of benefit as a motive would be an arson-for-hire case, or a young woman driving a car into a river and then reporting it stolen in order relieve herself of the payments. Other forms of insurance fraud provide examples of financial benefit resulting from filing false claims.

Field Interrogation Reports

Field interrogation reports (FIRs) may offer investigative leads by providing the names of individuals who were at or near the scene of a crime when it was committed. FIRs can demonstrate the suspect had the opportunity to commit the crime. Investigators may determine why a person was in that location at that time. For example, a detective may review reports of field interrogations conducted near the scene of a burglary and then request that the fingerprints of persons identified in the FIR be compared against any prints found at the scene.

In *Terry v. Ohio*, the Supreme Court authorized *investigative detention* as an investigative technique. The facts in *Terry* illustrate how patrol officers and investigators can use the technique to both inquire into suspicious activity and to develop leads that may be of use in follow-up investigations. Police Detective McFadden observed two men standing on a street corner in downtown Cleveland at approximately 2:30 p.m. on October 31, 1963. McFadden watched the two men, one of whom was later identified as Terry, walk from the corner to the middle of the block, where they looked through the window of a jewelry store. The two men appeared to be "casing" the store. A third man joined the men on the corner briefly but soon left. McFadden then observed the first two men rejoin the third man two blocks away. McFadden approached the men, identified himself, and asked for identification. One of the men made a mumbled response, at which time McFadden frisked all three men, finding that Terry and another man were carrying guns. Both were convicted of carrying concealed weapons.

The Supreme Court made it clear that investigative detention or "stop and frisk" is a valid investigative tool. A brief detention based on reasonable suspicion, rather than probable cause, is legal. Thus, a police officer may stop a person he reasonably suspects has been or is about to commit a crime; he may also frisk or pat down the outside of the detainee's clothing if he suspects the person is armed.

Every investigative detention should be documented with a field interrogation report for two reasons. (Figure 5.2) First, it documents that the person was in a specific location at a specific time. Thus, if detectives find that someone was near a crime, they can determine what that person was doing there. David

```
                    SOUTHEAST MISSOURI STATE LAW ENFORCEMENT ACADEMY
                            FIELD INTERROGATION CARD                    DATE & TIME

NAME (LAST NAME FIRST)                              NICKNAME

RESIDENCE ADDRESS                                  RESIDENCE PHONE

DOB      SSN       DRIVER'S LICENSE NO.            DRIV (X)   PASS (X)   PED (X)

LOCATION OF OCCURRENCE                             PLACE OF BIRTH

SEX   DESCENT   AGE   DATE OF BIRTH   HEIGHT   WEIGHT   HAIR   EYES   COMPLEXION

MARKS, SCARS, TATOOS, ETC.

CLOTHING WORN

YEAR AND MAKE OF CAR       BODY TYPE   COLOR (S)   LICENSE NO.          YEAR

                                  A
```

Figure 5.2A   Field interrogation card (front)

```
SUSPECT'S BUSINESS ADDRESS       (PH. NO. & SHIFT)      (IF JUVENILE, NAME OF SCHOOL & GRADE)

NAMES OF PERSONS WITH SUSPECT AT TIME OF INTERROGATION

REASON FOR INTERROGATION

DISPOSITION

OFFICER(S) REPORTING   (LAST NAME AND SERIAL NUMBER)       DIVISION            DETAIL

                                  B
```

Figure 5.2B   Field interrogation card (back)

Berkowitz, a.k.a. the Son of Sam, was identified from a parking ticket that was placed on his car while he was looking for victims. The investigators who contacted him to determine why he had been in that area felt that, given his responses to their questions, additional follow-up was needed.

A second reason for completing an FIR is to protect the officers against allegations that they harassed an innocent person. By stating the facts that justified the stop, the officer may avoid allegations of misconduct.

Identification

Fingerprints

Fingerprints are particularly valuable evidence. Jurors intuitively understand what fingerprints are and how they prove a person's presence at a specific location. It is absolutely essential to note where a print was found at a crime scene. Fingerprints are circumstantial evidence that merely place a suspect at a location. They do not prove that the person who left them committed a crime. A fingerprint found on the outside of a pane of glass only proves the suspect was there. A defense attorney can provide any number of plausible explanations of how the fingerprint came to be where it was found. A fingerprint found on the inside of a pane of glass indicates the suspect was inside the scene. A fingerprint found on a cash register puts the suspect at the place where the crime occurred. The closer the print is to the scene of the crime, the more likely the jury is to conclude that the person charged committed the crime.

Fingerprints have limitations, however. Fingerprints are circumstantial and therefore do not prove a suspect's guilt. Additionally, fingerprints do not identify themselves. An investigator must have some idea who a suspect is before prints found at a scene can be compared. In most cases in which fingerprints are used to identify a suspect, the investigator must request that the known prints of a specific person be compared with those prints that are on file. The investigator must have first identified the suspect using some other lead, such as an informant. Currently, in order to identify an unknown person from their fingerprints, the investigator must have all five digits from one hand, and ideally all 10 prints from both hands.

Automated Fingerprint Identification Systems

The technology to do computerized fingerprint searches for a single print, known as a cold search, is improving. The ability of a computer to scan thousands of 10-digit cards greatly expands an investigators' ability to use single prints found at a scene to identify a suspect. Several states have this capability or will have it in the near future.

Elimination Prints

Before submitting a print to an automated fingerprint system, investigators must obtain elimination prints from persons who have legitimate access to the crime scene. Elimination prints are necessary to prevent entering the fingerprints of an innocent person into the system. Once the print has been entered into a system, it will remain there until specifically purged from the system.

Reports from Hospitals or Other Medical Facilities

Most states have statutes that require medical personnel to report what appears to be gunshot wounds or evidence of a violent act to a law enforcement agency. Similarly, medical personnel must report any evidence of child abuse or neglect to the police. Missouri law states the following:

Gunshot wounds—physicians, nurses, therapists: duty to report, content—violation, penalty.

1. Any person licensed under Chapter 334 or 335 RSMo, who treats a person for a wound inflicted by gunshot shall immediately report to a local law enforcement official the name and address of the person, if known, and if unknown, a description of the person, together with an explanation of the nature of the wound and the circumstances under which the treatment was rendered.
2. Any person licensed under Chapter 334 or 335, RSMo, who knowingly fails to report the injuries described in this section is guilty of the offense of medical deception.
3. Medical deception is an infraction.

Other occupations are also required to report what may be child abuse or neglect. Children appearing in emergency rooms with unusual or unexplained injuries must be reported to the police.

Photo Lineups

Most law enforcement agencies take an arrestee's photographs as part of the booking procedure. Officers should be encouraged to maintain a catalog of persons who have been arrested who may be committing crimes in the community. When showing mugshots to witnesses of a crime, the investigator must take pains to avoid suggesting a particular suspect to the witness. Investigators seeking to identify a suspect should never show a single photograph to a witness. This procedure will almost certainly taint any identification. The recommended procedure is to show at least six or eight mugshots to a witness. One technique is to place the photos on a flat surface and to allow the witness to view them without interference from the investigator. Another technique is to place the photos in a small photo album and to allow the witness to examine each picture. Prior to looking at the picture, the witness should be instructed to look at each picture before selecting a suspect. If the witness identifies a suspect, the investigator should have the specific photo marked with the following information:

1. Case number
2. Date and time
3. Witness' name and signature
4. Investigator's name and identification number

All photographs should be collected, marked, and submitted as evidence. In the likely event that the defense moves to suppress the evidence, the prosecution must be prepared to prove that the investigator did not lead the witness to a particular suspect.

Lineups

Lineups are a useful investigative technique in crimes for which a witness has been located. Investigators must be particularly sensitive to avoid anything that would suggest a particular suspect to the witness or witnesses. In 1967, the Supreme Court handed down the first in a series of cases that clarify the use of lineups by police. In *United States v. Wade*, 388 U.S. 218 (1967), the Court said that a defendant has the right to legal counsel after the filing of a formal charge. In *Wade* a man with a small piece of tape on either side of his face entered a bank and forced a cashier and a vice president to place cash in a pillowcase. The robber than drove away with an accomplice. Wade was indicted for the robbery and was arrested. At the time of arrest, counsel was appointed for Wade. Fifteen days later, Wade was placed in a lineup without his attorney being notified. Both bank employees identified Wade as the robber. In court they again identified Wade, but they also testified that they had seen him in police custody prior to the lineup. Wade was convicted of bank robbery. The Supreme Court ruled that a lineup or other "face to face" identification procedure that occurred after the defendant had been formally charged was a "critical stage of the proceedings," and the accused had a right to have counsel present. The absence of counsel in this case rendered the identification inadmissible.

United States v. Wade left trial courts confused as to where in the pre-trial identification procedure the suspect had the right to legal representation. That question was answered in *Kirby v. Illinois*, 406 U.S. 682 (1972). In *Kirby*, a man reported that two men had robbed him of his wallet. The wallet contained the victim's social security card and traveler's checks. The following day, police stopped Kirby and a companion, and asked him for identification. Kirby produced a wallet containing three traveler's checks and the social security card of the robbery victim. Kirby and his companion were taken to the police station. At the station, the police checked their records and at that point they learned of the robbery. The victim was brought to the police station and immediately upon entering the station, he positively identified Kirby and the other man as the robbers. No attorney was present and neither suspect asked for an attorney. Kirby was convicted of armed robbery. The Supreme Court ruled that the defendant does not have the right to legal counsel at a lineup or other identification before the defendant is formally charged. The Court went on to say that the type of identification is part of the routine investigation procedures used by the police and was not a critical stage of the prosecution requiring legal representation to protect the defendant's rights.

Suspect Sketches

If there are witnesses to the crime, it may be worthwhile to have them work with a sketch artist to create a likeness of the suspect. In the past, sketches of this sort were done by artists hired by the department for specific cases. Over the last several years, however, several companies have developed kits that are used to recreate faces. As with eyewitness identifications, the investigator should be somewhat cautious in placing a great deal of faith in the accuracy of the sketch. Witnesses may be limited in their ability to recall a face seen only briefly in a stressful situation. It is possible that the sketch might be so inaccurate as to mislead investigators and to later become an asset to the defense in that they can argue that the defendant was incorrectly identified.

Serial Numbers

Serial numbers may also provide leads in a follow-up investigation. The success of investigators in identifying suspects in the World Trade Center and Oklahoma City bombings are examples how valuable vehicle license tag numbers and vehicle identification numbers can be to investigators. Anytime a law enforcement officer seizes an object with a serial number, the number should routinely be run through the National Crime Information Center (NCIC) operated by the FBI and through any state systems that are available. The investigator should always remember that information entered into the computer is not always accurate. In one case, patrol officers recovered a 20-gauge shotgun in a disturbance. When the officers ran the serial number through NCIC, they got a "hit" on the number as having been stolen in a burglary. The weapon listed in the computer, however, was a 12-gauge shotgun. Follow-up investigation revealed that the victim had inherited the gun and did not know the difference between various types of weapons and simply said it was a 12-gauge because she had heard the word used before. Every law enforcement agency should have a pawn shop detail that routinely checks items pawned in the previous week or two weeks to determine if any of those items were stolen.

National Crime Information Center (NCIC)

Investigators have access to the NCIC, which is operated by the FBI. The NCIC currently has the following databases:

1. **Article file:** records of stolen items
2. **Boat file:** records of stolen boats, trailers, and parts
3. **Foreign fugitive file:** records of subjects wanted in other countries for crimes considered felonies the United States
4. **Gun file:** records of stolen, recovered, abandoned, or seized guns
5. **Interstate identification index:** criminal history of individuals
6. **Missing person file:** records of missing persons under various conditions
7. **License plate file:** records of stolen license plates
8. **Off-line search file:** records of all persons and vehicles for which requests for information have been received
9. **Originating agency identifier (ORI) file:** records of agency information of all agencies receiving NCIC information
10. **Securities file:** records of serially numbered stolen, embezzled, and counterfeited securities and documents of all types
11. **Unidentified person file:** records of unidentified deceased persons, catastrophe victims, and body parts

12. **U.S. Secret Service file:** records of individuals who may pose a threat to the President and any other person given protection by the Secret Service
13. **Vehicle file:** records of stolen vehicles, vehicle parts, and vehicles wants in connection with felonies

In addition to NCIC, each state has records systems that deal primarily with driver's licenses and vehicle registration. Many states, however, are expanding their information processing capabilities to include various types of criminal history files.

Informants

Informants have long been a vital part of the investigative process. Until someone provides information directing an investigator to a specific suspect, an investigation will often lack direction. Lieutenant Michael Fiaschetti, head of the famed Italian Squad of the New York City Police Department, described the importance of informants more than 60 years ago:

> It makes me tired to hear how those bulls in the books solve mysteries with their deductions. In the honest to God story of how the detective gets his man, stool pigeon is the word. (Fiaschetti, 1930, p. 27)

Informant Motivation

When dealing with informants, particularly criminal informants, it is essential to understand why they are willing to cooperate with an investigator. Informants are often classified by their motivation. Some of the more common classifications of informants include:

- Fearful
- Mercenary
- Perverse
- Egotistical
- Repentant

Fearful Informants
Fearful informants may be afraid of criminal prosecution or of their associates in crime. In these situations, informants have usually been arrested and are willing to cooperate with the police and the prosecution by providing information about a criminal activity that is apparently more serious than the one for which they were arrested.

Mercenary Informants
Mercenary informants provide information for money. Television has left the impression that law enforcement agencies have substantial resources to expend on informants. In truth very few agencies have cash available to pay informants. Experienced investigators argue that mercenary informants are more difficult to control because the only hold the investigator has over the informant is money. If the money is not enough, or it stops, the informant will stop providing assis-

tance. Other investigators argue that mercenary informants are easier to deal with since they are paid a pre-determined amount for specific information. It then becomes the informant's decision to return to the officer in the future.

Perverse Informants

Perverse informants seek some special benefit for themselves by informing. While this is true of all informants, perverse informants give information about competitors in the hope of putting them out of business by using the police. Perverse informants may also try to trade information about criminal activity in return for information about investigations on themselves. Informants of this type may think of themselves as "double agents" and are often difficult to control. Investigators working with perverse informants should take pains to avoid becoming overly friendly with them to reduce the possibility that the informant will use the friendship to manipulate the investigator.

Egotistical Informants

Egotistical informants seek to enhance their self-esteem by emphasizing the importance of their contacts in the underworld. Egotistical informants enjoy the attention paid to them by officials from the law enforcement community. An investigator needs to lavish praise on egotistical informants to keep them under control.

Repentant Informants

Repentant informant's have "seen the light." Repentant informants have grown weary of the lifestyle they live and want to make amends for what they have done. In one case, a hardened ex-convict gave a veteran drug agent information on a large cocaine smuggling operation. In this case, the informant's wife, a woman who had remained married to him throughout the years he had been in prison, asked him on her deathbed to give up crime. The informant's information led to one of the largest inland cocaine seizures in history. Repentant informants may be difficult to deal with because their reasons for wanting to cooperate may change on the spur of the moment, and they often return to their former lives of crime.

Informant Control

Before entering into any agreement with an informant, several steps should be taken to provide for adequate control of the informant and to ensure that the informant does not embarrass the officer and the department at a later time. For example, informants should be photographed, fingerprinted, and required to complete a cooperating individual form, such as the form illustrated in Figure 5.3. In addition, some effort must always be expended to attempt to verify the potential informant's information. Local prosecutors must be contacted in order to determine if they are willing to sanction an agreement between the state and the individual. If the prosecutor is willing to allow the deal, then whatever has been agreed to must be put in writing so that all parties know in advance what they have agreed upon. This agreement is later made available to the defense on

CITY OF WINCHESTER POLICE DEPARTMENT

COOPERATING INDIVIDUAL RELEASE

On this _____day of _____, 19_____, I, _____

of _____, in

consideration of being allowed to obtain the unique experience of acting as an informant under

the rules and guidelines as wet by the City of Winchester Police Department, DO HEREBY

RELEASE, DISCHARGE, INDEMNIFY AND SAVE HARMLESS THE CITY OF

WINCHESTER, AND THE WINCHESTER POLICE DEPARTMENT AND ITS OFFICERS

AND EMPLOYEES from all liability to me, my employer, my heirs, assigns, executors, and

personal representatives NOW AND FOREVER for all loss or damage to my person or property,

whether by negligence or otherwise, during such time that I may be an informant for the City of

Winchester Police Department. I do recognize that acting as an informant for the Winchester

Police Department my be dangerous and that I may be physically harmed, and hereby at risk. The

rules and guidelines for the control and use of informants and the law pertaining to the use of

informants have been explained to me, and I fully understand and agree to abide by those rules

and guidelines.

_____

Informant

Witness:_____

Date:_____

Figure 5.3   Cooperating individual release form

discovery. Without taking these precautions, it will prove difficult to prosecute cases made on an informants' testimony. Drug investigations rely heavily on informants, and the use of drug informants is discussed in Chapter 12.

The experiences in the Marion Barry trial and the John DeLorean trial indicate that jurors are very skeptical of a criminal informant's testimony. In both cases, jurors later said that they believed the defendants were probably guilty, but the conduct of the informants was as reprehensible as that of the men on trial. The credibility of Michael Fortier was a major issue in the trials of Timothy McVeigh and Terry Nichols, the two men convicted of the bombing in Oklahoma City.

Using an Informant's Information

Hearsay information provided by informants may be used to establish probable cause. To understand how this is done, it is necessary to examine three leading cases: *Aguilar v. Texas*, *Spinelli v. United States*, and *Illinois v. Gates*.

In *Aguilar v. Texas*, the Supreme Court created what became known as the two-pronged test for establishing probable cause based on hearsay evidence. The two-pronged test required that (1) the credibility of the informant be established and (2) the reliability of the informant's information be established. The first prong of the test was usually satisfied by one of two techniques. First, an informant made statements against his penal interests, thus subjecting himself to potential criminal prosecution, which was generally considered proof of the informant's reliability. This technique is particularly useful when using an informant for the first time.

Second, after the informant has been used to provide information on more than one occasion, the investigator can use the informant's "track record" to demonstrate his or her reliability. A police officer, in preparing an affidavit for a warrant, can demonstrate the informant's reliability by showing that the informant has provided accurate information in the past that has led to a certain number of arrests and convictions. Demonstrating the reliability of the informant's information, the second prong of the test, is most commonly accomplished by stating that the informant has direct knowledge of the facts.

In *Spinelli v. United States*, the Supreme Court approved the use of corroboration as a means to establish probable cause. Under this concept, the Court suggested that facts, when combined in sufficient quantity, could add up to probable cause. Thus, traditional investigative techniques, such as surveillance, record checks, and neighborhood canvasses, could be of value in obtaining warrants.

In 1983, the Supreme Court handed down a decision that had a profound impact on the use of informants. In *Illinois v. Gates*, the Court established the "totality of circumstances" test to establish probable cause. In Gates, a police officer received an anonymous letter so detailed in its contents that a judge felt that the information contained in the letter was adequate to support the issuance of search and arrest warrants. At no point in the letter did the informant identify himself. The judge inferred the informant's credibility from the detailed information in the letter. The Supreme Court, in accepting the judge's reasoning, eliminated the "first prong" of the two-pronged test. Presently, the techniques set forth in *Aguilar*, *Spinelli*, and *Gates* may be used by an officer when using an informant's hearsay information to establish probable cause.

Protecting an Informant's Identity

Investigators must be careful to protect an informant's identity. The reasons for this are obvious: no one can be expected to assist the police by providing information if they will be ostracized, injured, or perhaps even killed. Two cases have established principles that determine circumstances under which trial court judges can compel disclosure of an informant's identity in court. In *Rovario v. United States*, the Supreme Court ruled that when an informant is a material witness in a criminal case, the police and the prosecution can be compelled to disclose the informant's identity in court. A material witness in a criminal trial is a witness whose testimony is crucial to either the prosecution or the defense. In many cases, a material witness may have been a participant in the crime. If this is true, the identity of the witness must be revealed to the opposing party, usually the defendant. This requirement stems from the Sixth Amendment right of the accused in a criminal case to confront his accusers. Thus, if informants are actually participants in a criminal transaction, such as making controlled buys of drugs, they will be required to testify about their role in the transaction. Informants who are to be used in this capacity must be told that they will be called upon to testify when these cases go to trial. In a later case, *McCray v. Illinois*, the Supreme Court held that when an informant, whose reliability has already been established, only provides evidence that establishes probable cause, the defense cannot compel the prosecution to divulge the informant's identity (McCray v. Illinois [1967]).

In some states an informant's identity may be protected as a privileged communication between the officer and the informant. Where the privilege exits, an officer may refuse to disclose the identity of an informant who has only provided information leading to probable cause. In those states where the privilege does not exist, an informant's identity may be protected as a matter of relevancy. A prosecutor may argue that as long as the informant is not a material witness, revealing his identity is not relevant. The trial judge will then make an in-camera determination on the need to reveal the informant's identity.

In order to further protect the informant and the department, policies should be established to govern the actions of informants and the officers who supervise them. A sample informant policy appears in Figure 5.4.

Jail or Prison Inmates as Informants

Inmates have been a source of leads, both reliable and otherwise, for years. Information provided by Floyd Wells, an inmate at the Kansas Penitentiary, directed agents of the Kansas Bureau of Investigation to Richard Hickock and his accomplice, Perry Smith, as suspects in the murders of the Clutter Family in 1959. The story of these brutal murders was recorded in Truman Capote's *In Cold Blood*. Wells, a former cellmate of Hickock's, had been an employee of Herbert Clutter. Hickock had seemed interested in the wealthy farmer as a means to make the "big score" that so many criminals are looking for. Wells traded his information for consideration of an earlier release date from prison.

Investigators receive a great deal of information from inmates who are hoping that the information they have will gain them some special consideration.

CITY OF WINCHESTER POLICE DEPARTMENT

GENERAL ORDER NO. 86-2

EFFECTIVE: January 27, 1997   INDEX AS: Criminal Informants
TO: ALL PERSONNEL
SUBJECT: CRIMINAL INFORMANTS

The purpose of this General Order is to establish procedural guidelines for the control and use of informants.

I. GENERAL:

Law enforcement agencies have as their primary role the protection of lives and property, the prevention and detection of criminal activity and the apprehension of offenders. In fulfilling the role, the Winchester Police Department recognizes the value and necessity of using criminal informants and the information that they provide. However, there exists considerable potential for abuse and/or misuse of such informants and their information. The guidelines provided herein are intended to minimize that possibility.

II. DEFINITIONS:

Informant - anyone who gives or serves as a source of confidential information to the police.

Confidential Informant - anyone who gives information to the police, and whose identity is concealed or confidential.

Informant File - a master file maintained by the OIC of Detectives with access strictly limited to those commissioned officers who can demonstrate a viable and legitimate "Need-to-Know."

Entrapment - an entrapment is perpetrated if a law enforcement officer, or a person acting in cooperation with such an officer, for the purpose of obtaining evidence of the commission of an offense, solicits, encourages or otherwise induces another person to engage in conduct when he was not ready and willing to engage in such conduct.

III. PROCEDURE:

A. Development of Informants

1. Informants may be developed by any member of the police department. Once developed, that informant is to be considered a confidential source of information to the department and not the property of any individual officer.

2. To protect the identity of an informant, each shall be given a designation known only to the investigator/officer and supervisors working with the informant.

3. All informants shall be photographed and fingerprinted. Photos and prints shall be maintained in the informants master file.

4. Each informant shall complete the personal information record form. (WPD Form #26 attached)

Figure 5.4   Informant policy (*Part 1 of 2*)

GENERAL ORDER NO. 86-2 (Page 2)

B. Control/Use of Informants

1. Informants shall be advised that they are not employees of this department, they have no enforcement powers and are not to represent themselves as police officers.

2. Informants are to be explained the laws pertaining to entrapment.

3. Each informant must sign a release form (WPD Form #91 attached) prior to his/her utilization by this department.

4. Informants shall not be allowed to commit crimes. Once an officer determines that the informant has committed a crime, the relevant facts shall be reported by the officer to his supervisor. If the facts indicate that prosecution is appropriate, the case shall be submitted to the prosecuting attorney.

5. Officers of this department are not authorized to offer immunity to informants or to enter into any other improper agreements in return for an informant's cooperation.

6. All information relevant to criminal activity will be placed in a master file which will be maintained by the OIC of Detectives. Access to this file will be limited to those persons who can demonstrate a legitimate "Need-to-Know". (Information which is a matter of public record, e.g., newspaper stories, are not to be included in informant files.)

7. Payment. No payment, or compensation of any kind, shall be made to an informant without prior approval of the OIC of the Detective Division. When such payment is made, it shall be properly documented and signed receipts maintained.

8. Juveniles - the department recognizes the need to obtain information from reliable sources without regard to the age of the person. The department also recognizes the goal of the juvenile court in preventing criminal conduct by youthful offenders. The decision to use a juvenile as an informant will be made by a panel consisting of the Chief of Police, the police officer who will actually work with the juvenile, the Prosecuting Attorney or his designated representative, the Juvenile Court Judge, and the juvenile's parents or legal guardian. All members of the panel must approve in writing the use of the juvenile as an informant. Approval may be granted only after all requirements of this policy have been explained to the juvenile and his parents or guardian.

BY
ORDER OF:_____
                    Ray Johnson, Chief of Police

cc: City Manager
        City Attorney

I have read and understand this General Order. Any questions I might have had have been satisfactorily answered by my supervisor.

_____

Figure 5.4   Informant policy (*Part 2 of 2*)

Information from such sources should be regarded with skepticism and used with caution, but it cannot be overlooked. Information from inmates can, of course, be used as intelligence, but under certain strictly defined situations it can also be used to prosecute a defendant.

In *Perkins v. Illinois*, the Supreme Court clarified the use of jailed informants. Lloyd Perkins met and befriended Donald Charleton, who was serving a six-year sentence for burglary. Perkins eventually told Charleton that he had committed a murder in East St. Louis, Illinois. Charleton relayed this information to the police, who then had Charleton introduce an undercover officer, who was posing as an inmate, to Perkins. The officer engaged Perkins in a conversation in which Perkins described the murder in East St. Louis in detail. Perkins was charged with murder on the following day. Prior to the trial, the defense moved to have Perkin's statements suppressed, arguing that they had been obtained without properly advising the defendant of his rights under *Miranda*. The Court rejected the argument, holding that, although the suspect was in custody and was being interrogated, the purpose of *Miranda* is to mitigate the coercive effects that are inherent in police interrogation. In Perkin's case, there was no psychological pressure compelling him to talk; indeed, he seemed to brag about his crime. The Court felt that when there was no psychological pressure brought on the suspect, no *Miranda* warnings were required. Perkins was convicted of murder.

In order to use a suspect's statements, no matter what the circumstances, the state must demonstrate that the statements were made voluntarily. In *State v. Fulminate*, the defendant was convicted of murder partially based on statements he had made to an inmate informant. The defendant, Fulminate, was reputed to have raped and murdered his stepdaughter. These rumors resulted in harsh treatment at the hands of other inmates. An inmate informant offered to protect Fulminate in return for the truth about what had happened. Fulminate described in graphic detail how he had killed the girl. The inmate informant later testified against Fulminate, who was convicted of the crime. The Arizona Supreme Court suppressed the inmate's testimony, holding that the statements were made in return for protection by the inmate informant and were not made voluntarily. *Fulminate* stands for the proposition that the state must show that statements were made freely, not in response to promises or threats by anyone.

The state must also be sensitive to the defendant's right to counsel. In *Massiah v. United States*, discussed earlier, the Court held that once formal charges have been filed against the defendant, no interrogation can take place without the defendant's attorney being present. Thus, no information obtained by an inmate informant can be used by the state against the defendant *about any crime he is currently charged with*. Because of *Massiah*, inmate informants can usually only testify about statements made about unrelated crimes. There is one exception to *Massiah* as it relates to inmate informants. If inmate informants only overhear statements made by another inmate, they may testify to what they heard, although the state bears a heavy burden to demonstrate that the statements were voluntary and that the inmate informant was not serving as an agent of the state. The investigators and prosecutors should anticipate that the inmate informant/witness will be cross-examined vigorously by the defense. Testimony offered by convicted inmates is viewed with skepticism by jurors. The entire case should be reviewed to determine what other evidence is available to demonstrate the defendant's guilt to avoid relying too much on the testimony of an inmate informant.

Patrol Officer as Investigator

Patrol is the backbone of American law enforcement. The men and women who wear the uniform and work the streets are responsible for protecting the residents of their community. The increasing professionalism of the modern law enforcement officer has resulted in the Supreme Court expanding the number of legal tools that may be used by patrol officers to enforce the law and to conduct investigations. One of the most important of these tools is the *vehicle stop*. Patrol officers must couple knowledge of the law with sound tactics in order to perform their duty to protect and serve the community in a safe and effective manner.

The purpose of this section is to review the law related to vehicle stops and to discuss how it guides the actions of law enforcement officers assigned to patrol. The decision to stop a vehicle begins with an understanding of the authority to arrest or detain individuals.

Authority to Make Vehicle Stops

Any time peace officers limit a person's freedom of movement, they have "seized" that person for Fourth Amendment purposes. Therefore, any stops must be reasonable as provided for in the Fourth Amendment.

In order to stop a vehicle, an officer must have probable cause to believe that a crime, including a traffic offense, was committed by someone in the vehicle or that evidence of a crime can be found in the vehicle. Officers may also stop a vehicle if they have a reasonable suspicion that some criminal activity is about to occur. Peace officers cannot arbitrarily stop vehicles to check the driver's license or the vehicle registration. Officers can, however, stop vehicles systematically, as in a roadblock or a driver's license check (Delaware v. Prouse, 440 U.S. 648 [1979]; Michigan Department of State Police v. Sitz, 110 S.Ct. 481 [1990]).

Whren v. U.S.

In June 1996, the Supreme Court handed down an opinion that has an impact on vehicle stops as well as the use of profiles. The Court ruled that temporary detentions of motorists that are supported by probable cause to believe that the motorist has committed a civil traffic violation are reasonable under the Fourth Amendment. This is true regardless of the actual motivations of the officers making the stop. It is also true even if reasonable officers in the same situation would not have made the stop. In *Whren v. U.S.*, 116 S.Ct. 1769 (1996), two plainclothes vice officers were patrolling an area that was known for its drug activities. They became suspicious when they saw the driver of a vehicle looking into the lap of the passenger while the vehicle was stopped at a stop sign for an unusually long time. The officers made a U-turn to follow the vehicle, which made a turn without signaling and sped away. The car was stopped because of the traffic violation and the police subsequently found drugs. The defendants argued that the police had conducted a "pretextual stop," that is, the police used a traffic offense as an excuse to stop the car to conduct a search or to investigate some other criminal activity. Writing for the majority, Justice Scalia stated that stops based on probable cause are valid under the Fourth Amendment. Therefore, police can stop cars for traffic violations and use the stop as a means or opportunity to initiate a criminal investigation.

Actions After the Legal Stop

A *search* is defined as a governmental intrusion into an area where a person has a reasonable expectation of privacy. If no government official is involved in a search or if police enter an area where the person has no recognized expectation of privacy, then, by definition, no search has occurred. The reduced expectation of privacy resulting from a vehicle being on a public street and the inherent mobility of a vehicle are the major factors in the Supreme Court cases related to stopping and searching vehicles.

The Warrant Requirement

Generally searches conducted without a search warrant are considered unreasonable unless they fall within certain clearly defined exceptions. Several exceptions are applicable to vehicles and must be understood by all patrol officers. These exceptions are as follows:

1. Search incident to arrest
2. Investigative detention
3. Vehicle exception searches
4. Plain view seizures
5. Inventory or impound searches
6. Consent searches
7. Abandonment

Search Incident to Arrest

When law enforcement officers make a custodial arrest, they have the authority to search the person arrested and the area under her immediate control. It is important to remember, however, that the authority to search incident to arrest is limited with regard to strip searches and body cavity searches. The difficulty in defining the extent of the search incident will be in determining what constitutes the area under the immediate control of the arrestee. The answer lies in the "wingspan" rule. The Supreme Court has ruled that police may search an area into which the arrested person could reach in order to obtain a weapon, to gain the means to escape, or to destroy evidence (Chimel v. California, 395 U.S. 752 [1969]). When a vehicle occupant is arrested, the officer may search the entire passenger compartment of the vehicle (New York v. Belton, 453 U.S. 454 [1981]). The scope of the search incident to arrest in a vehicle situation does not include locked containers or the trunk, unless probable cause is developed to believe that evidence or contraband is hidden in the car. Officers must also remember that search incident to arrest must be contemporaneous with the arrest. So, if an arrest is made at the scene, and the suspect and his car are taken to the police station, there is no longer authority to search the car incident to arrest.

Investigative Detention

Investigative detention is often referred to as "stop and frisk." Investigative detention is based on the authority of peace officers to stop and briefly detain persons when an officer has a reasonable suspicion to believe that a person is about to commit a crime (Terry v. Ohio, 392 U.S. 1 [1968]).

Establishing Reasonable Suspicion

Reasonable suspicion is determined by the totality of circumstances test (United States v. Cortez, 449 U.S. 411 [1981]). This means that the facts upon which the officer made the stop should be viewed as a whole package. For example, in *United States v. Sharpe*, a Drug Enforcement Administration agent observed a blue pickup truck with a camper shell traveling on a highway. The agent saw the vehicle in an area known to be frequently used by drug traffickers. The agent knew that campers are often used to transport large quantities of drugs. The truck also appeared to be heavily loaded and had the windows of the camper covered, which prevented anyone from seeing in. The agent requested assistance and a highway patrol car was dispatched. When the marked vehicle approached the truck, the driver accelerated and attempted to evade the trooper. The trooper stopped the truck and detained the driver until the agent arrived. When the agent arrived he asked for consent to search the truck but the defendant refused. The agent then smelled marijuana, at which time he searched the vehicle and found marijuana in the camper. The Court said that the facts amounted to a reasonable suspicion that criminal activity was occurring and the agent's actions were appropriate given the facts of the case (United States v. Sharpe, 470 U.S. 675 [1985]). Officers seeking to stop a vehicle on reasonable suspicion must be prepared to describe in detail the facts that led them to make the stop. An investigative detention should be documented to protect officers if their actions are later questioned and to provide investigative leads that may be of use in other investigations.

Drug Courier Profile

Law enforcement officers have relied on profiles to detect criminals for years. The practice of detaining people based on characteristics, however, continues to be controversial. For example, when does a profile amount to enough information to justify a stop? Does the presence of a male with particular racial characteristics in a Florida rental car, northbound on a major interstate highway, add up to reasonable suspicion that drugs are being transported in the vehicle? The answer is no, but profiles may be used with other information to establish reasonable suspicion. In *United States v. Sokolow*, the Supreme Court dealt with profiling as a basis for an investigative detention. Although the facts in *Sokolow* dealt with an investigative detention in an airport, the circumstances can be generalized to car stops. The Court held that a detention based upon facts, including a drug courier profile, is reasonable (United States v. Sokolow, 109 S.Ct. 1581 [1989]). However, a drug courier profile will not, standing alone, satisfy a court that the detention is valid. At this time, the Supreme Court has not decided any cases related to car stops based entirely on a profile. It seems safe to say that stops can be based on information including profiles, which when viewed from the totality of circumstances perspective, will be considered valid.

Controlling the Occupants of a Vehicle

Clearly when a person is under arrest, an officer may exert control over that individual. With investigative detention, the authority to restrain the individual is less clear. In *Pennsylvania v. Mimms*, Philadelphia police officers stopped a car for expired plates. The officers ordered the driver out of the car, at which time one of the officers noticed a bulge under the driver's coat. The officer immediately patted the outside of the man's clothing and felt what he believed to be a revolver. The officer reached inside the coat and removed a .38 caliber revolver. Mimms was convicted of carrying a concealed weapon. The Supreme Court held that once law enforcement officers have lawfully stopped a vehicle, they may order the driver to get out of the vehicle, even though the officer does not suspect any criminal activity or any imminent danger. Having done so, the officers may pat the driver down when they feel the occupant of the vehicle may pose a threat to them (Pennsylvania v. Mimms, 434 U.S. 106 [1977]).

Examining the Interior of the Vehicle

After a driver or passenger of a vehicle has been arrested, the entire passenger compartment of the vehicle can be searched. In *Michigan v. Long*, the Supreme Court defined the scope of vehicle search associated with an investigative detention. In *Long*, two officers in a rural area saw a car being driven erratically and at an excessive speed late at night. The driver lost control of the vehicle and drove into a ditch. As the officers approached the car, Long, the only occupant of the vehicle, met them at the rear of the car. Long was asked for a driver's license, at which time he walked back toward the open driver's door. One of the officers accompanied him and looked into the passenger compartment before allowing Long to enter. The officer saw a large hunting knife on the floorboard of the car. He stopped Long and shined his flashlight into the car, looking for other weapons. The officer saw a pouch under the armrest. He removed it to look for a weapon, and upon opening the pouch he found it contained marijuana. Long was arrested for possession of a controlled substance. The Court held that where officers reasonably suspect that dangerous weapons may be present, they may make a limited search of the interior of the vehicle to look for weapons that might be accessible to the person detained. If, while searching for weapons, police find incriminating evidence, it may be used to prosecute the individual (Michigan v. Long, 463 U.S. 1032 [1983]).

Vehicle Searches

The authority to conduct a warrantless search of a motor vehicle is one of the oldest yet most misunderstood exceptions to the warrant requirement. In *Carroll v. United States*, the Court held that peace officers may search a vehicle if three factors are present. First, the officers must have probable cause to believe that evidence of a crime or contraband is concealed somewhere in the vehicle. Second, the vehicle must be in a place where it is lawfully accessible to the police, such as on a city street. Finally, the scope of the search must be restricted to areas where the item searched for could be hidden. For example, police could not search for a stolen engine in a glove compartment (Carroll v. United States, 267 U.S. 132 [1925]).

In 1982, the Supreme Court expanded this vehicle exception in *United States v. Ross*. In this case police had information from a reliable informant that Ross had heroin in the trunk of his car. The informant described Ross, his automobile, and where his transactions took place in detail. Officers proceeded to the location and saw a man matching Ross' description. Ross was arrested and his car was searched. Officers found a gun and ammunition in the glove compartment. Officers then opened the trunk with Ross' keys, where they found a closed brown paper bag containing a substance later identified as heroin. They also found a leather pouch containing approximately $3200. The Court held that when police have probable cause to believe that a vehicle contains the fruits or instrumentalities of a crime or contraband, they may search the entire vehicle, including any areas that might contain the item they seek (United States v. Ross, 456 U.S. 798 [1982]). Unlike searches incident to arrest, vehicle searches need not be conducted at the time the vehicle is seized (Chambers v. Maroney, 399 U.S. 42 [1970]). Recreational vehicles and campers are subject to the vehicle exception as long as they are mobile and are in an area accessible to the police (California v. Carney, 471 U.S. 386 [1985]).

Sealed or Locked Containers

Officers often have to deal with locked or sealed containers. If the owner of the package in question demonstrates the intent to maintain privacy, police may be required to obtain a search warrant before opening the package. In *United States v. Chadwick*, Drug Enforcement Agency (DEA) investigators received information that a large locker, probably containing a substantial amount of marijuana, was being shipped from San Diego to Boston. DEA agents arrested the defendant as he placed the footlocker into the trunk of his car. They opened the footlocker about two hours later without a search warrant or consent. The Court ruled that the search was invalid because the owner had an expectation of privacy in locked or sealed packages and containers, and the search was neither incident to arrest nor within the scope of the vehicle search exception. Under these circumstances, police were required to secure a search warrant before opening the package. The fact that the package was in a vehicle did not automatically cause the situation to come under the vehicle exception (United States v. Chadwick, 433 U.S. [1977]).

In a 1991 case, the Supreme Court finally provided a "bright line" rule to guide police when dealing with closed containers in vehicles. In *California v. Acevedo*, police watched a house to which a parcel containing marijuana had been delivered. Approximately two hours after the delivery had been made, police saw the defendant, Acevedo, leave the house carrying a package about the size of one of the packages of marijuana. The package was placed in the trunk of a vehicle and the defendant began to drive away. The police stopped the car and removed the package from the trunk and opened it; the package did contain marijuana. Acevedo was subsequently convicted of possessing drugs. A California appellate court ordered the evidence suppressed, holding that the evidence was inadmissible under *Chadwick*. The United States Supreme Court reversed, holding that when police have probable cause to believe that a container in a vehicle holds contraband or evidence of a crime, they may search the container, even if probable cause does not extend to the entire vehicle. Therefore police are no longer required to obtain a warrant to search a package when they have probable cause to believe that the package contains something that may be seized, and the package is in a mobile vehicle. The Court cautioned that probable cause relating to a package does not provide justification to search the entire vehicle (California v. Acevedo, 111 S.Ct. 1982 [1991]). Once the evidence has been located, however, this may give rise to a reasonable belief that other evidence or contraband is located elsewhere in the vehicle, thereby providing legal grounds to search the rest of the vehicle.

Plain View Seizures

Police can seize contraband from a vehicle if three clearly defined criteria are met. First, officers must be prepared to prove that they were lawfully in the place where the observations were made. Second, they must observe something that they know to be subject to seizure. In most cases this will be contraband, such as an illegal firearm or some type of drug. Finally, the item must be readily observable. The requirement that the item be in the open is the reason why this act is referred to as a seizure and not a search. If the officer had to look for the item, then it is a search and cannot be justified as a plain view seizure (Coolidge v. New Hampshire, 403 U.S. 443 [1974]; Brown v. Texas, 443 U.S. 47 [1979]).

In *Colorado v. Bannister*, an officer approached a car parked in a gas station that he had earlier seen being driven at excessive speed. As he approached, two men got out of the car. The officer asked the driver for his license and looked through the window on the driver's side. Lights from the station illuminated the interior of the car. The officer saw chrome lug nuts on the console between the bucket seats and two lug wrenches on the floorboard. Similar items had been reported stolen earlier in the area. The officer then realized that the men matched the description of suspects in the reported theft of auto parts. The suspects were arrested and the items seized. The Court held that the evidence was in plain view and the seizure was valid (Colorado v. Bannister, 449 U.S. 1 [1980]).

Vehicle Identification Number

In *New York v. Class*, the Court ruled that motorists have no reasonable expectation of privacy with regard to the vehicle identification number (VIN). In *Class*, officers stopped a car for a traffic violation. During the stop, an officer moved papers on the dashboard of the car in order to see the VIN. While moving the papers, the officer saw the butt of a gun protruding from under the seat. Class was arrested for criminal possession of a weapon. The Court said that due to the lessened expectation of privacy and the limited intrusiveness of the search, the seizure was reasonable. Thus police can examine the VIN plate when they make a valid car stop (New York v. Class, 475 U.S. 106 [1986]).

Inventory or Impound Searches

Law enforcement officers are often required to take possession of a motor vehicle to protect the interests of the department, the individual officer, and the owner of the vehicle. When police impound a vehicle, they assume the role of *involuntary bailee*, that is, they have a limited obligation to see that the vehicle or property be placed in a location where it will be secure. Once the vehicle is impounded, police must inventory its contents to determine the presence of valuables or dangerous items. If while conducting the inventory police find contraband, the item may be seized and the owner prosecuted for possessing it (South Dakota v. Opperman, 428 U.S. 364 [1976]). Inventory searches are valid if:

1. The officer is legally in possession of the vehicle, such as impounding an illegally parked car
2. The officer is acting pursuant to a standard department operational procedure
3. The police are not acting in bad faith, or for the sole purpose of conducting an investigation to discover incriminating evidence (Colorado v. Bertine, 479 U.S. 564 [1987]; Florida v. Wells, 110 S.Ct. 1632 [1990])

Consent Searches

Police officers may ask permission to search a vehicle or container. In a consent search, the officer is asking the person to waive his or her Fourth Amendment right to refuse the search (Bumper v. North Carolina, 391 U.S. 543 [1968]). The search will be considered valid if the person giving consent does so voluntarily and has lawful control of the item or area to be searched. The person giving consent may limit the scope of the search and may withdraw consent at any time. When requesting consent to search, peace officers are not required to inform the person that they may refuse to give consent (Schneckloth v. Bustamonte, 412 U.S. 218 [1973]). Similarly, officers are not required to obtain a written waiver of rights form, although additional documentation are helpful in proving that consent was given voluntarily. Under no circumstances may officers misrepresent any facts or intimidate the person giving consent.

Abandonment

A person has no expectation of privacy in property or items that have been abandoned. Abandonment means giving up something without limitation as to any particular person or purpose. Thus, if someone throws an object from a vehicle or leaves something behind in an abandoned vehicle, that evidence can be seized and used against the defendant in a criminal case.

Car Stops and *Miranda*

Whenever peace officers ask questions of someone who is in custody, they must advise that person of his or her rights under *Miranda v. Arizona*, 384 U.S. 436 (1966). Thus when the officer makes a custodial arrest of a suspect from a vehicle, interrogation must be preceded by the *Miranda* warning. The use of the *Miranda* warning is less clear in cases where the officer is conducting an investigative detention rather than making an arrest. The Supreme Court dealt with this issue in *Berkemer v. McCarty*. In this case, police followed McCarty's car for two miles and watched it weaving in and out of the traffic lane several times. The car was stopped and McCarty was asked to step out of the vehicle. The officer making the stop decided that McCarty would be charged with a traffic violation. McCarty was asked to undergo a field sobriety test, which he failed. The officer asked him if he had been using intoxicants. McCarty replied that he had consumed two beers and had smoked marijuana. McCarty was then arrested and transported to jail, where he was given a blood alcohol test, which did not indicate alcohol in his system. The officer never advised McCarty of his rights during the investigation. McCarty was convicted of operating a motor vehicle under the influence of alcohol or drugs. The Court was called upon to determine if the *Miranda* warning was required in this situation. The Court held that *Miranda* is required in any situation where custodial interrogation exists. Thus, whenever a person is under arrest, they must be advised of their rights prior to being questioned no matter how minor the violation. The Court went on to state that roadside questioning of a motorist does not constitute custodial interrogation. Thus, in a typical stop for a traffic violation, police are not required to advise a defendant of their rights (Berkemer v. McCarty, 468 U.S. 420 [1984]).

Conclusion

Once the crime scene has been processed, investigators must develop and pursue leads. All leads will full under the acronym MOM - method, opportunity, and motive. Leads should be assessed in relation to established solvability factors. Both patrol officers and investigators can play role in the solution of crimes. One of the most important types of activities conducted from the patrol car is the proactive vehicle stop. The U.S. Supreme Court has provided patrol officers with an extensive array of legal tools with which to perform their duties to protect lives and property. Aggressive patrolling based on a thorough working knowledge of the law, coupled with sound tactics, results in making the community safer.

References

Berkemer v. McCarty, 468 U.S. 420 (1984).

Black's Law Dictionary, 5th ed. St. Paul, MN: West Publishing, 1983.

Brown, Michael F. "Criminal Informants: Some Observations on Use Abuse and Control." *Journal of Police Science and Administration* 13(3):251–256.

Bumper v. North Carolina, 391 U.S. 543 (1968).

California v. Acevedo, (1991).

California v. Carney, 471 U.S. 386 (1985).

Carroll v. United States, 267 U.S. 132 (1925).

Chambers v. Maroney, 399 U.S. 42 (1970).

Chimel v. California, 395 U.S. 752 (1969).

Colorado v. Bannister, 449 U.S. 1 (1980).

Colorado v. Bertine, 479 U.S. 564 (1987).

Coolidge v. New Hampshire, 403 U.S. 443 (1974).

Crawford, Kimberly Kingston. "Cellmate Informants: A Constitutional Guide to their Use." *FBI Law Enforcement Bulletin* 59(12):18–24, 1990.

Fiaschetti, Michael. *You Gotta Be Rough*. New York: Doubleday, 1930.

Greenwood, Peter W. and Petersilia, Joan. *The Criminal Investigation Process, Vol. 1. Summary and Policy Implications*. Santa Monica, CA: Rand Corporation, 1975.

Illinois v. Gates, 103 S.Ct. 2317 (1983).

Jacobson, Ben. "Informants and the Public Police." *Criminal and Civil Investigations Handbook*, Joseph J. Graw, ed. New York: McGraw Hill, 1981, p. 63–80.

Kirby v. Illinois, 406 U.S. 682 (1972).

Kleinman, David Marc. "Out of the Shadows and into the Files: Who Should Control Informants?" *Police* 13(6):36–44, 1980.

Kuhlman v. Wilson, 106 S.Ct. 2616 (1986).

Michigan v. Long, 463 U.S. 1032 (1983).

Miranda v. Arizona, 384 U.S. 436 (1966).

Morris, Jack. *Police Informant Management*. Orangevale, CA: Palmer Enterprises, 1983.

Mount, Harry, A. "Criminal Informants: An Administrators Dream or Nightmare?" *FBI Law Enforcement Bulletin* 59(12):12–16, 1990.

New York v. Belton, 453 U.S. 454 (1981).

Pennsylvania v. Mimms, 434 U.S. 106 (1977).

Rubin, Richard. "Computer Trends in Law Enforcement." *The Police Chief* 4:20–24, 1991.

Schneckloth v. Bustamonte, 412 U.S. 218 (1973).

South Dakota v. Opperman, 428 U.S. 364 (1976).

Sparrow, Malcom K. "Information Systems: A Help or Hindrance in the Evolution of Policing?" *The Police Chief* 4:26–44, 1991.

Terry v. Ohio, 392 U.S. 1 (1968).

Texas v. Brown, 460 U.S. 730 (1983).

United States v. Chadwick, 433 U.S. 1 (1977).

United States v. Cortez, 449 U.S. 411 (1981).

United States v. Ross, 456 U.S. 798 (1982).

United States v. Sharpe, 470 U.S. 675 (1985).

United States v. Sokolow, 109 S.Ct. 1581 (1989).

United States v. Wade, 388 U.S. 218 (1967).

Weston, Paul B. and Wells, Kenneth M. *Criminal Investigation: Basic Perspectives*, 5th ed. Englewood Cliffs, NJ: Prentice Hall, 1990.

Whren v. United States, 116 S.Ct. 1769 (1996).

6. Interviewing

"Pray compose yourself, sir" said Holmes, "and let me have a clear account of who you are, and what has befallen you."

Sherlock Holmes, *The Adventure of the Beryl Coronet*, Sir Arthur Conan Doyle

Information, one of the traditional three I's of criminal investigation, is the lifeblood of law enforcement. Information is usually derived through interviewing, another of the three I's. The ability to locate persons who have knowledge of crime and to get them to willingly provide that information is central to an investigator's ability to perform his or her job. All law enforcement officers have the ability to become good interviewers if they are willing to take the time and to devote the energy to developing the knowledge, skills, and attitudes necessary to do the job. Good interviewers are made, not born, and they must develop an array of interviewing techniques to choose from in any situation. The investigator's first task is to find witnesses or other persons who have information about a crime.

The Neighborhood Canvass

The neighborhood canvass is an essential part of any preliminary investigation and is usually conducted by uniformed officers. Despite recognizing the importance of the neighborhood canvass, Eck noted that in some law enforcement agencies officers often do not take full advantage of this resource. He went on to recommend:

> Greater effort should be devoted to canvassing neighborhoods for witnesses. Considerable evidence establishes the importance of witnesses in identifying suspects, and leading to arrests and convictions. Yet patrol officers often fail to canvass neighborhoods near crime scenes in order to find witnesses. Relying solely on victims and those witnesses immediately available at the crime scene obstructs the effectiveness of further investigative efforts. It is crucial that patrol officers conducting preliminary investigations routinely search for potential witnesses who are not at the crime scene when officers arrive. (Eck, 1983, p. xxvi)

Canvasses should be conducted at the time the officers arrive at the scene or shortly thereafter. If it is determined that the crime occurred at some other time of the day, investigators should return to interview others who might have been there at the time the crime occurred but then left. For example, interviewers should look for delivery personnel or other persons who might have been in the area where the crime took place. It is not uncommon to find that potential witnesses are nearby. For a number of reasons, however, witnesses are reluctant to cooperate with the police and to provide relevant information voluntarily. It is the investigator's job to find those witnesses and to encourage them to willingly provide what information they have.

Motivating Reluctant Witnesses

Dealing with the reluctance or outright refusal of witnesses of a crime to provide the information they have is one of the most frustrating aspects of the interviewing process. The investigator will, unfortunately, become accustomed to hearing witnesses put off requests for interviews by saying, "I don't want to get involved."

Reluctance to become a witness is understandable because the fear of reprisal is very real today. The investigator must use every legal and ethical means available to obtain the cooperation of witnesses. Interviewers are much like salespersons in this situation. They must sell witnesses on the idea of providing what information they have and of later testifying in court about what they saw and/or heard.

In a recent National Institute of Justice publication, researchers noted that victim and witness intimidation has become a serious problem in many jurisdictions, especially those that report substantial gang activity. Intimidation is of two general types:

Case-specific intimidation: Threats of violence are made to discourage victims and witnesses from testifying in particular cases.

Community-wide intimidation: The actions of gangs and drug-selling groups create a general atmosphere of fear and result in a general reluctance to cooperate with the police and the prosecutor.

The techniques for encouraging someone to talk to the police apply to victims and to persons who witnessed a crime, both of whom will be called upon to testify. In either case, the interviewer must treat the victim or witness with kindness and sensitivity. Witnesses should not be seen simply as sources of information but as human beings who have undergone a frightening, often emotionally devastating, experience. The interviewer should remember that victims, particularly victims of violent crimes, are only beginning to deal with the fact that they have been victimized. The victim will probably feel that she has been violated, and she may feel helpless or at least vulnerable to similar attacks in the future. Victims may often express anger at the police at the apparent inability of law enforcement to protect them from crime. As efforts to obtain information from victims and witnesses become more difficult, interviewers should not be surprised by the reluctance of witnesses to "get involved."

An investigator may begin the interview by explaining the importance of the witness' information and how that information will be used in court. Most people have only limited knowledge of how the criminal justice system works. A witness must be made aware that under the American legal system person's providing testimonial evidence must present that evidence in court, in person. This means the witness may have to take the witness stand. The witness must be told that under the Sixth Amendment, defendants in criminal cases have the right to confront their accusers. The defendant has the right to see the witness and ask questions of the person who is testifying against him. This means that the witness must take the witness stand to be examined by attorneys for both the prosecution and the defense. When explaining these legal requirements, the investigator should keep the witness' age, level of education, and intelligence in mind and adapt the description of how the criminal justice system works to the intelligence level and sophistication of the witness. At some point during the interview, it must be made clear to a witness that he or she will be called upon to take the witness stand and testify.

Another means by which to obtain a witness' cooperation is to explain how the information he possesses can help the community. In recent years, police administrators and educators have become increasingly aware of the importance of the community in dealing with crime. Robert Trojanowitz has described the need for police to maintain and enhance the sense of community in this way:

> Part of the challenge of community policing, therefore, is to help revive the idea that those who live in the same area can improve the quality of community life by understanding how they share a community of interest. Perhaps ironically, the threat of crime and disorder can be the catalyst to make people see that they share a community of interest based on mutual geography. Of great consequence as well is that unless this corrosive fear is channeled into positive change, it can degenerate into apathy— or into outbursts of vigilantism. Community policing holds the promise of using that fear and anger as the impetus and foundation for efforts to improve the overall quality of community life. (Trojanowicz, p. 80, 1990)

In many cases, investigators do not live on the beats where they work, and in some cases they do not even live in the city where they work. They must still remain sensitive to the concerns of the people who do live there. In a community, the residents look out for each other and have some sense of responsibility for other resident's well being. A witness may be encouraged to talk by explaining that the information he may provide can remove a criminal from the community. By taking that person out of society, the community is safer for everyone.

It is sometimes necessary to bring legal pressure to bear on the witness. For example, a witness may simply refuse to cooperate. In cases where this occurs, it may be necessary to tell a potential witness that he will be receiving a subpoena and will be required to testify before a judge or before a grand jury. The witness often responds by giving an interview at that time. Some states have expanded the investigator's ability to obtain a subpoena before a charge has been filed. For example, a Missouri statute allows:

> In the course of a criminal investigation, the prosecuting or circuit attorney may request the circuit judge to issue a subpoena to any witness who may have information for the purpose of oral examination under oath to require the production of books, papers, records, or other material of any evidentiary nature at the office of the prosecuting or circuit attorney requesting the subpoena. (RSMo 1995 560.085)

No matter what technique interviewers use to encourage a witness to cooperate in an investigation, they must recognize the witness' cooperation. A person who has summoned the courage to talk to the police and later testify should be thanked for his contribution to making his community safer.

Witness Advocate

The theme that runs throughout all these interviewing techniques is that both the witness and the investigator must do the "right thing." Investigators must not make any promises to the witness that they cannot or do not intend to keep.

Investigators will, in many cases, become the person who guides a witness through the complexities of the criminal justice system. Investigators may assume the role of advocate for the witness or, if a witness assistance officer is available, the investigator should arrange for that person to work with the witness as the case progresses through the criminal justice system.

Witness Rights

Some law enforcement agencies provide victims and witnesses with witness rights forms. These forms provide information on the rights, services, and/or compensation to which a victim or witness to a crime may be entitled. Witnesses have the right to be free of harassment from the persons against whom they are testifying. In some cases, crime victims may be entitled to compensation for injuries they received during the commission of a crime. A copy of a witness rights card appears in Figure 6.1.

Interviewing Techniques

After locating witnesses, it is essential to separate them immediately. Witnesses must be separated to prevent them from comparing recollections about how an event occurred. When a crime occurs, a sequence of acts takes place, usually in a matter of seconds. Each witness sees and remembers different parts of the total event. If witnesses have the opportunity to discuss the events with each other, individual, distinct recollections may merge with the recollections of other witnesses; as a result, none of them may be sure of what they saw. It is the investiga-

---

Witness Rights

You have the right as a victim of a crime to:

1. be free from intimidation.
2. be told about available compensation for your injuries.
3. be told about social service agencies which can help you.
4. be assisted by your criminal justice agencies.

Your District Attorney operates a special Victim-Witness Assistance Unit.

If you need help call: 1 (800) 555-1212

Figure 6.1   Witness rights form

tor's task to interview each witness separately and to combine individual stories into a more complete picture of what actually happened.

Witnesses may be separated by placing them in different parts of a building or in different police cars. Witnesses must be made comfortable and given the opportunity to compose themselves. It is important, however, to conduct an interview as soon as possible after a crime has occurred. This is the point at which the witness' recollection is most fresh; in addition, the witness has had less time to think about the possible negative consequences of cooperating with the police. Start by obtaining identification from the witness as soon as possible after the interview begins. This information may be useful when trying to contact a witness later for an interview in a more comfortable environment if he or she refuses to talk to the interviewer at the initial interview. Obtaining identification immediately also makes it possible to locate witnesses later if they disappear before they are needed to testify in court.

Try to keep the interview as casual as possible. The goal is to conduct the interview more like a conversation between friends than an adversarial cross-examination. An aggressive approach to an interview may frighten or anger a witness and cause him to refuse to talk.

Begin by asking the witness to describe what happened and allowing him to tell the story in his own words. At pauses, ask open-ended questions, such as "What happened then?" or "What happened next?" This should be done to encourage the witness to continue to reflect on what happened and to continue to talk. Asking these questions also shows the witness that you are interested in what he is saying. When asking witnesses to describe emotions such as anger or fear, request the person to describe what he saw by asking question such as "What gave you that idea?" In this manner, it may be possible to obtain more detailed and specific information. At the apparent completion of the witness' narrative, ask the witness to clarify points mentioned earlier in the interview. This should be done tactfully in order to avoid antagonizing the witness. Repeat this process until you are convinced that the witness has told all that he knows or all that he is willing to provide at that time.

At the close of the interview, ask the witness to take a few moments to review the whole incident and to think about what he has said. At this point you may wish to remind the witness that he may be called upon to testify later and that what he has told you will be the basis of your testimony. This may be enough to cause the witness to focus on the event more clearly or to provide more information. By emphasizing to the witness that he may be called upon to testify, he may be forced to reconsider the story he has told and to tell the truth if he has been deceptive up to that point. Always conclude the interview by thanking the witness for the help he has provided and leaving a business card so that he can reach you if he thinks of anything else relevant to the case.

The Cognitive Interview

Investigators have long sought better means to obtain all the information a witness possesses about a crime. At one time it was hoped that hypnosis would provide the answer to this dilemma. Over the past several years, however, trial and appellate court judges have consistently ruled against the use of evidence obtained during hypnosis. The potential for suggesting information to witnesses under hypnosis outweighs the benefits that might result from any additional evidence obtained from hypnotized witnesses or victims.

The development of the cognitive interview provides a technique to recover the information possessed by witnesses in a manner that is acceptable to the courts. The cognitive interview consists of four parts, all of which must be used in order to make the interviewing process work:

1. Reconstruction of the circumstances surrounding the event
2. Asking the witness to report everything
3. Having the witness describe the events in a different order
4. Having the witness change perspective

In the reconstruction phase, first ask the witness to try to picture the circumstances surrounding the crime. Next ask the witness to think about, or perhaps even visualize, the scene. Then ask the witness what the scene looked like, who was present or nearby, where the furniture was, what the weather was like, and any other questions that might help him focus on the event under investigation. As the final step in the first phase of the circumstance reconstruction, ask the witness to remember how he was feeling at the time the event occurred and how he reacted to the event as it happened.

Next attempt to have the witness report everything he heard or saw. Tell the witness that persons sometimes withhold information because they feel it is unimportant or irrelevant. Instruct him to tell the entire story, leaving nothing out. At this point in the interview, it is important to be patient and to let the witness tell the entire story as he recalls it.

Then ask the witness to recall the events of the crime in reverse order. This may be done by telling the witness that it is normal to recall events in the order in which they occurred, but that it might be helpful to retell the story in reverse order, or by beginning from the most significant event and telling the story from that point both forward and backward in time. Again the hope is that by telling the story in a different sequence, the witness may recall some additional bits of information.

The final step in the cognitive interview is to ask the victim to recall the event from different physical perspectives. These perspectives should be from a location other than where he was during the event. You might ask the witness what he might have seen from across the street. Ask the witness to assume the perspective of others who witnessed the crime. He should be asked what he would have seen or heard if he had been that person. Research has demonstrated that the cognitive interview does result in more information being obtained than in a standard interview (Fisher et al., 1989).

Witness Statements

Over the years, there has been considerable controversy about whether witnesses should write statements themselves or whether investigators should write the statement for the witness after the interview. The answer to that question depends on the intellectual ability and writing skills of the witness. If the witness is a fairly capable writer and understands that the statement must be detailed, then it may be appropriate to have him write his own description of the event. This approach has the advantage of providing information with which the police and prosecutor can monitor the witness' testimony. Witnesses are less likely to lie in a statement if they know they will later be called upon to explain what they said in court. Statements written in the witness' own hand provide insights into how he may perform as a witness on the stand. Having witnesses write their own statements may also make a case more complex. In one incident, a woman was shot in the face by her live-in boyfriend. The boyfriend was later charged with felony assault. Some of the most damaging evidence offered against the victim was contained in the numerous statements she had written to various people, including the police, her doctor, and friends while her jaw was wired shut. Because each statement was different, the defense was able to impeach her credibility by showing numerous prior inconsistent statements.

In cases where a witness is unable or unwilling to write a statement about the crime, include the witness statement in the report. Statements taken in this manner are more likely to be complete because investigators focus on obtaining the information needed to prosecute a case by reporting all that the witness said rather than what the witness may think is important.

Witness Competency

The investigator conducting the interview needs to evaluate the competency of the witness and to make a determination of how that person will perform on the witness stand. Witnesses must be able to understand the obligation to tell the truth. They must be able to communicate with the trier of fact, and they must have knowledge and recollection of what they are called to testify about. The prosecutor will ask the investigator how well the witness meets these requirements to serve as a witness. Of course, the trial judge will ultimately determine if a witness is competent to testify, but an investigator should be prepared to advise the prosecutor of a witness' willingness and ability to tell the truth.

Reporting the Interview in Writing

One of the realities of the contemporary criminal justice system is that cases do not come to court for months or even years after the crime occurs. For this reason, it is essential to document the events of the case in well-written reports. A report is a summary of all the facts that are known to the investigator. Reports will provide the basis for the investigator and witnesses' later testimony.

Qualities of a Good Report

Reports should answer six basic questions:

Who?

What?

When?

Where?

How?

Why?

Who Was Involved?

The officer needs to provide all identifying information about the victims and witnesses to a crime. This includes each person's full name, including middle name, nicknames, or aliases; address, both home and work; telephone number, both home and work; social security number; driver's license number; and date of birth.

What Happened?

The investigator needs to document how the crime occurred. This is done by describing the events in chronological order. Before writing the report, organize the information in an outline. This section of the report also provides a description of the actions of all victims and witnesses.

Where Did it Happen?

It is essential to report exactly where all victims and witnesses were at various times when the crime occurred. The report must also include information on where evidence was found. Information on where the perpetrator was seen and where he or she went after the crime is reported in this section.

When Did the Event Occur?

It is important to document as precisely as possible when the crime occurred. This can be done by checking times with dispatchers. Interviewers can often establish approximate times by using a frame of reference, such as television or radio programs or some other event that occurred at the time of the crime.

How Was the Crime Committed?

The "how" question is most often answered with a description of the criminal's *modus operandi*. In answering the "how" question, take advantage of the many checklists that are available to ensure that all key questions are asked.

Why Did the Crime Occur?

In this part of the report, describe why the crime occurred, including information on the perpetrator's motive. Summarize the facts and opinions provided by victims and witnesses. If opinions are included in the report, they should clearly be labeled as such. Avoid putting your own opinions in a report; it is your task to report the facts without comment. To do otherwise creates the appearance of an inappropriate personal interest in the case. Defense attorneys can easily take a police officer's opinions and turn them to the defense's advantage by making it appear that the officer has a personal vendetta against the defendant.

Report Format

Most law enforcement agencies use a standard offense/incident report form. Detailed report forms guide an investigator through an interview. They also help capture information that is useful for crime analysis and for identifying crime trends. Most report forms still require that a narrative report be written. The report should follow a standard format, as illustrated in Figure 6.2, beginning with a synopsis of the case.

Conclusion

Information is essential to solving any criminal case. Some of the most valuable information comes from persons who have knowledge of a crime. Investigators obtain that information by using a variety of interviewing techniques. Once an interview is complete, it is important to document every aspect of the interview in a report. Often, it will not be possible to determine the future value of an item

---

Synopsis:

Martha Smith reports being assaulted by her husband Robert at their residence 1501 E. Elm at approximately 2245 hours 9/15/90.

Complainant Description:

Martha Ann Smith, 45,W/F, DOB 2/2 1945, SSN 212-40-8888, residence 1501 E. Elm Street, South City, Illinois, Phone number (618) 555-1234,

At 2240 hours 9/15/91 I was dispatched to a domestic assault call at 1501 E. Elm. Upon arriving at that location I contacted a women who identified herself as Martha Smith. Mrs. Smith was seated in a chair in the living room. She was holding a towel on left side of her head. I briefly examined the wound which appeared to be a serious laceration approximately 4 inches above her left ear. I requested an ambulance at that point. She stated that her husband Robert had come home at approximately 2200 hours and was, in her words, "drunk again." She said when demanded to see his wallet at which time an argument ensued. Mr. Smith stated that her husband had walked into the kitchen where he took a bottle of beer from the refrigerator at which time she again demanded to see his wallet. He then said "You want something, I'll give you something" at which he struck her with the beer bottle. He then left the house through the front door.

Suspect Description:

The suspect in this assault is Robert James 45 w/m

Evidence Collected:

Three pieces of a broken Motor City Beer bottle were recovered from the floor. I collected these items after allowing them to air dry at the scene. The evidence was turned in at evidence locker number 1 in the South City Crime Laboratory at 0300 hours 9/16/90.

Doctors Statement:

See attached statement by Dr. Martin Jones

Figure 6.2   Sample offense report

of evidence; if there is a possibility that information will be useful in court, it should be included in the report.

References

Bennett, Margo, and Hess, John E. "Cognitive Interviewing." *FBI Law Enforcement Bulletin* 60(3):8–12, 1991.

Eck, John E. *Solving Crimes: The Investigation of Robbery and Burglary.* Washington DC, Police Executive Research Forum, National Institute of Justice, 1983.

Fisher, Ronald P., Geiselman, R. Edward, and Amador, Michael. "Field Test of the Cognitive Interview: Enhancing the Recollection of Actual Victims and Witnesses of Crime." *Journal of Applied Psychology* 74(5):22–27, 1989.

Geiselman, R. Edward, and Fisher, Ronald P. *Interviewing Victims and Witnesses of Crime.* Research in Brief, Washington, DC, National Institute of Justice, December, 1985.

Healy, Murphy Kerry. "Victim and Witness Intimidation: New Developments and Emerging Responses." Washington, DC, U.S. Department of Justice, Office of Justice Programs, National Institute of Justice, October, 1995.

Royal, Robert F., and Schutt, Steven R. *The Gentle Art of Interviewing and Interrogation.* Englewood Cliffs, NJ: Prentice Hall, 1976.

Skogan, W.G., and Antunes, G.E. "Information, Apprehension, and Deterrence: Exploring the Limits of Police Productivity." *Journal of Criminal Justice* 7(3):217–241, 1979.

7. Interrogation of Suspects

If I claim full justice for my art, it is because it is an impersonal thing—a thing beyond myself. Crime is common. Logic is rare. Therefore, it is upon the logic rather than upon crime that you should dwell.

Sherlock Holmes, *The Adventure of the Copper Beeches*, Sir Arthur Conan Doyle

An interrogation differs from an interview in that in an interview the investigator is generally seeking information about a crime from witnesses. In an *interrogation*, the investigator is seeking to obtain information from someone who has been identified as a suspect in a crime. Although many of the skills necessary to be a good interviewer are also of value in an interrogation, there are significant legal differences between how interviews and interrogations are conducted. In order to conduct a successful interrogation, the investigator must be knowledgeable about both techniques of interrogation and the law governing the admissibility of a suspect's statements, admissions, and confessions at trial.

The Law of Confessions

A confession to a crime is often a key element in obtaining a conviction in a criminal case. In *Bruton v. United States* the Supreme Court stated:

> The defendant's own confession is probably the most probative and damaging evidence that can be admitted against him. (Bruton v. United States, 391 U.S. 123, 139 [1968])

Because confessions can be so damaging to a defendant, the Supreme Court has handed down a series of cases that govern the admissibility of statements made by the defendant. The purpose of these cases is to protect a defendant's Fifth and Sixth Amendment rights in a criminal case. Presently there are three tests that must be used by a trial court judge to determine if defendant's statements may be used against him in any subsequent proceedings:

1. The due process or voluntariness test
2. The right to counsel test
3. The Fifth Amendment privilege against incrimination test

The Due Process or Voluntariness Test

Before any statements made by defendants can be used against them, the state must demonstrate that the defendant made them voluntarily. Any hint of force or coercion by the police in obtaining an admission or confession will result in the suppression of those statements by the trial judge. The difficulty in applying this test is that *voluntary* is an imprecise term that means different things to different people, particularly trial judges, defense attorneys, and prosecutors. The test is easy to apply in cases of physical torture, such as in *Brown v. Mississippi*. In *Brown*, sheriff's deputies beat the defendant in a murder case until he confessed to the crime (Brown v. Mississippi, 297 U.S. 278 [1936]).

Other forms of coercion may be equally compelling. For example, in *Spano v. New York* the defendant was arrested for murder. He was then contacted by a friend who was a rookie policeman. Spano told the young policeman that he had been severely beaten by the dead man and that he did not remember what he had done. Spano went to a police station accompanied by an attorney. The attorney advised him not to say anything to the police. The rookie officer then made four telephone calls to Spano telling him that he, Spano, had caused the officer a number of problems with his superiors. Spano initially refused to cooperate, but finally, after the fourth call, he agreed to tell the police about the shooting. The Court ruled that the confession in this case was not given voluntarily and ordered that it be suppressed.

When determining if a confession was made voluntarily, the trial judge will consider several factors, including:

· Age of the suspect
· Education of the suspect
· Whether the *Miranda* was given
· Length of the interrogation session
· Threats made to the suspect
· Promises of leniency

If there is evidence that a statement was obtained involuntarily from the defendant, then the trial judge may suppress it. This is true even though the police may have advised the defendant of his rights under *Miranda*. In the event that the defense moves to suppress a statement, admission, or confession, the judge will evaluate the conduct of the officers using the totality of the circumstances test. The trial judge will review the circumstances surrounding how the statements were obtained. No single fact will usually result in a statement being suppressed unless the police are shown to have used physical violence.

The Right to Counsel Test

The lack of clarity in the voluntariness test proved troubling for police, prosecutors, and judges. The Court took steps toward resolving the confusion in two cases, *Escobedo v. Illinois* and *Massiah v. United States*. These cases set the stage for the development of the "right to counsel" test for determining if a confession had been obtained legally. In *Escobedo*, the defendant, Danny Escobedo, was arrested for murder. He was interrogated for several hours at a police station. During that time, he repeatedly asked for a lawyer. His requests were denied and the police continued to interrogate him. After several hours, he confessed and was later convicted of the murder. The Supreme Court later suppressed the confession and reversed his conviction, saying that Escobedo had been denied his right to counsel during the interrogation. The Court went on to say, "where, as here, the investigation is no longer a general inquiry into the unsolved crime but has begun to focus on a particular suspect ... no statement elicited by the police during the investigation may be used against him at a criminal trial." The Court said that when an investigation focuses on a specific suspect, the police are required to inform the suspect that he or she has the right to an attorney while being questioned. This test created fertile ground for defense attorneys to argue that an investigation had focused on a suspect far in advance of when the police actually advised the client of his right to an attorney. *Miranda*, to be discussed below, subsequently provided a "bright line rule" to guide the police when questioning suspects about their involvement in a crime.

In *Davis v. United States*, 114 S.Ct. 2350 (1994), the Supreme Court once again dealt with the defendant's right to counsel. In *Davis*, the Supreme Court ruled that after the police have obtained a valid *Miranda* waiver, they may continue to question a suspect after the suspect has made an ambiguous or equivocal request to have an attorney present during questioning. The Court noted that while it is good police practice to attempt to clarify or obtain an unequivocal request from the defendant, it is not constitutionally required. In this case, the defendant, Davis, was a suspect in a murder case. Davis had waived his right to counsel but during the interview he said, "maybe I should talk to a lawyer." The interviewers clarified this statement and determined that Davis did not want a lawyer. Later in the interview, the defendant specifically requested an attorney, at which time the questioning ceased.

The defendant, Davis, moved to have the statements obtained during the interrogation suppressed. The lower courts denied the motion and the Supreme Court affirmed, holding that when, in custody, suspects waive their *Miranda* rights but later make ambiguous reference to an attorney, law enforcement officers are not required to stop questioning the suspect. In *Davis*, the Court reaffirmed *Edwards v. Arizona*, in which it was decided that when a suspect makes an *unambiguous* or *unequivocal* request for an attorney all questioning must cease. The Court in *Davis* made it clear, however, that if the request is ambiguous, it is reasonable for the interviewer to attempt to clarify the suspect's request and to continue the interview until the defendant clearly requests an attorney. Thus police are not required to stop an interview anytime a suspect makes reference to an attorney; rather, the police may continue until the suspect clearly asserts his or her request for legal counsel.

Another right to counsel case, *Massiah v. United States*, further complicated the issue of when defendants in criminal cases have the right to have legal representation during an interrogation. In *Massiah*, the defendant had been indicted for violating federal narcotics laws and was released on bail. Massiah had retained an attorney. While the defendant was on bail, federal agents sent an informant equipped with a tape recorder to engage Massiah in a conversation about the crime he had been charged with. These statements were used, over the defense's objections, in Massiah's trial. The Supreme Court held that the statements made after the defendant had been charged could not be used at trial. The Court said that this action violated the defendant's Sixth Amendment right to counsel. Thus, today police cannot talk to a suspect after they have been formally charged with a crime without the suspect's attorney present.

Minnick v. Mississippi

In the fall 1990 term, the Supreme Court provided a powerful indication of how strongly it planned to protect the accused's right to legal representation in order to ensure that he or she receive a fair trial. In *Minnick v. Mississippi*, 59 Law Week 4037 (1990), the Court held that after suspects have asserted the right to counsel, law enforcement officers cannot interrogate them without the defendant's attorney present.

In *Minnick*, the defendant was arrested on a capital murder warrant from Mississippi. FBI agents briefly interrogated Minnick until he requested a lawyer, at which time the interrogation ended. Minnick subsequently met with his appointed counsel two or three times. Clarke County, Mississippi, Sheriff's Deputy, J.C. Denham initiated an interrogation after Minnick was told that he could not refuse to talk to him. Minnick subsequently confessed to Deputy Denham. Minnick's motion to suppress his confession at trial was denied, and he was convicted of first-degree murder. The U.S. Supreme Court held that when counsel is requested, interrogation must cease and law enforcement officers may not continue the interrogation without counsel present, whether or not the accused has had the opportunity to consult with an attorney. This simply means that the police may not attempt to interrogate a suspect after the accused has asserted the right to legal representation during custodial interrogation.

Fifth Amendment Privilege Against Self-Incrimination Test

Escobedo v. Illinois did not provide the bright line rule needed by law enforcement officers in the field to determine if their actions were legally correct. This set the stage for *Miranda v. Arizona*. The Supreme Court had been waiting for a case with the appropriate facts to provide the clarification needed by officers.

Facts in *Miranda*

In *Miranda v. Arizona*, 23-year-old Ernesto Miranda was arrested for kidnapping and rape. He was interrogated for over two hours. Police obtained a written confession to the crimes. Miranda was subsequently convicted on both counts. The Supreme Court reversed his conviction, saying that police must inform a suspect that he or she has certain rights prior to custodial interrogation.

In *Miranda*, the Supreme Court moved away from the Fifth Amendment due process test and the *Massiah-Escobedo* Sixth Amendment test to determine the admissibility of statements. Along with the earlier tests, the Supreme Court established the Fifth Amendment privilege against self-incrimination test. The Court stated:

> The prosecution may not use statements, whether exculpatory or inculpatory, stemming from custodial interrogation of the defendant unless it demonstrates the use of procedural safeguards effective to secure the privilege against self-incrimination. (Miranda v. Arizona, 1966)

With *Miranda*, the Court established the Fifth Amendment as the primary standard for determining the admissibility of statements, admissions, or confessions. Prior to custodial interrogation, suspects in criminal cases must be advised of their rights under the Fifth Amendment. To protect a suspect's rights, the interrogator must inform individuals of their *Miranda rights*:

1. The right to remain silent
2. The right to be told that anything said can be used in court
3. The right to have the advice of an attorney before and during the interrogation
4. The right to have an attorney appointed by the court to represent them if they cannot afford one

Most law enforcement agencies issue "Miranda Cards" to officers. There is, however, no constitutional requirement that the warning be given in exactly the manner that appears on the card (Duckworth v. Eagan, 109 S.Ct. 2875 [1989]; California v. Prysock, 453 U.S. 355 [1981]). In addition, the suspect does not have a right to be told of the particular crime that is under investigation (Colorado v. Spring, 479 U.S. 564 [1987]).

In order to correctly apply the law, the interrogator must be clear on two points:

1. The investigator must determine when a suspect is in custody.
2. The investigator must determine when a suspect is actually being interrogated.

When Is a Suspect in Custody?

As long as the suspect is not in custody or is not being interrogated, the investigator is not required to advise suspects of their rights under *Miranda*. The first question is, then, was the suspect in custody? Custody occurs when a suspect's freedom of movement has been restricted by a law enforcement officer (Orozco v. Texas, 394 U.S. 324 [1969]). If suspects are not in custody, that is, they are free to end the interview or leave at any time, they are not in custody and the police are not required to advise them of their rights (Beckwith v. United States, 425 U.S. 341 [1976]; Oregon v. Mathiason, 429 U.S. 492 [1977]).

In *Stansbury v. California*, 114 S.Ct. 1526 (1994), the Court further clarified what constitutes custody. In *Stansbury*, the Court reaffirmed the principle that a police officer's uncommunicated suspicions about a suspect's guilt are irrelevant to the question of whether the suspect is in custody for purposes of *Miranda*. Custody is an objective determination based on facts and circumstances known to the suspect at that time. In *Stansbury*, the police were investigating the rape and murder of a 10-year-old girl. Initially the investigation focused on an ice cream truck driver. The defendant, Stansbury, an ice cream truck driver who had talked to the girl, was interviewed, although he was not a suspect at the time. In the course of the investigation, police contacted Stansbury at his home and informed him that he might be a witness in a homicide and asked him to accompany them to a police station, where they would take his statement. At the station Stansbury was interviewed about his activities on the day of the murder. During the course of the interview, he made incriminating statements regarding his vehicle and his criminal record. The interview was terminated and he was advised of his rights under *Miranda*; he invoked his rights and was arrested.

The lower courts ruled that the defendant was not in custody until the officer's suspicions focused on him. This decision is clearly a throwback to the earlier *Escobedo* decision. The Supreme Court reversed the lower court decision, concluding instead that the determination of when a suspect is in custody should not take into account the officer's uncommunicated suspicions. The Court emphasized that custody was to be determined by objective factors, such as arrest or a significant restraint of the suspect's freedom of movement. *Stansbury* should lay to rest the "focus of suspicion" test established in *Escobedo* that lingered after the Court instituted the Miranda warning in 1966.

When Is a Suspect Being Interrogated?

Police are required to advise suspects of their rights if they ask any potentially incriminating questions of an in-custody suspect. The so-called Christian speech case illustrates when a suspect is in custody. In this case a 10-year-old girl disappeared from a YMCA in Des Moines, Iowa. A witness said he had seen a man carrying a large bundle with "two legs in it, and they were skinny and white." Williams, an escapee from a mental institution with a religious obsession, was suspected of the crime. Williams was arrested in Davenport, Iowa, and arraigned. Williams retained counsel, who advised him not to talk to the police. Police officers from Des Moines informed the attorney that the defendant, Williams, would be returned to Des Moines and would not be interrogated. On the return trip from Davenport, one of the police officers began a conversation with Williams. During the course of the conversation, one officer commented that the girl should receive a "Christian burial." Williams then took the police to the child's body. The Supreme Court ruled that, in the confines of the automobile and that given the circumstances of the conversation, the officer was interrogating the suspect. The statements made by Williams were suppressed.

In a later case, *Rhode Island v. Innis*, 446 U.S. 291 (1980), the Court further clarified what constitutes an interrogation. Providence, Rhode Island, police arrested Innis for abducting and killing a cab driver with a shotgun. The arresting officers advised Innis of his rights, and Innis made no statements. Other officers arrived and again advised Innis of his rights, and he stated he wanted to see an attorney. Innis was placed in a police car to be transported to the police station. While being transported to the station, officers in the front seat began a conversation among themselves about the danger posed to children in a nearby school for the handicapped by Innis' shotgun, which had not been recovered. Innis interrupted the conversation and instructed the officers to return to the scene to show them where the gun was hidden. Innis was advised of his rights under *Miranda* again, and he showed the police where the gun was. Innis was convicted of robbery, kidnapping, and murder. The defendant later appealed his conviction on the grounds that he had been subjected to custodial interrogation without his attorney present. The Court disagreed, saying that the conversation of the officers was neither direct questioning nor the "functional equivalent" of custodial interrogation.

The Decision to Request Legal Counsel

In *Moran v. Burbine*, 475 U.S. 106 (1986), the Supreme Court held that the decision to request legal representation is individual in nature. If the uncharged defendant does not request an attorney, the police are not required to let an attorney talk to the suspect, even if an attorney demands to see the defendant. It is not at all uncommon for an acquaintance or family member of a person arrested to call an attorney to represent the suspect. The attorney will go to the police station and demand to see his client. If the client has not requested an attorney, the police need not allow the attorney to see the suspect. The Supreme Court stated:

> Events occurring outside the presence of the suspect and entirely unknown to him can have no bearing on the capacity to comprehend and knowingly relinquish a constitutional right . . . Once it is determined that a suspect's decision not to rely on rights was uncoerced, that he at all times knew he could stand mute and request a lawyer, and that he was aware of the state's intention to use his statements to secure a conviction, the analysis is complete and the waiver is valid as a matter of law.

The police must remain aware that any effort to interfere with the defendant's right to speak to an attorney will likely result in suppression of any statements made to the police. In *Edwards v. Arizona*, when the defendant was arrested, he said he wanted "to make a deal," but later changed his mind and requested an attorney. Two police officers went to the jail to interview him. He told the detention officer he did not want to see the police but was told he had no choice. Edwards was advised of his rights and then made incriminating statements after hearing a taped statement by an accomplice implicating him in a crime. The Court said that once defendants invoke the right to an attorney, police may not question them again without an attorney present, even though the *Miranda* is given again. In 1988, the Court extended the right to counsel to interrogations involving more than one crime. In *Arizona v. Roberson*, 486 U.S. 675 (1988), the Court said police cannot interrogate a suspect about *any* crime once the suspect has asked to see an attorney. In *Smith v Illinois*, 105 S.Ct. at 490 (1984), the court made it clear that when the suspect invokes or attempts to invoke the right to counsel or the right to remain silent, interrogation must cease. In *Smith*, the suspect was arrested and advised of his rights. After being advised he said, "uh, yeah I'd like to do that." Police officers, however, continued to interrogate. The Court ruled that Smith had invoked his rights and that his statements were not admissible.

Resumption of an Interrogation by the Suspect

When a defendant invokes either the right to remain silent or the right to have an attorney present during an interrogation, all attempts to question the suspect must cease. However, if the suspect voluntarily resumes the interrogation, the police can continue to ask questions. In *Oregon v. Bradshaw*, the suspect ended the custodial interrogation by invoking his right to have an attorney present. He then asked the arresting officer, "what is going to happen to me now?" The officer advised Bradshaw that he did not have to talk, explained the charges to him, and suggested that he take a polygraph examination. Bradshaw agreed to the examination. Bradshaw was again advised of his rights and took the examination. The examiner told Bradshaw that he did not believe his story, at which time Bradshaw confessed to the crime. The Supreme Court held that Bradshaw had made a valid waiver of his rights under *Miranda*. Thus, if suspects voluntarily resume an interrogation after invoking the right to remain silent or the right to have an attorney present during the questioning, and if the police again advise the defendant of his rights, statements made to the officer may be used in court against the defendant. (Oregon v. Bradshaw, 462 U.S. 1039 [1983])

Miranda Revisited

On June 26, 2000, the Supreme Court issued its review of the Miranda warning. In a 7 to 2 opinion, the Court held that Miranda and subsequent cases govern the admissibility of statements made during custodial interrogation in both state and federal courts. The Court considered a Fourth Circuit ruling in the *Dickerson v. United States*. In Dickerson, the Fourth Circuit overturned a lower court decision to suppress a confession obtained in violation of the Miranda warnings. The Fourth Circuit held that the admissibility of the confession should be viewed in light of federal statute, codified at Title 18 Section 3501, which requires federal courts to apply a voluntariness standard to confessions in lieu of the Miranda warnings. (Dickerson v. United States, 121 S.Ct. 183, 530 U.S. 428 [2000])

Dickerson v. United States, The Facts

On January 24, 1997, an individual armed with a semiautomatic pistol robbed a bank in Old Town Alexandria, Virginia. An eyewitness provided police with a description of the robber and the getaway car, including a license plate number. Police determined that getaway car was registered to Charles T. Dickerson. Shortly thereafter, several FBI agents and a local police officer went to Dickerson's apartment. The officers observed an automobile matching the description of the getaway car. The agents knocked on the door and were greeted by Dickerson. After a brief conversation, Dickerson was asked if he would accompany the agents to the FBI office in Washington, DC. Dickerson agreed; he further agreed to ride in an agent's car. Dickerson later said at a court proceeding that he had no choice but to accompany the agents to the office.

Before leaving the apartment for the office, Dickerson asked if he could get his coat from his room. As he picked up his coat, an agent observed a large amount of cash on the bed. Dickerson explained that the money was winnings from a recent gambling trip to Atlantic City. Agents later testified that at the time they left Dickerson's apartment, he was not under formal arrest, and he was not handcuffed. Several agents stayed in the vicinity of the apartment after Dickerson left for the FBI office.

Once at the FBI office, Dickerson denied any involvement in the bank robbery, but admitted that he had driven to Old Town Alexandria to look for a restaurant. He stated that while he was in Old Town he met a friend who asked for a ride to Maryland. At this point, agents stopped the interview, and a telephonic search warrant for Dickerson's apartment was requested. The warrant request was based on facts summarized by the agent; the agent noted that Dickerson was not under arrest and could easily return to his apartment and destroy or remove evidence. The warrant was served and the search uncovered numerous items of evidence implicating Dickerson in the robbery.

The agent requesting the telephonic warrant returned to the interview room and advised Dickerson that his apartment was about to be searched. At that point, Dickerson said that he wanted to change his story and admitted that he had driven the getaway car in several bank robberies. Dickerson identified someone else as the actual robbery. Dickerson was arrested after he completed his statement.

Dickerson was charged with bank robbery. He later moved to suppress the statements and the evidence seized at his apartment. The defense argued that he had not been properly advised of his rights under Miranda.

The district court concluded that the confession was voluntary under the Fifth Amendment, but suppressed the statements because they were obtained in violation of the Miranda. At the suppression hearing, the timing of the Miranda warnings was in dispute. There was a discrepancy when they were given. The defense argued that the Miranda warnings had not been given prior to Dickerson's admission that he was the getaway driver. The district court judge concluded that the statements were obtained in violation of Miranda. The judge further concluded that, without challenge from the government, Dickerson was in police custody for purposes of the Miranda at the time he was brought to the FBI office. The judge concluded that the Miranda had been violated and that Dickerson's statements should be excluded.

The government appealed, requesting a review of the district court's decision. The appeal was made on two grounds: (1) that the Miranda was not violated because there was a discrepancy with the time the warning had been given and (2) even if the Miranda had been violated, the statement should be admitted because it was voluntary, therefore consistent with Title 18 U.S.C. Section 3501, and should be admitted against the defendant.

The Department of Justice withdrew the appeal with regard to the use of Section 3501, on the grounds that Congress did not have the right to overrule Miranda, and they would not advocate application of a potentially unconstitutional statute.

The Fourth Circuit, however, concluded that it had the authority to apply Section 3501 to Dickerson's statements writing:

> Because the Department of Justice will not defend the constitutionality of Section 3501—and no criminal defendant will press the issue—the question of whether the statute, rather than the Miranda, governs the admission of confessions in federal court will most likely not be answered until a Court of Appeals exercises its discretion to consider the issue. Here, the district court has suppressed a confession that on its face, is admissible under the mandate of Section 3501. As a result, we are required to consider the issue now.

Title 18 Section 3501

Section 3501 was intended to restore the totality of circumstances test to the admissibility of confessions and restore the principle of voluntariness as the key factor in determining if a confession should be admitted in federal courts. Section 3501 includes a number of factors that may be considered by a trial court judge in determining if a confession was obtained voluntarily without a defendant's privilege against self incrimination.

Factors Affecting Voluntariness Identified in 3501

Congress identified several factors that could be used by a trial court in determining if a statement, admission, or a confession should be admitted under the totality of the circumstances test including:

- The time elapsing between arrest and presentment of the defendant making the confession, if the confession was made after arrest and before the presentment
- Whether the defendant knew of the nature of the offense that he was charged with or suspected of at the time of making the confession
- Whether the defendant was advised or knew that he was not required to make any statement giving the Miranda warning would satisfy (This issue could be satisfied by given the traditional Miranda warning to the suspect)
- Whether the defendant understood he had the right to have an attorney present during interrogation
- Whether the defendant was questioned without an attorney present
- Advice of rights to a suspect in the future

The factors listed above may be used by a trial judge when determining the voluntariness of a statement. In the end, however, the Miranda is clearly required prior to custodial interrogation.

Preparation for an Interrogation

Before attempting to interrogate a suspect, investigators must prepare themselves mentally, physically, and emotionally for whatever they may experience in the interview. Mental preparation begins by becoming informed about the progress of an investigation up to that point. This will be done by reviewing:

- Witness statements
- Police reports
- Information on the *modus operandi*
- Physical evidence gathered
- Laboratory reports

Before the interrogation session begins, the investigator should be able to reconstruct the events of the crime as accurately as can be done, given the information available at that time. Being able to reconstruct the crime will result from doing the necessary background work. There is no excuse for an investigator not to take the time needed to complete the necessary preparation.

Physical preparation refers to the investigator's stamina, the investigator's ability to last through an extended interrogation with a suspect. Although explaining the length of an interrogation session sometimes presents legal difficulties at trial, the Supreme Court has ruled that as long as the suspect in custody does not invoke the right to remain silent or the right to have an attorney present during the interrogation, the investigator need not terminate the session. The fact that an interrogation session lasts several hours does not mean that investigators have worn down the suspect's will to resist. In some cases, the opposite may be true—the suspect may be trying to cause the investigator to give up the interrogation. In effect, the suspect takes advantage of the investigator's lack of patience and resolve. The interrogator must be ready to complete an interrogation without regard to how long it takes.

Emotional preparation refers to the ability of the interrogator to obtain incriminating information from a suspect without showing emotion. At the point at which a suspect admits involvement in a crime, it is essential that the interrogator not stop the flow of information by verbally or physically demonstrating to the suspect that the interrogator considers the suspect's actions offensive. The interrogator must remain calm throughout the session, never showing anger or revulsion. Later, investigators can release frustration or anger, out of the suspect's presence.

Physical Setting of the Interrogation

Privacy is absolutely essential to a successful interrogation. Suspects cannot be expected to admit guilt or involvement in a crime in front of a crowd of onlookers. Interrogation sessions should be conducted in rooms that are removed from groups of people, such as booking areas or squad rooms. Ideally, the room should be soundproofed and have only one door. It should be painted in colors that soften the environment, such as blues or earth tones, and there should be nothing in the room that reminds suspects that they are in custody or that they may be sent to prison. It is important that an interrogation room not be painted in "institutional colors," such as gray or lime green, and that there are no bars on the windows.

The room should be sparsely furnished with only two chairs, which are placed in the center of the room. The suspect's chair is bolted to the floor, while the interrogator's chair is on rollers. This makes it possible for the interrogator to control the suspect's actions and to create a higher degree of tension in the suspect by taking advantage of the proxemics and kinesics.

An interrogator should direct the suspect to his chair and then position himself with his knees near the suspect's knees before the suspect closes his knees or crosses his legs. This action places the suspect on the defensive and puts the interrogator in control of the session.

The Interrogation Session

The most problematic area of interrogation is the actual exchange between the suspect and the interrogator. The dynamics of an interrogation are not fully understood. Several factors determine the course of events in an interrogation. The amount of information available to the interrogator, the suspect's motives for telling some or all of the truth, and the interrogator's skill at conducting the session all have an impact on the outcome. The interrogator must prepare a list of questions that she wishes answered before the session begins. At the same time, the interrogator must be ready to digress from prepared questions if the session takes an unanticipated turn.

Dress and Appearance

The interrogator's personal appearance will have an impact on how quickly a rapport may be established between the investigator and the suspect. In general, the interrogator should dress in appropriate business attire. It is very difficult to interrogate a suspect while in uniform. The trappings of authority, the uniform, the shield, and the gun all serve to create a powerful impression of government authority in the mind of a suspect who is about to be interrogated. An investigator is more likely to be successful in obtaining a confession from a suspect if the person being interrogated is not being constantly faced with the trappings of government and its power to punish criminals due to the attire of the person seated across from him. It is advisable to wear a business suit of gray, navy blue, or some other conservative color. Clothing accompanied by a good professional demeanor may serve to impress the suspect. The message conveyed by the professional appearance of the investigator is that the interrogator is someone of importance to be treated with respect. The hope is that the suspect may respond to the investigator by telling the truth.

Structure of the Interrogation Session

The actual steps of an interrogation session will consist of several distinct, but related steps:

- Establish the initial control
- Tell the individual that he or she is the suspect in the case
- Do not allow the suspect to deny involvement in the crime
- Use specific questions
- Take the confession, statements, or admissions
- Thank the suspect for his or her cooperation

Initial Control

Once the interrogator has fully prepared, the suspect should be brought into the interview room by an investigator. At that point, direct the suspect to his chair and take your seat while moving into the suspect's space. Once in position, suspects who are in custody and are about to be interrogated must be advised of their Fifth and Sixth Amendment rights. In *California v. Prysock* the Supreme Court ruled there is no specific format in which the *Miranda* warning must be administered. The Court instead ruled that the true issue in determining whether statements should be admitted into evidence is whether the accused was adequately informed of his or her rights and whether the accused understood those rights. Thus, the *Miranda* warning is not required by the Court. The safest approach to administering the suspect's rights, however, is to read the warning from a Miranda card or from a Waiver of Rights form.

Once in position to begin the interrogation, do not allow the suspect to smoke. Smoking may allow the suspect to relax, and handling a cigarette provides the suspect with a number of opportunities to break eye contact with the interrogator.

Tell the Suspect that He Is Involved

Once the suspect is seated, stand above the suspect and tell him that the investigation up to that point has shown that he, the suspect, is involved in the case. It is possible that the suspect might confess at this point. He may be compelled by guilt or by the hope that he can obtain some consideration from the investigator. At the outset of the interview, show great interest in what the suspect has to say. You may actually sit on the edge of your chair and lean toward the suspect. If the suspect cooperates, continue to demonstrate to the suspect that you are paying close attention to him. If, however, the suspect lies, convey to suspect that his story is not believable. This may be done through facial expressions, by showing the suspect a look of irritation or disbelief. As the suspect realizes that you do not believe his story, he may change it at that time. As always, your goal as an investigator is to determine the truth, but if the suspect lies, then this information can be tested against other evidence. Inconsistencies can be presented as admissions in later proceedings.

Questions

The investigator must prepare a list of questions to be answered before the session begins. One of the most difficult aspects of an interrogation is to continue the interrogation after the prepared questions have been asked and the suspect has denied or refuted allegations against him. At the beginning of the interrogation, ask the suspect to tell his story. The suspect should be allowed to talk until he has completed his narrative. Do not interrupt the suspect, even if he is obviously lying. This is done for two reasons:

1. To confront the suspect in a lie at such an early point in the interrogation would likely impede any further communication between the interrogator and the suspect.
2. Getting the suspect to lie may be almost as valuable to the prosecution as the truth. Once the suspect's lies have been documented, it is possible to check his story against other witness statements or physical evidence. Such inconsistencies may be admissions and may be very incriminating.

Phrasing Questions

The interrogator's goal is to obtain the truth from the suspect. In the pursuit of that goal, you may be tempted to deceive the suspect. Although the Supreme Court has accepted the use of "artifice, stratagem, and deception," the public and the prosecutor may have reservations about the practice of lying to a suspect. For example, an interrogator may inform a suspect that he may as well tell the truth because his fingerprints were found at a crime scene or witnesses have positively identified him when this is not, in fact, true. The result may be that the suspect, after weighing his situation, may choose to admit his involvement in the crime. The defense can then use the same set of facts to demonstrate that the state engaged in conduct that, although effective, may be questionable in the minds of a judge or jury.

To avoid this dilemma, you may wish to change statements into questions. For example, instead of telling a suspect that his fingerprints were found at the crime scene, it may be better for presentation in court to ask the suspect, "Is there any reason why your fingerprints would be found at the scene?" or "Why would someone say they saw you there?" Instead of accusing the suspect of doing something illegal, you are asking the suspect a question to which the suspect can give either a truthful or deceptive response. If you are later asked on the stand by a defense attorney if you told the defendant that his fingerprints were found at the scene, you can answer that you did not. The decision as to how to answer is left to the suspect. There are a number of ways to phrase statements as questions. After the question is asked, watch for a cluster of behaviors that indicate deception or a lack of behaviors that indicate the person is being truthful. In other situations, simply ask a probing question, and watch and listen for a truthful or deceptive response. The following questions may be used at an appropriate point in the interview:

> *Who do you think had the best opportunity to commit the crime (or to do this)?* An innocent person would provide an answer that made sense, such as giving the names of the persons who had an opportunity to commit the act. A guilty person would try to implicate the largest number of people possible.

> *What do you think should happen to the person who did this?* An innocent person would likely respond that the person should be prosecuted. A guilty person might say that the person needs help or should be given a break.

> *How do you think this happened?* An innocent person would again give an answer that made sense, even if the answer implicated himself. A deceptive person would want to create the largest number of suspects.

Other useful questions are:

> *Who do you suspect or whom do you think might have done this?*

> *Where were you when this happened?*

> *Did you do this?*

> *Is there any reason why we would have found your fingerprints at the scene?* If there is a reason, the person interviewed should give an answer that explains why he was there.

> *Is there any reason why someone would have said he saw you there?*

> *Is there any reason why we cannot eliminate you as a subject?*

> *How do you think you would do if you took a polygraph (lie detector test if the person does not understand the term polygraph)?* An innocent person would say he would pass whereas a guilty would give excuses, such as having a nervous condition or a fear of machines.

> *Can you vouch for someone or rule out someone as a suspect?* An innocent person would be more likely to speak for someone she really trusts or has confidence. A guilty person would wish to create the largest pool of suspects possible to divert attention from himself.

> *Where were you at the time the crime occurred?*

> *How do you think the person who did this feels?* (if the crime is a sex offense or violent crime). This question accompanied by sympathetic demeanor may induce the suspect to make an incriminating statement.

After asking the questions, watch for signs of deception. If the suspect gives an evasive or equivocal response, you may respond by giving a facial expression indicating doubt or suspicion. It may be useful to ask, "Are you sure?" This is a way to indicate doubt and may be enough to cause the suspect to tell the truth or to change his story.

Taking the Confession

In addition to watching for signs of deception, watch the suspect for physical indicators that he is about to confess. These indicators may occur so quickly that you may miss them if you are not alert. Perhaps the best indicator is the suspect giving a large sigh. Any parent who has been pestered by a child into giving her what she wants is familiar with this behavior. You can recall giving up, sighing, and telling the child she will get what she wants. The moment of confession is often emotional. The suspect's head may drop to his chest, his hands may open as if beseeching the interrogator to understand what he did, and he may become tearful or even physically ill. He will then admit his involvement in the crime.

Thanking the Suspect

At the point at which a suspect confesses, avoid exhibitions of victory or condemnation of the suspect. The suspect must be treated with respect as a person. More pragmatically, however, the suspect's confession should be tape-recorded, and if the interrogator has angered or offended the suspect she may refuse to cooperate in the future.

Verbal and Physical Signs of Deception

Interrogators have long known that a suspect under stress will exhibit physical cues or say things that may indicate he is being deceptive. For example, the following set of instructions were given by Vedas of ancient India to detect deception over 2,000 years ago:

> A person who gives poison may be recognized. He does not answer questions, or they are evasive answers; he speaks nonsense, rubs his great toe along the ground, and shivers; his face is discolored; he rubs the roots of his hair with his fingers; and he tries by every means to leave the house ... (Palmiotto, 1983, p. 206)

Under the stress of an interrogation, a suspect may indicate she is lying by both verbal and physical indicators. It should be noted that no single word or behavior will indicate the suspect is lying. The interrogator must look for behaviors in clusters. A *cluster* may consist of both words and physical actions.

A suspect's eye movements may give some indication that he is being deceptive. Although it is not true that a guilty person cannot look an interrogator in the eye, either refusing to look at an interrogator in the eye or, conversely, excessive eye contact may indicate he is lying. In order to break eye contact in an apparently normal manner, the suspect may appear to be rubbing his eyes or cleaning his glasses. This is why it is recommended that the suspect not be allowed to smoke during an interrogation. When the suspect is lighting, smoking, or putting out a cigarette, he can break eye contact in a seemingly normal manner.

The suspect's mouth may also indicate deception. A nervous suspect may bite his lips, squeeze them together, or lick them. Gulping or excessive swallowing may also indicate stress resulting from attempts to be deceptive.

Avoiding Pitfalls in an Interrogation

The following is provided to assist interviewers/interrogators to identify problems that may arise in an interrogation and how to deal with them. Remember, the terms *interview* and *interrogation* are used interchangeably. In addition, it must be remembered that interviewing and interrogation are not yet sciences, therefore, from time to time some advice on how to conduct interviews may seem somewhat inconsistent. Techniques will change as the circumstances in an interview change.

People seem to dislike silence and they do not want to appear rude, at least not early on in an interview. Therefore, a pause after asking a question or making a statement may cause the person being interviewed to continue to speak. The more they talk, the more likely they are to reinforce their story or to make a mistake that the interviewer can take advantage of.

Remember, an innocent did not commit the crime. A person can deny involvement and will resist any efforts to link himself to the crime. If the person being interviewed deviates from the position that he did not commit the crime then the interviewer should be alert to the possibility of a confession or, more likely, the person will indicate that he knows something about the crime but was not involved directly. Interviewers should probe areas of consistency for complete explanations.

It is difficult for individuals to keep track of lies they have told in the past. They must constantly remind themselves of what they have said. If in an interview, the subject invokes his right to an attorney or to remain silent, the interviewer knows that additional follow-up on this person is warranted.

How an investigator frames a question can indicate to the subject what type of answer the investigator wants to hear. For example, if an investigator asks the subject, "There really isn't any reason to talk to anyone else about this, is there?" The interviewer has provided an end to the interview. In this case, the investigator appears to be trying to end an interview or even an investigation and is leading the subject to the answer what the investigator desires. The investigator should remember to ask open-ended questions.

Do not accuse the subject of lying if you are not sure he is lying. Belief in a subject's deception must be more substantive than mere suspicion. Any number of factors can explain inconsistencies in a story. Accusing an innocent person of lying will anger him or cause him to become defensive. To accuse a guilty person of lying will allow or force him to stay with the story he is telling. If evidence reveals that the person is lying, the investigator should turn statements into questions and attempt to obtain clarification, which may lead to the suspect making a truthful statement.

Throughout an interview or while reading a suspects' statement, investigators should pay particular attention to that person's use of pronouns. Do not disregard other parts of speech, but the pronouns are some of the best indicators of an effort by a suspect to shift or diffuse blame to others. Readers should review the section on statement elsewhere in this chapter for additional ideas on the use of pronouns.

On important questions, avoid framing the questions that may provide a negative response. For example, by starting a question with "I have to ask you a sensitive question," the interviewer is providing time to a guilty person, which may allow them the opportunity to create a deceptive response or find an effective means to stall or end the interview.

Do not argue with the subject. Strong denials are often a means to deflect attention from the purpose of the interview. To lose one's temper and to be lured into an argument will not result in obtaining the truth, nor will it result in obtaining any additional information. At times, it will be necessary to press the person to explain statements he has made or clarify inconsistencies, but arguing with the suspect will only bring an end to the interview.

Remember, there are no unimportant questions. If, during an interview, the subject asks a question, this is an indication that the issue is important to them. When someone asks a question, the interviewer should make note of it. The interviewer should also use this time as an opportunity to reinforce, in the mind of the person being interviewed, that the police will conduct a thorough investigation, which will lead to a prosecution.

Along with questions, the interviewer must be alert to any extraneous information introduced into an interview. The purpose of the interview is to obtain the truth to the best extent possible. Apparently unrelated information could be an attempt to divert the interviewer away from a sensitive subject. It may also signal an attempt by the subject to introduce another story that the subject hopes will be more believable to the investigator. Efforts to introduce additional, apparently unrelated, information is usually an indication that something important is about to occur in an interview.

Interviewers should be alert for out of sequence information. Events have a beginning, middle, and end. Most stories are told in the sequence in which they occurred. When a subject jumps ahead in a story or attempts to review part of a story, the interviewer should seek to explain why the person wishes to discuss particular events at a particular time. The investigator should be alert to seemingly coincidental events or comments.

Recording the Session

Judges and juries are innately suspicious of confessions. It seems unnatural for a person to willingly say something that will lead to criminal prosecution and punishment. One of the best ways to dispel the hint of coercion by an interrogator is to make an audiotape or videotape of the session. Improvements in taping technology have made it possible to tape sessions without significant logistical problems. If the session is taped, make sure that the required equipment is in working order. This means taking the time to check everything before the session begins. Use only new tapes, and once the session is over, handle the tape like any other item of evidence. A complete record of the chain of custody on any tape should be maintained to prevent possible suppression resulting from the chance that the tape could have been altered in some way.

When the taping session starts, begin by identifying all parties in the room, including law enforcement officers, the defendant, and the defendant's attorney. Then advise the suspect of his rights. If any promises have been made to the defendant, note them at this time. Then give the suspect the opportunity to tell his story without interruption. Attempt to avoid "question and answer" confessions, although, in reality, it may be impossible to elicit the required information from the suspect without asking leading questions.

Statement Analysis

Investigators continue to search for means to improve their ability to determine the truth or falseness of a person's statements. Analysis of someone's written statements offer another means to ascertain the truthfulness of what someone has written or said. For example, when Susan Smith was interviewed before the media, she consistently used the past tense when she referred to her little boys. In other cases of child abduction, parents will cling to any hope that their child is still alive. Susan Smith spoke of her children in the past tense because she already knew that the boys were dead. Her inadvertent use of the past tense led investigators to identify her as a suspect early in the investigation.

Analysis of a written statement allows investigators to review the words in the document independent of the facts of the case. Analysis can sometimes uncover deception. Statement analysis, at its simplest level, consists of reviewing the parts of speech and the balance of the statement.

Taking a Statement

A statement should be written by hand in ink. Handwritten statements are not as easily edited. The writer may use a particular phrase or word and may then want to make a correction. When the desire to make a change occurs, the writer must scratch out the unwanted word or phrase. The desire to make a change can be most informative. In the event the writer is in custody, the appropriate legal warning must be given. The existence of a handwritten statement would strongly suggest that the statement was written voluntarily.

Norming

The technique begins with the process of "norming" the statement. Norming refers to establishing what a typical truthful statement made by the person would be. After reading as many statements or samples of the person's written work, the investigator will then read a statement to look for deviations from the norm.

Actual analysis of a statement begins with an examination of the parts of speech. Investigators must pay particular attention to pronouns, nouns, and verbs. After establishing the norm, investigators should seek to determine why any deviation exists. Statement analysis begins with a review of the pronouns.

The policeman told me to write what happened so this is generally what happened. I come to work early like usual. I like to talk to the clerk coming to see what been going on. It was quite. At about 1 in the morning I see this guy come walking into the store. Looked at him but dont know him. Hes wearing blue jeans white tee shirt & running shoes. Hes maybe 6 foot & white with brown hair. He goes to the back of the store to the coolers & then comes up to the counter & asks for a pack of Winstons. When I hand them to him I see the gun. Its a black semiautomatic, He says put the money in bag or maybe he said sack. The money goes in the bag & he says get on the floor & dant call the cops. Heard ~~him~~ him go out the door & just staid there for a long time, Then I called the ~~cops~~ police. I cant believe this happened ~~again~~. We been robbed three times in the last year. I was in two of them, That guy is really lucky we usually strip

Figure 7.1 Handwritten statement

the till at 1:30 but he got here before it got done because it was busy. This is getting to be a rough naborhood. I dont know if I will quit work here any more. That is pretty much the way it happened this time

John Q Victim
5/30/2000

Figure 7.1 Handwritten statement *(Continued)*

Pronouns

Pronouns are the parts of speech that take the place of personal nouns. The most commonly used pronouns are I, me, you, he, she, we, they, and it. Special attention should be given to the personal pronouns "I" and "we," and to all possessive pronouns such as my, our, your, his, and her.

Truthful people usually refer to themselves in the first person singular "I" when writing or speaking. Any deviation from this practice could be an indication that the person is not totally committed to the fact in the statement and may not be telling the whole truth. Changing from "I" to "we" may be an attempt to shift or diffuse responsibility for an act to someone else.

Possessive Pronouns

Possessive pronouns include my, our, your, his, her, and their, and may indicate an attachment of the writer or speaker to a person or an object. In a statement, when the speaker or writer changes the pronoun or drops it completely he is attempting not to show possession or admit association with a particular object or person.

Nouns

Nouns refer to persons, places, or things. The meaning of a noun may change depending upon who uses it and how it is used. When examining a statement, the investigator must note any changes in the use of nouns. Such changes suggest an effort by the person to hide certain facts. If the writer substitutes another word, they may be telegraphing that something has changed in their lives. Lan-

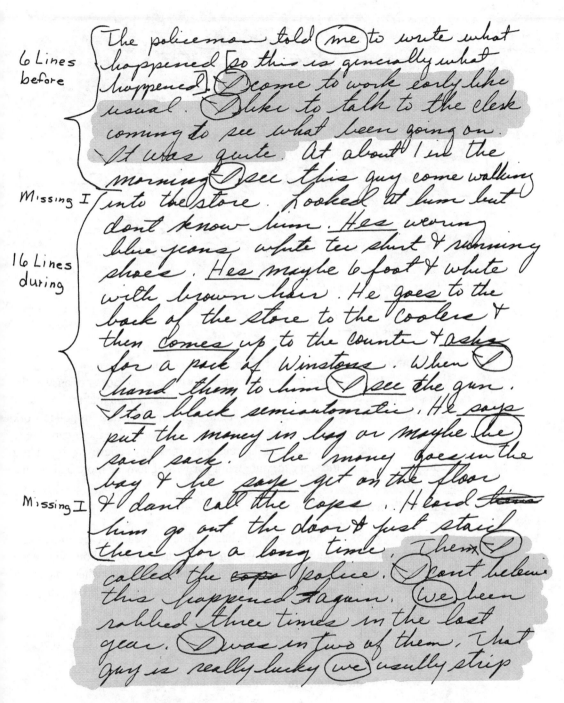

6 Lines before

Missing I

16 Lines during

Missing I

Figure 7.2   Analysis of handwritten statement

guage changes can always mean a change in reality, but those changes may be observed more frequently with nouns.

Verbs express action either in the past, present, or future. In statement analysis, the tense of the verb is extremely important. In a truthful statement, the writer or speaker uses the past tense because it relates to an event that has already occurred.

13 Lines
after
much of
which is
extraneous

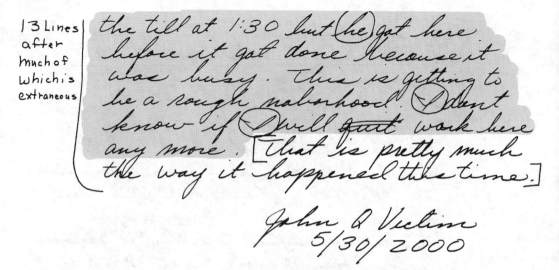

the till at 1:30 but (he) got here before it got done because it was busy. This is getting to be a rough naborhood. I don't know if I will quit work here any more. [That is pretty much the way it happened this time.]

John Q Victim
5/30/2000

Figure 7.2 Analysis of handwritten statement *(Continued)*

Extraneous Information

In a truthful statement, the writer or speaker will recount the events in a chronological and typically concise manner. Any information that does not answer the question presented to the individual is extraneous. The person making the statement may feel the need to justify his actions. It is an old axiom in police work that it takes longer to lie than it does to tell the truth. Truthful persons can simply recount the facts in a logical order. Deceptive persons may believe that by adding unnecessary detail, the story they are telling or writing may be more believable.

Lack of Conviction

A truthful person can simply say, "I didn't do it." A deceptive person cannot undo what they have done. They must concern themselves with about how much information an investigator has been able to uncover. Thus, when making a statement, they demonstrate a lack of commitment to a statement. They may use statements such as:

"I don't recall."

"I don't remember."

"I was so drunk, I don't know what happened."

Such statements simply lack credibility. Other examples of a person hedging are:

"I think."

"I believe."

"To the best of my knowledge."

"Kind of."

Balance of the Statement

A normal, truthful statement consists of three parts, each of which will be approximately the same length. The first part of the statement will be the chronology of the events that occurred prior to the incident. The second part will be a description of the event itself. The third part will to describe what happened after the incident. The more balanced the three parts are, the more likely the statement is to be true. A statement, which can be divided into three, approximately equal parts, can be described as the norm.

Analyzing the Statement

The investigator can conduct a preliminary review of a statement by completing the following steps.

Pronouns: Circle all the pronouns; indicate missing pronouns in the margin of the statement.

Verbs: Underline all changes in the verb tense.

Nouns: Underline changes in the language.

Extraneous information: Highlight information that does not respond to or otherwise answer a question.

Lack of conviction: Place brackets [ ] around words or phrases that demonstrate a lack of conviction.

Check the balance of the statement: Divide the statement into before, during, and after, and check the balance.

Sample Statement Analyzed

As with any investigative technique, statement analysis will not provide absolute proof of a person's willingness to tell the truth, but it can serve as an additional resource for the investigator.

The person who wrote this statement should be viewed as a suspect. A key pronoun is missing and the verb tense was changed when he begins to describe the incident. Overall, the statement is not balanced. His reference to an earlier crime suggests a pattern of till topping or accomplice crime. This sentence, coupled with other extraneous information would lead an investigation to be suspicious. The lack of connection exhibited in "that's pretty much what happened" shows a lack of commitment. Finally, the statement is not balanced. Viewed in its totality, the statement does not appear to be a completely truthful recounting of the fact.

The Polygraph

The polygraph examination, when conducted by an experienced operator, can provide valuable information to an investigator. The polygraph should be viewed as an investigative tool that may be appropriate in certain situations, not as an all-purpose indicator of deception. The polygraph measures three basic physio-logical responses over which the body has limited control:

· Respiration
· Heartbeat
· Galvanic skin response (GSR)

Under stress, these functions are altered: breathing increases and becomes irregular, the heartbeat accelerates, and the electric impulses in the skin (the GSR) increase. If the polygraph examination is administered correctly, the examiner can make an accurate assessment of the suspect's truthfulness. The examination itself begins with the exam-iner explaining how the machine works. This may be done be instructing the suspect to give incorrect answers to questions and then showing her how the machine responded to the false information. If the person taking the test believes that the polygraph can detect deception, the results are more likely to be accurate.

The examiner then goes through all the questions that the suspect will be asked in the examination without the machine turned on. This gives the suspect the opportu-nity to tell the truth or it alerts him to the knowledge that he will be asked incrimi-nating questions in the next session. All questions must be phrased so that the subject can answer "yes" or "no;" narrative answers are not allowed on a polygraph exami-nation. In being informed ahead of time of the questions, the subject begins to build toward the "peak of tension," which is essential for accurate results. The examiner then conducts the examination with the machine on, asking exactly the same ques-tions in the same order. As the questioning moves toward the key questions, the sub-ject should become tense. When the question is asked, the tension should be released with a truthful answer or should increase when the subject lies. The body's response is measured at this point. The questioning should continue through a series of routine questions to allow the subject to calm himself. After a brief rest, the examination should be repeated as before. At least two tests should be performed in order to com-pare the results. The examiner should thank the subject and advise him that he will be notified of the results of the test in a few days.

The possible results of the polygraph test are:

1. The person was telling the truth
2. The person was being deceptive about some part of the test
3. The results are inconclusive, that is, the investigator cannot tell whether or not the person was telling the truth

At this point, the investigator must make decisions about what direction the investigation should take. A particular set of results should not determine if an investigation should be continued or not. For example, in a robbery case, one of two identical twins held up a jewelry store. During the robbery, he looked directly into a camera. Both brothers were arrested and both naturally denied any involvement in the crime. Both were given a polygraph examination and both passed according to the examiner. What this meant was that one was prob-ably telling the truth, and the other was an expert liar. However, in extremely emotional cases, such as sexual abuse, the mere mention of the crime could cause such a powerful response that the results would be inaccurate. In all cases a thorough investigation should be conducted prior to the polygraph test.

Conclusion

An investigator's ability to interrogate suspects develops over time. An interrogator must be a good communicator as well as a good listener. A professional interrogator must also be completely knowledgeable about the current law regarding the admissibility of statements, admissions, and confessions. Effective interrogations result from a merger of knowledge of the law and interrogation techniques.

References

Adams, Susan H. "Statement Analysis: What do Suspects' Words Really Reveal?" *FBI Law Enforcement Bulletin*, Vol. 65, No. 10, p. 12–16 1996.

Arizona v. Roberson, 486 U.S. 675 (1988).

Beckwith v. United States, 425 U.S. 341 (1976).

Berkemer v. McCarty, 468 U.S. 420 (1984).

Brewer v. Williams, 430 U.S. 387 (1977).

Bruton v. United States, 391 U.S. 123 (1968).

California v. Prysock, 453 U.S. 355 (1981).

Colorado v. Spring, 107 S.Ct. 851 (1987).

Davis v. United States, 114 S.Ct. 2350 (1994).

Dickerson v. United States, 121 S.Ct. 183, 530 U.S. 428 (2000).

Duckworth v. Eagan, 109 S.Ct. 2875 (1989).

Ekman, Paul. *Telling Lies: Clues to Deceit in the Marketplace, Politics and Marriage.* New York: W.W. Norton, 1985.

Inbau, Fred. E., Reid, John E., and Buckley, Joseph R. *Criminal Interrogation and Confessions*, 3rd ed. Baltimore, MD: Williams and Wilkins, 1986.

Miner, Edgar M. "The Importance of Listening in the Interview and Interrogation Process." *FBI Law Enforcement Bulletin* 53(6):12–16, 1984.

Minnick v. Mississippi, 59 Law Week 4037, 1990.

Miranda v. Arizona, 384 U.S. 436 (1966).

Moran v. Burbine, 106 S.Ct. 1135 (1986).

O'Hara, Charles E., and O'Hara, L.O. *Fundamentals of Criminal Investigation*, 5th ed. Springfield, IL: Charles C. Thomas, 1980.

Oregon v. Bradshaw, 462 U.S. 1039 (1983).

Oregon v. Mathiason, 429 U.S. 492 (1977).

Orozco v. Texas, 394 U.S. 324 (1969).

Palmiotto, Michael J. "An Historical Review of Lie-Detection Methods Used in Detecting Criminal Acts." *Canadian Police College Journal* 7(3):206–212, 1983.

Regini, Lisa A. "The Supreme Court Revisits Miranda." *FBI Law Enforcement Bulletin*, Vol. 69, No. 3, p. 27–32, 2000.

Rhode Island v. Innis, 446 U.S. 291 (1980).

Smith v. Illinois, 105 S.Ct. at 490 (1984).

Stansbury v. California, 114 S.Ct. 1526 (1994).

Weston, Paul B., and Wells, Kenneth M. *Criminal Investigation: Basic Perspectives.* Englewood Cliffs, NJ: Prentice Hall, 1990.

8. Crimes of Violence: Assaults, Injury, and Death Investigation

There's the scarlet thread of murder running through the colorless skein of life, and our duty is to unravel it, and isolate it, and expose every inch of it.

Sherlock Holmes, *A Study in Scarlet*, Sir Arthur Conan Doyle

A badly handled violent crime investigation can leave unanswered questions that may plague an investigator and the agency for years to come. Because of the sensitive nature of violent crimes and unnatural death, many of the investigators skills will be tested. It is essential, however, that all necessary steps be taken to ensure that questions about an unusual death be answered as completely as possible. Anytime an investigator learns of a violent crime or death that appears to have occurred under questionable circumstances, it is essential that it be investigated as thoroughly as any criminal homicide would be.

Homicide

Law of Homicide

The word *homicide* is sometimes confusing. Legally, *homicide* means the killing of a human by a human. As such, a homicide is not necessarily a criminal act. Homicides are of three general types:

· Excusable
· Justifiable
· Criminal

Excusable homicides tend to be accidental. For example, imagine a man driving home from work through a residential neighborhood when a small child darts out into the street from behind a parked car. The driver is unable to apply the breaks before the auto strikes the child. The child is thrown to the street and suffers head injuries, resulting in his death. Assuming that no aggravating circumstances are present, such as driving while intoxicated or speeding, this type of event will likely be ruled an accidental death or excusable homicide.

Justifiable homicides tend to be the result of some legally required duty. For example, peace officers are, on occasion, required to use deadly force to make an arrest, as when preventing the commission of a violent felony. In addition, when the warden of a state penitentiary carries out an execution, he is performing a legally required duty. From an investigator's standpoint, the most common type of justifiable homicide will be the result of an apparent case of self-defense.

Criminal Homicide

There are two types of *criminal homicides*: murder and manslaughter. From a legal standpoint, murder is usually defined as the unlawful killing of a human by a human with malice. As with any legal definition, several words must be defined and understood from that perspective. *Unlawful* means simply that the homicide was neither excusable nor justifiable, and therefore by process of elimination must be criminal.

By far the most important concept in the law of murder is *malice*. Perkins defines *malice* this way:

> In brief, malice in the legal sense imparts (1) the absence of all elements of justification, excuse or recognized mitigation, and (2) the presence of either (a) an actual intent to cause the particular harm which is produced or harm of some general nature, or (b) the wanton or willful doing of an act with the awareness of a plain or strong likelihood that such harm may result. (Perkins, 1982, p. 860)

Malice, from a legal standpoint, connotes more than simply ill will. The investigator must provide the prosecutor with the evidence needed to demonstrate that the defendant intended to cause the death or serious physical harm that would be the logical consequence of an act. For example, if someone drives a car into a crowd of people because he dislikes someone in the crowd, he has committed an act that he would know is likely to cause death or serious physical injury and should be held accountable for that act.

Killing with malice is usually defined as murder in the second degree. The additional element of premeditation is required to raise the crime to first-degree murder. *Premeditation* is defined as thought of beforehand "for some length of time, however short" (Perkins, 1982, p. 131). The investigator must look for evidence that shows the defendant was acting after giving the matter some thought. As noted in the definition, the time needed to form premeditation may be quite brief.

Voluntary Manslaughter

Voluntary manslaughter may be defined as:

> Unlawful homicide committed without malice aforethought. (Perkins, 1982, p. 84)

In order for a felonious homicide to be manslaughter, several elements must be present: (1) there must be adequate provocation, (2) the killing must have occurred in the heat of passion, (3) the heat of passion must have been sudden, and (4) there must be a connection between the provocation of the passion and the fatal act. The key to understanding voluntary manslaughter is to realize the act is a so-called crime of passion and that there is some type of "provocation" that will reduce the act from what would otherwise be murder in the second degree. Provocation may occur in many recognizable legal forms:

- Mutual quarrel or combat
- Battery
- Assault
- Words (on a very limited basis)
- Trespass

Involuntary manslaughter is a catchall concept including other types of criminal homicide not covered in the other crimes. The most common type of involuntary manslaughter is homicide resulting from criminal negligence. For example, a woman left her three young children in a locked car while she visited her boyfriend at the county jail. The outside temperature was well over 100 degrees, making the temperature substantially hotter inside the car. Two of the children died of heat stroke, and the other suffered irreparable brain damage. A jury felt the she was criminally negligent in causing the death of her children. She was convicted of involuntary manslaughter.

Motives

In criminal homicide cases, it is important to determine why the crime occurred as quickly as possible for two reasons. First, the identification of a motive often provides the most productive leads in a homicide case. Once investigators determine who had a reason to commit the crime, they can focus on that suspect until a case has been built or leads prove to be unsuccessful. Second, it is important to establish a motive to help prove the defendant's guilt at trial. Although it is not a legal requirement that a motive be proven, it is invaluable for the prosecutor to show the jury why the crime occurred. The motive pulls the evidence in a case together and makes the story complete for the trier of fact. Motives for most criminal homicides fall into one or more identifiable patterns.

Anger Killings

Anger killings are spontaneous outbursts resulting from arguments or other disputes. This type of homicide may or may not involve weapons and often begins as assault. Crimes of this type are usually second-degree or voluntary manslaughter.

The Love Triangle

In homicides of this type, spouses or lovers become unhappy with their partner and kill them to free themselves from the relationship. Love triangles may involve both heterosexual and homosexual relationships. In homicides of this type, jealous lovers or former partners will gain revenge by killing the object of their jealousy. In cases of this type, the killer may also be motivated by anger or be part of a love triangle as well.

Profit

In cases of this type, the killer is acting out of the desire for some immediate personal gain. The gain in most cases is financial, as then the killer is the beneficiary in a life insurance policy.

Sexually Motivated Homicides

Homicides of this type are linked to a sexual assault, such as rape, sodomy, child molesting, or some other form of perversion. Sexual homicides are often bizarre and brutal. In one case a 13-year-old boy murdered his younger brother and a friend in a "sex game." In the game, the killer strangled the boys while he masturbated them. He apparently unintentionally killed his brother, which resulted in a charge of involuntary manslaughter and then killed the second boy to cover up his crime, which resulted in a charge of second-degree murder.

Serial Murder

Killings of this type are sometimes referred to as recreational murder. The murderer kills whenever the desire and the opportunity converge. Serial homicides are often sexually motivated. How many serial killers are active at any time is unknown, but they are considered to be a factor in the large number of unsolved homicides in this country. Serial murderers are difficult to identify and apprehend because of their mobility and knowledge of how to avoid detection by the police. The Violent Criminal Apprehension Program (VICAP) and the Homicide Investigation Tracking System (HITS) have been developed to help locate and arrest serial killers.

Murder-Suicide

In murder-suicide cases, the killer will often kill members of his family or a significant other and then take his own life. The killer is often suffering from some personal problem, such as an incurable disease, and decides to take his own life. He also decides to kill close relatives or acquaintances, apparently to protect them from a life or a fate similar to his.

Felony Murder

Felony murder occurs when someone causes the death of another in the commission of a dangerous felony. Felonies of this type are usually robbery, burglary, rape, kidnapping, or sodomy. In cases of this type, the murderer is acting to eliminate the only person(s) who can link him to a crime. Felony murders may be prosecuted as first- or second-degree murder, depending on state statutes.

Law of Assault

Assault is often described as the unlawful application of force to the person of another. Assaults are usually distinguished as felonies or misdemeanors, depending on the amount of force involved or the extent of injury to the victim. For example, shooting someone could be a first-degree assault, shooting at someone and missing could be a lesser degree of felony, while pointing a gun at someone could be a misdemeanor assault.

Post Mortem Observations of the Body

Investigators should be familiar with the conditions in which a human body may be found after death. The forensic pathologist will have the responsibility for making a more precise determination as to the time and cause of death. The investigators, especially those who arrive at the scene where a body has been found, may gather information that may be very useful in follow-up investigations. If the person is clearly deceased, then every effort should be made to protect the crime scene.

Observing the Deceased's Eyes

If the deceased died with her eyes open, she will remain that way until they are closed. The pupils may become irregular in shape and unequal in size as the body loses moisture after death. As the eye dries, the exposed surface will become rigid and a thin opaque film will cover the eyeballs. The film may be observed approximately one hour after death, particularly in a dry environment. As decomposition begins, the eyes will lose their firmness and will begin to subside into the socket. The white will begin to yellow and eventually turn red and then brown (Figure 8.1).

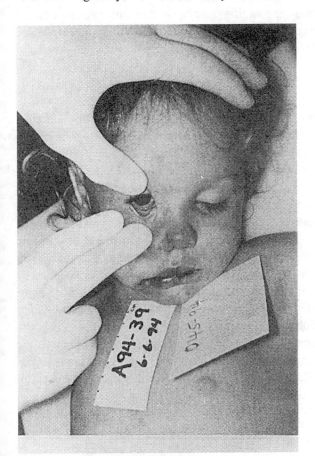

Figure 8.1   Observing the victim's eyes can give clues as to the cause of death

The investigator should begin by attempting to determine the body temperature at the scene. This may be done by touching to corpse and noting whether the body is still warm in relation to the surrounding area. If a medical examiner is at the scene, it may be possible to determine body temperature by inserting a thermometer into the victim's liver which is usually the last part of the body to cool. The body will cool at various rates depending on a number of factors, including air temperature, wind, amount of clothing on the body, and body size.

Rigor Mortis

After death, a body will generally experience stiffening of muscles in the body brought about by chemical changes. The onset of *rigor mortis* will vary considerably depending on temperature, wind, and humidity. It is difficult to determine the time to death based on rigor mortis. Generally, however, rigor will set in two to seven hours after death, with the body being in full rigor in 10 to 18 hours after death. Rigor will pass off 24 to 36 hours after death. At one time, it was believed that rigor mortis began in the head and spread to the feet. More recently, it has been determined that rigor mortis begins in the small muscles of the body and spreads to the larger ones. Since there are thousands of muscles in the face and shoulders, it may appear that rigor began there. Investigators should determine the extent of rigor by gently lifting an arm or leg on the corpse and noting the stiffness of the limb in the report.

Post Mortem Lividity

One of the most common characteristics of a dead body is the discoloration found on the lower parts of the body known as *post mortem lividity*. The discoloration is caused by blood settling to the lowest part of the body. Lividity will usually become apparent approximately 30 minutes after death and will be pronounced about four hours after death. Lividity can confuse inexperienced officers since it often appears to be bruising on the body. Bruises, however will often be accompanied by scratches and abrasions. In addition, lividity will usually be around a "blanched" area. Blanching occurs when blood is unable to flow into an area that is in contact with a hard, flat surface such as a floor. Capillaries are crushed by contact with the surface, leaving a pale white color surrounded by lividity. In most cases lividity will be purplish in color; however, in freezing or carbon monoxide deaths, lividity will be cherry red. In asphyxial deaths, lividity will be a darker, almost blue color.

The location of the lividity on the body will be helpful in determining if the body has been moved. It may also be helpful in determining the approximate time and cause of death. The location and extent of lividity should be noted in the investigator's report.

Cadaveric Spasm

Occasionally investigators will encounter a cadaveric spasm or "death grip." For example, in cases of suicide involving a firearm, the weapon may still be clutched tightly in the victim's hand. In other cases, drivers killed in automobile accidents have been found with both hands gripping the steering wheel, even though the arms may have suffered numerous fractures on impact. The cause of this phenomenon is unknown at this time. Cadaveric spasm is, however, associated with violent death and is thought to be largely psychological in origin. Actual cases of cadaveric spasm are rare. Unlike rigor mortis, a cadaveric spasm will not pass off over time.

Putrefaction

Putrefaction refers to the decomposition of the human body. The onset of putrefaction will vary depending on a number of factors, including temperature, humidity, air currents, and moisture (Figure 8.2). Decomposition is related to contact with oxygen. As a rule of thumb, one week of exposure to the air is the equivalent to two weeks in the water. Under normal conditions, putrefaction will begin 24 to 72 hours after death. The first signs of decomposition will be a greenish discoloration on the sides and abdomen. Bacteria in the intestines will cause gas, which enters the blood vessels and tissues and results in bloating in the abdominal region, and will eventually cause the entire body to bloat. Blisters filled with gas and fluid will appear on the skin, and lighter skinned bodies will gradually turn darker.

Higher temperatures will accelerate the onset of decomposition; in hot humid climates, it may be apparent in two or three hours after death. Cold weather slows decomposition, and freezing of a body stops the process until the body

Figure 8.2   A body exposed to extreme heat and high humidity will decompose quickly and attract maggots.

thaws. Bodies that have been exposed to kerosene or contain arsenic decompose more slowly.

Adipocere

Bodies that have been in water or located on wet soil may have a waxy yellowish-white substance on them. This substance, *adipocere*, often called "grave wax," is decomposed fat from beneath the skin. Adipocere can occur in both salt and fresh water.

Identifying the Body

After securing the scene, investigators should identify the body as quickly as possible. According to the *FBI Uniform Crime Reports*, the clearance rate by arrest for murder and non-negligent manslaughter is approximately 68 percent. Statistically, this means that a person who takes the life of another feloniously has approximately a one in three chance of avoiding apprehension and conviction. This figure is an oversimplification of problem, but it does demonstrate the changing nature of homicide investigation. Much of the decline in clearance rates stems from the inability of investigators to identify the victim's body. Investigators must identify the remains before they proceed to develop leads.

Visual Identification

The first means of identifying a body is to look for identification on the body. These means of identification include a driver's license, credit cards, or a social security card. If the body is decomposed, investigators should confirm the identification using one of the means later discussed. If the body is intact, the investigator may have someone who knew the deceased visually identify the body. It is recommended that the investigator get two independent visual identifications. This is to prevent the possibility of misidentifications by an emotionally overwrought friend or relative of the deceased.

Fingerprints

Bodies may be identified from the fingerprints if certain conditions exist. First, the body must not be so decomposed that it is not possible to take fingerprints. Second, for the present at least, the investigator must be able to recover prints from at least five digits from one hand. Third, the print must be on file in a database accessible to the investigator. These databases are usually in an FBI system or, more recently, state system. Thus if a body is found intact, investigators can take the prints, classify them, and send them to the FBI or the appropriate state agency; if the prints are on file, it will be possible to identify the body. However, if the fingerprints are not on file in any source known to the investigator, it may not be possible to identify the person using this technique.

Other Identification

In the event the body is decomposed or partly decomposed, it may be possible to identify the remains from dental records, skeletal remains, or distinctive features, such as scars or tattoos.

Forensic Odontology

A forensic odontologist, someone who is trained to identify human remains from dental work, can identify remains from the teeth if particular information is available. The average healthy adult has 32 teeth, which will normally have five distinct surfaces. The teeth and surfaces will, in turn, have 160 surface areas from which it may be possible to make identification. The odontologist will look for any unique characteristics, including placement of teeth, shape and size of teeth, cavities, fillings, bridges, plates, dentures, or any other possible identifier. The investigators must have some idea of who the deceased was so that they can request the individual's dental records. In addition, there must be dental records against which the remains can be compared. If the investigators have no idea who the person was or if there are no records, it will not be possible to identify the remains.

> **CASE STUDY**
>
> An elderly, retired college professor was not seen for several days. Concerned neighbors contacted the police, who determined that the case should be treated as being suspicious. The woman was never seen alive again. Approximately six months later, skeletal remains were found in a ditch several miles outside the city were she had lived. It was not possible to identify the remains visually or from fingerprints. The victim's dentist, who had an interest in forensic odontology, identified the remains based on dental records. The victim in this case had bridgework in her mouth using a technique that had not been employed by dentists for several years. Based on this, the dentist was able to determine conclusively that the remains were those of the professor. After the identification, the police were able to continue to build a circumstantial murder case against a young, male neighbor.

Skeletal Remains

It is also possible to identify remains from bones. This technique may be particularly valuable in cases where animals have scattered the remains and very little of the body is recovered. Again, limitations of this technique do exist. Police must have some idea who the deceased was and there must be records against which the bones may be compared. In one case, a 12-year-old African-American boy disappeared one evening. Months later, some children, while playing, found a skull and other bones in a shallow depression covered by leaves and boards. The skeleton was largely intact, some hair was still on the skull, and the bones were still in the deceased's high-top tennis shoes. Despite the obvious similarities between the description and the recovered remains, it was not possible to make a positive identification because the boy had never been treated for a broken bone and had never been to a dentist.

Distinctive Characteristics

Distinctive characteristics may be used to identify a body. These include peculiarly shaped or irregular teeth, scars, and tattoos. In one case, a body was brought into a city morgue. When the body was prepared for autopsy, attendants found that the deceased had a morgue tag tattooed to her foot with all the necessary identifying information on it. Apparently she assumed that, given her lifestyle, she would end up in a morgue eventually so she provided the staff with the means to identify her.

Deoxyribonucleic Acid (DNA)

DNA may well provide a promising means to identify remains in the near future. It will be possible to compare bone or dental pulp with DNA samples recovered from personal belongings of the missing person, such as hair from a brush. The technology currently exists but remains beyond the financial capabilities of many departments.

Transporting the Body

Before transporting a body to a morgue or funeral home for a post mortem examination, it is essential that investigators ensure that the body arrives substantially in the same condition in which it was found. Investigators should follow the "white sheet rule," that is, the body should be wrapped in a clean white sheet before placing it in a body bag. This will ensure that any objects falling from the body will not be lost. A body may be wrapped in a plastic tarp if no other materials are available. The body should be removed from the plastic as soon as possible to prevent decomposition. Figure 8.3 illustrates the importance

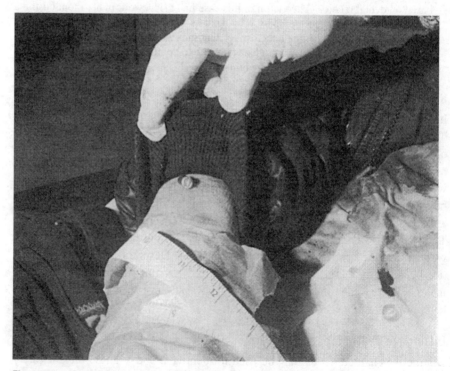

Figure 8.3   Protecting against loss of evidence

of the white sheet rule. A bullet had passed through the victim's jacket sleeve and through the forearm; however, it lacked the velocity to penetrate the opposite sleeve. The bullet was located inside the sleeve. In this situation the evidence could have been lost. Bagging the hands also helps prevent the loss of evidence (Figure 8.4).

Recognition of Wounds

Law enforcement officers should have a working knowledge of the various types of wounds they will encounter when investigating violent crimes. The most common wounds encountered are gunshot wounds, stab wounds, puncture wounds, incised wounds, lacerations, and blunt trauma.

Gunshot Wounds

Approximately 68 percent of felonious homicides and 23 percent of aggravated assaults involve a firearm (Federal Bureau of Investigation, 1996, p. 18, 32). It is vital that the investigator know a great deal about wounds caused by firearms.

Entrance and Exit Wounds

The ability to determine if a bullet hole is an entrance or exit wound is important in determining if the fatal injuries were inflicted intentionally or accidentally (Figure 8.5). The position of entrance and exit wounds on the body can tell a

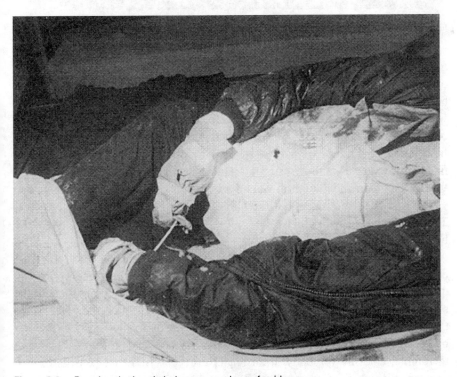

Figure 8.4　Bagging the hands helps prevent loss of evidence

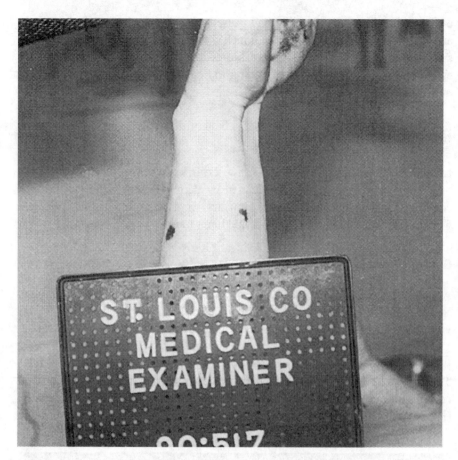

Figure 8.5   It is sometimes difficult to distinguish between entrance and exit wounds.

great deal about where the victim and the shooter were at the time of death. In one case, the deceased had what appeared to be four different bullet holes in his body. The assailant claimed he had fired only once in self-defense. Witnesses who were located in the neighborhood canvass stated that they had heard only one shot. Examination of the body revealed that only one shot had, in fact, been fired. The first entrance wound was in the palm of the deceased's left hand. The first exit wound was in the back of left hand. The second entrance wound was in the left shoulder, and the fourth wound was in the back of the left shoulder. The victim had been shot once, but the bullet has passed through his body twice. This fact, coupled with other information, led investigators to believe that the homicide was in fact justifiable.

Entrance wounds are normally smaller in diameter than the projectile that caused them because of the elasticity of the skin. Generally, entrance wounds do not bleed a great deal. An entrance wound will generally be approximately the shape and size of the projectile. This is only a generalization, however, since the elasticity of the skin may distort the injury. The projectile may not enter the body directly, as when it ricochets off another surface. The projectile may begin to tumble, entering the body at an angle, especially if it has passed through another object, such as a body. Entrance wounds will sometime have gunpowder residue near the wound. If the wound was inflicted at very close range, smudging or a residual ring of gunpowder may be present (Figure 8.6). Smudged gunpowder can be removed by wiping it off. If, however, the weapon was a few inches away from the skin, *tattooing* or *stippling* may occur as unburnt powder is blasted into the skin. Tattooing cannot be washed off. If the person is shot at a distance of 18 inches or less, there may be both smudging and tattooing.

Contact Gunshot Wounds

Contact gunshot entry wounds will sometimes be much larger than the typical entry wound, especially if the weapon was pressed against a hard surface, such as the victim's skull. A contact wound of this type will be characterized by a stellate or star-shaped tearing of the skin. This type of contact wound results when gases discharged from the weapon come in contact with the skin without being able to dissipate in the air. Gases from the muzzle are forced between the skin and the skull, and then move outward, resulting in large star-shaped wounds. Wounds of this type are often associated with suicides and execution murders.

Exit *wounds* are usually larger than entry wounds and often bleed profusely. If the victim was shot with a high-velocity jacketed projectile, the wound can be massive. Investigators should not expect to find an exit wound with every gunshot. Small-caliber projectiles may well expend their energy in the victim's body. Small-caliber bullets may actually be deflected by a skull, or they may break the skin at an angle and may stop under the skin. In recent years, ammunition has been designed to launch projectiles that dissipate their energy in the object they strike; thus the damage will be internal, leaving no exit wound.

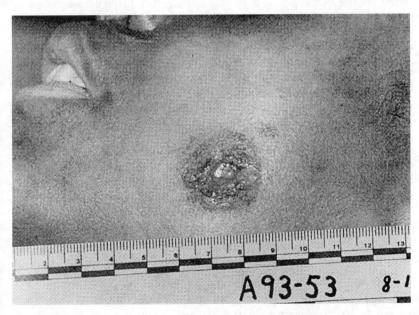

Figure 8.6   If a person is shot at a distance of 18 inches or less, there may be both smudging and tattooing.

Shotguns

Shotguns are involved in a number of shootings. A shotgun is a smoothbore, usually shoulder-fired, weapon. The ammunition fired through a shotgun will be multiple pellets or a single-rifled slug. The bore of a shotgun barrel is given in gauges rather than calibers, as with a handgun or rifle. Gauges are determined by starting with a pound of lead and dividing it into a set number of equal parts, and then forming a perfect sphere with that amount of lead. For example, a 12-gauge ball would be 1/12th of a pound of lead rolled into a ball .729 inches in diameter. A 16-gauge shotgun would fire a 1-ounce projectile that is .662 inches in diameter. This system of gauges is consistent for shotguns, with the exception of the 410 shotgun, pronounced 4–10, which has a diameter of .410 inches. Shotguns are usually used to fire shot shells that range form 00 buckshot, which is a pellet .33 inches in diameter, down to No. 9 shot, which is a pellet measuring .08 inches in diameter.

The entrance wound from a shotgun will vary depending on how far the muzzle of the shotgun was from the victim. If the shot was fired from less than 12 inches away, the wound will be approximately 3/4 inch in diameter. Powder tattooing may be present as the distance between the muzzle of the shotgun and the victim increases. At 3 to 6 feet the pattern of the shot extends to about 1/2 to 2 inches and the wound may have scalloped edges. From 6 feet and beyond, pellets will separate greatly, usually leaving no discernible pattern.

The wad that separates the powder from the shot will sometimes be propelled into the wound at distances of 15 feet or less. The wad may enter the wound or strike the body near the wound. Investigators should be aware of this possibility while conducting the investigation.

A firearms examiner can make determinations as to the distance the muzzle of the weapon was from the victim at the time it was fired. The examiner will begin be determining the size of the wound at the autopsy and then firing the same weapon using the same shells into sheets of paper until the pattern has been approximated.

Gunshot Residue Analysis

In cases where a firearm has been used, investigators should move quickly in order to prevent the destruction of evidence, particularly firearms evidence. In *Cupp v. Murphy*, 93 S.Ct. 2000, 412 U.S. 291 (1973), the Supreme Court provided the legal basis for emergency searches to prevent the loss of "evanescent evidence."

Cupp v. Murphy. Murphy voluntarily went to a police station to be questioned after learning that his estranged wife had been killed. Murphy met his lawyer at the station. Police observed a small spot on Murphy's finger, which they suspected might be dried blood. Murphy refused an officer's requests to take a sample of scrapings from his fingernails. At that time, Murphy placed his hands behind his back began to rub them together, apparently attempting to remove the spot. The police obtained samples from Murphy without his consent and without a search warrant. The samples were determined to have traces of the victim's skin and blood cells, and fabric from the victim's nightgown. Murphy was convicted of second-degree murder. The Supreme Court ruled that in situations such as this, where evidence might disappear or be destroyed, the police need not wait to obtain a search warrant prior to searching for and seizing the evidence. In this case, the suspect could have destroyed the evidence simply be washing his hands. Investigators have reported incidents of suspect's dipping their hands in motor oil, gasoline, or even urinating on them to destroy firearms evidence.

Defense Wounds

Defense wounds occur when victims attempt to protect themselves from an attack. Defense wounds are typically located on the victim's hands or forearms.

Incised Wounds

Incised wounds are often referred to as cutting wounds and are inflicted with a sharp-edged instrument, such as a knife or razor (Figure 8.7). Incised wounds

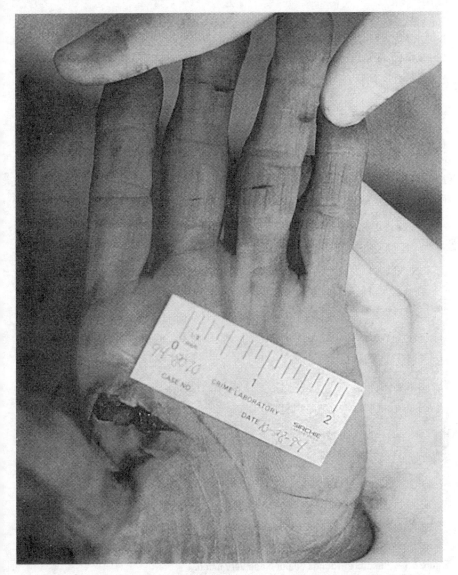

Figure 8.7   Incised wounds often occur when a person attempts to protect himself from an assailant using a sharp-edged instrument.

tend to be narrow on the ends and wider toward the middle of the wound. Wounds of this type bleed profusely. Death from incised wounds usually results from cutting the victim's throat, severing a major blood vessel, or striking a vital organ.

Puncture of Stab Wounds

Puncture wounds occur in assaults where the weapon was an ice pick, a screwdriver, or a knife. Puncture wounds do not bleed a great deal, and medical personnel may find it necessary to perform exploratory surgery to determine how deep or serious the wound is (Figure 8.8).

Lacerations

Lacerations are characterized by irregularly shaped wounds with profuse bleeding and substantial bruising around the injury. Lacerations are often the result of blunt trauma inflicted by baseball bats, pipes, pieces of reinforcing bar, garbage can lids, or other blunt objects (Figure 8.9).

Bite Marks

Bite marks can occur in any violent crime but are most often found in crimes such as homicide, sex offenses, and child abuse. Like burns, bites may be classified by degrees. A *first-degree bite* is well defined and results from a great deal of pressure; however, the skin is not broken or bruised. First-degree bites tend to disappear quickly.

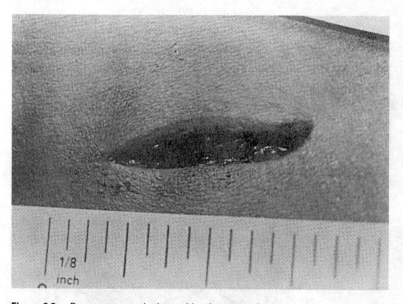

Figure 8.8   Puncture wounds do not bleed very much.

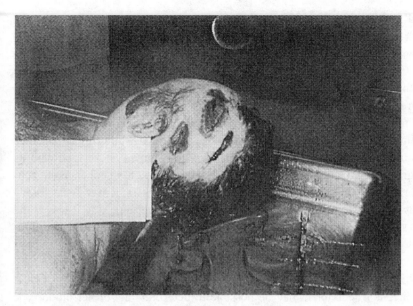

Figure 8.9   Lacerations are characterized by irregularly shaped wounds with profuse bleeding and substantial bruising.

The *second-degree bite* mark is the bite wound most commonly encountered by the investigator. A second-degree bite results in tissue damage and bruising, but the skin is not broken. Abrasions and more severe bruising are also common, resulting from the person being bitten pulling away from the bite.

Third-degree bites are characterized by broken skin. This type of injury can result from biting pressure or, again, from efforts of the person being bitten to free themselves. The skin may be torn, but as long as it remains attached it will be classified as a third-degree bite.

In a *fourth-degree bite*, the wound may be characterized by skin and tissue being torn from the body. It's not uncommon to encounter cases where someone has had their nose, ear, or even cheek bitten off in an altercation. Under common law, this type of act was prosecuted as *mayhem*.

Recovering Bite Mark Evidence

Evidence recovered from bite marks can either have class or individual characteristics. Investigators must make every effort to recover all bite evidence. If the subject from whom the evidence is to be recovered is alive, the investigator must act quickly to avoid loss of evidence as the body's healing mechanisms begin to work. As always, the investigator should be sensitive to the feelings of the person, especially if the person is a sexual assault victim.

The first step in the recovery process is to conduct a complete visual examination of the subject's body. This should be done under normal lighting, but it should also be repeated using ultraviolet or infrared light, which may reveal evidence not observable under normal lighting conditions. This is particularly true when examining dark-skinned persons. The visual examination should be repeated at least once more, approximately 24 hours after the initial observation.

Photographing the Bite Mark

As with any evidence, photographs should be taken of any bite marks. If the case under investigation is a homicide, then the body should be photographed at the scene. Once transported to the morgue or if the subject is at the emergency room, then a series of photos should be taken. At least two photos of each significant area should be taken, one without a ruler and another with a measuring device to make a one-to-one comparison possible later on. Pictures should be taken in color. The investigator may also use black-and-white film to enhance the contrast in the picture. The camera should be mounted on a tripod with its own light source. Oblique lighting may also be used, again, to enhance the contrast. Several pictures should be taken from different angles. It may be necessary to reposition the body in order to stretch the skin in the same way it was at the time of the attack. A complete photographic log should be maintained throughout this phase of the investigation.

Swabbing the Bite Mark

If the biter is a secretor it may be possible to determine his or her blood type from the saliva. Swabbing should be done as quickly as possible because evidence of this type is easily destroyed. Swabbing is begun by using a sterile cotton swab dipped in distilled water. The investigator must avoid touching the swab end to prevent contamination of the swab. The recovery begins by swabbing the outside of the suspect area and slowly moving to the center of the bite, moving the swab in concentric circles, being careful to overlap with each circular movement. After the swabbing has been completed, the swab should be placed in a sterile, dry vial to be transported to the laboratory. The investigator must also obtain a control sample from some other area of the subject's body, which should also be transported to the laboratory.

Making a Cast of the Bite Mark

After photographing and swabbing, it may be possible to obtain an impression of the bite mark using silicone rubber. It may be also possible to recover an actual, life-size impression of the bite mark. As with other attempts to make an impression, the investigator may need to build a dam around the bite mark to prevent the casting material from running. Before attempting to recover the impression, the bite mark should be carefully cleaned and the area saved. The actual cast should be larger than the bite itself to ensure complete coverage. The impression should then be marked and submitted like any other evidence, beginning with the chain of custody form.

Drawing and "Dusting" the Impression

It may also be possible to make a drawing of the bite mark. The investigator may tape a transparent plastic overlay over the bite so the mark is visible. Then, using a waterproof felt tip marker, trace the outline of the individual marks. It may also be possible to dust the bite mark and then "lift" the mark like a fingerprint. These steps may not provide much useful evidence for court purposes, but they may aid the forensic odontologist, so they should be attempted only after the bite mark has been photographed, swabbed, and an impression made.

Investigation of Suicide

Any death that appears suspicious should be investigated as if it were a criminal homicide; this is particularly true in an apparent suicide. Criminal homicide can be made to look like suicide without a great deal of effort or ingenuity on the part of the killer. In suicides, it is particularly important to investigate the victim's background in order to determine if the death was in fact suicidal. Some of the common reasons why people may be driven to take their own lives are ill health, unhappy relationships, financial setbacks, fear of being alone, or revenge against a loved one. These motives, coupled with physical evidence, may be adequate to justify a finding of suicide by the coroner. Over the years, eight methods of suicide have been identified: firearms, hanging, pharmaceutical, drowning, cutting and piercing instruments, ingestion of poisons and gases, and jumping from high places.

Suicide by Firearm

It is sometimes difficult to determine if a shooting death was a suicide or accidental. The position of the wound will indicate a great deal about the nature of the act. A wound to the temple and the trajectory of the bullet may indicate that a victim placed the weapon to his own head. In addition, it will be essential to perform gunshot residue analysis on the deceased's hands. In one case, a shooting victim was brought into an emergency room with a gunshot wound through his right eye. The man reported that he had been handling a gun when it accidentally discharged. However, after careful interviewing of the victim, he said that he had attempted to kill himself and had flinched at the last instant causing him to shoot himself through the eye. The injury was, in fact, a hesitation wound.

Suicide by Hanging

Another common technique by which to commit suicide is hanging. Inexperienced investigators assume that victims' necks will be broken and that their feet will be off the ground. In most cases the victim will have made some type of device to cut off the blood, and therefore the flow of oxygen to the brain. This is a relatively painless process. Once victims lose consciousness, their weight will fall against the noose or ligature, and the victim will die an asphyxial death. Hanging victims may be found on their feet, on their knees, or in sitting positions. In these cases the force will not be enough to break the victim's neck. When moving the body, it is absolutely essential that the knot on the noose or ligature be recovered intact. The ligature should be left on the victim until it can be removed at the morgue. At that point it should be photographed and then cut off away from the knot. The cut ends should be clearly marked.

Postmortem lividity will be most obvious in the lower portions of the body. Increased blood pressure caused by strangulation may cause petechial eruptions or hemorrhaging on the face, and particularly on the eye. Petechial eruptions appear as small specks on the eyeball or around the mouth.

Suicide by Drugs

Drugs, particularly sleeping pills, such as phenobarbital, have been a means of committing suicide for a number of years. Investigators should follow all the usual steps of a homicide investigation. Friends and relatives of the victim should be interviewed about the victim's background. All physical evidence should be reviewed before concluding that the death was a suicide.

Investigators in cases of this type must be alert to the possibility that deaths resulting from drug overdoses may also be accidental or intentionally administered as a means to commit murder. For example, barbiturates and alcohol are powerful depressants, which when taken together result in a "synergistic" effect leading to death. The investigator may also encounter a phenomenon known as *automatism*. Automatism is an unintentional or accidental overdose. In these cases, the victim takes a sleeping aid and doses off to sleep. The person then wakes up a few minutes later and takes another pill. This process, if repeated often enough, may lead to an accidental fatal overdose.

Suicide by Drowning

Drowning may be an accident, a suicide, or a criminal homicide. It is essential to determine if drowning was the cause of death and if the victim was killed elsewhere and placed in the water. Observations made at the scene and the autopsy report can answer most of these questions. One of the most distinctive characteristics of drowning noticeable at the scene will be white foam around the victim's mouth, which forms as a result of mucus mixing with water.

> **CASE STUDY**
>
> The body of a white female was found in a ditch in a mobile home park. Her nude body was found in about 3 feet of water left from a heavy rain the previous night. The scene was secured and the fire department pumped water from the ditch. No evidence was found at the scene but her clothes were found neatly folded about 200 yards away on the banks of a stream that had been nearly flooded the night before. The autopsy revealed that the water in her lungs was similar to that found in the ditch. A neighborhood canvass revealed that she had been drinking at a party the night before and had become quite intoxicated. She had gotten into an argument with others present and had left during the storm. She had apparently left to return to her home, which was on the other side of the stream. She had taken off her clothing and tried to cross, and was either unsuccessful or changed her mind. She was then unable to find her clothes and became disoriented and fell into the ditch. The case was ruled an accidental death.

Suicide by Cutting and Piercing Instruments

Suicide victims may use sharp-edged or piercing instruments to commit suicide. The most commonly used sharp-edged instrument is a razor blade or knife, but broken glass and electric carving knives have been used. In most cases, the victim will sever the artery in the wrist or throat and bleed to death. In suicides of this type, the investigator may find "hesitation marks" where the victim tried to cut herself but was unable to complete the act, at least at first. Suicides of this type are usually quite grisly, causing investigators to doubt that the act was a suicide. For example, in a small southern town a victim cut his throat by placing his neck down on the blade of a large table saw.

Suicide by Poisons

A variety of substances have been used as poisons. The victim will sometimes use acids and lyes to cause death. When this occurs a number of injuries will be obvious. When a victim ingests a poison, the body will immediately reject it by vomiting. In the aftermath, investigators will find blood mixed with vomit and pieces of the victim's stomach and esophagus. Blisters and burning will be apparent around the mouth. Since death does not occur immediately, the victim may resort to some other means to finish the task.

Poisons are seldom employed as a means to commit murder, although the possibility should never be ruled out, at least initially. In one case a women mixed antifreeze, which contains polyethyleneglycol, into her husband's orange juice over a period of several months, thereby causing his death. As in all unnatural deaths, the pathologist's report is an essential part of the investigation.

CASE STUDY

Poisonings are often accidental. In one case the victim was a teenage male who had a history of drug abuse. The deceased's stepfather worked in a hospital. The stepfather heard that he could purchase antifreeze cheaply from a friend, but he would need to provide his own container. The man took an empty 1-gallon cough syrup bottle from the hospital to transport the antifreeze. The empty bottle was still labeled "cough syrup with codeine." Upon returning home the man placed the gallon jug on a shelf in the garage. The boy, seeing the container, apparently assumed his stepfather had hidden the jug. The boy drank a lethal dose of antifreeze. This story is not that difficult to believe because antifreeze tastes sweet. In many cases, however, poisonings are suicides.

Suicide by Gases

Carbon monoxide is the gas most commonly involved in deaths of this sort. Again, the death can be either intentional or accidental. Faulty vehicle exhaust systems are responsible for a number of accidental deaths each year. When carbon monoxide is used as the means of suicide death, the victim will take steps to ensure that outcome. For example, the victim may run a hose from the tail pipe of an auto to the passenger compartment, where he will sit with the windows rolled up. In other cases, the victim may place rugs under a garage door and sit or lay by the tail pipe. In carbon monoxide deaths lividity is cherry red.

Jumping from High Places

Deaths of this type may be difficult to investigate because it is equally likely that the act could have been an accident, a suicide, or a murder. Investigators need to interview witnesses who saw the victim at or shortly before the time of death.

Suicide Notes

Investigators should look for a suicide note and other indications that the victim had been contemplating taking his or her life. The presence or absence of a suicide note is not definitive evidence of what happened because a person contemplating suicide may not take the time to write a note. In other situations, the victim's friends or family may find the body and alter the scene to make the incident look like an accident to reduce the trauma experienced by the family or other loved ones.

Investigating Child Abuse

Child abuse is among the most difficult crimes to investigate, in part because children are the least capable of all victims to defend themselves, both in and out of court. There are several reasons for this: child abuse victims are often too young both physically and mentally to protect themselves. The crimes of physical and sexual abuse occur in private, where there are no witnesses. Child abusers seldom boast about, or even talk about, their crimes. Youthful witnesses are often viewed by investigators, prosecutors, and juries as less than competent witnesses. One of the most difficult problems is that the criminal investigation is often concurrent with civil legal proceedings, such as a divorce or child custody decision. Investigators may not handle the case well because of lack of experience, lack of interest, or burnout. Finally, one of the most difficult aspects is denial of the fact that child physical or sexual abuse even occurs. For all of these reasons, investigating all forms of child abuse is very difficult.

Indicators of Physical Abuse

Physical abuse is often the easiest form of abuse to recognize because injuries and other indicators are observable. Most states require various professionals, such as health care workers and teachers, to report suspected child abuse. Investigators should err on the side of caution when evaluating a child's injuries. The assistance of medical professionals should be obtained whenever possible. The location and extent of injuries may indicate physical abuse. Investigators may also attempt to obtain the child's medical history to look for patterns of injury or any inconsistencies.

Bruises and Welts

When children fall they often receive abrasions on the elbows, knees, the heel of the hand, and chin; injuries on other parts of the body should be examined with considerable care. Bruises on infants, especially facial bruises and welts may result from pinching, slapping, or bilateral grab marks on the face. Investigators must pay particular attention to bruises on the posterior of the child. These bruises may exhibit unusual patterns from the instrument used, such as a looped electrical cord wire, coat hanger, or belt buckle. In one case, a male infant was pronounced dead on arrival at a nearby hospital. The position of the child's injuries suggested that the child had been subjected to physical abuse. A pathologist examined a bruise on the child's penis and concluded that it resulted from a clothespin being placed on the penis to prevent the boy from wetting his diaper. The body's father later confessed to the crime. A pattern of bruises may also reflect a handprint or may show where a child was gripped tightly by a larger person, such as when holding a child by the arms and shaking him violently. Bite marks may also leave bruises, which may result from bites from other children or be inflicted on the child by an adult as a punishment for biting.

Skeletal Injuries

Lacerations

Lacerations of the lip, eye, ear, or any part of the child's face should alert mandatory reporters and investigators to the possibility of child abuse. Any laceration or abrasion to the child's external genitalia should be investigated and adequately explained.

Burns

Burns are often encountered in child abuse cases. Burns may be of several types, including immersion, cigarette, clothes iron, rope, and dry burns. Burns can be associated with assaults, criminal homicides, or accidents. As always, the investigator's goal is to determine the truth. In these cases, the investigator must determine if the incident was an accident, a punishment, or the result of negligence.

Burns are the most painful of all injuries. Burns damage the skin, the largest organ of the body. The skin is a two-layered organ, consisting of the epidermis and dermis. The epidermis, the upper layer, is thickest over the palms and soles of the feet and thinnest on the abdomen, eyelids, and over the flexor surfaces of the arms. The dermis is the deepest layer of the skin, thickest on the back and thinnest on the eyelids. Burns can cause permanent damage, requiring continuing medical treatment, lack of mobility, and disfigurement, both physically and emotionally. Burns result from thermal energy being applied to the skin. The source of thermal energy can be heated liquids, heated solids, direct flame, and heat conversion from electrical, chemical, and microwave sources.

The seriousness of the injury is determined by a number of factors, including:

- The agent that caused the burn
- The temperature of the agent
- The length the agent was in contact with the skin
- The location of the burn, thicker skin is more resistant to burning
- The age of the child (younger children burn more easily)
- The presence of clothing: clothing may prevent the agent from coming in contact with the skin; conversely, clothing may hold the agent closer to the skin, thus causing a more severe burn

Classification of Burns   Burns are classified as first, second, third, and fourth degree. First-degree burns involve only the top layers of the epidermis. Burns of this type are characterized by redness, with no blisters or infection. Examples of first-degree burns are minor sunburns and superficial scalding from a hot liquid such as coffee.

Second-Degree Burns   Second-degree burns extend into the dermis to some extent. Superficial partial-thickness burns are painful, with blisters. Burns of this type will heal without scarring in about two weeks. Deep partial-thickness burns extend almost through the dermis. Burns of this type are painful but may result in some loss of sensation due to damage to nerve endings. These burns heal slowly over one to four weeks and may leave scars. Without treatment, deep-partial thickness burns may become infected and turn into a full-thickness third-degree burn.

Third-Degree Burns   Third-degree burns result in damage to the entire dermis. The burns may not be painful as a result of damage to nerve endings. Third-degree burns heal slowly and result in scarring; skin grafting is often required. They will not heal properly without treatment. The skin may appear deep cherry red, dry, and leathery. Third-degree burns result from immersion or flame.

Fourth-Degree Burns   Fourth-degree burns extend beyond the subcutaneous tissue. Burns of this type may extend to the bone, joints, or muscle.

Immersion Burns   Most burns to children result from hot liquids, usually hot water. Immersion burns indicate that the child was dunked in a hot liquid. Glove or sock burns occur on the child's hands or feet, and a doughnut-shaped burn will be found on the victim's buttocks.

Immersion burns may be unilateral but are usually bilateral, that is, they appear on both sides of the body. Burns that are bilateral and symmetrical are a strong indication that they were inflicted and intentional. They are often associated with toilet training. Children who have received immersion burns may die of shock or infection. The burn pattern and history of injuries may help determine if the injury was accidental or intentional. The caretaker may often relate that the injury took place in another location and give a story that is inconsistent with the physical evidence. She may also have delayed in obtaining medical assistance, trying instead to treat the injury herself. As always, a complete crime scene investigation should be conducted in a timely manner. Photographs should be taken as the injuries become more apparent or begin to heal. Complete reports should be obtained from all medical personnel.

Splash Burns   Splash burns may result from a child pulling a hot cup of coffee from a table or pulling a skillet from a stove. With splash burns it is difficult to distinguish whether they were accidental and intentional, and other investigative evidence is needed to confirm that a crime has occurred.

Contact Burns   Contact burns may leave the impression of the object that caused the injury. Intentional burns are usually deeper and more regular than accidental injuries. Contact burns are often caused by steam irons, curling irons, and cigarettes.

Internal Injuries

When assessing a child's injury, it is important to consider the injury in relation to the age of the child. Children under the two years old rarely experience accidental internal injuries. In other words, such injuries are likely to be inflicted on a child. If the child is older than two years, the injury could have a plausible accidental explanation, such as being incurred while playing football or landing on a hard object.

Head Injuries

In many physical abuse cases, the head is the injured area. In these cases, injuries may be hidden by the scalp, and there may not be any noticeable swelling. Head injuries may not be immediately apparent but will be observable after two or three days; therefore, the child should be watched and injuries documented with photographs as they appear. Abusers often seek to explain a child's injuries by reporting that the child fell. Certainly falls do cause injuries; however, it is important to remember that falls of less than 6 feet generally cause relatively minor injuries, such as:

· Simple bumps and bruises
· Single simple bone fractures
· Uncomplicated linear skull fractures
· No brain injury, except for mild concussions

While all the injuries mentioned thus far are serious, especially to a conscientious parent, they could occur by accident. Other unexplained injuries should also be investigated as possible abuse. Absence of hair as well as hemorrhaging beneath the scalp may result from violent hair pulling. Serious head injuries usually result from tremendous force being applied to the head, a force equivalent to that experienced when falling 15 to 20 feet; even this force may not result in external bruising or a skull fracture. However, injuries of this sort can result in immediate loss of consciousness, seizures, or death.

Establishing that Child Abuse Has Occurred

The determination of child abuse is usually made when the stories told by the caretaker are inconsistent with the injuries on the victim. In some situations, no explanation is given at all. In other cases, the explanation is inconsistent with the injury based on the child's age and the severity of the injury. The child may accuse one of the parents, especially in custody disputes. An abuser often delays in obtaining medical attention. Suspected abusers should be interviewed at least twice to establish that they tell the same story in the same way each time, and investigators should be alert to inconsistencies.

In addition, investigators should look for other factors associated with abuse, including:

· A recent family crisis or stress
· A triggering event, such as spilling milk, refusing to eat, or toilet training

- An increasing severity of injuries reported over time
- An abuser who was abused as a child
- Social isolation of the family and lack of a support system
- The injured child being taken to a different doctor or hospital after each injury
- An adult making a statement such as, "the child doesn't love," or "she did that to hurt my feelings," or "he is evil"

Indicators of Child Neglect

A crime can be an intentional *act* or an intentional *omission*. Parents are required to provide their children with a reasonable standard of care; that is, they must do their best to provide for the child's physical and emotional health. If they fail to do so, they may be guilty of child neglect. Some of the more common examples of neglect are inadequate supervision, inadequate clothing or hygiene, inadequate medical or dental care, inadequate nutrition, or inadequate adequate shelter.

Battered Child Syndrome

In *Osteal v. McGuire*, the Supreme Court recognized the existence of the battered child syndrome in a criminal. The syndrome may be recognized by repeated acts of intentional trauma inflicted on young children, resulting in injuries that are identifiable as nonaccidental. The child is beaten after little or no provocation. Injuries are most commonly directed at the head. It is common for the victim to have old bruises, especially on the back and buttocks. The victim may have old burns and fractures, and thus the investigator should request x-rays. As in other cases of abuse, the caretaker's story may not be consistent with the physical injuries. The story told by the caretaker may be inconsistent and change as it is retold. He may describe how the child fell from bed, fell from his arms, or fell down the stairs. As mentioned earlier, in these cases the caretaker may delay in seeking medical attention.

Impulse or Anger Homicide

The impulse or anger homicide, as the name suggests, is the result of a sudden act of violent behavior resulting in fatal injuries to a child. The act is often preceded by minor or trivial provocation. The child often appears healthy except for the injury. Again, there may be a delay in obtaining medical attention. The caretaker may avoid contact with medical personnel or leave the emergency room as soon as possible. The caretaker should be interviewed as soon as possible and a story obtained. Because the abuser in this type of act is not an experienced criminal, he or she is more likely to confess than offenders in other types of crime.

Shaken Baby Syndrome

The shaken baby syndrome occurs when a child is held and shaken violently and, in some cases, then struck against a solid object such as a wall or floor. The child is often held by the chest or upper arms, which results in bilateral bruising. In addition, the child may endure rib injuries resulting from chest compression. Children in these cases are usually under one year old, although they may be older. Since the force needed to cause injury is severe, the perpetrator is usually an adult or larger person. Medical findings usually indicate a subdural hematoma and retinal hemorrhaging. The caretaker should be interviewed as soon as possible, and the investigator should obtain a written statement describing the event, thus locking the caretaker into a story.

Munchausen Syndrome by Proxy

Munchausen Syndrome by Proxy (MSBP) is the name given a phenomenon in which a mother harms her child in order to receive attention from various medical and other professional personnel. In MSBP, the child is subjected to repeated medical treatment as the result of a fabricated illness or real injury created by the parent. The parent will deny any knowledge of the cause of the injury or illness. The child usually recovers when kept from the parent for extended periods, or when kept under close observation. The child's mother is responsible in almost every case, and the mother sometimes has some medical training or an illness that provides her with some knowledge of medical procedures. The child's father is almost always absent. The mother does not become upset when the child's illness is not diagnosed, as she does not want the attention to end. In those cases, that have been detected, the mother is usually observed by hospital staff actually attempting to harm the child.

Sudden Infant Death Syndrome (SIDS)

Sudden infant death syndrome (SIDS) is defined as "[t]he sudden unexplained death of an infant one week to one year of age" (Brodeur, Monteleone, 1994, p. 329). In a SIDS case, death remains unexplained after the performance of a complete postmortem investigation including an autopsy, an examination of the scene of death and a review of the case history" (NICHHD, 1989). The unexplained death of an infant is most common among children between the between the ages of two and four months, and 90 percent of cases occur in children less than six months of age. Approximately 60 to 70 percent of deaths occur in male babies, and 30 to 40 percent of deaths are in females. Most SIDS deaths occur in the winter months and are more common in multiple births. The risk of death increases if the mother smokes. Many states have created child death review procedures requiring that the death of a child under a specified age be investigated. These procedures have reduced the number of questions that accompany the unexplained death of a child.

Autopsy

The purpose of an autopsy is to observe and record as soon as possible the minute and gross anatomical peculiarities of the recently discovered dead body as they are observed by a forensic pathologist. (Moenssens, 1986, p. 274)

In cases where there is doubt as to the cause of death, responsible law enforcement officials should insist that an autopsy be performed. Autopsies can provide invaluable information on how an event occurred. Before a body is transported to the morgue or funeral home, it should be placed on a clean white sheet in order to catch anything that might fall from it.

CASE STUDY

Two men held up a "Mom and Pop" grocery store. As the robbers left, the owner picked up a revolver from under the counter and gave chase. As the robbers ran up the street, the owner fired three shots at the robbers and, in his words, "hit one of them in the ass." About 45 minutes later, a patrolman found the body of a man matching the description of one of the robbers lying behind a building a few blocks away. The man had a gunshot wound to the head but was alive at that time. He died shortly after arriving at the hospital. At the autopsy a lead bullet similar to those in the gun used by the old man was removed from the victim's right hip. The other bullet removed from his skull was a copper-jacketed projectile. In this situation, the old man had hit the deceased in the location he described. When the robber was apparently unable to keep up, his associate had shot him in the back of the head and left him.

Autopsies can answer a number of questions, including:

- What was the approximate time of death?
- What was the cause of death?
- Which wound(s) was(were) fatal?
- What type of weapon was involved?
- Did the deceased live after the assault?
- Was the body moved after death?
- Were injuries antemortem or post mortem?
- Are there drugs or alcohol in the victim's body?
- Are there foreign bodies in or on the body?
- Are there defense wounds on the body?

Violent Criminal Apprehension Program

In the 1980s and 1990s approximately 68 percent of criminal homicides were cleared by arrest. Statistically this means that approximately one in three criminal homicides will remain unsolved. Although the complete implications of this figure are not fully understood, experts believe that serial killers may be responsible for a substantial number of these crimes. Investigators may now draw on the resources of the National Center for the Analysis of Violent Crime (NCAVC). The center is located in the FBI's Academy at Quantico, Virginia, and is administered by the Behavioral Science Unit. The Violent Criminal Apprehension Program (VICAP) within the NCAVC is a nationwide data information center charged with the responsibility for gathering, collating, and analyzing information on specific violent crimes. Currently the VICAP is accepting cases that meet the following criteria:

1. Solved or unsolved homicides or attempts, especially those that involve an abduction; are apparently random, motiveless, or sexually oriented; or are known or suspected to be part of a series

2. Missing person, where the circumstances indicate a strong possibility of foul play and the victim is still missing
3. Unidentified dead bodies, where the manner of death is known or suspected to be homicide

The purpose of VICAP is to provide law enforcement agencies with timely information on crimes with similar characteristics in order hasten the identification and apprehension of violent criminals. Investigators may submit the VICAP Crime Analysis Report on crimes that meet the criteria listed above.

VICAP Crime Analysis Report

Investigators working unsolved homicides will be requested to complete a VICAP crime analysis report. From the report, VICAP analysts seek to identify patterns, leads, or suspects by analyzing all available information on:

· *Modus operandi*
· Victimology
· Physical evidence
· Suspect description
· Suspect behavior before, during, and after the crime

Among the more useful services offered through VICAP is the criminal profile (Douglas and Burgess, 1986, p. 9). In the criminal profile, analysts identify the major personality and behavioral characteristics of the offender. The profile is based upon information gathered from the crime(s) committed by offender. The profile usually consists of seven steps:

1. Evaluation of the crime itself
2. Evaluation of the specifics of the crime scene
3. Comprehensive analysis of the victim
4. Evaluation of preliminary police reports
5. Evaluation of the medical examiner's autopsy
6. Development of a profile with critical offender characteristics
7. Investigative suggestions based on the profile

The NCAVC has become a valuable resource for criminal investigators assigned to the investigation of violent crime. As the body information on serial criminals increases, the clearance rate for homicides may improve.

Conclusion

Criminal homicides, murder and manslaughter, have occurred at record rates for the past several years. Statistically, the clearance rate for these crimes is approximately 68 percent. It is essential that investigators use every legal resource available to them to increase the number of these crimes that are solved.

Acknowledgment

Much of the information used in this chapter was obtained from the Medicolegal Death Investigator's School presented by the St. Louis University School of Medicine.

References

Brodeur, A.E., and Monteleone, J.A. *Child Maltreatment: A Clinical Guide and Reference*. St. Louis, MO: G.W. Medical Publishing, Inc., 1994.

Charon, Jacque. *Suicide*. New York: Charles Scribner's Sons, 1972, p. 56.

Crime in the United States, 1995. Uniform Crime Reports. Washington. DC: U.S. Government Printing Office, 1996.

Cupp v. Murphy, 93 S.Ct. 2000, 412 U.S. 291 (1973).

Douglas, John E., and Burgess, Alan E. "Criminal Profiling: A Viable Investigative Tool Against Violent Crime." *FBI Law Enforcement Bulletin* 55(12): 9–13, 1986.

Douglas, John E., Burgess, Ann W., Burgess, Allen G., and Ressler, Robert K. *Crime Classification Manual: A Standard System for Investigating and Classifying Violent Crimes*. New York: Lexington Books, 1992.

Geberth, Vernon J. *Practical Homicide Investigation: Tactics, Procedures, and Forensic Techniques*. New York: Elsevier, 1983.

Howlett, James B., Hanfland, Kenneth A., and Ressler, Robert K. "The Violent Criminal Apprehension Program VICAP: A Progress Report." *FBI Law Enforcement Bulletin* 55(12): 14–22, 1986.

Keppel, Robert D., and Weis, Joseph G. *Improving the Investigation of Violent Crime: The Homicide Investigation and Tracking System*. Washington DC: National Institute of Justice: Research in Brief, August, 1993.

Moenssens, Andre A. *Scientific Evidence in Criminal Cases*, 3rd ed. Mineola, NY: Foundation Press, 1986.

Osteal v. McGuire, 112 S.Ct. 475 (1991).

Perkins, Rollin M., and Boyce, Ronald N. *Criminal Law*, 3rd ed. Mineola, NY: Foundation Press, 1982.

Svensson, Arne, Wendal, Otto, and Fisher, Barry A.J. *Techniques of Crime Scene Investigation*. New York: Elsevier, 1981.

VICAP Crime Analysis Report, Washington, DC, National Center For The Analysis of Violent Crime, Federal Bureau of Investigation, U.S. Department of Justice.

9. Sex Offenses

"Have you any reason to suspect any one of them more than the others?"
Soames hesitated. "It is a very delicate question," said he. "One hardly likes
to throw suspicion where there are no proofs." "Let us hear the suspicions. I
will look after the proofs."

Sherlock Holmes, *The Adventure of the Three Students*, Sir Arthur Conan Doyle

Sex offenses range from vicious acts, such as rape and sodomy, to less serious nuisance offenses, such as indecent exposure. Sex offenses may also include the conduct of mutually consenting adults. Given the delicate nature of so many of these acts, it is essential that any officer charged with the responsibility for investigating crimes of this type be sensitive to the needs of the parties involved as well as the need to determine the truth.

CASE STUDY

Sheriff's deputies were called to a summer church camp to "take a report." Upon arriving, the deputies contacted the camp director, who introduced them to two girls aged 14 and 15. The girls said they had been in the pool taking swimming lessons from a young minister who was a swimming instructor and summer camp counselor. They said that while they were in the water the minister/instructor had repeatedly placed his hands between their legs and on their breasts. The girls said they had been afraid to say anything since they didn't want to "get him into trouble." When asked for his side of the story, the minister, who was unmarried, denied touching the girls or having any other contact with them. Later, another camper said she had heard the girls laughing and talking about how they had "set up the preacher" so they could go home. In another interview, one of the girls admitted that she had gone along with the other girl because she was angry at her parents that they had "stuck her out in the woods" to "get rid of her." The allegation was proven to be untrue. The minister may have been guilty of poor judgment but not a crime. The allegation had very serious consequences for the young man's future.

Difficulties in Investigating Sex Offenses

Sex offenses are some of the most difficult crimes a police officer may be called upon to investigate. The difficulties arise for several reasons. Physical evidence is often lacking or has been destroyed. For example, a rape victim will often shower or bathe as quickly as possible after an attack, thereby destroying evidence. There may also be a lack of corroborating evidence or witness testimony to support a case. In date rapes, for example, the case may well be based on the victim's word versus the defendant's word.

Because of the traumatic nature of the crime, the victim may be unable to give a good description of the assailant. Crimes of this sort often occur in the dark, thereby making an eyewitness identification very difficult, if not impossible. The emotional and mental state of the victim may be a barrier to gaining accurate information about the assailant. The victim will often fear media attention resulting from the assault and be reluctant to cooperate in the investigation. Along with the fear of media attention, the victim may fear ostracism from friends, family, or the community. Finally, the investigating officer's own attitudes toward the case may present a problem. Any experienced investigator knows the difficulty in solving and subsequently prosecuting crimes of this type and may not pursue the investigation with enthusiasm.

Gender of the Sex Offense Investigator

Some departments routinely assign female investigators to work sex offenses under the assumption that women can relate better to the victims of sexual assault. It should be remembered, however, that a trained, sensitive, and motivated investigator of either sex can investigate a sex crime. The victim, whether male or female, is likely to come in contact with males in the criminal justice system, either as prosecutors, defense attorneys, or judges. Victims must begin to deal with males as soon as possible to improve the chances of a successful prosecution and to begin the process of healing both physically and emotionally.

Because of the extreme sensitivity of both the victim and the investigator in these cases, the investigation should be conducted with the utmost professionalism. Sexual assault victims often are reluctant to report and prosecute because they fear the reactions they may receive from police, prosecutors, judges, juries, and even their own friends. An understanding of the delicate nature of sex offense investigations begins with a review of the types of rape and the rape syndrome.

Sex Offenses as Defined by Law

Rape

Rape is usually defined as unlawful sexual intercourse with a female by force or against her will. These terms have specific meanings under the law that may be inconsistent with the common usage of the term.

Unlawful

Unlawful means the act occurred between two unmarried parties. Thus, in many states it is legally impossible for a married man to rape his wife. This requirement has come under attack over the last several years and has lead to the creation of several "marital rape" laws. Under these laws, a married man can be prosecuted for the rape of his spouse. In those states that do not have a marital rape law, a man could be charged with assault and battery, however (Perkins and Boyce, 1982, p. 203).

Sexual Intercourse

Sexual intercourse is sometimes referred to by the common law term, carnal knowledge. Any penetration of the female genitalia of the victim is sufficient to complete this element of the *corpus delicti* of rape. Thus, an emission is not necessary to complete the act.

With a Female

That the victim be a female was a common law requirement and is still a requirement in most states. If the attacker is a male and the victim is a male, the crime will be prosecuted as sodomy, "the abominable and detestable crime against nature" (Perkins and Boyce, 1982, p. 466). Some statutes state that if someone over a specified age, such as 17, has sexual intercourse with someone of the opposite sex who is less than a specified age, such as 14, the act is rape regardless of the "victim's" consent or cooperation. Crimes of this sort are usually defined as statutory rape. Thus an 18-year-old female babysitter who has sexual intercourse with a 13-year-old boy can be prosecuted for rape under these statutes.

By Force or Against her Will

The final requirement to complete the *corpus delicti* of rape is that the act must have occurred by force or otherwise against the victim's will. The victim's resistance may be overcome by physical assault or the threat of assault. In addition, rape is said to occur when the victim is unable to give consent because of limited intelligence or unconsciousness.

CASE STUDY

One rapist would choose his potential victims based on her seemingly limited intelligence. He would lure the victim to an isolated area and rape and sodomize her. His expectation was that the victim would be unable to testify against him. At least six such crimes were committed, until he mistook alcohol intoxication for limited intelligence and attempted to attack a woman, who in turn stabbed him with a pair of scissors. He was arrested when he sought medical attention at a nearby emergency room.

In a 1990 Wisconsin case, a man was found guilty of rape because he had intercourse with a woman who had a multiple personality disorder. The defendant argued that the woman consented to the act and thus no rape occurred. The jury believed, however, that he had taken advantage of the victim's mental state and found him guilty.

Types of Rape

The Power Rape

In all types of rape, it must be remembered that the crime is an act of violence in which the sexual act is only the means to commit the violence. The power rapist seeks to control or dominate his victim. He often stalks his victim, looking for particular characteristics. His goal is to terrorize his victim. If the victim resists, the rapist will escalate the violence to the point of killing the victim. The power rapist may be a serial rapist attacking on a seven- to fifteen-day cycle. When interrogating a power rapist, the investigator should use a friendly, low-key approach,

> **CASE STUDY**
>
> The rapist was a 6'3", 235-pound, 20-year-old male who had recently been cut by the local college football team. He drove around the city until he identified a victim— a young mother who was working in the home until her baby was a few years old. The man gained access to the house by asking to use the telephone. Once inside the man forced the victim to disrobe and raped her at knifepoint. The victim had asked if she could take the baby into another room where she would be safe and the rapist granted the request. After the attack the rapist left in his car. He was arrested later the same day based on the description of his car provided by a witness found in a neighborhood canvass. He was wearing the same clothing he had on at the time of the rape. The man was convicted of rape and armed criminal action and received a 27-year sentence.

Anger Rape

The anger rapist leads what appears to be an otherwise normal life but as pressures begin to build, he will look for a victim on whom to vent his anger. Anger rapists can be as violent as a sadistic rapist, especially if the victim resists. The anger rapist does not operate on a cycle but commits a rape when the pressures and frustrations become too much for him. When interviewing an anger rapist, the investigator should take a business-like approach.

The Sadistic Rapist

The sadistic rapist's motive is to torture or kill his victim. These crimes tend to be extremely brutal and bizarre. Although they are rare and account for approximately 4 percent of all rapes, sadistic rapes have a devastating impact on the community.

Working with the Victims of a Sexual Assault

The investigator must remember that everyone touched by a sexual assault is a victim. The person attacked, either adult or child, has survived a terrible ordeal and must be given help to begin the difficult process of rebuilding her life. The parents of a sexual assault victim are also victims in that they experience guilt because they did not protect their child. Parents will fear that their child will be mentally and physically harmed for life. Husbands and boyfriends of sexual assault victims may find their relationships altered forever by the act.

Rape Trauma Syndrome

Sexual assault victims, particularly rape victims, are likely to experience the *rape trauma syndrome*. The rape trauma syndrome has four distinct phases: acute reaction, denial, anger, and resignation. While attempting to interview a sexual assault victim, the investigator must be aware of the various stages of the rape trauma syndrome and the related reactions of the victim being interviewed.

Acute Reaction Phase

In the acute reaction stage, the victim may be in shock, may appear to be in a trance, may be giddy, or may be crying or hysterical. During the acute stage, the victim may experience sleeping difficulties, including insomnia or nightmares.

Denial Phase

In the denial phase, the victim may appear to be adjusting and resuming a normal life. The victim will show little interest in the investigation and may avoid the investigator. The victim's goal is to forget what happened, and she may even deny that anything occurred.

Anger Phase

In the anger stage of the rape trauma syndrome, the victim's fears, frustrations, and anger emerge. The victim may literally see her attacker wherever she looks. The victim will have a great deal of difficulty sleeping and may experience numerous aches and pains and imagined illnesses. She may call the investigator often about the progress of the case or to report a new suspect. She will often be angry with the police for not making an arrest in the case and will let her dissatisfaction be known.

The victim in the anger stage will also have difficulty with her family and friends. Family members may not understand the victim because, on the one hand, she is saying that everything is fine and, at the same time, she is depressed and prone to lose her temper. Victims in the anger stage of the rape trauma syndrome are the most difficult to deal with.

Acceptance or Resignation Phase

In the final stage of the rape trauma syndrome, the victim accepts the idea that the rape did occur and places the blame on the rapist, where it belongs. The victim's anger is directed at the attacker, and she is now more able to lead a normal life.

Gathering Physical Evidence

One of the difficulties in prosecuting a rape case is the lack of physical evidence. Efforts to protect and preserve physical evidence should begin when the police first learn of the assault. Dispatchers can be trained to advise the victim how to avoid the destruction of evidence. The victim's clothing should be secured as quickly as possible. The victim should also be instructed not to take a bath or shower until a complete examination has been completed. This should include all outer and under garments as well as sanitary napkins and tampons. Experienced investigators often carry a change of clothes with them in the event the victim may not have the opportunity to change. These items of clothing may be made available to a victim, if necessary. As with any physical evidence, maintaining the chain of custody is absolutely essential. Evidence should be air dried in an evidence locker. Any area where the assault may have occurred should be thoroughly searched. Areas such as beds, couches, the back seat of a car, or a floor should be thoroughly searched and vacuumed. A black light can be used to discover semen stain.

Physician's Report

A medical doctor should examine the victim and submit a report. The report should note any wounds to the victim, such as cuts, bruises, abrasions, or irritations. These injuries should be photographed at the time of the preliminary investigation and over the succeeding days to show the seriousness of the injuries as they become more apparent. The doctor should note the presence of foreign material, such as blood, semen, or hair on the genitalia, pubic area, legs, or stomach. The doctor may also take fingernail scrapings from the victim.

The investigator should take hair samples from the victim and the suspect. Samples should be taken from the head, eyebrows, armpits, legs, and pubic area of both parties. Blood samples should also be taken. Since it is now possible to positively identify a person from his or her DNA, blood, semen, or hair may prove to be the key evidence in a case of this type.

Sexual Assault Kit

Many crime laboratories make sexual assault kits available to area law enforcement agencies to facilitate the collection of evidence and thereby increase the likelihood of successful prosecution. Agencies should work with local medical facilities to prevent the destruction of evidence by well-meaning but uninformed medical personnel. Following is a sample checklist for evidence collection in a sexual assault:

- Use the comb provided to collect any foreign pubic hairs that may be tangled in the victim's pubic hair. Place the comb and the hair in the envelope provided.
- Pull several pubic hairs from the victim, seal them in the appropriate envelope, and label them as such.
- Collect fingernail scrapings from the victim using the toothpicks provided and put them in the designated envelopes. Seal the envelopes with tape and mark them as either the right or left hand.
- Draw a tube of blood using the provided purple-top vial. Use this blood to stain the piece of white fabric that is attached to the white card enclosed Allow the stain to air dry before placing it into the evidence collection kit.
- Take a saliva sample from the victim. You may do this by folding a piece of round filter paper in half and having the victim moisten the paper with her saliva. Do not allow the paper to become wadded in the process. Circle the saliva-stained spot with a pencil and allow it to air dry. Place the dry paper in the envelope provided, seal it with tape, and indicate its contents on the outside.
- Recover the victim's clothing if any suspicious dry stains are observed. Place each item in a separate paper bag, seal it, and indicate the contents of each bag.
- Take vaginal smears using the dry cotton swabs provided. Four swab specimens should be taken. Transfer each swab specimen to a slide by smearing. Allow the slide to air dry and place the slide in the envelope provided. Label the slide as a vaginal swab.

- Allow the cotton swab used for the vaginal smear to dry, and then place the swab in the enclosed envelope. Do not dilute the secretions on the slide or smear.
- If necessary, take a rectal smear using a separate cotton swab. Prepare the slide using distilled water as a solvent. Allow the slide to air dry before sealing it in the designated envelope. Label the envelope as a rectal specimen.
- Allow the rectal specimen swab to air dry before placing it in its envelope. Seal and mark this envelope appropriately.

When recovering evidence of sexual assault, the investigator may wish to request the assistance of trained hospital personnel.

Interviewing the Victim

Even well-experienced investigators may be reluctant to interview victims of sexual assault. Any investigator who approaches the interview with sensitivity, compassion, and a commitment to determine the truth can successfully interview a sexual assault victim. The key to the interview is to be honest with the victim. The investigator must explain what the investigation will entail and why various procedures are being followed. The victim does not need to experience any more unpleasant surprises from either the investigator or hospital personnel. The victim should be encouraged to go to a hospital for a pelvic examination and should be told that she will be asked to provide samples of head and pelvic hair as well as nail clippings. She should be advised to take extra undergarments because hers may be taken as evidence.

Victims are often reluctant to go to the hospital, and the investigator may need to explain why the examination is necessary: First, the victim should have any physical injuries treated. Second, the examination is necessary to recover physical evidence. Finally, it is advisable for the victim to be tested for pregnancy and venereal diseases.

In the interview, the investigator should use the cognitive interviewing technique to help the victim recreate the event. Clearly, in many cases the victim will not want to relive the event, but the investigator must obtain her trust and confidence in order to prepare her to participate in a successful prosecution. In addition, the interviewer should determine what the victim was doing in the hours and days prior to the attack.

CASE STUDY

A series of six rapes that occurred approximately two weeks apart had left a community nearly paralyzed. The victims resembled each other in appearance but other than that no other similarities could be identified. Analysis of the *modus operandi* clearly indicated that the rapes had been committed by the same man. The victims were interviewed about their activities prior to the attack. Each was asked to remember every detail, no matter how seemingly insignificant. One victim said she had stopped at a grocery store to make a purchase. Later, another victim recalled stopping at same store. Investigators had what they hoped was the first connection among the victims. The other victims were interviewed again, and each was asked if she had made any purchases before being attacked. Questioning of this type must be conducted carefully to avoid the possibility of suggesting an answer to the victim. Under these circumstances, a defense attorney will try to make the interview appear to be a coaching session in which the police provide the victim/witness with the desired answers. In the interviews, five of the six victims remembered stopping at the store and paying for their purchases with a check. Police determined the approximate time of day the purchase was made and then determined who was on duty at the time. The clerk was identified and his criminal history was checked. It was discovered that the clerk was then on parole from the state Department of Corrections for a rape conviction. The victims then identified the clerk from a photo lineup. He was subsequently arrested and convicted on all counts.

The following questions should be asked to determine the *modus operandi* of the attacker:

- *Location of the attack:* bar, party, residence, school, sporting event, park, etc.
- *Solicited/offered:* food, drink candy, ride, assistance, money, drugs, etc.
- *Suspect's actions:* ripped/cut clothes, took clothes, used lubricant, raped more than once, unnatural sex acts, etc.
- *Telephone:* pulled/cut cord, used cord to tie up complainant, called first, etc.
- *Force:* bound, hit, bit, shot, covered face, choked, cut/stabbed, etc.
- *Characteristics:* body odor, abnormal genitals, ejaculated, unable to achieve erection, etc.
- *Complainant was:* elderly, mentally retarded, intoxicated, physically disabled, juvenile

The interviewer should determine how the act actually occurred and obtain detailed information on the attacker's physical appearance. These are the most difficult questions to ask: Did he have any scars or tattoos? Any genital deformities? Was he circumcised? Did he have difficulty maintaining an erection? Did he ejaculate? Did he demand oral or anal sex? What did he say to the victim? All these questions should be answered if possible.

Finally, the victim should be asked how the attacker left—on foot or in a vehicle? The interviewer should obtain a detailed description of the attacker. It is vital that the interviewer thanks the victim for her cooperation and sees that she is in contact with a trained victim advocate before leaving her.

False Sexual Assault Reports

In sexual assault investigations, as in any type of investigation, some of the cases that come to the attention of the police will be false. The alleged victim will make up a story for any number of reasons, such as to avoid being caught in an indiscreet situation, to gain revenge, or to attract attention. Whatever the motive, the investigator must proceed with the investigation until evidence shows that there is no substance to the charge. A question that is often asked is, "Is it possible to rape a prostitute?" The answer is yes, but any investigator will know the difficulties in building and prosecuting a case of this type before a jury.

CASE STUDY

A patrolman was dispatched to take an assault report. When he arrived he was met by a nearly hysterical woman. After calming her, he asked what had happened. She said that she had been abducted and nearly raped about an hour earlier. The officer then proceeded to interview her in detail about what had happened. She said a man had followed her into the parking lot from a department store. He walked up behind her, took her by the arm, and guided her to a car, a Porsche. He ordered her into the car, slammed the door behind her, and got into the car on the driver's side. He then attempted to pull her clothing off. The officer doubted her story because of the traffic through the particular parking lot that she made reference to and the difficulty of attacking someone inside a small sports car. He then went through the interview again, hoping for more details. Eventually he was able to determine that she had been talking to the man inside the store, and he had invited her to look at his car. She had accompanied him voluntarily to the car. Once in the car, she had kissed him, again voluntarily. She then became nervous that she would not be home when her husband returned from work and attempted to get out, and she was unable to find the door handle. The man then opened her purse and removed her driver's license so he could call her later. In the end, it appeared that the only crime that had been committed was misdemeanor theft of her driver's license.

Obtaining Evidence from a Sexual Assault Suspect

The investigator needs to recover evidence from the suspect as quickly as possible to prevent its loss or destruction. The suspect's clothing, particularly his undergarments, should be seized for laboratory examination. In addition, his clothing may have provided the basis for the arrest because the suspect matched a description put out over the air after the assault.

It may be necessary to obtain a search warrant before recovering some pieces of physical evidence, such as dental impressions and photographs of the suspect's teeth for bite mark comparisons. The investigator may also need samples of head and pubic hair, as well as saliva samples, for comparison with evidence recovered from the victim or the crime scene.

Interviewing the Suspect

As with any interrogation, the interviewer should become completely familiar with all evidence available before initiating the session. In addition, all legal requirements imposed in a custodial arrest situation must be observed. Perhaps the most important preparation the interviewer should make is to prepare himself emotionally for whatever he may hear from the suspect. The interrogator must set aside opinions and attitudes about the crime in order to get the truth. It is vital to avoid injecting personal feelings into the session.

Defenses in a Sexual Assault Case

As in any criminal case, the prosecution needs to anticipate any defense that might be encountered. The most common defenses are that the police identified the wrong suspect, and that, although sexual intercourse did occur, the act was not rape. In the first scenario, the victim can expect to be vigorously cross-examined by the defense attorney in the hope of getting her to make inconsistent statements or to indicate that she is not absolutely sure of the defendant's identity. At this point the defense attorney may seek to introduce evidence of the victim's past sexual conduct and experience. Most states have "rape shield laws," which prevent the use of evidence of past sexual experience in open court unless the judge finds that evidence of this nature is relevant. The trial judge will make this determination in camera, that is, in chambers away from the jury.

Recent advances in DNA research make the possibility of an incorrect identification of the male far less likely. Courts have accepted DNA as positive identification since 1988 (Andrews v. State, 533 S. 2d.841 [1988]).

Date Rape

In the second scenario, the defendant will take the witness stand in his own defense and testify that intercourse did, in fact, occur but that the woman consented. In the absence of any evidence of physical injury, the case will rest on how the jury perceives the credibility of each witness. The "it didn't happen" defense is most often used in "date rape" cases. Occasionally the investigator may request the parties to this type of case to submit to a polygraph in order to get a sense of what happened.

Sexual Abuse

Sexual abuse is often an event more difficult to investigate and prosecute than other types of sex offenses. The reasons for this are similar to those for other sex offenses, with some compounding factors. It is not possible to detect sexual abuse, such as fondling, and sexual intercourse cannot be detected by simply looking at the victim. Allegations of sexual abuse must be taken seriously and investigated to the fullest extent possible.

CASE STUDY

In one case, a patrol officer took an 11-year-old female runaway into custody. As she was being transported to a juvenile detention facility, she asked if her father would be coming for her. The officer asked why she was concerned. She answered that she did not like the things he did to her. He asked her to describe what she meant. She then described oral, anal, and vaginal intercourse. The officer wrote a supplemental report, which resulted in an investigation of the father.

Complete medical examinations must be conducted by trained medical personnel to detect any evidence of sexual abuse. Even trained professionals may not find evidence after injuries have healed. Lack of physical evidence does not, of course, mean that the act(s) did not occur. Investigators should remember several points:

- Fondling, kissing, oral sex, and pornography do not typically result in physical harm.
- Anal intercourse does not necessarily result in physical harm, and resultant redness and swelling may disappear after a few days.
- Minor tears, abrasions, and bruises can heal completely over time.
- Medical evidence can confirm the sexual abuse has occurred, but it does not indicate who caused it. However, increased availability of DNA testing may reduce this problem in the future.

The presence of one or more sexually transmitted diseases may provide some evidence of sexual abuse. However, some diseases are more difficult to detect in young children. Gonorrhea and Chlamydia cannot be detected without a laboratory culture. Even this may not be definitive because Gonorrhea may have been transferred to the child from the mother if the child is under six months of age. Similarly, Chlamydia in a child under two years of age may have come from the mother. The mother should always be tested to determine if she has a sexually transmitted disease in order to rule out that possibility.

Child Sexual Abuse and Pornography

Child pornography is the visual depiction of a child engaged in sexual conduct or the lewd display of the child's genitalia. Much child pornography today is homemade as a result of the availability of inexpensive video recorders. The pornographer may also take Polaroid pictures or use print film if the person has access to film developing laboratories. Photo developing labs are required in most states to inform their local police departments of any suspicious photographs involving children.

Interviewing Children

Interviewing is an essential skill for any investigator. The interviewer must develop the ability to gain truthful information from victims and witnesses of a crime. Nowhere is this more important than when interviewing children. The competency of a child witness is always an issue at trial. Defense attorneys can be expected to cross-examine children vigorously and will raise the issue of suggestibility, that is, that the interviewer planted the idea in the child's mind.

Preparation for the Interview

The interviewer should prepare before talking to the child. He or she should be aware of known facts and circumstances of the case. Questions to be answered should be prepared before the interview begins.

Location of the Interview

The interview should be conducted in private. The room should be quiet and comfortable for the child. The child should be allowed bring a toy or blanket if she wishes to make her feel more comfortable. Of course, it is important for the interviewer to give the child his or her undivided attention.

Taping the Interview

While any interview will be reduced to a report, the interviewer may wish to use a videotape or audiotape. Tapes can be shown to the trier of fact to dispel an allegation that the interviewer led the child to an answer or fabrication.

The Interview

The investigator should begin by introducing herself and then should explain what she will be doing. The child should be given permission to ask for clarification when she does not understand a question or is not sure how to go about answering a question. Interviewers should determine who the primary caretaker is, and where he and/or she was at the time of the abuse. The interviewer must also determine who was in the child's residence at the time the act occurred. Lastly, it is important to learn the names the child uses for her different body parts.

During the interview the following questions should be answered, as appropriate:

- Was there oral, vaginal, penile, or anal contact?
- Was there fondling, penetration, or masturbation?
- What acts did the perpetrator do to the child?
- What acts did the child do to the offender?
- What objects, contraceptives, or lubricants were used?
- Were pornographic pictures or videos shown to the child?
- What did the offender say to the child before, during, and after the act?
- What did the child say before, during, and after the act?
- Was there or is there now any pain, bleeding, or discharge?
- Did the offender ejaculate?
- If the offender ejaculated, where did it occur, when did it occur, and how was it cleaned up?
- Please describe the offender's genitals.
- Please describe the offender's clothing. Did the offender disrobe or stay dressed?
- Describe what happened after the abuse. Were promises or threats made? Did the offender demand secrecy? What were the elements of the secrecy?
- The interviewer should obtain a complete description of the perpetrator, including the name and relationship of the offender to the victim.

As the interview progresses, the interviewer should establish:

- Where the abuse occurred
- How many times the abuse occurred
- How old the child was at the time the abuse began
- When the abuse began
- What time of the day the abuse occurred
- How well the child recalls the incident(s)
- Where, specifically, the abuse occurred—in a house or vehicle?
- What location looked like—furniture, bedding, anything the child can remember
- What the perpetrator specifically said
- Whether anyone else was present and where other members of the household were at the time of the act
- Whether other offenders were involved
- Who first reported the crime and how they became aware of it
- Whether the victim knows of any other victims

Once the interviewer is satisfied that all the necessary questions have been asked, she should close the interview. First summarize what has been heard and ask the child to review what she said. Then ask the child if she might have forgotten anything. The child should be reminded that she can ask questions and should feel free to call the investigator at any time. Finally, thank the child for her help.

Interviewers should prepare themselves emotionally before a potentially difficult interview. Specifically keep in mind the following points:

· Don't skip the introduction.
· Remember that children have short attention spans, so the interview should be kept moving.
· Don't assume that you understand the child's emotions by saying such things as, "I know this is embarrassing," or "I know you are scared."
· Don't touch the child unless she requests it.
· Don't assume the child wants the offender to be punished.
· Let the child tell the story in her own words; don't lead her.
· Don't pressure the child to tell her story; let her tell the story when she is ready.
· Don't rush through the details, especially when the child is describing the sexual contact.
· Do not become emotional and show anger or revulsion.

Search Warrants

Because child abuse—physical, emotional, and sexual—is one of the most difficult crimes to investigate and prosecute, investigators should use all investigative techniques available, including search warrants. Search warrants can be used to recover physical evidence from the crime scene, such as the suspect's or child's underwear, blood, hair, camera or video equipment, and DNA evidence. They can provide information to corroborate the child's story by describing the suspect's dwelling and may even lead to the discovery of other victims and suspects. Search warrants can also be used to recover contraband, such as drugs, weapons, and child pornography.

Move quickly to obtain a search warrant because evidence in cases of this type can be moved or destroyed easily. Attempt to obtain consent to search if you think you may not be able to obtain a search warrant or it is necessary to move before a warrant can be issued. Of course, the search investigators should be both photographed and videotaped. Documenting the scene in this way creates a permanent record of the scene for later use.

The Child Victim as a Witness

Testifying in court can be a terrifying experience for a child. If a child is made to confront the person who abused her, it can cause the experience to be even more devastating. For these reasons, the courts have wrestled with how to protect the defendant's Sixth Amendment right to confront his accusers while still making it possible for the victim to testify. The Supreme Court has provided guidelines governing the circumstances under which the victim and the defendant may both, to some degree, be protected. First, the trial court judge must determine if the witness is competent.

Child Witness Competency

Juries tend to be inherently supportive of child witnesses. This attitude is supported by research that shows children are truthful about sexual abuse (McGough, 1994, pp. 251–252). In addition, a child's ability to accurately describe sexual activity beyond his or her years is an indicator of the child's reliability (United States v. Dorian [1986]). At the same time, the trial judge must determine that the child can understand his or her obligations as a witness before the child's testimony can be considered proof beyond a reasonable doubt.

The next issue is whether or not the accused must actually be allowed to confront the accuser in these cases. This was discussed in *Coy v. Iowa*, 487 U.S. 1012, 108 S.Ct. 2798 (1988), and *Craig v. Maryland*, 497 U.S. 836, 110 S.Ct. 3157 (1990). In *Coy*, the defendant was charged with sexually molesting two 13-year-old girls. They were the only witnesses against him. The defendant requested a jury trial. An opaque screen was placed between the witnesses and the defendant in the courtroom. The judge and jury were able to see both the witnesses and the defendant. Justice Scalia, writing for the majority, wrote that the confrontation clause of the Sixth Amendment requires a face-to-face meeting between the accusers and the accused.

In *Craig v. Maryland*, the Court once again considered the scope of the confrontation clause. In a five to four decision, the Court held that the Maryland statute that authorized judges to allow child witnesses to testify via closed circuit television did violate the defendant's right to confront her accusers. Under the Maryland law, if the judge determines that the child would undergo serious emotional stress such that the child could not communicate, then the judge could authorize the use of television. The witness, the prosecutor, and the defense attorney were with the witness while the judge, the jury, and the defendant remained in the courtroom. The accused could not see the witness; however, she could communicate with the defense attorney at all times during the examination of the witness.

In *Craig*, the defendant was the operator of a preschool. She was prosecuted for crimes against Brooke, a six-year-old. There were, however, other children who testified against the defendant. Brooke's therapist testified that the child feared retaliation by the defendant and that the presence of the defendant would make it difficult for Brooke to testify. She further stated that Brooke became so distraught that she had difficulty breathing. Experts testified that other children would also have difficulty testifying. The trial judge ruled against placing the children on the stand in front of the defendant and that Brooke could testify via closed circuit television.

Clearly, under *Coy* the judge's decision should be reversed; however, Justice O'Connor, writing for the majority, stated that the "central concern" of the confrontation clause was the right of cross-examination. She noted also that a strict interpretation of the confrontation would eliminate many of the exceptions to the hearsay rule. She wrote that the confrontation clause is satisfied when four conditions are met:

1. The physical presence of the witness
2. The understanding of the oath
3. The opportunity to cross-examine
4. Observation of the demeanor by the trier of fact

Consideration of these factors would ensure that the defendant's right to confront the accuser would be protected. She went on to write that confrontation was preferred, but not absolutely required.

As a result of *Coy* and *Craig*, a trial court judge must determine if the child will be further traumatized by taking the stand in front of the alleged abuser. If so, the judge can order the use of television or perhaps some other technique to screen the child from the alleged attacker. The decision cannot be made solely based on a statute, however. The decision must be made on a case-by-case basis, such that the rights and needs of both parties are taken into consideration.

The prosecutor will be called upon to argue that the witness should not be required to confront the defendant. The investigator can help the prosecution by gathering evidence of the following facts:

· Reactions of the victim to the perpetrator on prior occasions. This is particularly useful when the child has actually confronted the defendant; the prosecutor will have some idea of how the child will react to the defendant.
· How the child reacted when the topic of testifying was discussed in therapy or in the home.
· Whether the child shows signs of anxiety or stress as the date to testify approaches. Parents and caregivers should be interviewed to monitor the child's emotional state.
· The condition of the child's mental health. Opinions on these issues may be obtained from interviews with the child's psychiatrist or psychologist.
· Whether any threats have been made against the child, a parent, or a caregiver. The defendant or his associates may attempt to intimidate the child to prevent her from testifying.
· How a face-to-face confrontation with the child might affect the child's ability to testify. In other words, will the child panic or withdraw on the witness stand?
· The results of any psychological tests conducted to evaluate the child's trauma. (Myers, 1992)

The investigator will need to provide information on all of these matters, and it must be made known to the prosecutor.

Conclusion

Sexual assaults are among the most difficult crimes an investigator will encounter. The difficulties include societal attitudes, investigator attitudes, and the lack of evidence. These problems, however, cannot be allowed to prevent investigators from documenting every aspect of the case as completely as possible in an effort to prosecute sexual predators.

References

Andrews v. State, 533 S. 2d. 841 (1988).

Burgess, Ann Wolbert, and Holstrom, Linda Lytle. "Rape Trauma Syndrome." *American Journal of Psychiatry* 131:981, 1974.

Coy v. Iowa, 487 U.S. 1012, 108 S.Ct. 2798 (1988).

Craig v. Maryland, 497 U.S. 836, 110 S.Ct. 3157 (1990).

Hazelwood, Robert R., and Burgess, Ann Wolbert. *Practical Aspects of Rape Investigation: A Multidisciplinary Approach*. New York: Elsevier Science, 1987.

Hazelwood, Robert R., and Warren, Janet. "The Criminal Behavior of the Serial Rapist." *FBI Law Enforcement Bulletin* 59(2): 11–17, 1990.

International Association of Chiefs of Police, *Interviewing the Rape Victim: Training Key # 210*. Gaithersburg, MD, IACP, 1974.

Lanning, Kenneth V., and Hazelwood, Robert R. "The Maligned Investigator of Criminal Sexuality." *FBI Law Enforcement Bulletin* 57(9):1–10, 1988.

McGough, Lucy S. *Child Witnesses: Fragile Voices in the American Legal System*. New Haven & London: Yale University Press, 1994.

McIlwaine, Blaine D. "Interrogating Child Molesters." *FBI Law Enforcement Bulletin* 63(6):1–4, 1994.

Myers, J. *Evidence in Child Abuse and Neglect Cases*, Vol. 1, 2nd ed. New York: Wiley Law, 1992, p. 60.

Perkins, Rollin M., and Boyce, Ronald, N. *Criminal Law*, 3rd ed. Mineola, NY: The Foundation Press, 1982.

United States v. Dorian, 803 F. 2d. (1986).

10. Robbery, Burglary, and Stealing Investigation

"Come Watson Come!" he cried. "The game is afoot. Not a word! Into your clothes and come!"

Sherlock Holmes, *The Adventure of the Abby Grange*, Sir Arthur Conan Doyle

Legal Elements of Robbery

Robbery is stealing from the presence of another by force. Thus, the investigator most be prepared to prove all the elements of the crime of stealing, theft, or larceny plus the added element of force. The question that sometimes arises is, "How much force will be necessary to change a theft to robbery?" Clearly, when the assailant uses a deadly weapon or dangerous instrument, then the act is robbery. For example, when the assailant takes property from another at the point of a gun or with a knife or galvanized steel pipe, then the *corpus delicti* of robbery are there. In other cases, what began as a purse snatch may become a robbery. For example, an elderly woman may see a young thief running toward her. As he approaches she may tighten her grip on the shoulder strap of her purse to prevent the thief from taking it. When the purse-snatcher then tries to wrench the purse from the victim, he pulls her from her feet, causing knee and head injuries. This act should be prosecuted as robbery.

The 1998 Uniform Crime Reports provide figures on the how robberies are committed:

- 38.2 percent involved a firearm
- 8.8 percent involved a knife or cutting instrument
- 13.4 percent involved some other type of weapon
- 39.7 percent were strong-armed robberies (mugging) (Federal Bureau of Investigation, 1996, p. 29)

Weapons other than firearms or knives could be bricks, bottles, or some other blunt instrument. In approximately 38 percent of robbery cases, the robber had no weapon, but relied on brute force and violence to accomplish the robbery.

CASE STUDY

A series of brutal robberies occurred in which the victims were seriously injured by the assailant. The crime was staged by the perpetrator, who requested a cab to pick up a fare at an isolated location. The passenger/robber then gave an address to the driver. The address was always another isolated location. When the driver arrived at the destination, the robber indicated that he had only a large denomination bill, which required change. During the delay, the robber, a large man, dragged the driver from the cab, violently threw him to the ground, and then kicked and stomped him until he was unable to defend himself. In this case the robber wore cowboy boots with high heels, which were used to inflict serious injuries to the victim's face.

Profile of the Robber

What kinds of people commit robbery? Robbers tend to be young: Sixty-four percent of robbery suspects arrested in 1996 were under 25 years old. Robbery is almost exclusively a male activity, with 91 percent of those arrested being male. Fifty-nine percent of arrested robbers were black, 39 percent were white, and the remainder were from all other ethnic groups (Federal Bureau of Investigation, 1999 p. 31). Knowledge of the types of people who tend to commit robberies may provide additional evidence to justify an investigative detention or arrest.

Developing a profile of a robbery or a pattern of robberies can be as valuable as the profile of the robber. For example, some bank robbers may select banks that are near major thoroughfares or are in isolated areas to facilitate their escape. By the time the police can respond and organize a search, the robber can be miles away. Robbers may examine a possible robbery location, or "case it" prior to selecting a suitable victim or location. They will be looking for various security precautions, such as security guards, cameras, volume of customer traffic, and number of personnel on duty. Robbers are less likely to select targets that may have a number of potential witnesses. For example, convenience stores that have more than one clerk on duty at all times and stores that have video games that are used by customers late at night are less likely to be robbed. Robbers often select buildings that have no windows facing a street or windows that are covered. In this situation, witnesses cannot see the crime occur and victims cannot see accomplices or escape vehicles. Experienced robbers tend to use a stolen car in the commission of the crime anyway. Robbers may select only female victims, either because they present less of a threat of resisting the robber or because they may also be targets of opportunity for a sexual assault. If a robber has had particular success with a certain robbery in terms of financial gain or ease, he may rob the same location more than once.

CASE STUDY

In a small town in the rural Midwest, the same robber robbed the same bank four times in four years. The crimes were linked by the suspect's *modus operandi*. A suspect was identified by information provided by an informant. The suspect was ultimately arrested as a result of the investigator's knowledge that he was a stock car racing fan. The suspect's photograph was shown to vendors and concessionaires at racetracks. A reward was also offered for information leading to capture of the suspect. Ultimately, he was arrested at a racetrack in an adjoining state.

Robbery is a crime of violence in which the actor enjoys the thrill of controlling the victim. Senseless violence is often associated with armed robbery. For example, in a midwestern city an elderly widow was robbed and beaten in her own home. The robber severed her ring finger with a knife when he was unable to pull her wedding ring off.

Interviewing Victims and Witnesses

One advantage for the investigator in a robbery investigation is that there is usually a living witness who can provide at least some information about the suspect. The investigator must have the patience to walk victims through the interview slowly, encouraging them to remember as many details as they can. The cognitive interview may be particularly useful when interviewing a robbery victim. It is important to be sensitive to the victim's fears, both real and imagined. Police officers, who are taught to believe they can protect themselves in all types of difficult situations, may sometimes not fully understand how a victim feels. The feeling of being at the mercy of another person can be devastating and can take months or even years to recover from. Investigators should conduct themselves in a thoughtful yet professional manner.

Types of Robbery

Robbers tend to select particular types of targets. In some cases, the robbery victim may be the unfortunate "target of opportunity" selected by a mobile bandit armed with a "Saturday night special." Other robberies may be carried by experienced criminals who are following out carefully developed plan. Generally robberies tend to be aimed at specific types of objects or victims: commercial, residential, people on the street, and vehicles.

Commercial Robberies

Commercial robberies usually occur in business establishments and banks. They are often aimed at small businesses, such as convenience stores, liquor stores, gas stations, restaurants, and bars. The robber may select targets at times when there are few customers in the business, at late hours, to reduce the possibility of later being identified. This situation sometimes leads to the murder of the only witness who could identify the robber.

Bank Robbery

Bank robbery is thought of as being the work of professional criminals who carry out carefully conceived plans. To some extent this remains true, but because most banks and savings and loans have security devices, they are not as attractive targets as they once were. Today, bank robberies are often an act of desperation or impulse. For example, in one bank robbery the robber was apprehended a block from the bank he had robbed. He had forgotten where he had parked his car. When he was later interviewed, he reported that he had lost his job and, consequently, his family health insurance. His wife and children had serious, long-term illnesses, which had resulted in large medical bills. He had concluded the only option left to him was to rob a bank.

That bank robbers may be impulsive does not mean they are less dangerous than other types of robbers. Quite the contrary, since they have been driven to this point, they may, in fact, be more dangerous than other, more rational criminals.

Most bank robberies involve taking money at the teller's window; seldom today does a robber attempt to get money from the safe. When the safe is the target, the robber will strike early in the morning or late in the day, when there are fewer customers in the bank. More experienced bank robbers may use a holdup note rather than drawing attention to their crime by loud demands and threats. They will also take the note with them to avoid leaving evidence at the scene. When an experienced bank robber uses a car, it is usually a stolen vehicle.

Residential Robberies

Residential robberies are sometimes referred to as *home invasions*, a name that, in part at least, captures the victim's sense of being violated. Occasionally the robbery may be an unanticipated result of a burglary.

CASE STUDY

A young woman returned home from her 4 p.m. to 12 a.m. job. After she changed into the pajamas, she went to the closet to hang up her clothes. Upon opening the door she found a man, apparently a burglar, standing there. He had been inside the apartment when she had returned home and had hidden in the closet until she had opened the door. He slashed at her with a knife and she fainted. He then removed a necklace from around her neck, thus making the crime a robbery. As is often the case in a robbery, the victim was unable to provide a good description of the robber or to pick him from a photo lineup. No arrest was made for these crimes.

In actual home invasions, the robber will gain entry into the house by force or trickery. For example, he may claim to be a deliveryman or utility meter reader. As in any robbery, the object is immediate financial gain, although robbers may enjoy the feeling of power and control they temporarily have over their victims.

Street Robberies

Street robberies or "muggings" are crude, vicious crimes. Often they are little more than a robber confronting a victim and demanding money. In other cases, the victim may be assaulted to overcome or prevent resistance. These crimes may involve the use of a weapon, usually a rock, bottle, or brick.

Vehicle Robberies

Recently police departments in several cities have reported an increase in vehicle robberies or "car jackings." The object of the robbery is to obtain an expensive automobile, which can then be handled like any other stolen vehicle. Unlike traditional auto theft, however, where the victim steals the car under concealment, the robber, or car jacker, takes the car directly from the driver by force. As in any robbery, resistance by the victim will likely be met with further violence. Car jacking may be solved by having officers do thorough canvasses of the area where the crime occurred and where the suspected perpetrator may live. The car jacker may actually want to be seen in the stolen car. It may be viewed and used by the thief as a "trophy," a symbol of his prowess as a car thief that he wants to show off. This is a rather chilling idea, in that the car jacker either expects nothing to happen as a consequence of his actions or does not fear any consequences of his actions.

Determining the Robber's *Modus Operandi*

When investigating a robbery, it is particularly important to examine the perpetrator's *modus operandi*. Robbers tend to be habitual in their performance of a crime. The investigator should begin the investigation by determining the suspect's actions prior to and during the robbery. While no list of suspect actions is exhaustive, several types of action may be identifiable. For example, the investigator should ask if the robber engaged in any of the following actions:

1. Did the robber physically assault the victim before or during the robbery?
2. Did the robber bind or otherwise restrain the victim?
3. Did the robber demand a particular item, such as jewelry or drugs?
4. Did the robber ask for cigarettes or beer, or some other type of merchandise before or during the robbery?
5. Was the robbery a shoplift or purse snatch that became a robbery when the victim resisted?
6. Was prostitution involved?
7. Did the robber use a lookout or was he acting alone?
8. Did the robber use distinctive word or actions?
9. Was the victim sexually assaulted?
10. Did the robber use a stolen vehicle?
11. Did the robber fire shots during the robbery or as he was leaving the scene?

This list of actions taken by a robbery suspect is not exhaustive, but it provides a starting point for an investigator.

The robber's *modus operandi* may also be determined by establishing how the suspect made contact with the victim. For example, the robber may:

1. Appear to need help for a stalled vehicle
2. Ask for a ride
3. Request information, while appearing to be lost
4. Ask to use the telephone
5. Request money
6. Request or offer sex
7. Rip off drugs

Instructions given to the robbery victim may also be of value in establishing a robber's *modus operandi*. For example, the robber may order the victims to lie down or sit on the floor. He may order the victims to go into a bathroom, closet, or cooler. The robber may order the victim to go to the rear of the store building. The victim may be forced to disrobe, either to enable the robber to sexually assault the victim or to make it more difficult for the victim to look at the robber or summon help. Finally, the robber may force the victim to place money or other items in a bag or sack.

CASE STUDY

In a series of robberies, a robber entered a convenience store late at night when there were few, if any, customers. The robber pulled a gun on the clerk and forced him to lock the doors. At that time, the robber ordered the clerk to remove the money from the register and place it in a bag from under the counter in the store. The clerk was then taken to the back of the store, where his hands and feet were taped together. Tape was then placed over the victim's mouth and wrists. The robber threaded a piece of chain through the tape on the victim's wrists and looped the chain over a water pipe on the back wall of the store. The chain was tightened until the victim was pulled up with his arms behind him, leaving only his toes on the floor. The chain was then secured with a padlock taken from a display in the store. This was a particularly cruel crime, in that the victim was left in this excruciatingly painful position until someone unlocked the door and let the victim down. The suspect in this case was later determined to be a former employee of the convenience store chain.

Robbers may also select particular types of victims or certain times and locations to commit crimes. For example, victims are vulnerable while they are opening or closing businesses. Robbers may also victimize certain types of victims:

- The mentally ill
- Persons with disabilities
- Intoxicated victims
- Victims who are alone
- Females
- The elderly
- Victims who have been gambling
- Prostitutes

Use of Informants

Robbers often brag about their exploits, thus making informants particularly valuable in this type of investigation. Occasionally the viciousness of an attack will cause informants to assist the police, as in the convenience store robberies just described. Robbery investigators must be familiar with the means by which to take advantage of all types of information provided by informants.

Arresting Violent Felons

Robbery detectives were once identifiable because they frequently carried two handguns. In this manner, old-timers recognized the potential for violence that has always existed when attempting to arrest a violent felon such as an armed robber. Arrests of a violent felon generally occur in two situations: when officers stake out a potential robbery scene and when they have an arrest warrant for a suspect. In either situation, the safety of the officer and the public are the foremost considerations.

The Stakeout

Stakeouts usually occur when police have a tip that a crime is likely to occur at a specific location or when crime-analysis pattern-identification information leads them to believe that a crime may occur at one or more potential targets. In the case of a tip, it is advisable to substitute an undercover police officer in place of a potential victim, such as a clerk or salesperson. Trained police officers are better prepared to deal with dangerous situations. In addition, police have both an ethical and legal obligation to protect innocent persons in situations where they might be harmed. In *United States v. Watson*, the Supreme Court held that police do not need an arrest warrant to apprehend a suspect who commits a crime in a public place. Thus, if police actually observe a robbery of a liquor store, for example, they may take the suspect into custody as soon as it is safely possible to do so.

When a suspect is identified after the robbery has taken place, police need to make the arrest as soon as possible. As soon as the suspect is known, police obtain an arrest warrant for that individual. Legally, the officer's actions are guided by two cases, *Payton v. New York*, 445 U.S. 573 (1980) and *Steagald v. United States*, 451 U.S. 204 (1981). In *Payton*, the Court held that police must, in the absence of exigent or emergency circumstances, obtain an arrest warrant for a suspect before they may enter a private residence to make a felony arrest. In *Steagald*, the Court ruled that an arrest warrant does not authorize police to enter a third party's home to make a felony arrest. Thus, if police believe that a suspect can be found in a residence other than that of the suspect, they must obtain a search warrant to enter the other residence to arrest the felon.

Arrest Tactics

When law enforcement officers make an arrest, particularly a felony arrest, the potential for violence exists. To reduce the possibility of injury to or death of anyone involved, it is essential to prepare for any foreseeable consequences. At a minimum, attempt to determine the floor plan of the structure where the suspect is thought to be in order to enter as quickly and effectively as possible. Planning should include a discussion of:

1. Equipment needed, such as raid jackets, ram, weapons, flashlights, body armor, first aid kits, etc.
2. Where the suspect will be taken after the arrest
3. What to do with third parties, such as a spouse and children
4. Where the closest medical facilities are located

Legal Aspects of Burglary

Burglary is one of the most common felonies committed in the United States. In 1999, 2,099,739 burglaries were reported to the FBI. Estimated dollar loses associated with burglary run upwards of millions of dollars per year. Burglary can have a profound psychological impact on its victims. The burglar may have violated the victim's most intimate space. It is common for patrol officers, when investigating a burglary, to hear the victim ask if the officer believes that the crime was committed by youth or "kids." It may somehow be comforting for the victim to think that the intruder was a child and therefore less likely to be a threat to the victim. The thought of an adult entering and violating the victim's privacy and potentially attacking her is terrifying.

The common elements of *burglary* are as follows:

- The breaking
- and entering
- of an inhabitable structure
- with the intent to commit a crime therein.

Under common law, the additional element that the act occurs "in the night-time" was also required. Today, most modern statutes have eliminated the requirement, although some jurisdictions make the punishment more severe if the act occurred during the hours of darkness.

Breaking

Breaking refers to making forcible entry into the structure. The most common means used to gain entry are pry bars, screwdrivers, channel locks, vice grips, and pliers. Under contemporary case law, forced entry is not required. For example, placing tape over the bolt in a doorknob or simply entering through an unlocked door are enough to complete the element of entering.

The element of breaking may also be completed by a "constructive" break, in which the defendant did not use force to gain entry, but rather secreted himself somewhere in the building or used some type of ruse to gain entry. Under Missouri law, for example, a burglary may be committed if the person "enters" or "remains" in the structure.

Entering

To satisfy the element of entering, the prosecution must show that some part of the suspect's body broke an invisible plane surrounding the structure. Thus, simply raising an unlocked window and removing an object completes the elements of breaking and entering.

Inhabitable Structure

In order for a burglary to occur, the breaking and entering must be of an inhabitable structure. In most cases, the structure will be a building of some sort, such as a house or office building.

Intent to Commit a Crime

Finally, the defendant must be shown to have entered the structure with the intent to commit a crime. It is not uncommon to have transients break into buildings seeking shelter during inclement weather. If these persons are apprehended while in the building, they may be guilty of trespass, but not burglary. In some jurisdictions, the illegal entry must have been made for the purpose of committing a felony. Thus, if the person breaks and takes a small amount of property, the appropriate charge will be trespass and stealing. In most states, however, the commission of any crime is sufficient to complete this element.

Burglaries are often categorized as first and second degree, or simple and aggravated, burglary. In these cases, all the elements of burglary are present plus the additional element that a burglary occurred while the structure was occupied or the burglar was armed. Of course, the burglar had to be apprehended to determine if he was armed. The risk of death or injury to an innocent victim in these situations calls for more severe punishment upon conviction.

Elements of Burglary

Burglar's Tools

Possession of burglar's tools is usually a felony. In some jurisdictions, it is necessary to arrest the burglar in the act of committing a burglary, actually using the tools, in order to successfully prosecute the individual. In some states, it may be possible to prosecute an individual in possession of instruments that have been modified for use in a burglary.

Some of the more common burglar's tools are pry bars, cold chisels, punches, axes, glasscutters, pliers, and vice grips. One of the best indicators that tools have been used for burglary are finding tools such as a sledge hammer with its handles sawed off and taped for use in close quarters. Power drills, various types of tape, and acetylene torches are also widely used by safe burglars.

Modus Operandi

The identification of a unique *modus operandi* may be particularly useful in burglary investigation. When completing the preliminary investigation, the patrol officer should take particularly care to obtain answers to the following questions:

- Where did the burglar gain entry? Through the front, rear, or side of the building; through a window, a sliding glass door, the wall, an open door, a duct, or vent?
- Where did the burglar leave the structure?
- How did the burglar gain entry?
- What did the burglar do in the structure?
- Where was the victim when the burglary occurred?

Points of Entry and Exit

The investigator should begin his investigation by determining where the burglar gained entry to the building. Did the perpetrators enter through the front, rear, or side of a building? Did they come in through a frame door, window, sliding door, through a duct or vent, through an adjacent building, or through the wall? Burglars will also gain entry through the roof of a building or through an open garage door. The same questions should be answered when determining how the burglar left the building. Did they go out the same way they went in, or did they leave by some other route?

How Did the Suspect Gain Entry?

The investigator will next attempt to determine how the burglar gained entry. One of the simplest is a "smash and grab." In this type of burglary, the perpetrator uses a brick or garbage can or whatever item is available, throws it through a window or door, scoops up whatever is within reach, and flees immediately. A more experienced burglar makes less noise when gaining entry. He may break out or cut a small pain of glass in order to unlock a door from the inside. The burglar is vulnerable at this point, as his attention is focused on getting into the building. He may cut himself when removing shards of glass from a windowsill, or he may leave fingerprints on the glass as he pulls the glass from the frame. It is very important to examine pieces of glass for blood or prints, and to note whether the glass was inside or outside the building.

A burglar may pry or "jimmy" a door. In this type of burglary, it is particularly important to look for tool impressions left by the prying device that might be recovered or cast for later comparison. In some cases, the burglar removes an obstacle, such as an air conditioner or exhaust fan, or a door panel or louver.

When there are no signs of forced entry, this may indicate the burglar entered through an open or unlocked door. This is a common means of entry in rural areas. This may also indicate that the burglar had a key to the building. In the latter case, present and former employees and everyone who had access to the keys should be investigated. If there is no evidence of forced entry, it may mean the burglar hid somewhere in the building.

The instrument used by the burglar to gain entry will reveal something about his *modus operandi*. Did he use a key, prying tool, saw, drill, bolt cutters, or chopping tool? Did he use channel locks, vice grips, or did he tape the bolt with masking or electrical tape?

Actions of the Suspect at the Scene

The investigator needs to determine what the suspect did once inside the scene. Some burglars ransack the building and engage in senseless destruction of the building's contents. They may spend time at the scene looking through the building and perhaps eating or drinking. If this is the case, it is important to search for fingerprints and to allow wet items, such as glasses or beer and soda cans, to air-dry in the hopes of recovering fingerprints. Conversely, it is important to determine if a burglar wiped the scene clean of prints before leaving.

If the burglar knew of hidden places in a house or building where valuables are kept, this suggests that perhaps a relative or former employee committed the crime. In a residential burglary in a rural area, a burglar removed the cover from a hidden compartment in a wall of the victim's home. The victim kept his firearms hidden there. Unfortunately, it was later found that the victim liked to brag about the compartment at a local restaurant, thus making his secret public knowledge.

Occasionally a burglar may defecate at the scene. The reasons for this are unclear, but it is possible that under the stress of the moment a burglar may lose control of his bowels and be forced relieve himself at the scene. Another explanation is that the burglar may be showing his contempt for the victim or society as a whole. For example, in cases where the suspect defecates, the burglary is often characterized by extensive property damage. In one case, the burglar defecated in the center of a queen-sized bed and in another the burglar defecated in women's purses.

Noting what the burglar took may be valuable in identifying his *modus operandi* and will certainly increase the chance of tracing stolen property. The officer needs to gather as much detailed information as possible regarding the items taken so that this information may be entered into National Crime Information Center's (NCIC) database.

Victim's Actions

Intentionally or unintentionally, a victim may contribute to the commission of a crime. A burglar may have been watching the victim to determine where the victim goes at certain times. For example, a burglar may commit her crimes while victims are at school, at work, or out of town. If a pattern is identified, it may be appropriate to target particular suspects or to stake out specific types of locations where the burglar may attack.

Confession of an Old-Time Burglar

There are individuals who tend to commit particular types of crime. These people become known for their expertise as burglars, robbers, or car thieves. Following is the transcript of the confession of a career criminal who had spent much of his adolescence and adult life either committing burglaries or serving prison sentences for burglary. His confession, while full of self-pity, provides some insight into how burglars operate. It was dictated to a detective after uniformed patrol officers arrested the burglar in a building:

> I would like for you to write a statement for me, as I tell you. It seems like this thing is done on an impulse, most or all of the time when I have been drinking. When I'm sober I'm scared. The thing of it is, when I get drunk, I get lonely and melancholy, with the attitude, if they catch me, they catch me, it they don't, they don't. There are times I go a long time without "going in anywhere." The 10 years I was married I never thought of breaking in any place. Since my divorce two and a half years ago, the majority of my burglaries have been here on the Cape. I have done security work, and I know the Cape has the poorest individual building security I have ever seen. There are always windows left open, doors unlocked, and one time I found the key in the front door of the Dairy Queen. Louvered windows provide no security. Martin Oil, the louvered windows weren't closed all the way. Cape merchants are obviously lax in the security of their businesses. Some of the banks, the mercantile in the plaza, you walk in, the cashier's back is to you, and the money is within reach. The first bin is $100 bills. Jim Dandy's bar, you can crawl under and with a keyhole saw, go through the floor so easily. I will gladly go through the reports with you, and you can list the burglaries I did. I'll tell you how I got in and everything. Not only am I doing this to help me mentally, to get it off my chest, I want to help you to cut down on burglaries. Maybe it can help someone like me. If it weren't easy, I wouldn't have been doing it. The majority of the door locks in this town can be picked with a penknife. I remember the first one I got in was the First Presbyterian Church. I guess it was the only time I broke a window and that was to get into the office. The door to the school area was left unlocked. I can't remember what I got, maybe $60. I got in there two or three times; the last time I got in, I picked the boiler room door with a pen knife. I got in and unlocked a window one time and didn't take anything. One time I stood and looked at that big safe for a long time, wondering if I could get in.

Cape Marina, I stood outside that building, down by the river. I studied it. The first time I went in I found that I could go up the fire escape. On the roof there is a trap door. The first time I didn't have a flashlight so I had to let myself down carefully into the top part of the building, which is abandoned, almost rat infested. You go down the stairs and pick the lock to the business. I got in two other times. I got money from the beauty shop two times, but the last time they were closed for vacation. It was funny. They put a chain lock on the back door. That didn't slow me much. While I was in there I looked out and see this police car. I stooped down and stayed a long time and waited. Finally got the register opened with my crowbar and belly crawled out. Only got a few dollars in change. Guess he, the police, wasn't there when I came out. The Algiers Lounge was easy. I locked myself in a bathroom in the building that is not used. They are locked, but they can be picked with a penknife. I would get in, sit down, and go to sleep. Sleep a couple hours, wake up, and go to work. I don't remember how much I got; I broke open the machines and I think that's where one of my moneybags came from. Boy was that stuff heavy. I rolled all the quarters, took it to the bank, Farmers and Merchants at Spring and Good Hope, and bought traveler's checks. I got in both times by staying in that unused bathroom. The grate in front of Rosetti's raises up and goes into the Moonlight Lounge, although I never used that way in. World Travel Agency, were all the same night, I was staying at Sunny Vale. Went in Houston Oil through the louvered windows, popped one hasp with a screwdriver to get in the back room. At O'Reilly's, I got in the bathroom window, the one by the car lot. Got about $7 in there, in Houston Oil I got nothing. I saw the big safe in O'Reilly's, they probably store furs in there.

I've already told you about World Travel. I did it first, and then worked my way home from the plaza. I wasn't wearing gloves that night. Sometimes I did, sometimes I didn't wear gloves. My prints aren't on file anywhere so until you catch someone, his fingerprints are useless.

I don't know why I thought of Shakey's. I was walking down Ellis, saw there was no padlock on the outside of the back door. I pulled on it and could see the hasp and lock on the inside. I popped it with the crowbar and went in. Only way to lock a door like that is with a bar. I assumed the money was in the little filing type thing, I didn't even have to pop the lock, just pry it up a little and pull the bottom part of the bar, and there it was—open. I don't recall how much was in there.

Many times I would read how much I got in the newspaper and know there was an insurance rip-off by the proprietor. I played the piano in Shakey's for a while.

Did I ever get upset when I read about the Pink Pony! The paper said $325 cash and a lot of booze. I didn't get but maybe $100. No booze, I don't take anything like that to carry. That night it was about 2:30 a.m. I got in through the back door. Couldn't push the door open because of a cross bar, so I took off the frame and opened it out, instead of in. Inside, door was the same way. That night a police car came around as I was leaving, as he went behind the notary public, I ran across home. Couldn't understand why the policeman didn't see that door back there behind Pink Pony. Boy, that booze was a real rip-off, I didn't take it.

Night before last, Thursday night, I went in the Marina then on to the Natural Cosmetic Studio. That's a well-protected place, has a dark alleyway, no night light at all; you could stand back there in a white suit and never be seen. I'm surprised someone didn't hear me there, that prying on tin is noisy. I was heading home when a policeman stopped me. He asked to look in my bag, so I let him. I had some rolls of money in there, but I told him I worked at the Elbow Room, so he let me go. It scared me some.

Last night 07-16-76, I was really drunk. I had been to the Purple Shamrock with two friends. We came back in a cab to their residence, then I headed home, but I was going by Shakey's to get something to eat. I stopped at Themis and Pacific to take a leak. I went behind the building there. So I opened it up and popped the screen. It had ivy all over it, growing in the window. I climbed in, went to the front and saw it was a sporting goods store. Then I saw a man walk by with a shotgun just after I had gotten the money from the register. I saw the shotgun and panicked. I tried to hide in the overhead, fell through, and then I just froze. I just stood there in the bathroom. I put the money on the sink. When the lights came on, I put my hands out in front of me, I asked them not to hurt me. They were not rude to me, they were very nice. They said they wouldn't hurt me. I was brought down here and that's where I met you. I consented to a house search and here we are.

I guess I must have six bank bags, no seven, and the tools you saw there are the ones I have been using. All the keys you saw, I have picked up in burglaries and some I found. The money, the rolls of coins, and the money I had on me last night, is mine. It is not stolen money. The tools I bought, that crow bar is a good one that cost me $10 up in Seattle, Washington. I will go with you if you want to get the things at my house that are stolen.

For the past two and a half years I have been everywhere. I got to the Cape on 03-11-76 and went to work for Mr. Hahs about a week later. Me and a friend went to Hawaii, we flew out of St. Louis, left here on 05-06-76. Got back to the Cape on 05-31-76. I went back to work for Mr. Hahs on about 06-14-76.

I am positive this is all I have done on the Cape. I have done things in other places, but I won't go into that. I never burglarized a residence; I hit basically small businesses, but never insurance or finance or construction companies. They never have any money around. I would never hurt anyone or threaten to; if I were challenged I would run. I always felt if I don't, I don't. I don't have anyone; Mom and Dad could really care less. I was adopted when I was four. I guess I wanted to get caught. That's it, I guess.

Legal Aspects of Stealing

The terms *stealing*, *theft*, and *larceny* are used interchangeably in different jurisdictions to represent the act of unlawfully taking the property of another. Larceny is defined under common law as:

A trespassory taking and carrying away (transportation) of the personal property of another with the intention of depriving the owner of its use.

Under common law, fraud (theft by deceit) and extortion (theft by coercion) were separate laws. The trend today is to merge fraud and extortion into a single statute. The distinction between felony and misdemeanor stealing will be determined by the value of the property taken or the theft of certain objects. Felony stealing is usually theft of property valued at more than $150, and the theft of vehicles, drugs, firearms, or credit cards usually constitutes a felony.

Types of Stealing

Stealing can be as simple as placing an object in one's pocket and walking out of a store. Events of this sort probably number in the millions. As thieves become more experienced and bolder, they may begin to develop an interest in stealing certain types of objects, with an accompanying expertise in acquiring them.

Shoplifting Theft Rings

Shoplifting can be nothing more than a thief walking into a store and placing an object in his pocket and walking back out. Some shoplifters have become quite sophisticated at this type of activity.

CASE STUDY

In this case the thieves were several juveniles, both male and female, who were not old enough to have drivers' licenses. They had been organized by a 19-year-old, who would drop them off at one of several malls in the city with a "shopping list" of things to steal. The lists varied from sunglasses to items of clothing. The 19-year-old had given each juvenile an alias and had given him or her instructions that in the event that they were arrested they could call him instead of their parents. Since the juveniles were too young to have a driver's license, it would be difficult to identify them. When they were arrested, they were to say their parents had abandoned them and that they were living with an "uncle," the 19-year-old. He would arrive at the juvenile section, where the child was being held, and request that the child, his "nephew," be released to his custody, which was routinely done. The child would be issued a notice to appear before a juvenile court under the alias. The child would then be given a new alias and instructions on how not to get caught the next time and sent back to the malls. Eventually a 13-year-old was arrested and was unable to make contact with the "uncle." The boy, who did have parents, broke down sobbing to a juvenile officer and told the story. The ring had been active for approximately two years by this time. The "uncle" was arrested and convicted of contributing to the delinquency of a minor.

Shoplifters make use of a number of props in their operations, including booster boxes, bloomers, extra pockets sewn into their clothing, and a variety of diversion techniques.

CASE STUDY

In a relatively simple, albeit ambitious, scheme, a woman would enter a chain store during a busy time of day and take a shopping cart, which she then filled with objects that would be useful in an office, such as typewriters, or floor fans. She removed all the tags or any other form of identification from the items. She then took the items to the service desk, in the same store, and told the clerk that an assistant who purchased the items had lost the receipt. She would then state that the items were not what were needed and demanded to return them. If the clerk objected, the woman created a disturbance. In most cases, the money was given to the thief. Ultimately she was arrested and convicted because she had targeted the same chain too many times, and police officers and store security personnel had warned other stores throughout the region. In order to make a prosecutable case in a situation of this sort, someone, usually a store security officer, needs to observe the acts of the shoplifter and be able to testify that the suspect removed price tags and any other identifiers from the objects.

Instructions for Shoplifters

The following text is a verbatim transcript of a much-copied set of instructions that were found on a shoplifter arrested in a large midwestern department store. At the time the shoplifter was booked into the city jail, her property was inventoried and the instructions were found. The spelling and grammatical errors are those of the original author.

CONFIDENTIAL

DRESSING ROOM: This method should not be used unless you can't do it "off the floor," or the opportunity is obvious. Of course, many stores have dressing room counters and this prevents their use. The most important thing to remember in working the dressing room is to make sure no one can tell how many and what specific pieces you have taken in, needless to say, if you are planning to take four or five pieces, it is necessary to take into the dressing room at least twice that many. Of those that you take in, it is essential that the pieces be similar, this is because if a salesperson or security sees you, they see a certain print or style go into the dressing room and if it is not there when you are finished, it will tip them off. So, whatever pieces you decide to take, make sure you have at least one other of that print. A good way of disguising how many pieces there are is to hang the piece you want to take on the one you're not going to take.

Never wander around with any of the pieces you are planning to take, because not only will the salespeople want to help you or hold them for you or put them in a dressing room for you; all of which defeat your purpose, but it gives security a chance to count how many you have. Figure out which pieces you want to take and either swing them around to one rack, or when the sales people are not paying any attention to you, quickly gather them up and go into the room. Try not to look too obvious about this because you never know if security is watching. Once in the dressing room, separate out which pieces you want to take and try to hide them by putting them on a chair, covered by your jacket. Often saleswomen will come in and check on you and when this happens, your pieces are protected. Most dressing room doors have slits in them, which face in for direction. These allow people on the outside to see in. These were designed specifically for this purpose because before security can make a bust, they have to be absolutely sure that you have taken something and the best way to do this is to observe you. One way to guard this is to hang some clothes on the door itself, so they cannot see in. You can see if someone is observing you by bending down low and looking up through the slits, or opening the door and seeing if someone is out there. Once you have taken your pieces, leave the remaining ones in the dressing room. This gives you more time to leave the store undetected, because, by the time someone goes back there to see what's left, you will be on your way out.

If you feel uneasy about something and you want to test if security is suspicious, take the remaining pieces out and see if they are paying attention or acting funny. One thing to your advantage is that when a salesperson is suspicious, they will almost always show it by acting rude or looking you up and down, etc.

OFF THE FLOOR: This seems a lot more nerve wracking than in the dressing room, because you are practically doing it in front of people around you. The best ones are those that block you from view of any and all people around you, the best ones are those that shield you from both sides. Of course, you can't have anyone close by, but as long as no one can see you, don't be stopped by other people in the department. The only thing you have to worry about is observation windows and three-sided mirrors. Also, many stores have disc shaped mirrors in the corder, which reflect down. However, these are not too dangerous unless you're standing close by them. Besides, somebody has to be looking close, and you should notice if they are. The last thing you must be concerned with is a two-way mirror or observation windows. These are usually small dark little holes located towards the top of the wall. Most of the time, there is never anyone in there, but if they can be avoided, do so. If not, you can usually tell if someone is behind them by standing directly under them.

One nice thing about working off the floor is that if someone has seen you, they will let you know because they get crazy. If it is a customer, they will usually look twice to make sure they saw what they thought they saw, and then run and find a salesperson to tell. If a salesperson sees you, they will have a suspicious expression on their face and either go tell someone, or pick up the phone to call security. Security can be contacted by three methods: phoning the security office and tell them where the suspected thief is, or using walkie talkies, or having a system of dings that will go off in the store, to notify them. I'm sure you have heard them, and in large department stores, they are going off constantly. Unfortunately, no one has the code to be able to figure out which department has called them, and most of the time, you should ignore the bells. However, if you think a salesperson is suspicious, and you see them pick up the phone or push something and you hear the bells go off, then be aware, because they could be for you.

If you have gotten your pieces all right and there is no detacher, you can get ready to leave the store. Check in a mirror to see if you look all right and there are no belts or tags hanging out. Remember, because you know those pieces are there, you can see them, but nobody else can. Also, as you're getting ready and getting closer to the door to leave, be double-checking security, because they will not grab you until you are out that door. How to spot security will be described later, but be suspicious of anyone who is around you a lot or following you, if they were around when you took the pieces, and if they are around you when you're leaving—watch them. Security people almost always give themselves away by using their walkie talkie, which will be in their purse or some shopping bag. They will stare at you from behind racks; they will keep looking at you, follow you, etc. Never, ever leave the store without checking for them, no matter how cool you thought you were. If, for some reason you think someone is onto you, don't panic, because they can't do anything unless you leave that store. Keep walking around from department to department, just casually shopping, and if they're still around, give them back their merchandise. Quickly go behind a rack and dump it or go into a dressing room and leave it. At that point, security knows what you're doing and you know who they are, but you haven't broken the law. They might even say something to you, but just act like you don't what they are talking about, and leave. Do not go directly to your car, because they know you are a pro, and that you probably have other pieces in your car, so if they can get your plates, they will call the police and get you searched. Just walk around and see if someone is following you, and if no one is, then go to your car. If someone is, call J. S., and arrangements can be made. Your car is very important; it can keep you from getting busted. Always park it as close to the store entrance as possible, the further away it is, the further you may have to run. Leave the door unlocked so you can jump in as fast as possible, and as soon as you get in, close and lock the door. Make this a reflex action because once you are in that car, you are almost home free.

After you leave, put the pieces in the trunk and take your trunk key off the ring and put it somewhere else. This way, if you do get pulled over and they want to search your trunk, tell them you don't have the key. The police can then either take you and the car in, and get a warrant and search your car and you're sunk, or they will probably bust open the trunk, and this is illegal search and seizure and though you might go to jail, the case will not hold up in court. Always check for people tailing you. Sometimes they will let you leave the store, but a plainclothes will follow you from store to store, waiting for you to finish so they can bust you and get more charges against you. If you are being tailed, get out of the city, and if they try to pull you over, ignore them. You could always claim you didn't believe they were police. If you have pieces in the car, rip off the price tags and throw them out because without these they have no proof.

DETACHERS: *These are a royal pain in the –. They are designed to sound an alarm as you leave the store. As I'm sure you have seen, they are white plastic and must be taken off with the proper tool. At one time, only about 50 percent of the stores had them, but now all of them do, so they must be dealt with. When working off the floor, take your pieces as usual and then go into the dressing room, but make sure you take some clothes in with you. This is necessary when you take the detachers off; you will have no place to put them. Put them on the clothes you have taken in, they clip on. Put them in the seams because that is where the stores place them. Don't put more than one on in there, if for some reason you don't have enough clothes to put them on, put them in your pocket and then put them in pockets of clothing out on the floor.*

Quite often, you can sort through the pieces and find some that are undetached, but always feel the pieces because you may not be able to see them. This brings up another point, there are other forms of this; little pieces of cardboard. However, these can be ripped off. These usually say "Inventory Control" on them, but sometimes stores, especially smaller ones, try to disguise them by putting them in plastic and putting the store name on them. Because they are small, they are tricky to find, so make sure you check the garment inside and out. Be extra sure, and if you're not, go into the dressing room and double check.

Finally, some stores have really slick methods. Always check the door to see if they have alarms; they will take different forms; white or wood pillars, overhanging ones, or things that sort of resemble gates. If you see any of these, be clued that there is something on the clothes. If you can't find anything on them, hang out by the cash register and see what they do to the clothes when something is bought. If the beeper does go off, you have to make a decision whether to run for it or give back the pieces. In smaller stores, if your car is close by, you might as well run for it. In a department store, if you can walk back into the store and drop off the pieces without too much attention, go ahead. If your car is real close, run, but that is a decision you have to make.

SECURITY: As I mentioned earlier, security people almost always give themselves away, but nevertheless, there are some that are as slick as you are. The one thing most of them have in common is their mentality, I mean it takes a certain type of person to have a job where you suspect everyone and send people to jail. This mentality expresses itself as most security look like real ---. (They get off on the power they think they have.) When they're working, they will be sneaking looks at people, looking over racks, or hiding behind things trying to spy on whoever. Most often, security works in couples because they can see more that way and more importantly, a man has the strength to grab you and keep you. They almost always carry a walkie talkie, so if you see a woman sort of talking into her purse, be careful. The men carry theirs inside their jacket or in a bag like they bought something. They also try to dress down and usually wear blue jeans because they are trying to look like your average shopper. If you see a supposed customer talk to a salesperson like they know them, be suspicious, or if you see two customers who aren't together, stop and briefly talk to each other, that is another good sign. When they're suspicious, they will keep looking, because they have to make sure that you have taken something. Sometimes they will even bump into you to see if they can feel something on you. If you act cool, however, there is no reason for them to be suspicious of you, unless of course they see you doing something. Security looks for people who look nervous, or minorities. They are always suspicious of blacks, chicanos, etc. Sometimes this works against you, because if there are some around you in a store, you can be pretty sure security is around. However, most of the time, security will be so worried about them, they won't be paying any attention to you. One should be more careful when working the dressing room, because security is real aware of this method. When you go into the dressing room, because security is real aware of this method. When you go into the dressing room, be aware, and if they leave when you do, the odds are real high that is who they are. I would try and make it a practice never to leave through a men's department. This is because if you are being followed by a man, he will be much more obvious if you're in a women's department than in a man's. The reason this is important is as I mentioned earlier, is that a man can grab you. If a woman tries to bust you by herself, you will probably be so scared that you will have the strength to get away, and if that involves kicking her or hitting her, do so, because you really don't want to go to jail. Some stores also have security people who wear red jackets and although they are obvious, they should be paid attention to. Also, some of the smaller stores have armed guards, and if you can avoid dealing with these, it would probably be better.

APPROACH: Where to go. You should have a list of stores, when you are first starting out, go to the smaller stores until you build up your confidence, then the bigger stores. Remember, you have to keep going back into these same stores every couple of weeks, so the less attention you draw to yourself, the better. The bigger stores have different departments, which helps, because you can go in one department one week and a separate department the next.

Mostly, you have to use common sense and act cool, and you shouldn't really have any trouble. If you are careful and alert, you should never get caught. Remember too, that it is better to come home with no pieces than to get busted, don't force it. If God forbid, you do get caught, don't panic, you will be out in several hours. Do not tell security or the police anything expect your name. They will also try to ask you to confess or tell them about your "man," etc. They will indicate that they are being told they can get you on another charge of racketeering. Tell them they are for yourself or they are presents.

Whoever prepared these instructions was not an amateur thief. The writer had given a great deal of thought to preparing and conducting stealing operations. Investigators and police officers should be alert to the ruses and tricks mentioned in these instructions.

Confidence (Con) Games

Confidence games are another form of stealing that continue to plague law enforcement throughout the country. Confidence men or women rely on the greed or gullibility of their victims to make their crimes succeed. Stealing committed in this manner is sometimes referred to as fraud or theft by deception. Some of the more common types of con games are:

- Pigeon drop or Jamaican switch
- Bank examiner scheme
- Selling bogus home repairs

Pigeon Drop

The pigeon drop is often directed at older men. The drop begins with a confidence man approaching a potential victim or mark in a public parking lot. The con man will show the mark the contents of a bag, which will usually be what appears to be several thousand dollars in used small denomination bills. The con man will then ask the mark, "What are *we* going to do with all this money?" The con man will then tell the victim that he will call his attorney for legal advice. The mark will be told that the lawyer advised that if no one claims the money in 30 days the finders can keep it. The old man will be excited by the prospect of easy money. The con man will suggest that the old man keep the money with him but that he put up some "good faith" money to ensure his honest intentions. The old man will then draw a sum of money from his bank account and give it to the con man, who leaves the bag with the victim. The con man has switched a bag filled with cut-up paper for the bag of cash in the meantime. By the time the victim discovers what has happened, the thief will have fled. The victim in a case such as this will often delay reporting the crime to the police because of embarrassment.

The Bank Examiner Scheme

The victims in these cases are often elderly persons, living alone. The confidence man appears as a well-dressed law enforcement officer, who presents himself as an FBI or IRS agent, or a representative of some other federal agency. The bogus agent tells the victim that the agency they are with is conducting an investigation of a local bank where the victim has an account. The "investigator" asks the victim to withdraw a large sum of money from the bank so that the investigator can mark it and then it will be redeposited. The deposit will then be "traced" in order to identify the thief in the bank. The confidence man sometimes embellishes the story by telling the victim that the local police are not involved because there is some question about their integrity. As soon as the victim delivers the money, the con man disappears after telling the victim he will be back in contact in a few days. By the time the crime is reported, the thief is gone.

Bogus Home Repairs

In this scheme, the thieves present themselves as contractors offering home improvements at a modest price. After the work, which is often no more than spray painting a roof with aluminum paint or some other sham operation, the con men send the victim a large bill. If the victim protests, the confidence man threatens her with a lawsuit. At this point victims, fearful of losing their homes, will pay the bill. A payment schedule may be established, which may result in the victim paying even more for the bogus repairs. This type of crime may be particularly difficult to prove in court because it may be difficult to prove the difference between shoddy workmanship and outright schemes to steal a victim's money. In some cases, the confidence man will have operated on the fringes of the law for years before being shut down. Occasionally the thief may be willing to make restitution or complete the job he originally contracted to perform. Once this happens the victim will usually be satisfied with the result.

Confidence games are particularly cruel, in that the victims targeted for this crime are often the elderly, members of society who are less able to defend themselves. Crime prevention workshops aimed at informing the elderly about the risks of this type of crime are particularly useful.

Vehicle Theft

In 1999, 1,147,305 vehicles were reported stolen in the United States. Generally vehicles were stolen for a specific purpose, such as:

- Joy riding
- Stealing for use in another crime
- Stealing for profit

Joy Riding

Joy riding usually involves young males who steal a car to use as quick transportation or simply to ride around in. They may, of course, take property from the vehicle, and they may steal parts and accessories. The youths often attack a target of opportunity by taking a car with the keys in it or by hot wiring a car to get it started. Joy riders will often take the same type of vehicles once they become familiar with the make and how to get it started. In most cases, the joy riders abandon the vehicle within a few hours after it is stolen when it runs out of gas. Carjacking is, in some cases, a violent form of joy riding.

Stealing for Use in Another Crime

In these cases, criminals will steal a vehicle that cannot be traced to them. Once the vehicle has been used in a crime, it is abandoned, often even before the owner has reported it stolen. When vehicles used in other crimes are recovered, they should be very carefully searched to recover any trace of evidence the perpetrators might have left behind. In one case, an elderly woman was abducted, raped, and murdered; her body was then placed in the trunk of her car and transported to an isolated location, where it was buried in a shallow grave. The major break occurred when police officer observed the killer, a teenager, asleep in the car. The officer conducted a field interview but was unable to check to vehicle license plate because the computer was down at that time. The officer was later able to testify that she had seen the boy in the deceased victim's car. The car was seized as evidence, and the victim's hair and clothing fibers were found in the trunk, which was enough to provide additional circumstantial evidence to support a conviction.

Stealing for Profit

In the past, vehicles were stolen and transported to another part of the United States, where they were resold to unscrupulous drivers who did not care where their vehicle came from.

International Vehicle Theft

A new trend seems to be emerging in vehicle theft, that of stealing vehicles for resale in another country. Luxury cars may sell overseas for twice what they would normally bring in the United States. A vehicle is stolen near a port city and driven to a cargo ship, where it is placed in a cargo container and shipped abroad. This crime has been reported in New York City, several cities in New Jersey, Houston, Boston, Philadelphia, and Tampa. This type of crime is difficult to investigate because the public tends to think of vehicle theft as a victimless crime. The vehicles that are most commonly stolen are usually insured; thus the cost is passed on through higher future premiums, and the owner does not suffer a large immediate loss. In addition, the insured is often more interested in a cash settlement than in recovering the car (Beekman, 1990, p. 14).

Chop Shops

Historically one of the more successful stolen vehicle operations is the "chop shop." Thieves steal vehicles and then disassemble them in "chop shops." The parts can be sold and distributed individually to auto repair shops or auto salvage yards. Normally, used auto parts are purchased from salvage yards that have purchased auto bodies that have been "totaled out," that is, contain damage that is too extensive to repair, from insurance companies. The wrecked vehicle is sold by an insurance company to a salvage operation, and the parts are sold legally. In a chop shop operation, an auto repairman or salvage yard owner may even contact a thief with instructions to steal a particular kind of vehicle. The desired parts of the vehicle, such as a front-end assembly are sold to the repairman, and the remainder of the auto parts are stripped and the parts sold for a substantial profit.

Identifying a Stolen Vehicle

Since 1956, American automobile manufacturers have been required to place an individual vehicle identification number (VIN) on all new vehicles. The VIN includes information on the manufacturer, the model, the model year, the type of engine and transmission, the plant where the vehicle was produced, and the sequential production number.

On U.S.-made vehicles the VIN plate is attached on the left side of the dashboard, on newer vehicles, the ends of the VIN are placed under a ridge on the dashboard making them more difficult to reach. The plate is attached to the dashboard with stainless steel pop rivets with rosette heads. These rosette rivets are only produced by certain manufacturers, and distribution is limited. Damage to the rivet heads indicates that someone has tampered with the VIN. Thieves may attempt to alter the VIN in a number of ways. A crude technique is to create a new number and simply place the number where the original was. Another technique is to alter the numbers on the original VIN. For example, a 1 may be turned into a 4 or a 3 into an 8.

In some situations the thief may simply remove the VIN from a vehicle that has been totaled and place it on another stolen vehicle of the same type. The thief removes the VIN plate from the dashboard of the stolen car and replaces it with the plate from the salvaged car. If a police officer runs the VIN through a federal or state information system, it will not be reported as stolen. Officers should note that VIN plates are attached to the dashboard with pop rivets with rosette-shaped heads. If the rivet appears to have been tampered with, the investigator should be alert to other indications that the vehicle might be stolen.

Confidential VIN

The confidential VIN or CVIN will be stamped on parts of the vehicle, such as the frame, engine block, or transmission. The CVIN may be the complete number or a derivative of the number. When examining auto parts, the investigator should check the CVIN using the manual published by the National Auto Theft Bureau (NATB). The NATB manual contains information on passenger vehicle identification. These manuals are available only to investigators. Investigators should check numbers found on the vehicle against the manual to determine the authenticity of parts.

Observing the Vehicle Identification Number

In *New York v. Class*, 475 U.S. 106 (1986), the Supreme Court ruled that a VIN is not covered by the Fourth Amendment. In that case, two police officers stopped an automobile for a traffic violation. The driver voluntarily got out of the car. At that point, one of the officers moved some papers on the dashboard to see the VIN. He then saw the butt of a revolver, which he seized, and the driver was arrested for carrying a concealed weapon. The defendant appealed his conviction on the grounds that he had a reasonable expectation of privacy in that the officers had no legal justification to look under the papers on the dashboard. The Court held that there is no reasonable expectation of privacy in the VIN because of the more important role of the VIN in governmental regulation of automobiles. The VIN is considered to be in plain view, and the fact that the defendant placed papers over it did not create an expectation of privacy on the defendant's part. Thus, police officers can examine the VIN as part of a routine traffic stop.

Federal Safety Standard Sticker

Since 1970, all vehicles produced in the United States have been required to have a federal safety standards sticker on the driver's-side doorpost. Several items of information are printed on the sticker, including the serial number, vehicle weight, and production information. When tampered with, these stickers are designed to come apart or to read "void." With patience, however, a car thief can remove the sticker and place it on another vehicle. It is also possible to alter stickers or produce counterfeits that can pass a superficial examination.

Credit Card Crime

At one time, the increased use of credit cards was heralded as the beginning of the cashless society in anticipation of virtually all financial transactions being conducted using "plastic money." Not only has increased credit card use not resulted in a reduction in robbery and stealing, it has also added yet another responsibility for criminal investigators. Credit cares may be defined as:

> . . . a card, booklet, credit card number or other identifying symbol or instrument evidencing an undertaking to pay promptly for property or services delivered or rendered to or upon the order of a designated person or bearer. (Oregon State Statutes 165.055)

Credit cards may be obtained in a number of ways. They may be the fruit of other crimes, such as robbery, burglary, or stealing. In one simple case, a victim became distracted after making a gasoline purchase while on vacation and left the card at a gas station. By the time she realized the card was missing, the clerk and his girlfriend had made purchases of over $1,600, being careful to keep the charges to under $50 to avoid having the purchase checked.

In other situations, credit cards may be the object of the crime, as in a purse snatch or by a pickpocket, who then uses the card or sells it to a professional thief or fence. Prostitutes sometimes steal cards from their customers. In cases such as these, the victim is usually reluctant to report the crime or reports the card as lost rather than stolen. Cards may be stolen from the mail by thieves who specialize in illegal card usage. This type of theft sometimes involves postal employees.

In perhaps one of the simplest crimes of all, a thief can use the card number to order property over the telephone simply by using a valid number and having the property delivered to a location before the police can arrest him. The victim does not learn of the transactions until the bill arrives or the credit card company informs the cardholder of a large number of transactions.

Stolen credit cards must be used quickly before the victim becomes aware that the card is missing. Criminals often work with an accomplice who creates a diversion, such as arguing with a clerk, urging the clerk to move more quickly, etc. In other cases, the card user may be working with a store clerk who shares in the profits.

Computer Crime

Computers have entered every aspect of modern life, including crime. Estimates are that computer thieves may be stealing $3 billion to $5 billion a year (Conly and McEwen, 1990). Most law enforcement agencies are not prepared to respond to this new type of high technology crime. Computer crime is defined as:

> [a]ny illegal act for which knowledge of computer technology is used to commit the offense. (Conly and McEwen, 1990, p. 3)

Computers have been involved in most types of crimes encountered by criminal investigators, including theft of all types, drug offenses, burglary, crimes of violence, sabotage, and pornography (Parker, 1989, p. 3).

Computer crimes are of general types:

- Internal computer crimes
- Telecommunications and telephone crimes
- Computer manipulation crimes
- Computers used in support of crimes
- Thefts of hardware and software (McEwen, 1989, p. 2)

Internal Computer Crimes

Internal computer crimes involve alterations of programs that cause the system to perform unauthorized functions. Planting a "computer virus" is an example of this type of crime. Crimes of this type are usually committed by programmers to sabotage a system. A number of internal computer crimes are known, including Trojan Horse, logic bombs, and trap doors.

Telecommunications and Telephone Crimes

Telecommunications crimes involve illegally accessing or using computer systems over telephone lines. The *hacker* uses programs to find valid access codes for a computer system by continually dialing randomly generated codes. Once a valid code is identified, the system is diverted to an unknowing innocent person. Telecommunication crimes also involve *phone breaking*, involving electronic devices that emit tones signaling normal long distance calls that should be charged to a legitimate number, but are not.

Computer Manipulation Crimes

Computer manipulation crimes involve altering existing data or creating new records to commit a crime. For example, embezzlements at financial institutions usually involve the creation of false accounts into which the thief diverts funds.

Computers Used in Support of Crimes

This category involves the use of computers to facilitate the commission of another crime. Drug dealers keep records on microcomputer systems, and in one case, the operators of a prostitution ring established a database, including the names and credit card numbers of all active customers.

Thefts of Computer Software and Hardware

Software and hardware thefts are often simply software piracy, in which someone makes an unauthorized copy of a proprietary software package and then sells the copies for a profit. Stealing trade secrets also falls into this category of crime and is usually committed for the personal gain of the thief. Thefts of hardware, ranging from component parts to large mainframe computers, are aimed at acquiring the machines needed to perform specific functions, thus providing leads in the case.

Investigation of Computer Crimes

The investigation of computer crime begins with an understanding of how a computer works. A computer is basically an electronic machine capable of accepting data and performing mathematical and logical operations on them. The investigator must develop an awareness of the points at which a computer criminal is vulnerable and concentrate on those areas in order to build a case. One of the more promising approaches to the investigation of computer crime is the dedicated crime unit (Conly and McEwen, 1990). The success of a computer crime unit will be based on the commitment of the chief executive and the officers assigned to the unit. Before undertaking such a project, the department should identify personnel who have an interest in computers or are willing to learn the skills needed to perform these types of investigations. Computer literacy is rapidly becoming a necessity for all law enforcement officers.

Conclusion

Robbery, in all its forms, is a crime of violence. Robbers prefer to take property from their victims in an atmosphere where the offender is able to dominate the victim through force or the threat of force. Apprehending a robber inherently presents an opportunity for a violent confrontation between the police and the criminal. Burglary, on the other hand, is a crime that requires secrecy to succeed. Burglars seek to avoid confrontation. Burglary, however, is an act that leaves the victim with a feeling of having been violated. The victim is left with the knowledge that intruder has entered the victim's home or place of work, and has gone through his or her most private possessions. Burglary victims report a profound sense of having been violated. Burglary victims often ask the investigating officers if the officers, in their professional judgment, think that the burglar was a young person. In may be easier for a victim to cope emotionally with the unknown perpetrator by imagining the intruder as a youth incapable of harming the victim than as an adult who might be capable of greater violence.

Stealing is a crime that also leaves the victim with a sense of having been violated. The property, which was paid for with hard-earned dollars, is no longer available and, if possible, must be replaced, thereby placing an additional strain on often limited financial resources. Identifying, apprehending, and helping to prosecute robbers, burglars, and thieves is one of the most gratifying aspects of an investigator's job.

References

Beekman, Mary Ellen, and Daly, Michael R. "Motor Vehicle Theft Investigations: Emerging International Trends." *FBI Law Enforcement Bulletin* 59(9):14–17, 1990.

Burke, Tod W., and O'Rear, Charles E. "Armed Carjacking: A Violent Problem in Need of a Solution." *The Police Chief* 40(1):18–21, 1993.

Butler v. City of Detroit, 386 N.W. 2d. 645 (1985).

Colvin, Bill D. "Computer Crime Investigators." *FBI Law Enforcement Bulletin* 48(7):9–15, 1979.

Conly, Catherine H. and McEwen, J. Thomas. *Computer Crime*. U.S. Department of Justice, National Institute of Justice. *NIJ Reports* 218, January–February 1990.

Crime in America, Uniform Crime Report for the United States, 1995. Washington, DC: U.S. Department of Justice, Federal Bureau of Investigation, 1996.

Crime in the United States; 1993. Washington, DC: U.S. Department of Justice, Federal Bureau of Investigation, 1994.

Ealy v. City of Detroit, 375 N.W. 2d. 438 (1985).

Ford v. Childress, 650 F. Supp. 110 D.C. III (1986).

Krueger v. Fuhr 991 F2d 438 8th Cir. (1993).

McEwen, J. Thomas, *Dedicated Computer Crime Units*. Washington DC: U.S. Department of Justice, National Institute of Justice, 1989.

New York v. Class, 475 U.S. 106 (1986).

Parker, Donn B. *Computer Crime Criminal Justice Resource Manual*. Washington DC: U.S. Department of Justice, National Institute of Justice, 1989.

Payton v. New York, 445 U.S. 573 (1980).

Perkins, Rollin M., and Boyce, Ronald N. *Criminal Law*, 3rd ed. Mineola, NY: Foundation Press, 1982.

Rhiner v. City of Clive, 373 N.W. 2d. 466 (1985).

Ryder v. the City of Topeka, 814 F. 2d. 1412 (1987).

Schaefer, James, and Latzen, Murray A. "Knock-out Dates: Flirting with Danger." *FBI Law Enforcement Bulletin* 62(1):7–9, 1993.

Steagald v. United States, 451 U.S. 204 (1981).

Tennessee v. Garner, 471 U.S. 1 (1985).

Trejo v. Wattles, 654 F. Supp. 1143 (1987).

Wright, Richard T., and Decker Scott H. *Burglars on the Job: Streetlife and Residential Break Ins*. Boston, MA: Northeastern University Press, 1994.

11. Arson and Bomb Investigation

I have already explained to you that what is out of the common is usually a guide rather than a hindrance. In solving a problem of this sort, the grand thing is to be able to reason backward.

Sherlock Holmes, *A Study in Scarlet*, Sir Arthur Conan Doyle

Arson is defined in the FBI's *Uniform Crime Report* as "any willful or malicious burning or attempt to burn, with or without intent to defraud, a dwelling house, public building, motor vehicle, personal property of another, etc." In some states, arson only occurs when real property such as buildings are burned, while fires of other types of property will be classified as another crime, such as "knowingly burning" property. Arson is one of the fastest growing crimes in the United States.

Incendiary, Suspicious, and Accidental Fires

Fires are of three types: incendiary, suspicious, and accidental. Incendiary fires that are deliberately set for the purpose of burning the property. Suspicious fires are those in which the cause and origin of the fire is difficult to determine. Due to the unusual circumstances of these fires, they are suspected of being incendiary in origin. Accidental fires are those that were not willfully or maliciously set. Fires of this type are often associated with accidents, such as smoking in bed, children playing with matches, or an unsupervised trash fire. Accidental fires also result from defective heating equipment, such as space heaters or kerosene heaters. Accidental fires may result from cooking equipment, smoking, energized electrical equipment, accidental ignition of flammable liquids, open flames or sparks, spontaneous combustion, fireworks, dust explosions, or lightning. Investigators may be involved in the investigation of all three types of fires, although when a fire is determined to be accidental in origin, the criminal investigation will usually cease.

Motives for Arson

Using the previously discussed acronym MOM, the investigator will begin by reviewing possible motives for arson or incendiary fire.

Profit

One of the most obvious motives for setting a fire is direct profit to the arsonist. The most common scenario is an insurance fraud in which a business that was insured for more than its appraised value burns under suspicious circumstances. This type of crime is most often associated with businesses, although occasionally homeowners will burn their houses or other property for the insurance settlement.

Business fires may be started for several different reasons:

1. To collect an insurance settlement, and thereby start over with the cash received from the insurance company
2. To dispose of unsalable or excess inventory
3. As a "real estate speculation" scheme, most often seen in large cities, in which dilapidated or condemned property is purchased and then insured for more than its market value. After a period, the building burns and the owner collects from the insurance company.

Private persons set fires for basically two reasons: to get out of mortgage payments or to obtain cash needed to replace old clothing or furnishings in the house. Persons who are deeply in debt are good suspects in these cases.

Elimination of Competition

Unscrupulous business people may use arson to eliminate competition by burning or otherwise damaging a competitor's ability to operate. Arson may also be a means to stimulate business by destroying the property of a customer, who will then need to restock its inventory from the arsonist.

Concealing Another Crime

Arson may also be used to conceal another crime, such as murder or stealing. Anytime investigators discover a body in a fire scene, they should insist that an autopsy be performed to determine the cause of death. An investigator should determine what types of records were destroyed in a fire in order to determine who might have a reason to start that fire. A careful examination of all filing cabinets and desk drawers should be made as part of the following case.

Jealousy or Revenge

An arsonist might have personal reasons for starting a fire. The arsonist may be acting out of jealousy or a desire to obtain revenge. In some cases, old boyfriends have been identified as having set fires.

Desire for Recognition

In some cases, security personnel for firefighters have started fires and then immediately reported them or put them out to appear that they are alert on the job.

Pyromania

Pyromania has been defined as "an irresistible impulse to start fires" (Gold, 1962, p. 407). Pyromaniacs are sometimes described as psychopaths, although there is no consensus among experts as to whether fire setters suffer from any specific psychiatric disorder.

Inspecting the Crime Scene

Obtaining Legal Authority to Enter a Possible Crime Scene

The investigator will need to consider whether to obtain a search warrant before processing the fire scene for evidence. In *Michigan v. Tyler*, the Supreme Court ruled the need to control and extinguish the fire is the immediate responsibility of responding fire personnel. Once the fire has been put out, the emergency has ended. If it appears that the fire may be of suspicious origin, it is advisable to obtain a search warrant before processing the scene (Michigan v. Tyler, 436 U.S. 499 [1978]).

Michigan v. Tyler

Shortly before midnight on January 21, 1970, a fire broke out at Tyler's Auction, a furniture store in Oakland County, Michigan. The building was leased to Loren Tyler, who conducted the business in association with Robert Tompkins. According to the trial testimony of various witnesses, the fire department responded to the fire and was "just watering down the embers" when Fire Chief See arrived on the scene around 2 a.m. It was the chief's responsibility to "determine the cause and make all reports." See was met by Lt. Lawson, who informed him that two plastic containers of flammable liquid had been found in the building. Using portable lights, they entered the gutted store, which was filled with smoke and steam, to examine the containers. Concluding that the fire "could possibly have been an arson," Chief See called the police, who arrived around 3 a.m. A police detective took several pictures of the containers and the interior of the store, but stopped because of smoke and steam. Chief See looked through the building in an attempt to determine the cause of the fire. By 4 a.m., the fire had been completely extinguished, and the firefighters left. The containers were turned over to the police as evidence. Investigators had not obtained consent or a search warrant to examine the scene or to remove evidence.

Four hours after See had left the fire scene, he returned with another investigator whose job it was to determine the cause and origin of the fire. They found a number of suspicious items, including burn marks on the carpet and pieces of tape with burn marks on them on a stairway. Investigators left again to obtain tools needed to recover the evidence.

On February 16, another investigator returned to the scene to take pictures and to recover any other evidence. Again, entries were made without consent or a search warrant.

The defendants were arrested and convicted of arson. They appealed their conviction on the grounds that the evidence had been seized in violation of the Fourth

Amendment. The Supreme Court held that the entries were clearly detached from the initial exigency and warrantless entry. Since all of the searches were conducted without valid warrants and without consent, they were invalid under the Fourth and Fourteenth Amendments, and any evidence obtained as a result of these entries must be excluded. The Court went on to say that an initial entry to fight the fire requires no warrant, and that once in the building, officials may remain there for a reasonable time to investigate the blaze. After that, however, any entries must be made pursuant to a warrant or consent.

Fire Investigation Procedure

Once on the scene, the investigator should begin to look for clues about the cause and origin of the fire. The age of the building provides some clues about the nature of the fire. Most newer buildings are less susceptible to fire because of construction building codes and sprinkler systems. Usually, once a fire has started in a new building, it does not spread very rapidly through a building, so rapid spreading should be noted. Similarly, if fires are burning in more than one location in the building, the fire should be considered suspicious.

Begin the investigation by noting the condition of the interior of the building. Obviously, this will be difficult given the extent of smoke and water damage that usually results from efforts to extinguish a fire. Record if the contents of the building appear to have been removed prior to the fire. Determine if file cabinets were opened and the contents removed. One experienced arson investigator noted that he always determined if the residents of a fire scene had a pet. If the pet was not in the residence at the time of the fire, he often found the fire to be suspicious. Examine doors and windows to determined if forced entry was made or if the arsonist placed objects in the path to delay firefighters' attempts to gain entry to the fire scene. Also, photograph or videotape the crowd at the scene for later follow-up investigation.

Point of Origin

Establish the point or points of origin at the fire scene. The point of origin is the actual location where the fire started. If more than one point of origin is found, this is a strong indication of an arson fire. The point of origin can be determined by interviewing witnesses and by processing the physical evidence found at the scene.

Determining the Cause and Origin of a Fire

One of the first difficulties encountered in an arson investigation is the differing attitudes of law enforcement and fire personnel toward the scene. In the event the fire appears to be of suspicious origin, the investigator will wish to keep the scene in substantially the same condition it was in when the fire was extinguished. Firefighters, on the other hand, will often begin to clean up the scene shortly after the fire has been put out. Under these circumstances, the investigators should request the fire personnel to delay the cleanup until the investigation of the scene is complete.

Interviewing Witnesses at the Scene

The first person to be interviewed is the person who reported the fire. The investigator should ask the following questions:

- Where was the witness when he or she first saw the fire?
- What was the exact location of the fire when the witness who first saw it reported it?
- How big was the fire?
- How rapidly did the fire spread?

The investigator also needs to interview fire personnel at the scene. Trained fire fighters can provide a great deal of information about the fire.

Inspection of the Debris

The investigator should carefully inspect the debris left at a fire scene for clues as to the cause of a fire. Evidence should be examined layer by layer. The investigator must look on the surfaces present for V patterns, alligatoring, and spalling.

Locating the V Pattern

Fire investigators often begin the search for the point of origin of a fire by locating the *V pattern*. Normally fire expands upward and outward resulting in a distinctive V-shaped burn pattern. The shape may not be an exact V, however, it may be vertical, horizontal, or at an angle. V patterns may result from secondary fires, which can mislead the investigator.

Alligatoring

Alligatoring may aid in the determination of the point of origin. Alligatoring is the pattern of charring on the surface of wood as it burns. If a fire is extinguished shortly after is begun, charring will be minimal and the alligatoring will be more pronounced. The longer the fire burns, the deeper the charring and the smaller the alligatoring pattern.

Evidence Indicating the Presence of Flammable Liquids

Flammable liquids are often used by arsonists to accelerate a fire and to cause more damage. The accelerants used at a fire scene are readily available. The investigator should be aware of several possible indicators of accelerant use. One of the most obvious and common indicators is a rapid lateral spread of the fire, that is, the entire building seems to burst into flames.

The color of the smoke and flame may indicate accelerant use. Flammable petroleum distillates usually burn with a red or orange flame. They also produce a black sooty smoke. Alcohols give off a blue flame with little smoke.

It is sometimes possible to trace the path of an accelerant as it was poured by the arsonist. Liquids, such as gasoline, alcohol, or turpentine, will run to the lowest spot in the area and flow around any fixed objects in its path. Occasionally unburned pools of the accelerant may found at the scene or drops of the liquid may have been splashed onto furniture or walls. When recovering evidence of accelerant use, the items should first be photographed, measured, and sketched before being moved. The evidence should then be placed in an airtight container, such as a clean unused paint can, to prevent evaporation of the liquid. Unused paint cans can be obtained from paint or hardware stores.

Concrete Spalling

Concrete *spalling* occurs when concrete explodes after it is exposed to extreme heat. When a liquid accelerant, such as gasoline or kerosene, burns on top of a concrete floor, spalling will occur because of the formation of steam pockets in the area where the accelerant was applied. When examining the scene, be careful to look for fragments of concrete. If the arsonist used an accelerant that resulted in spalling, rather than finding fragments of concrete, just the ingredients of the concrete, such as gravel or sand, will be seen.

Distinct Burn Patterns

Accelerant poured from a container may conform to the shape of the container. Once the liquid is poured, it will flow to the lowest spot and accumulate. After ignited, the liquid will tend to burn and char the floor or floor covering in a puddle configuration. Liquids burning in this way leave distinct lines of demarcation between the burned and unburned or lightly charred areas near the fire.

Downward Burning

Fire normally burns upward unless something causes it to burn in another direction. If a flammable liquid is poured down an area, such as a staircase or sloping floor, and then ignited at the top, the flames will burn down to the lowest point where the liquid and vapors spread.

Holes in the Flooring

Since liquids flow to the lowest point, they will penetrate the lowest spots in the area, such as cracks in the floor and floor joints. Because the liquid gets concentrated in those areas, it will burn more rapidly there, which results in holes being burned at joints and cracks in the floor.

Burning Beneath Floors

Liquids sometimes penetrate cracks and joints, and flow beneath the surface. At the same time, the liquid will begin to vaporize and sink into lower areas. Once ignited, the fire may burn beneath the surface such as a floor.

Burning in Protected Areas

Objects such as furniture and appliances obstruct the expansion of flames. If a liquid has been poured under an object, it will burn more quickly than expected and char the underside more than the top or upper surface.

Straight-Up Burn Patterns

Flammable liquids poured at the base of a wall burn in a wider area than a fire that originated from a smaller single source, such as an electrical outlet.

In addition, the V pattern usually found with a fire is not as pronounced in these cases.

Explosions

Clear glass found 5 feet or more from a structure often indicates an explosion. Other indications of an explosion include walls being pushed out at the bottom. This occurs when accelerant fumes are allowed to accumulate and are suddenly ignited.

CASE STUDY

A man was on his way to work at approximately 5 o'clock in the morning. He had to break quickly to avoid hitting another man who suddenly appeared in his headlights. The driver realized that something was wrong when he observed smoke rising from the man's body. The pedestrian ran in front of the truck and opened the door on the passenger side, at which time the truck's dome light came on. The driver observed the man had been seriously burned: His skin was dripping from his fingers and much of his clothing was burned to his skin. The burned man asked for a ride as he stepped into the truck. The driver, being aware that a hospital was nearby, began driving toward the hospital. The injured man asked where the driver was going. When the driver responded that he was taking him to a hospital, the man said, "I can't be goin' to no hospital," and jumped out of the truck. The driver continued on until he found a telephone and called the police. At approximately the same time, the local fire department was responding to fire at a Harley Davidson dealership. The firemen reported seeing several signs of accelerant use, including the smell of gasoline. The police searched the area but could not find the man or his body. All hospitals within a 500-mile radius were contacted, but over the next few days no one with serious burns sought medical assistance at any of these facilities. Investigators concluded that the case involved an outlaw motorcycle gang member who set the fire and was inadvertently caught in an explosion of the gasoline fumes. The arsonist, after jumping from the truck, might have called a friend to pick him up, but it's probable that he died later and was buried in an unmarked grave since it's unlikely that anyone could survive burns of this nature without medical attention.

Fire-Starting Mechanisms

One of the keys to proving that a fire was of suspicious origin is to recover evidence of an ignition device. Ignition devices can be quite simple, such as matches, or they can be more complicated devices with timers, which provide the arsonist with the time needed to leave the scene.

Matches

Matches are the devices of choice for starting most fires. They are simple to use and readily available. Unsophisticated fire setters and pyromaniacs may pile up rubbish and ignite it. More experienced arsonists want a delay before the fire ignites to allow them time to escape. This may be done by attaching matches to a lighted cigarette or by placing a lighted cigarette in a matchbox.

Gelatin Capsules

Gelatin capsules are also used by arsonists. The fire setter uses silver nitrate-magnesium powder or sugar-sodium peroxide packed into a capsule along with water or sulfuric acid. When the capsule disintegrates, the flame created ignites the accelerant.

Candles

Like matches, candles can be very effective ignition devices. The arsonist simply lights the candle and lets it burn down to the accelerant. An arsonist can experiment with candles of different diameters to determine how fast each will burn. A candle 3/4 of an inch in diameter will burn at approximately 1 inch per hour. The limitation of this technique is that obvious physical evidence will be left behind.

Timing Devices

An arsonist may use an electrical timing device to delay ignition.

CASE STUDY

An arsonist seeking to burn a large warehouse used an electric charcoal lighter to start a fire. The starter was placed in a pile of old newspapers in a pool of diesel fuel and then plugged into an electrical socket. The plan worked until the flames hit the diesel. The arsonist failed to consider that diesel fuel has a high ignition point; thus, the accelerant only smoldered until the fire department arrived.

Chemicals

Experienced arsonists often use phosphorous as an ignition device because it ignites when it comes in contact with air. The arsonist fills a balloon with a mixture of water and phosphorous. He then makes a pinhole in the bottom of the balloon to allow the water to trickle out. As the water seeps out it evaporates, and then the phosphorus ignites when it dries. Other chemicals ignite when they come in contact with water; thus, they can be ignited by the flushing of a toilet or by a rain shower. Fires started this way are uncommon because the characteristic odor of the chemicals used creates suspicion and because most arsonists are not sophisticated enough to use such techniques.

An arsonist can use natural gas to start a fire by preventing the gas, which is lighter than air, from venting. The gas initially rises to the ceiling and then gradually sinks down to the level of the pilot light. When the gas reaches the pilot light an explosion results, often followed by a fire. In addition, the arsonist may place a candle on a higher object to shorten the time to explosion.

Evidence Collection

An arson investigator must obtain answers to the following questions:

- Where did the fire start?
- How did the fire start?
- Was the fire of suspicious origin?

Arson is among the most difficult crimes to investigate because most of the evidence is destroyed in the fire. The investigator must methodically process evidence at the scene and accumulate as much circumstantial evidence as possible.

The search for physical evidence focuses on the point of origin of the fire. Fire evidence is difficult to identify and easily destroyed. A flammable accelerant is particularly likely to evaporate. Charred rags and paper may contain evidence of a flammable fluid. Evidence of this type should be photographed, sketched, and placed in an airtight container.

Any suspected ignition devices should be recovered and transported to the laboratory. Determining how the fire was set is crucial for formulating the arsonist's *modus operandi*. Burned documents are often found at the scene. These items should be placed intact into a cardboard box. If the fire occurred outdoors, soil samples should be taken. It is necessary to sift the debris at the scene through a screen sieve to ensure that nothing is lost.

The investigator should take all the normal steps associated with any criminal investigation including:

- Determining who reported the fire
- Conducting a neighborhood canvass
- Interviewing fire personnel
- Interviewing owners of the property

Follow-up Arson Investigation

The Paper Chase

Quite often in an arson fire, a suspect is readily apparent, but the difficulty is in linking the suspect to the crime. As long as the person responsible for the fire remains silent, it is quite possible he could be successful in avoiding being charged with his crime. In some cases, an informant comes forward with the needed information and is willing to testify. When this occurs it is usually because the informant has been caught in another crime and is willing testify in return for lenience in his case. Informants may also respond to substantial rewards offered by insurance companies. In most cases, however, the only impetus for an informant to cooperate is when he hopes to receive some special consideration with regard to his own legal problems.

In most cases, an investigator must build a circumstantial case relying on available records. Begin by examining courthouse records. These records include the register of deeds, which shows who owns the building, who it was purchased from, and for what cost. City and county tax records may also list the owner of the building and its appraised value. Building inspection records may indicate whether the structure was in poor condition, whether any structural violations were involved, and/or if it was condemned.

Lastly, it is necessary to obtain all insurance records, which indicate when the building was insured and for how much. It is very important to determine who the beneficiary of the insurance policy is and who submitted the claim.

Bank Mortgage Records

It is important to determine if the owner was behind in making mortgage payments. Mortgage records may also show if the owner made any false statements regarding the ownership or value of the property.

Bombing Investigation

Bombings are particularly vicious crimes and result in terrible suffering and injury to the victim. The incredible devastation in terms of loss of life and property damage to the federal building in Oklahoma City, Oklahoma, illustrates the harm that can result from the use of a massive explosive device. Bombers tend to place explosive devices in locations that are likely to result in harm to a number of innocent parties. Bombs have long been the instrument of choice of terrorist organizations, but they have been used by organized crime as well as by single individuals as a means to commit murder.

Leads in a Bombing Case

All leads in a bombing investigation begin with the bomb itself. Every effort must be made to recover as many pieces of the explosive device as possible in order to determine how the bomb was made. Once this has been done it may be possible to determine who made the bomb. The bombing of Pan Am flight 103 left debris over an area of approximately 845 square miles, thus easily making it the largest crime scene in history. Yet, despite the enormity of the area, searchers and investigators were able to find the container in which the bomb was housed, a portable radio case, among the debris. Once they had found the container, they were able to determine the suitcase in which the bomb was hidden, and then to trace that suitcase to Malta, where they gathered the information necessary to identify the suspects.

Once an explosion has been determined to have been caused by a bomb, it is usual to proceed in one of four ways: (1) Determine what the components of the bomb were (a job usually carried out by laboratory personnel) and then attempt to link them to the specific person who bought or made them; (2) Proceed on the assumption that the bombing was an act of revenge or extortion and then delve into the victim's background to determine who might have a reason or the opportunity to undertake this crime; and (3) Determine how the bomb was made in order to connect it with other bombs of the same type. In this case, the bomber's *modus operandi* may point to specific individual or group. Indeed, the construction of an explosive device may be so unique as to provide the bomber's "signature." In the Unibomber case, Theodore Kaczynski was extraordinarily successful in avoiding detection for more than 20 years by being careful to leave little or nothing to point to him, including making his own bomb parts.

Finally, investigators should never overlook the possibility of finding useful evidence amidst the debris. When a bomb detonates, its components do not disintegrate but are rather blasted into smaller pieces. It may possible to recover a fingerprint from the package found at the scene. In both the Oklahoma City bombing and the World Trade Center bombing the primary leads came from the recovery of the confidential vehicle identification numbers on axles of the vehicles that were used to deliver the bombs. In both cases, the bombs were transported in rented trucks. As is often the case, making an identification of the bomber is a combination of high technology, traditional investigative techniques, and persistence.

Explosives

The bomber must start with some type of explosive. An explosive is a material capable of rapid conversion from either solid or liquid to a gas, with resultant heat, pressure, and loud noise. Explosives may be either high or low explosives.

Low Explosives

The most common low explosive is black powder, which is a mixture of potassium or sodium nitrate, sulfur, and charcoal. Black powder is sensitive to heat, impact, friction, and sparks. When compacted, as in a pipe bomb, it can be very destructive. Because black powder is easy to obtain and ignite, it is one of the more common explosives used in homemade bombs.

Smokeless powder is also readily available and is therefore used in some homemade bombs. Smokeless powder is of two types, single base and double base. Single base is made of nitrocellulose, and double base is made of nitrocellulose and nitroglycerin. Smokeless powder is less sensitive than black powder, but should be handled with extreme care because it is more powerful.

High Explosives

There are two types of high explosives—primary and secondary. High explosives are usually detonated by shock, have a much greater detonation velocity than low explosives, and do not need to be confined to explode.

Primary explosives detonate when subjected to heat and shock. They are most often used to ignite other larger charges of high explosives, such as blasting caps and firearm primers. Blasting caps may be electrically or nonelectrically ignited. Blasting caps are usually 1 to 3 inches in length and 1/4 inch in diameter. Typically they will be cased in aluminum, copper, or bronze.

Secondary explosives are detonated by shock from a primary source. Detonation velocities of secondary explosives range from 3,300 feet per second to 29,900 feet per second, depending on the explosive used. The Federal Bureau of Alcohol, Tobacco and Firearms has jurisdiction in cases of this type and can provide support to local investigators.

Conclusion

Fire and explosives have been the tools of choice for terrorists throughout history. The motives for an arson attack or bombing may be as simple as an act of revenge by a former boyfriend or an attempt to frighten competition away from a business. Conversely, an arson or a bombing may be an incredibly vicious and indiscriminate act, such as the World Trade Center bombing in New York City or the bombing of the Alfred P. Murrah Federal Building in Oklahoma City. The investigation of arson and bombing cases will test an investigator's skill and patience, but the success of investigators in the World Trade Center bombing demonstrates that teamwork and perseverance can lead to the prosecution of these criminals.

References

Bates, Edward B. *Elements of Fire and Arson Investigation*. Santa Cruz, CA: Davis, 1975.

Department of the Treasury, Bureau of Alcohol, Tobacco and Firearms, *1993 Explosive Incidents Report*. Washington, DC: U.S. Government Printing Office, 1994.

Lindsey, Robert. *A Gathering of Saints: A True Story of Money, Murder and Deceit*. New York: Simon and Schuster, 1988.

Michigan v. Tyler, 436 U.S. 499 (1978).

Sillitoe, Linda, and Roberts Allen. *Salamander: The Story of the Mormon Forgery Murders*. New York: Signature Books, 1988.

12. Drug Investigations

"But consider!" I said earnestly. "Count the cost! Your brain may, as you say, be roused and excited, but it is a pathological and morbid process, which involves increased tissue-change and may at least leave a permanent weakness. You know, too, what a black reaction comes upon you."

Dr. Watson to Sherlock Holmes, *The Sign of Four*, Sir Arthur Conan Doyle

The use of illegal drugs continues to be one of the most serious problems facing the United States and the American criminal justice system. Indeed, the use and abuse of illegal drugs is a global problem. Research has demonstrated a strong link between the use and abuse of illicit drugs and crime. In one study, approximately half of men arrested for felonies in 23 major cities had traces of one or more illegal substances in their systems at the time they were arrested (Drug Use Forecasting, 1995). The problem posed by illegal drug use is not only the concern of law enforcement agencies, it is also a problem requiring the attention of all Americans.

Effective law enforcement efforts can reduce the opportunity for drug dealers to distribute their products and for abusers to use them. Law enforcement should be seen as only one part of a comprehensive strategy to reduce the demand for illegal drugs. As long as drug abusers seek some substance that will allow them to escape reality or to make themselves feel better, at least for a little while, drugs will be abused. Efforts to reduce demand are the only long-term solution to the problem. Unfortunately treatment programs can only be effective when the user decides to quit abusing drugs. It is therefore incumbent upon law enforcement agencies to make every effort to reduce the availability of illegal drugs in the United States.

Proactive Investigations

Drug investigations tend to be proactive in that investigators use an array of covert investigative techniques against known drug dealers or users. They may use every investigative technique available at some point in an investigation. It is important to remember that the goal of an investigation is to develop a case that demonstrates the defendant's guilt beyond a reasonable doubt. If a drug dealer is involved in another crime or his guilt may be proven by more conventional investigative techniques, no opportunity should be missed to obtain a conviction. For example, if a package of marijuana is discovered as it is sent through the mail, the contents should be carefully examined for fingerprints. If prints are found on the inside of the package, especially on the container in which the drugs are found, this may be offered as evidence that the defendant was in possession of the package.

Similarly, many drug arrests result from vehicle stops made be uniformed patrol officers. A number of major drug seizures have been made by patrol officers as a result of routine vehicle stops that led to probable cause to search the vehicles or the officers requesting consent to search the vehicles. In order to take action, the patrol officer must have a thorough knowledge of the law of search and seizure, especially as it relates to vehicles.

Drugs of Abuse

Knowledge of drugs and their effects is important to law enforcement officers for two reasons. First, it is essential that the criminal investigator be able to identify illegal drugs and their symptoms in order to determine if a commitment of investigative time and effort is appropriate. Second, as part of the law enforcement officer's responsibility to educate the public about illegal drugs, officers must be prepared to give accurate information about drugs and their effects to persons requesting such information. This is particularly true when dealing with young people. If the officer's descriptions of drugs and their effects are not consistent with a young person's experiences, then he or she is more likely to reject the information as propaganda.

Comprehensive Drug Abuse Prevention and Control Act of 1970

Illegal drug use in the United States is regulated by the Controlled Substances Act (CSA). The act applies only to federal officers, but it has served as a model for state statutes for the regulation of the more common drugs of abuse. Under the CSA, drugs are classified or scheduled as I through V according to the extent to which each drug may be abused.

Schedule I drugs have a high potential for abuse and have no currently recognized medical use in the United States. Some states are reconsidering medical uses for marijuana. Ultimately the United States Supreme Court will determine if these laws violate the Constitution. Schedule I drugs lack accepted safety standards for use under medical supervision. Schedule I drugs include heroin, LSD, methaqualone, and marijuana.

Schedule II drugs have a high potential for abuse and have a currently accepted medical use in the United States. Abuse of schedule II drugs may lead to severe psychological or physical dependence. Schedule II drugs include cocaine, morphine, and codeine.

Schedule III drugs have a lower potential for abuse than Schedule I or II drugs and have a currently accepted medical use in the United States. Abuse of these drugs may lead to moderate physical dependence or severe psychological dependence.

Schedule IV drugs have a lower potential for abuse of than Schedule I, II, or III drugs and have an accepted medical use in the United States. Use of Schedule IV drugs may lead to limited physical or psychological dependence relative to Schedule III drugs.

Schedule V drugs have a low potential for abuse relative to Schedule IV drugs and have a currently accepted medical use in the United States. Abuse of these drugs may lead to limited physical or psychological dependence relative to Schedule IV drugs.

Narcotics

One of the most commonly used and misused terms in drug enforcement is the word *narcotic* itself. The term *narcotic* is used generically to describe any substance that may be listed under the CSA. Medically, the term has a much more specific meaning. Medically, a narcotic is "a drug that in moderate doses depresses the central nervous system, thus relieving pain and producing sleep, but in excessive doses produces unconsciousness, stupor, coma and possibly death" (Taber's, p. 1274).

Narcotics can be natural or synthetic. Natural narcotics are usually derivatives of the opium poppy, *Papaver somniferum*. The opium poppy grows in India, Turkey, China, Mexico, and in both southeast and southwest Asia. Raw *opium* is obtained by slashing the fruiting capsule of the plant and then collecting the resulting latex exudate, which may be smoked. *Morphine* is a purified alkaloid extracted from opium and is about 10 times as strong as unrefined opium. *Heroin* is a semisynthetic compound produced by chemically altering morphine. The chemical conversion of morphine to heroin is one to one, so there is no loss of product in the process, although heroin is a much more potent and addictive drug. Narcotics may be injected intravenously, swallowed in pill form, inhaled, or smoked, depending on the type and availability of the specific drug.

Symptoms of Narcotic Abuse

Investigators must be able to recognize individuals who are under the influence of all types of drugs, including narcotics. Symptoms of narcotics use are as follows:

- Constricted pupils
- Slowed respiration
- Nausea
- Drowsiness
- Euphoria
- Constipation
- Tolerance to the drug
- Physical dependence

Narcotic use may begin with an initial "rush" in which the user experiences a feeling of euphoria, exhilaration, and a warm tingling feeling in the skin. In the next phase, the user may become semiconscious and lethargic. Fatal and near fatal overdoses are common with narcotic use.

Cannabis

Cannabis, commonly called *marijuana*, is the botanical name for a tall, annual, dioecious (bearing male and female flowers on separate plants) herb. There are a number of species of *Cannabis*, including *Cannabis sativa*, *Cannabis indica*, and *Cannabis americana*. The marijuana plant may grow to a height of 20 feet but is usually 8 to 10 feet high. In recent years, marijuana growers have begun growing plants in isolated areas in the United States or in small plots to avoid detection from the air and because of state and federal asset forfeiture statutes. The marijuana plant grows on a fluted stock and produces an odd number of palmate leaves with distinctive saw-toothed edges.

The marijuana plant produces a number of pharmacologically active compounds, called *cannabinoids*, the most important of which, from a law enforcement perspective, is delta-trans tetrahydrocannabinol (THC), the psychoactive ingredient in marijuana. In the past, the THC content in wild marijuana or "ditch weed" was about 3 to 4 percent. Through careful cultivation of plants, marijuana growers have been able to increase the THC in some plants to 10 to 11 percent. It is suspected that increased emergency room admissions related to marijuana use may be related to these higher THC levels. Marijuana is known to reduce nausea, which is why it is sometimes used for cancer chemotherapy patients.

Most drug abusers seldom restrict themselves to one substance of abuse. Marijuana is often taken in combination with another drug, usually alcohol. When alcohol and marijuana are consumed at the same time, it is thought that the THC may act to suppress the body's natural tendency to reject excessive quantities of alcohol (though nausea and vomiting), which may thus lead to alcohol poisoning or another alcohol-related problem.

Marijuana is usually smoked and produces a number physical and psychological symptoms. Users report feelings of euphoria, well being, and relaxation, and may also report increased sensory perception and occasionally hunger.

Investigating Violations of Marijuana Laws

As mentioned earlier, a variety of investigative techniques may be used to reduce the sale, distribution, and production of marijuana. These techniques include the search of open fields, aerial surveillance, as well as traditional and covert investigations.

Open Fields

Because much marijuana production often occurs outdoors, investigators must be knowledgeable of the law of search and seizure as it relates to open fields and aerial surveillance. Increased use of aerial surveillance by law enforcement agencies has caused marijuana growers to change their cultivation techniques to planting in small plots located in isolated areas. Many growers now plant marijuana in national and state forests to avoid the consequences of federal and state assets forfeiture laws. Under the latter laws, after conviction of a drug-related offense the violator may be compelled to forfeit the means by which the crime was committed, including money, land, vehicles, or other items involved in the commission of the crime.

In order to locate plots where marijuana is being grown, investigators work from both the air and ground. In *Oliver v. United States*, the Supreme Court placed the "open fields" exception to the search warrant requirement on solid legal footing. In *Oliver*, two Kentucky state policemen, acting on a tip that the defendant was growing marijuana on his farm, went to the farm to investigate.

They drove past Oliver's house to a gate that was posted with a "No Trespassing" sign. A footpath led away from one side of the gate. The officers followed the path to a field of marijuana, which was approximately 1 mile from the defendant's house. Oliver was later arrested and convicted of manufacturing a controlled substance. The Court held that open fields were accessible to the public and therefore the defendant did not have a reasonable expectation of privacy in the fields surrounding his house. As a result of *Oliver*, the police may make warrantless entries into an area outside the curtilage of the house to search for and seize items of evidence.

Aerial Surveillance

In *California v. Ciriaolo*, the Supreme Court clarified the law related to aerial surveillance. Police received an anonymous tip that Cirialo was growing marijuana in his backyard. The officers went to the house to investigate. After they found that they could not see into the area from ground level where the plants were alleged to be, they then rented a private airplane and flew over the defendant's backyard. The officers, who had been trained to identify marijuana, saw the plants in question and took aerial photographs of them. Using this evidence, the officers obtained a search warrant and subsequently seized several marijuana plants. Cirialo was convicted of manufacturing marijuana. The Court ruled that no search warrant was required for naked-eye aerial observations of the suspect's backyard, even in the curtilage around his house.

The Supreme Court provided additional guidance on how far the curtilage of a residence extends in *United States v. Dunn*. In *Dunn*, police learned that a codefendant had purchased large quantities of chemicals and equipment that are used to produce controlled substances. Police placed a tracking device in some of the equipment, which led them to Dunn's farm. Officers entered the property by climbing over several fences and walked to a barn that was 50 yards from the defendant's house. The offices had been led to the barn by strong chemical odors and the sound of a motor running. Without entering the barn, the officers stood at a locked gate and shined a flashlight into the building, where they saw what appeared to be an illegal laboratory. Using this information, the officers obtained a search warrant and seized the lab. Dunn was convicted of conspiracy to manufacture a controlled substance. The Court said that the barn was not within the curtilage of the house. The determination of what is part of the curtilage is based on four factors:

1. The proximity of the area to the house
2. Whether the area is an enclosure surrounding the house
3. The nature and uses of the area
4. The steps taken to conceal the area from public view

Aerial surveillance provides an effective mechanism to limit the outdoor production of marijuana. Marijuana producers no longer grow marijuana in large plots. Instead, three or four plants are grown close together in small, isolated clusters, thus making them more difficult to locate. In addition, many plants are produced in indoor "hot house" growing operations.

Stimulants

Stimulants are substances that accelerate the central nervous system. Stimulants can be natural or synthetic. Natural stimulants are adrenaline, ephedrine, caffeine, and methylbenzyl ecgonine, or as it better know, cocaine. Synthetic stimulants include amphetamines, phenmetrazine, and methylphenidate, which sells under the trade name Ritalin.

Stimulants trigger the body's fight or flight response. They produce an increase in blood pressure, an increase in energy level through the release of stored sugar, and an increase in the pulse rate. Stimulant users report feelings of increased alertness, excitation, and euphoria and tunnel vision.

Methamphetamine

One of the more commonly encountered stimulants is methamphetamine. Methamphetamine is commonly known by the street names of *crystal, crystal meth, speed*, and *crank*. The term *crank* allegedly comes from the long association of methamphetamine with outlaw motorcycle gangs that are involved in the production and distribution of methamphetamine. Crank refers to the act of "cranking over" a motorcycle to start it.

Methamphetamine may be inhaled, swallowed, or snorted through the nostrils. The preferred means of use is intravenous injection of a solution of the drug. Recently a new form of methamphetamine that can be smoked, called *ice* because of its resemblance to that substance, has appeared on the streets. The attraction of this form of methamphetamine is its ability to produce a feeling of euphoria within seconds after being inhaled. The effect of the drug may last for four to six hours and may be quite intense. Methamphetamine users often drink alcoholic beverages while using the drug to moderate the effects of the stimulant on the body, a practice referred to as "cutting the edge off the speed."

Repeated use of amphetamine produces an increased tolerance for the drug. Although it remains unclear whether and to what extent physical dependence develops with extended methamphetamine use, it does appear that it can produce psychological dependence.

Symptoms of Stimulant Abuse

Stimulant abusers may be recognized by the following common symptoms:

- Excitation and hyperactivity
- Restlessness and insomnia
- Extreme loss of appetite
- Dilated pupils
- Increased perspiration
- Dry mouth
- Disorientation and panic

Stimulant abusers withdrawing from drug use often appear apathetic, depressed, irritable, and disoriented. They may sleep for periods of as long as 20 hours or more a day.

Cocaine

Cocaine, in its many forms, is presently one of the most commonly abused stimulants in the United States. Cocaine use and abuse is not a new phenomenon. Andean Indians, living over 3,000 years ago, used to chew coca leaves to extract their stimulatory alkaloids, and coca leaves were used by priests and nobility in religious ceremonies of the Incas. Today most coca plants are grown in Bolivia and Peru. The primary laboratories where cocaine is extracted from coca leaves are currently located in Columbia.

Cocaine Production   The coca plants, *Erythroxylum coca* and *Erythroxylum novogranatense*, are grown from seed and usually mature in about 18 months. Leaves may be harvested three or four times a year, and a plant may produce for 50 years. Approximately 150 pounds of coca leaves are required to produce 1 pound of cocaine. The refining of cocaine begins by extracting cocaine alkaloids from the leaves. This process produces a crude paste, called *basuko*, which is refined into cocaine hydrochloride (cocaine HCl), the street form of the drug.

Cocaine Usage   Cocaine HCI is a white crystalline powder that may be inhaled or injected. Users feel the effects of the drug within approximately 30 seconds when it is inhaled and within about eight seconds when injected. The effects of a smokable form of cocaine, commonly referred to as *crack*, are felt within as little as five seconds.

Cocaine HCI cannot be smoked and is converted into a smokable form by users via any of a number of techniques. While cocaine HCI is being processed into a smokable form, it makes a "cracking" sound, and hence the name *crack*. The stimulatory effects of cocaine use, in any form, last for only 10 to 15 minutes. Because of the relatively short duration of the drug's effects, a habitual cocaine user's life often becomes a continuous search for the drug and the money to buy it.

Symptoms of Cocaine Abuse   Extended cocaine usage results in general physical deterioration. The user suffers from loss of energy, insomnia, and headaches, and often a sore throat, a runny nose, and nosebleeds, especially if the drug is inhaled. Heavy cocaine use produces seizures and convulsions, breathing difficulties, and an irregular heartbeat. Cocaine users may appear anxious and depressed, or conversely, extremely excited. Sharp mood swings are common, and regular users find it increasingly difficult to maintain a job or other normal relations. While physical dependence may not develop with its use, psychological dependence is commonly seen.

Hallucinogens

Hallucinogens are sometimes referred to as *psychedelics*, but the latter term is generally avoided by law enforcement personnel to avoid implying that the use of this class of drugs may produce romantic or pleasurable experiences. Hallucinogens may produce altered perception, thoughts, and feelings. Users of hallucinogens reported heightened awareness of sensory stimuli, distorted perception, feelings of detachment, poor perception of time and distance, and entering into trancelike states.

Lysergic Acid Diethylamide (LSD)

Lysergic acid diethylamide (LSD) is the prototypical hallucinogen. Its action in the brain is not clearly understood. Users report experiencing the general effects of hallucinogens already described, as well as others, including *synesthesia*, the ability to "feel" colors and "touch" sounds.

Physical symptoms of LSD use include:

- Dilated pupils
- Tremors
- Drowsiness
- Headaches
- Nausea
- Irregular breathing
- Increased blood pressure
- Burning sensations in the skin

The dosage forms of LSD are measured in micrograms, that is, one millionth of a gram. LSD may be ingested by taking tablets, placing liquid LSD on a sugar cube and eating it, or by placing liquid LSD on a piece of paper and chewing the paper.

Phencyclidine (PCP)

Phencyclidine (PCP) was originally developed in 1957 as an anesthetic. It was found to be too powerful for human use and was later marketed as an animal tranquilizer. PCP is sold under the street names of angel dust, hog, whack, water, and sernylan, usually as a clear liquid in small glass or plastic vials. Users dip a cigarette into liquid PCP and then smoke it. Alternatively, powdered PCP may be sprinkled onto a cigarette, marijuana, or parsley flakes and smoked. PCP use may produce hallucinations, depression, stimulation, and/or unpredictable and violent behavior. Because PCP acts on the nervous system as an anesthetic, the user does not feel pain, a state that, when coupled with the unpredictable behavior it often invokes, makes any situation involving PCP users potentially quite dangerous.

Depressants

Depressants are drugs that depress the activities of the central nervous system. They are classified as hypnotics, that is, drugs that produce or induce sleep, and as sedatives, drugs that produce relaxation or sleep. Some of the more commonly abused depressants include phenobarbital, glutethimide, which is marketed as Doriden, and methaqualone, which used to be marketed as Quaalude or Sopor and is commonly called *ludes*. Methaqualone is now a Schedule I drug, although it is still produced outside the United States and is smuggled into the country. Among the less powerful tranquilizers that are abused are the benzodiazepines, which include the prescribed drugs Valium (diazepam) and Librium (chlordiaz-epoxide), and the carbamate derivative, Miltown (meprobamate). Depressants are often taken with alcohol, which may enhance the effect of the drug on the user.

Symptoms of Depressant Abuse

An abuser of depressants may manifest symptoms resembling alcohol intoxication, especially if one of the more powerful depressants, such as phenobarbital, has been used. Depressant users may exhibit sluggishness, difficulty following instructions, and poor memory. Abuse of depressants may produce extreme mood swings and even suicidal ideation and behavior. Withdrawal of drug use in chronic barbiturate abusers can produce severe symptoms that can even lead to death from cardiovascular collapse or respiratory failure.

Investigating Drug-Related Crimes

The investigation of drug abuse involves a variety of techniques, both reactive and proactive. One of the most common and effective techniques used by law enforcement is the purchase of drugs by undercover police officers or informants.

Controlled Buys of Drugs

Controlled drug buys require having a knowledgeable informant. An informant is a person who gives information to law enforcement officials regarding violations of the law. Informants are specifically used to:

· Furnish information from sources not readily available to an investigator
· Make observations or perform assignments in situations where a stranger would be suspect
· Make controlled buys and conduct undercover operations
· Provide intelligence information on street activity

The use of informants can be very problematic. The problems most commonly associated with the use of informants include:

1. Control of the informant
2. Credibility of the informant
3. Agency embarrassment
4. Entrapment

Investigators must determine what is motivating the informant to cooperate with the police. The most common motivations are:

· Fear of associates and/or legal punishment
· Revenge
· Perversity
· Egotism
· Jealously over women, drugs, or money

- Desire to discover what the law agency knows about the suspects
- Diversion of suspicion
- Identification with law enforcement
- Desire to be well regarded by the law
- Desire to magnify one's own importance
- Mercenary (to grain money)
- Repentance (to atone for past transgressions)

Developing and Controlling Informants

1. Everyone arrested should be approached as a potential informant.
2. The best success comes with being sociable and having a pleasing personality.
3. Techniques for developing informants are limited only by the investigator's imagination and his or her ability and desire to be a proficient, well-rounded investigator.
4. Proper interviewing techniques can often secure the cooperation of hesitant informants.

Interviewing Potential Informants

When attempting to objectively evaluate a potential informant and the information he or she is offering to provide, the following questions should be answered:

- What is the informant's motivation?
- Has the informant been reliable in the past?
- How intelligent is the informant?
- How did the informant gain the knowledge he or she is offering?
- Does the informant have a personal interest in the case?
- Does the informant have direct knowledge of the events being discussed or is it simply street gossip?
- Does the informant have access to additional related information?
- Does the informant have a reason to be vengeful toward the violator?
- Does the informant have experience with the criminal justice system that will make it possible to report the information accurately?
- Is the informant withholding information? The answer to that question is almost always yes.
- Has the informant fabricated information in the past?
- Is the informant willing to testify in court? If not, he or she cannot be used to make controlled buys.

If most of the above questions can be answered, the investigator should be able to objectively evaluate the informant and his or her information.

Control and Handling of Informants

1. The investigator directs and controls the investigation, not the informant.
2. The investigator should not promise monetary payments or make any other promises that cannot be kept or are outside his or her authority.
3. The investigator must maintain proper control of the informant and the direction of the investigation, including:

- Making frequent personal contact with the informant at a prearranged, secure meeting place
- Avoiding the use of official buildings for meetings
- Having a second officer present as a witness (to corroborate anything said or done at the meeting)

Entrapment

Entrapment means enticing or procuring a person to commit a crime that he or she did not contemplate or would have not committed, for the sole purpose of prosecuting that person. The following examples illustrate facts that indicate entrapment:

Example 1

Involving a first-offender in a scheme in which the illegal act is only incidental to the plan. For example, an informant, who was a low-character individual, enticed a physician into a scheme to bet on racehorses injected with heroin. The physician referred the informant to the defendant, a first-offender of high reputation, to acquire the drug. On mentioning the physician's name, the defendant was persuaded to buy the heroin from a dealer, induced by the chance of making large winnings.

Example 2

Playing on the sympathies of a first-offender to alleviate the pain or suffering of another. For example, an addict, placed under arrest and promised release if she produced results, persuaded a first-offender to procure morphine for her, at personal profit, to enable the addict to keep her job.

Example 3

Giving narcotics to a first-offender and inducing him to sell it over his objections. For example, an informant gave 25 marijuana cigarettes to a student and told him to sell them. The student tried to return them, but the investigator refused. He was subsequently arrested for possession. The student had no prior record of possession.

Do's and Don'ts of Dealing with Informants

Do's

Do determine if the informant can do what he claims. In difficult situations, such as when an informant has been arrested, he may make any number of promises and claims to escape the problem he is in.

Do determine and understand the motivation of the informant.

Do ensure that the informant has a clear understanding of what he or she is allowed to do and not do. The informant should be required to complete the cooperating individual agreement.

Do question, evaluate, and verify the content of the information provided by an informant, and verify how the information was obtained.

Do maintain security through good meeting and reporting procedures and other such practices.

Do instruct the informant on agency operational procedures and legal issues.

Do direct and channel the informant's efforts to obtain desired results.

Do practice "need to know" procedures in discussing the informant with others, even other police officers.

Do practice "need to know" procedures in discussions with the informant. Maintain a one-way flow of information with the informant unless a particular investigative goal is served by talking to the informant.

Do establish and maintain good lines of communication with the informant. Ensure that the informant can be reached at a later time.

Do maintain a strictly professional relationship.

Do objectively evaluate the information provided.

Do maintain control over the informant (always make it clear that you are the boss).

Do be sensitive to the feelings and needs of the informant. Avoid using derogatory terms, such as snitch or stool pigeon.

Do remember that the informant may have perverse motives for cooperating.

Do remember to thoroughly debrief the informant on first contact, obtaining as much information as possible. This may be the best opportunity to obtain truthful information from the informant.

Do evaluate and weigh the information that is provided by an informant.

Do continuously compare and correlate newly acquired information with old information.

Do verify information received from an informant with other sources.

Do continuously work to develop and maintain sources of information by improving your communication and investigative procedures, rather than by relying strictly on power and obligation.

Do approach every encounter or interview with the informant in an organized manner. The purpose of the meeting is to gain information.

Do obtain a signed receipt for all payments made to the informant.

Do obtain a photograph, fingerprints, and background information from an informant at the first meeting. If the informant is to be paid, also obtain a handwriting sample.

Do determine if the informant is currently or has previously worked as an informant for another investigator or agency.

Do document an informant's activity and productivity.

Don'ts

Don't bring the informant to the police facility.

Don't hold the meeting in a location where the investigator's or the informant's security may be compromised.

Don't tell the informant anything other than what he must know to accomplish his mission (information flows based on "need to know").

Don't allow the informant to run the show.

Don't become emotionally attached to the informant. Investigators must maintain a professional relationship.

Don't become romantically involved with the informant.

Don't accept any information at "face value." An investigator must verify everything.

Don't make promises to an informant that cannot be kept.

Don't allow any information to be obtained by illegal means. In one case, an informant was giving information to the investigator that his girlfriend, who was working as a clerk in the police record section, was stealing from police files she had access to.

Don't allow the informant to engage in unrelated criminal activity. Being an informant is not a license to commit crimes.

Don't take the word of an informant over that of another police officer.

Don't continue to use an informant who has gone "sour" or has become unproductive.

Don't allow an informant to carry weapons or function as a law enforcement officer.

Don't give an informant any controlled substances for any reason.

Don't expose an informant to other informants or undercover officers.

Once the individual has agreed to cooperate, the case officer must thoroughly debrief the individual. Through skillful interviewing, the investigator must attempt to learn everything the informant knows about drug trafficking and other types of criminal activity. Remember that informants usually withhold and distort information to protect themselves against immediate prosecution. Informants also withhold information that may be of use in some future legal difficulties they may be involved in. For these reasons, it is virtually impossible to learn everything an informant knows. Interviewers should always view an informant's information with skepticism.

After debriefing the informant, the investigator must corroborate the informant's information. The most common means to corroborate information are:

· Department records
· State police records
· Surveillance reports
· Other law enforcement agency records

While debriefing the informant, the investigator must avoid making any promises to the informant. Peace officers have no authority to make deals on behalf of the prosecutor. Any unauthorized agreements will make successful prosecution much more difficult. The informant's involvement in any transaction must be completely voluntary and not based on unauthorized promises of leniency or special considerations by the police. Any agreements made with the informant should be written and should be made available to the defense on discovery. Investigators should use every available technique to determine an informant's reliability and dependability.

> **CASE STUDY**
>
> Police are continually looking for potential informants. In one case, a police officer assigned to drug investigations obtained the release of a pre-trial detainee who was in a county jail awaiting trial on a charge of receiving stolen property. The officer had the inmate released on a personal recognizance bond with the expectation that the man would begin to make controlled buys of drugs for the police. While free on bond, the new, and as yet unused, informant was arrested and charged with first-degree murder after he killed a man who had befriended him after his release. Although the murder had no apparent links with the other crime for which the defendant/informant had been jailed, questions were raised by the media and the deceased's family about the practice of obtaining release for criminal defendants to work as informants.

The possibility of encountering problems with informants can be reduced, but certainly not eliminated, by following policies regulating the use of informants. As long as informants are used by the police, particularly in drug investigations, episodes of this sort will occur. If investigators are acting pursuant to a standard policy, the potential for problems will be reduced but not be eliminated.

Intercepting and Recording Conversations

The informant should contact the subject of investigation on the telephone. In most states, intercepting electronic transmissions is legal if one of the parties to the conversation, the informant in this case, is aware the conversation is being intercepted.

Law of Electronic Intercepts

Traditional investigative techniques often do not yield the information necessary to prosecute drug cases. Police are therefore required to employ a variety of investigative techniques for this purpose. One of the most effective techniques for gathering information is electronic surveillance. Electronic surveillance is governed by Title III of the Omnibus Crime Control and Safe Streets Act of 1968. While this is a federal law, it serves as a model for states, which create similar statutes. The law states:

> Procedure for interception of wire, oral, or electronic communications
>
> (1) Each application for an order authorizing or approving the interception of a wire, oral, or electronic communication under this chapter shall be made in writing upon oath or affirmation to a judge of competent jurisdiction and shall state the applicant's authority to make such application. Each application shall include the following information:
>   (a) the identity of the investigative or law enforcement officer making the application, and the officer authorizing the application;
>   (b) a full and complete statement of the facts and circumstances relied upon by the applicant, to justify his belief that an order should be issued, including (i) details as to the particular offense that has been, is being, or

is about to be committed, (ii) except as provided in subsection (11), a particular description of the nature and location of the facilities from which or the place where the communication is to be intercepted, (iii) a particular description of the type of communications sought to be intercepted, (iv) the identity of the person, if known, committing the offense and whose communications are to be intercepted;

(c) a full and complete statement as to whether or not other investigative procedures have been tried and failed or why they reasonably appear to be unlikely to succeed if tried or to be too dangerous;

(d) a statement of the period of time for which the interception is required to be maintained. If the nature of the investigation is such that the authorization for interception should not automatically terminate when the described type of communication has been first obtained, a particular description of facts establishing probable cause to believe that additional communications of the same type will occur thereafter;

(e) a full and complete statement of the facts concerning all previous applications known to the individual authorizing and making the application, made to any judge for authorization to intercept, or for approval of interceptions of wire, oral, or electronic communications involving any of the same persons, facilities or places specified in the application, and the action taken by the judge on each such application; and

(f) where the application is for the extension of an order, a statement setting forth the results thus far obtained from the interception, or a reasonable explanation of the failure to obtain such results.

Obtaining a Search Warrant for a Electronic Intercept

Prior to intercepting a wire, oral, or electronic communication, law enforcement officers must obtain a search warrant. The investigator must demonstrate all of the following to a judge:

1. Probable cause to believe that the person whose communication is about to be intercepted has committed, is committing, or is about to commit murder, kidnapping, robbery, extortion, bribery of public officials, gambling, drug trafficking, escape, or counterfeiting
2. Probable cause to believe that the particular communications can be obtained through the interception
3. That normal investigative procedures have been or will be unsuccessful in obtaining the required information and/or that other investigative procedures might prove too dangerous
4. That the facility from which the intercept is to occur is being used in connection with the suspected crime and that the name listed on the lease or title is in the name commonly used by the suspect

Issuance of the Search Warrant

If a judge issues a search warrant, the order authorizing the interception must specify all of the following:

1. The identity of the person whose communications are to be intercepted
2. The nature and location of the communications facilities for which, or the place where, authority to intercept is granted

3. A particular description of the type of communications sought to be intercepted, and a statement of the particular offense to which the communication relates
4. The identity of the agency authorized to intercept the communication and the identity of the person authorizing the application
5. The length of time for which the interception is authorized

Execution of the Search Warrant

Once a search warrant authorizing the interception of a wire, oral, or electronic communication is issued, the order must be carried out as soon as possible. Delays in the execution of the order may be allowed if the agency conducting the interception is able to explain the delay.

Title III and similar state statutes require that the interception be conducted in such a manner that the interception of unauthorized communications is held to a minimum. The determination of what communications are included in the order is made by a judge using the objective reasonableness test. In the event that investigators intercept communications that relate to crimes other than those that were specified in the order, the investigator can request the prosecutor to contact the judge who issued order. A request may be made to obtain judicial approval to disclose the evidence in court. Without prior judicial approval, the newly discovered evidence may not be used.

Once the authorized interceptions have resulted in obtaining the objective specified in the warrant, the interceptions must cease. In any case, the interceptions must cease within 30 days. Extensions may be granted, but only after the agency conducting the interception has reapplied for another order or warrant.

Once the interception has been terminated, the agency must deliver the recordings to the judge who issued the order. The recordings are then sealed under the judge's order. Sealing the recording is done to prevent tampering, to maintain the chain of custody, to protect confidentiality, and to ensure judicial oversight of the electronic surveillance. Finally, after the interceptions have ended, the agency must, within a reasonable time, but not later than 90 days, notify the persons named in the order of the surveillance. In addition, other persons whose communications were intercepted must also be notified. The judge who issued the order may delay the notification if it appears that the delay may be in the interest of justice.

An electronic surveillance of this sort is an enormously time-consuming and expensive undertaking. While it is a valuable tool against drug trafficking and other crimes that are committed in secret, its use is limited usually to joint municipal, county, state, and federal task forces.

Consensual Electronic Intercepts

The principle of consensual intercepts provides the authority to use body wires and tape recorders under similar circumstances. Unlike other forms of electronic surveillance, consensual interceptions do not require prior judicial approval. When one party to a communication consents to the interception of the communication, no prior judicial approval is required. Law enforcement officers or private citizens may intercept and record communications without violating the

Fourth Amendment or Title III. Evidence obtained in this manner can be invaluable in the prosecution of drug cases. The equipment needed to tape a phone conversation may be purchased at most electronics stores. A microphone is taped to the earpiece (top) of the telephone and then plugged into a tape recorder. Once the call has been completed, the tape should be removed and the tabs of the cassette broken off to prevent taping over the conversation. The tape should then be submitted as evidence, ensuring that the chain of custody is maintained.

Setting a Location for the Buy

As part of the telephone conversation, the informant should attempt to set up the meeting place in a location that will provide the greatest opportunity to conduct surveillance. Ideally the meeting should take place during daylight and out of doors. Remarkably, a convincing informant can provide a plausible explanation for wanting such a meeting site. In addition, assets forfeiture laws have forced dealers to conduct transactions at locations other than their own homes.

Briefing Other Officers

The case officer should next brief other officers assigned to the investigation. Officers must also be told the informant's description as well as the description of the defendant. The officers conducting the surveillance should be in place well before the transaction is to take place. Under no circumstances should any covert transaction be conducted without surveillance. This is required for two reasons:

1. Surveillance is necessary for the undercover operative's safety.
2. Officers on the surveillance can provide needed corroborating evidence in later criminal proceedings.

Searching the Informant

Prior to the transaction, the informant must be strip searched in order to ensure that he has no other drugs or money on his person. This must be done to reduce the possibility that the defense will argue that the informant sold additional drugs to the defendant or that the defendant kept part of the buy money. The informant must also be searched after returning from the transaction for the same reasons. At this point in time, the investigators may wish to place a recording device or transmitter on the informant. The law allowing the use of body wires is the same as the law governing consensual interceptions of communications discussed earlier.

Buy Money

The informant should then be given marked money with which to make the purchase. The recommended practice is to record the following information from each bill:

· Serial number
· Series number

· Date the bill was issued
· Denomination

The informant should be given cash in many different denominations to avoid arousing the dealer's suspicions. If the informant can deal skillfully and credibly with the suspect, he or she should attempt to negotiate with the suspect to obtain a better price on the drugs. A customer who suddenly agrees to pay a price he or she previously considered to be unacceptably high is likely to arouse suspicion and might cause the suspect to refuse to make the sale.

Discussing the Story with the Informant

The investigator must tell the informant what to do. At this point the investigator and the informant must develop a plausible cover story for the informant. A simple scenario that is similar to what the informant has done in the past with the subject is most effective. The investigator should also work with the informant to discuss possible snags in the transactions and to develop contingency plans for different situations.

One question that frequently arises is the issue of advancing or "fronting" money to the dealer. One of the cardinal rules of drug investigations is NEVER FRONT THE MONEY. In any business transaction, individuals do not pay money in advance hoping to receive something in return later. Buying illegal drugs is a business transaction for the parties involved. In order to be convincing, the informant must insist on certain terms before a deal is transacted.

The investigator should instruct the informant to complete the transaction as soon as possible and then leave the defendant's premises. The investigator should try to set a time limit of 30 to 45 minutes for the informant to complete the transaction. Without setting a time limit, surveillance officers may wait hours for the informant to return.

The informant must be instructed to avoid entrapping the defendants. *Entrapment* is the enticing or procuring of a person to commit a crime he was not otherwise predisposed to commit. Entrapment is not often successful, primarily because the defendant must admit involvement in a criminal transaction on the stand. Defendants are understandably reluctant to do that. Entrapment also involves bringing undue pressure on the defendant, such as begging for drugs or threatening defendants to force them to sell the drugs.

Several factors, however, reduce the possibility of a successful entrapment defense, such as when the defendant sets the price on his own, when the defendant supplies the drug immediately to the informant, or when the defendant has had a recent conviction for a related crime. Making two or more buys from the same defendant also makes the use of the entrapment defense unlikely.

After the buy has been completed, the case officer must meet with the informant immediately to recover the evidence. This is the next link in the chain of custody of the evidence. The evidence should remain in the case officer's possession until it is turned into the appropriate location, such as an evidence locker at a laboratory. The officer may wish to field test the drug using a commercially available test kit so that the informant can later praise or complain about the quality of the drug in a later telephone call.

After recovering the evidence, the buyer should be strip searched again for the same reasons as listed earlier. The informant's actions during the buy should be documented, with special attention being paid to events that occurred when he or she was out of sight of the surveillance officers. It is generally best for the officer to take the statement from the informant and then write a report. An informant will seldom provide the necessary detail required by a prosecuting attorney. A sample witness statement and report appears in Figure 12.1.

The informant should next make a follow up phone call to the suspect and discuss the transaction and the quality of the drug. The call should be taped and the tape should be handled in the same manner described earlier. The informant can now be released with instructions on how and when to contact the case officer.

Undercover Officers

In general, it is preferable to use undercover police officers rather than informants in covert drug investigations. This is because undercover officers are trained investigators who are prepared to testify in court on any transaction in which they were involved. The steps in an undercover investigation are basically the same as in an informant buy, except that the officer is making the transaction. In cases of this type, an informant is used to introduce the undercover officer. After the officer's credibility with the drug dealer has been established, the informant is removed from the operation and used in some other capacity. Undercover investigations involving commissioned police officers are preferable to informant buys because:

· The officer is a believable witness.
· The officer will gain information immediately, rather than needing to wait to debrief the informant. This will allow the officer to alter an operational plan in order to develop new evidence or new cases.

Drug Possession Cases

Patrol officers often make cases for possession of a controlled substance, especially drug possession. This type of case may lead not only to convictions of drug users but also to information on drug activity in the community. Controlled substance possession cases are of three types:

1. Actual possession
2. Constructive possession
3. Joint constructive possession

Actual Possession Cases

Persons can be prosecuted for having a controlled substance in their possession. The prosecution must be prepared to prove that the defendant knowingly and intentionally possessed the drug and was aware that the substance was a drug. Possession may be shown by circumstantial evidence. The circumstantial evidence should be inconsistent with the defendant's guilty plea and show guilt beyond a reasonable inference. Thus possession can be proven when the substance is

IN THE CIRCUIT COURT OF SOUTH COUNTY, MISSOURI

STATE OF MISSOURI   CASE NO._____

COUNTY OF SOUTH

COOPERATING INDIVIDUAL FORM

The following statement was taken by Detectives Robert Smith and William Jones of the King County Sheriff's Department from SIF-90-0000 on March 15, 1994 at 11:15 p.m. at the Sheriff's office in Louisville, Missouri.

At about 3:00 p.m. on March 15, 1995 I got a phone call from John Doe at my house in St. Louis. John told me over the phone that he was going to get three "cars" in later that night, and wanted to now if I was interested. The word "car" is a code that John uses when he is talking over the phone about kilograms of cocaine. I told him I would call him back a little later and let him know if I was interested in buying any accessories, meaning smaller quantities of cocaine. I called Detective Smith immediately, and we made plans to meet.

At about 4:30 p.m. I met Detectives Smith and Jones, and I made a tape recorded call to John, and told him I was interested in buying a couple ounces, and he said they would be "one" apiece, meaning one thousand dollars each. I agreed to the price, and he told me to come by his house about 10:00 p.m. John told me not to come by before then, because he would have company from out of tow. I took this to mean his source of supply from Miami.

At about 6:00 p.m. I met with Detectives Smith and Jones again at a Target Store a few blocks from Johns house. There were some other agents there also. Detective Smith sent the other agents over to watch John's house, and then I got in the back of a van where Detectives Smith and Jones searched me. Detective Jones then searched my car and Detective Smith had me sign for $2,000.00 of Government money that I was going to spend for the cocaine. Detective Smith concealed a recorder and a transmitter on me, and then we just waited around.

About 9:30 p.m. one of the other police contacted Detective Smith by the radio and told him that a blue Ford van with Florida plates had just arrived at Johns house, and a guy went in with a suitcase. About 15 minutes later Detective Smith instructed me to go to Johns house and buy the two ounces of cocaine and see how much I could get fronted. I drove to John's followed by Detectives Smith and Jones. I knocked at the door and John answered. John told me I would have to come back later but I told him I had family problems out of state and needed to leave.

John let me in and he took me to a bedroom just off the living room. I looked into the kitchen on the way to the bedroom and I saw at least five (5) kilograms of cocaine on the kitchen table. There was a dark complexioned man standing by the table and I asked John who the guy was. John said he was the 'main man" from Florida and he asked me how much cocaine I wanted. I told him I had the money for two ounces, but said I could get rid of a full kilogram within 48 hours.

John left the room and came back about five minutes later with my two ounces in a plastic bag. The two ounces was in a big chunk like it was cut right off a kilogram brick. He told me he talked with the "main man" and he would allow John to front me a kilogram of cocaine on a front, but I would have to pay $28,000 for the cocaine within one week. I agreed and John walked back to the kitchen. I waited a couple minutes and John started to walk back to the bedroom so I just left the bedroom and met him before he could get out of the kitchen. I gave the $2,000 to John for the 2 ounces and he handed me a grocery bag. I opened the grocery bag and inside was one kilogram of cocaine.

I shook the dark complexioned guys' hand and thanked him. I asked him his name and he said "Jaime". I told John I would see him in about three days and then I left. Detectives Smith and Jones followed me back to the Target Store where I turned over the cocaine to Detective Smith. The detectives searched me again in the back of a van and they searched my car again. A few minutes later we left and I followed the detectives to the sheriff's office.

The above statement is true to the best of my knowledge. no threats or promises were made to me in return for this statement.

Investigators who were involved in the case will also write reports detailing their observations and actions.

OFFICE OF THE PROSECUTING ATTORNEY

By:_____

                           ᵛJames Smith #12345

Subscribed and sworn to before me this ___day of ____, 19____.

_____

                           CIRCUIT COURT JUDGE

TIME:

Figure 12.1 A sample witness statement and report

removed from the person or from the clothing of the person arrested during a search incident to arrest. Possession may also be shown if the substance is removed from the defendant's car in a vehicle search or if it is found while serving a search warrant on the defendant's dwelling.

Constructive Possession

The facts of a case may be adequate to demonstrate that the defendant was in constructive possession of a controlled substance, which occurs when the defendant can be shown to have knowledge of the presence of a controlled substance, even though it is not actually in the defendant's presence. If the defendant is in exclusive control of a premise where the drugs were found, this will usually lead to a reasonable inference by the jury that the person possessed the drugs.

Joint Constructive Possession Cases

Joint constructive possession cases are among the more difficult drug possession cases to prove in court. These cases occur where more than one person has access to a premise or vehicle. For example, drugs found on a kitchen table would probably be adequate to prove that the residents of that dwelling were in possession of the substances found there.

Possession with the Intent to Distribute

Possession of a controlled substance is usually a felony unless the arrest is for a first offense of small quantities of marijuana, approximately 30 grams. In order to prosecute dealers, particularly street-level dealers, most state legislatures have provided statutes that allow the prosecution of sellers for possession with intent to distribute. These statutes provide significant penalty enhancements upon conviction of this crime. The most common means to prove possession with the intent to distribute is to actually make a hand-to-hand buy from the seller. This may be done by modifying the steps listed earlier for a controlled buy. Most drug task forces conduct transactions of this type and document the events using audiotape or videotape. It may also be possible to prove the intent to distribute by showing other types of evidence, including:

- Quantity of the drug
- Packaging of the drugs
- Purity of the drugs
- Possession of large amounts of cash
- Possession of weapons, particularly assault-style rifles, high-capacity magazine semiautomatic pistols, or sawed-off shotguns
- Possession of drug paraphernalia

Quantity of the Drug

Perhaps the best means to prove that suspect intended to distribute drugs will be the quantity of the drug seized. In some states, the weight is specified by statute. If the investigator seizes pounds or kilograms of marijuana or ounces of cocaine, methamphetamine, or heroin, for example, the prosecutor can likely demonstrate that the defendant intended to sell some of the drugs in his or her possession.

Packaging of the Drugs

If the drugs seized are packaged in numerous small bags or containers, then the prosecutor can show that the defendant intended to distribute the drugs. The number and type of packages seized should be included in the investigator's report.

Purity of the Drugs

Many drugs, such as heroin or cocaine, are cut with some substance to increase the weight and therefore the profitability of transactions for the suspect. If the investigator seizes drugs that are pure or unadulterated, this fact can be offered to show intent to distribute. Investigators must be prepared to testify about the relative purity of locally available street drugs to demonstrate that the drugs offered in this case are more pure than is usual.

Possession of Large Amounts of Cash

Financial gain is the primary purpose of drug dealing. Street-level drug transactions are conducted with cash. Therefore, the presence of large amounts or cash is evidence of possession of drugs with the intent to distribute. Serial numbers should be noted to determine if the dealer was been involved in recent controlled buys.

Possession of Weapons

Drug trafficking is often a violent activity, and therefore dealers tend to be armed. The weapons of choice include assault weapons and other firearms that have large magazine capacities that can fire numerous rounds. Investigators may also encounter sawed-off shotguns or expensive firearms. In the event an illegal firearm, such as a shotgun, a rifle with a barrel length less than 18 inches or a sawed-off stock, or an automatic weapon, is found, the Federal Bureau of Alcohol, Tobacco and Firearms should be contacted. The dealer can be prosecuted for possession of these firearms. In addition, if the person arrested is a convicted felon, he can be prosecuted as a felon in possession of a firearm under federal statute, and usually under state law as well.

Possession of Drug Paraphernalia or Instrumentalities

The presence of the instrumentalities needed to process and package drugs can be used to demonstrate the intent to distribute. These instrumentalities or paraphernalia include scales, cutting agents, sifters, spoons, drug residue, bags, chemicals, and film containers. Investigators should also look for beepers and large numbers of telephones or other types of communications and security equipment. Heavy foot or vehicle traffic, especially by known drug dealers, users, or gang members, reflects on the suspect's intent to distribute drugs. Finally, when searching after a drug arrest, investigators should look for notebooks and ledgers of transactions kept by dealers. Telephone and beeper records should also be seized.

The factors mentioned here may not, by themselves, be adequate to demonstrate the intent to distribute drugs but, taken in combination, may create a strong circumstantial case against the suspect.

Conclusion

Drug abuse and crime are closely related. Whether drug abusers commit crime to support their drug use or people who commit crimes are pre-disposed to abuse drugs remains unclear at this time. For the time being, investigators must use every legal means available to reduce the availability and use of illegal drugs in society.

References

Drugs and Crime 1989. Drug Use Forecasting Annual Report. Washington, DC: National Institute of Justice, U.S. Department of Justice, June 1990.

Drugs and Crime 1990. Drug Use Forecasting Annual Report. Washington, DC: National Institute of Justice Research in Action, U.S. Department of Justice, 1991.

Drug Use Forecasting, 1993. Annual Report on Adult Arrestees: Drugs and Crime in America's City. Washington, DC: U.S. Department of Justice, Office of Justice Programs, National Institute of Justice, November 1994.

Drug Use Forecasting Annual Report Adult and Juvenile Arrestees. Washington, DC: National Institute of Justice, U.S. Department of Justice, Office of Justice Programs, 1995.

Geberth, Vernon J. "Narcotics Buy Operations." In: *Criminal and Civil Investigation Handbook*, Grau, Joseph J., ed. New York: McGraw Hill, 1981.

Hayeslip, David W., Jr. and Weisel, Deborah L. "Local Level Drug Enforcement." In: *What Works in Policing? Operations and Administration Examined*, Cordner, Gary W., and Hale, Donna C., eds. Cincinnati, Ohio: Anderson Publishing, 1992.

Marx, Gary T. *Under Cover: Police Surveillance in America*. Berkeley, California: University of California Press, 1988.

Source Debriefing Guide. Washington, DC: Office of Intelligence, Drug Enforcement Administration, U.S. Department of Justice.

Taber's Cyclopedic Medical Dictionary, 17th ed. Thomas, Clayton, ed. Philadelphia, Pennsylvania: F.A. Davis, Co., 1989.

United States v. Carneiro, 861 F.2d 1171 (9th Cir. 1988).

United States v. Smith, 909 F. 2d 1164 (8th Cir. 1990).

United States v. Van Horn, 789 f. 2d 1492 (11th Cir. 1986).

Wilson, James Q. *The Investigators: Managing FBI and Narcotics Agents*. New York: Basic Books, 1978.

13. Fugitive Investigation, Case Preparation, and Presentation of Evidence

One should always look for a possible alternative and provide against it. It is the first rule of criminal investigation.

Sherlock Holmes, *The Adventure of Black Peter*, Sir Arthur Conan Doyle

Fugitive Investigations

After the identification of a suspect, the investigation becomes what Sanders (1977) calls a "Where are they investigation?" This is the fugitive phase of the investigation. A fugitive is someone for whom an arrest warrant has been issued. The investigator should begin a fugitive investigation by entering necessary information about the suspect into the appropriate state and national information systems, including:

- National Crime Information Center (NCIC)
- El Paso Intelligence Center (EPIC)
- State Information Systems
- Regional Information Sharing Systems (RISS) Programs

Searching for the Fugitive

After information on the fugitive has been entered, the investigator must take steps to find the individual. The first step the investigator should take is to confirm that the suspect is still at large. A phone call can prevent the waste of several investigative hours looking for someone who is already in custody. Investigators should be particularly sensitive to "pickups" or pickup orders. These terms were widely used in law enforcement in the past. The past practice was for detectives to issue pickups for suspects and if patrol officers or detectives located the suspect, he or she was to taken into custody or "picked up" for questioning. Today, law enforcement officers must be certain of the legal authority upon which they are arresting or detaining a person before restricting someone's freedom of movement. Officers cannot detain an individual unless they have reasonable suspicion to believe that the person stopped is engaged in some type of criminal activity, thus supporting an investigative detention. Similarly, officers must have probable cause or an arrest warrant based on probable cause to arrest a person. Before attempting to interfere with a person's freedom, the officer must be clear as to the legal authority upon which he is acting. The quickest way to confirm the authority upon which the action is to be taken is to contact the agency and the investigator assigned to the case.

The investigator should review the laws of arrest in the jurisdiction where he is working. For example, in most states, arresting officers need not have a copy of the arrest warrant with them at the time of the arrest. The investigator should determine that an arrest warrant for the suspect is still outstanding before attempting to make an arrest.

The investigator should next gather all the documentation available on the fugitive. This will include:

- Fingerprints
- Photographs (particularly the most recent arrest photos of the fugitive)
- Booking sheets from other agencies (if they are available)

The investigator should also contact detectives assigned to the case to see if they have insights into the fugitive's personality to determine how the suspect might avoid apprehension or if he is capable of violence. Background information on a fugitive can be used to develop a profile on suspects to determine where they might go for help.

This information can then be placed in a wanted poster along with other information about the fugitive, including:

- Locations where the suspect might seek help
- Associates the suspect might try to find
- Whether the suspect is considered dangerous

Thought should be given to where the flier should be distributed. In addition, the agency issuing the bulletin should attempt to recover or cancel the fliers once the fugitive is apprehended.

The investigator should determine if a reward has been offered for the fugitive. Even a modest reward can be a powerful incentive to cooperate with the officer. Occasionally investigators may serve as brokers between someone who is providing a reward and persons with information about a suspect's location.

Sources of Leads in a Fugitive Investigation

Once the preliminary steps have been taken, the investigator will actually begin looking for the fugitive. The first step is to contact the fugitive's family. An investigator's interviewing skills will be important as he tries to overcome the family's loyalty to the relative. The investigator should not be surprised if the family cooperates, especially when family members have been victimized by the fugitive. The investigator should make repeated contacts with all members of the family because the suspect will likely make some effort to contact his relatives eventually.

Law Related to Fugitive Investigation

As investigators interview persons who may have knowledge of a fugitive's location, they may wish to remind the person that there are several crimes related to protecting a fugitive, such as:

- Aiding in an escape
- Harboring a fugitive
- Hindering prosecution
- Accessory after the fact

These crimes are usually felonies and carry stiff penalties. Investigators should carry copies of the appropriate statutes to refresh their recollection about the law and to demonstrate to the person the seriousness of helping a fugitive to avoid apprehension.

Bondsmen

If the fugitive was free on bond at the time he absconded, it is worthwhile to contact the fugitive's bondsman. Bondsmen have a financial interest in having the fugitive found and returned to stand trial. Bondsman may have information on the fugitive's addresses and associates.

Credit Records

If the fugitive does not have large amounts of cash available, he may find it necessary to use his credit cards. The investigator can obtain the records on credit card usage with a court order or grand jury subpoena.

Phone Records

Telephone toll records can be very valuable in determining a fugitive's associates. It is necessary to obtain a court order or grand jury subpoena to obtain toll records.

Altering the Fugitive's Facial Appearance

When a fugitive has been at large for an extended period of time, it is to be expected that his or her appearance will change. To compensate for this, the fugitive's last known photograph can be altered by an artist to age the individual. It may also worthwhile to have the fugitive's photograph drawn with varying lengths of hair as well as different styles of facial hair.

Mail Covers

The investigator may request the U.S. Postal Service to place a mail cover on the fugitive's mail or mail to relatives of the fugitive. The postal service can record the postmarks and return addresses on the mail of someone suspected of having contact with the fugitive. The investigator may not open the mail without a search warrant.

Trash Searches

Discarded letters and other items may provide leads to a fugitive's location. Law enforcement officers may examine someone's trash after the individual has relinquished any claim to it. In *California v. Greenwood*, the Supreme Court ruled that the Fourth Amendment does not prohibit a warrantless search and seizure of trash left for collection in an area accessible to the public. In *Greenwood*, police set up surveillance on the defendant's house after receiving information that he was engaged in drug trafficking. Officers observed several vehicles stop briefly at the house at odd hours. One of the vehicles was followed to another residence, where trafficking was also suspected. Officers asked the local trash collectors to pick up the trash bags at Greenwood's residence and to return them unopened to the investigators. In the bags, investigators found evidence of drug use. Based on this information, investigators obtained a search warrant for Greenwood's residence. The search revealed quantities of cocaine and hashish. Greenwood and a co-conspirator were arrested on felony drug charges.

Officers later received new information that Greenwood had returned to drug dealing after being released on bond. Officer's again seized Greenwood's discarded trash and again found evidence of drug activity. Officers obtained another search warrant and again found evidence of illegal drug activity. Greenwood was arrested and charged a second time. The Court ruled that the defendant had no expectation of privacy in the trash once it had been placed outside the curtilage of the house. The Court went on to say:

> The warrantless search and seizure of the garbage bags left at the Greenwood house would violate the Fourth Amendment only if respondents [Greenwood] manifested a subjective expectation of privacy in their garbage that society accepts as objectively reasonable . . . It may well be that respondents did not expect that the contents of their garbage bags would become known to the police or other members of the public. An expectation of privacy does not give rise to Fourth Amendment protection, however, unless society is prepared to accept that expectation as objectively reasonable . . . Here we conclude that respondents exposed their garbage to the public to defeat their claim to Fourth Amendment protection. It is common knowledge that plastic garbage bags left on or at the side of a public street are readily accessible to animals, children, scavengers, snoops, and other members of the public . . . (California v. Greenwood [1988])

Trash searches can reveal a great deal about a suspect's habits, activities, and location. Most fugitives are captured because they revert to the types of activities at which they are comfortable. It is the investigator's task to identify those habits and to use them to locate the fugitive.

Major Case Squads

Police departments and sheriffs' offices are being required to develop creative responses to crime on limited budgets. Law enforcement agencies respond to crime in one of three ways. First, patrol units can be better allocated to crime-prone areas through crime analysis. More patrol units will be available at times when they are more likely to be needed. Second, crime prevention programs can be implemented. Crime prevention programs are intended to reduce the opportunities to commit some crimes or to make stolen property easier to recover. Many have some impact on crime, particularly if the program is vigorously pursued by the agency and the public.

Finally, efforts can be made to improve the agencies' ability to perform follow-up investigations. Such efforts may be restricted by jurisdictional boundaries, many of which are artificial. Although criminals do not stop at county or state lines, information possessed by law enforcement agencies about them very often does. This situation benefits only the criminal offender. Major case squads made up of representatives from area agencies can work together to investigate serious crimes in those communities.

Advantages of Major Case Squads

There are a number of obvious advantages to forming a major case squad, including:

- A partial solution to problems posed by jurisdictional limits
- A forum in which to exchange information about offenders and crime patterns
- An opportunity to take advantage of skills possessed by the different agency representatives

At one time, it was possible for a law enforcement officer to cross city or county lines to contact witnesses or make arrests. While the practice was sometimes questionable, the informality of law enforcement in the past made these practices possible. In a multi-agency operation, the pairing of officers from different jurisdictions makes it possible to conduct searches and to make arrests more easily. For example, it is easier for a local officer to apply for search and arrest warrants. A squad member's knowledge of local practices and personnel could expedite the investigative process and the paperwork associated with it.

The creation of a major case squad can also facilitate the exchange of information between law enforcement agencies. Collection, analysis, and dissemination of criminal intelligence have always presented a problem in police work. The realities of police work have largely prevented the dissemination of timely and accurate information; fragmentation of police agencies created physical and attitudinal barriers. It is time consuming and tedious to meet to exchange information. A major case squad, however, if properly structured and supervised, can overcome most of these barriers.

The levels of expertise of different agency personnel present another barrier to the exchange of information. Experienced investigators are sometimes reluctant to exchange information with inexperienced personnel, who may not know how to use the information correctly.

A third advantage of major case squads is that they provide an opportunity for different agencies to take advantage of each other's facilities and personnel. The cost of advanced training for investigators and specialized equipment is frequently beyond the reach of many agencies. For example, polygraphs and polygraph operators, hypnotists, and field evidence technicians cannot be cost effective in a small department. The purchase of essential equipment or the training of personnel could be made possible through the cooperative efforts of several agencies. In addition, the use of jointly funded regional crime laboratories is becoming increasingly popular. The demand on state crime laboratories often makes the delays in processing physical evidence a severe hindrance in prosecuting cases. Regional labs allow better utilization of scarce resources.

Structure of a Major Case Squad

The structure of a major case squad will vary depending on a number of factors. For example, informal meetings and telephone calls may provide for an adequate exchange of information in some situations. In many cases, however, a more formal structure may be required. A major case squad should be governed by a board of directors made up of one representative from each agency participating in the squad, chosen by the agency they represent. Each member of the board of directors should have one vote. The idea of "one agency one vote" is necessary to ensure the feeling of equal treatment among squad participants, particularly among representatives of small agencies.

The board of directors should be specifically charged with the following responsibilities:

· Establish all major policies
· Develop necessary operating procedures
· Make final decisions on controversial issues
· Determine the goals of the squad
· Appoint command and supervisory personnel from the members of the squad
· Screen applications for squad membership
· Appoint or remove persons from the squad

Activation of the Squad

Normally, the squad will be activated at the request of a member agency for homicides, major sex offenses, and robberies or burglaries with substantial losses. The chief executive of the agency requesting assistance should contact the squad commander, who in turn will determine the nature of the incident. If it is determined that the incident is more than eight hours old, the squad commander may decline to activate the squad. Normally, an investigation will not extend more than 72 hours unless unusual circumstances require an extension. The decision to extend the investigation must be made by the board of directors.

Squad Composition

As with the board of directors, members of the squad should be full-time, salaried, commissioned law enforcement officers drawn from the agencies that comprise the squad. Squad members must be experienced investigators. While a number of qualities are desirable in a squad member, two qualities are indispensable: the ability both to work with minimal supervision and the ability to work with other equally capable investigators.

Squad members should be selected to fill specific positions, following a formal screening process conducted by the board of directors. A functional major case squad should have the following positions, with an alternative also designated for each one: a squad commander and a deputy, a personnel officer, an equipment officer, an evidence officer, a report officer, and enough investigators to complete necessary assignments.

The squad should be under the overall control of one commander, who should be both an experienced investigator and a supervisor. While the squad commander is in complete control of the investigation, he should solicit the assistance of all members of the squad.

When the squad is requested, it will be the commander's responsibility to contact the agency to determine the details of the case. The squad commander should then obtain the authorization of at least one member of the board of directors before entering the case. Within 24 hours from the time the squad is called, however, the board should meet to review the decisions to enter the case. The squad commander or a supervisor designated by him will take direct charge of the investigation.

Although squad members are expected to be trained and experienced at the time they are appointed, some further training may be appropriate. For example, squad members must be oriented to the squad's goals and objectives. In addition, refresher courses and training in new investigative techniques are useful.

Command and Control

The ranking officer or someone designated from the agency that requested the squad will be designated as the Officer in Charge (OIC). The authority of the OIC must be restricted to his usual jurisdiction. The OIC should serve as an advisor and facilitator to the squad. In the event of a disagreement with regard to an aspect of the investigation, the OIC may appeal, in writing, to the board of directors. Routinely, the OIC will be responsible for the following:

- Arranging for office quarters for the squad
- Providing proper equipment for the investigation
- Providing sources of information as necessary
- Making arrangements for vehicle maintenance and repair, and purchase of gas and oil at any time of the day
- Arranging for transportation and communication facilities, as needed
- Arranging for special equipment, such as helicopters, airplanes, diving suits, etc., as needed
- Establishing liaison with criminal investigative laboratories or other public or private firms that can aid in the investigation
- Making general preparation for introducing into an area a large investigative group and their attendant needs, both personal and official
- Maintaining constant liaison with the prosecuting attorney for solution of legal problems that might prejudice the case
- Providing squad members with identification authenticating their temporary but official duties in the area (This should be in the form of a card limited to a specific span of time, identifying the officer's home agency and certifying his official capacity in the jurisdiction.)

Personnel Officer

The personnel officer will be responsible for identifying appropriate lodging and headquarters facilities. This information should be recorded and updated at least twice a year. A personal information card should be maintained on each squad member, containing necessary information as well as particular skills. The personnel officer, after notification by the squad commander, should select and dispatch appropriate squad members to the agency that requested assistance.

Evidence Officer

The evidence officer will be responsible for the collection of all evidence. He must pay particular attention to three aspects of evidence control:

· Chain of custody
· Storage and security of all evidence
· Maintaining a record of mailed exhibits in order to trace lost packages

Report Officer

The report officer will be responsible for receiving, editing, indexing, filing, collating, and summarizing all case reports. This officer will also supervise clerical personnel. The report officer, as a collator, must have an eye for detail. His numerous responsibilities include:

· Requiring each investigator to use and properly complete the forms provided for reporting
· Requiring reports in triplicate or as required (Additional copies may be made if necessary to assist the investigative staff in its duties.)
· Requiring investigators to submit individual reports for each suspect investigated
· Placing only productive information in the main case file (No report of elimination of suspects should be included in this file.)
· Placing all nonproductive information (elimination of suspects, etc.) in a secondary (or bulky exhibit) file (All extraneous investigative data, including extra copies of reports, are placed in this file.)
· Preparing a daily or general progress report as determined by the squad commander
· Upon termination of the squad's participation in the investigation, preparing a general report of the findings (with a summary introduction) that is indexed and divided according to chronology of events and categories of investigation
· Upon successful solution of a case by the squad, preparing an indexed prosecuting summary, listing the facts of the crime, the criminal history of the defendant, and the evidence to be presented and by whom
· Serving as a historian for the entire case
· Exercising discretion in preventing disclosures that could possibly hamper future investigation or endanger witnesses

- Maintaining memoranda containing facts of the case and the background of the suspect and victim, including biographical data and photographs
- Maintaining a file of case news clippings for use as required
- Serving as liaison officer between the squad commander and the OIC relative to press releases, and suggesting means of using press facilities to assist the investigators
- Preparing information for press releases, which shall be released to the various news media only by the OIC, who shall release only information agreed upon between himself and the squad commander

Equipment Officer

The equipment officer should be responsible for the availability of all property and equipment that may be required in the investigation. It must be made clear that all expenditures must be approved by the squad commander and OIC. The equipment officer must work closely with the squad commander in order to be apprised of the equipment needs of the investigation. In order to meet the squad's equipment needs, he should maintain lists of equipment and persons capable of operating that equipment.

Squad in Operation

Investigators should work in pairs, not so much for the protection of the investigators (although this is a factor), but to reduce the jurisdictional impediments. Specialists such as polygraph operators and evidence technicians should be available on limited notice. Expenses such as overtime and equipment costs should be borne by the requesting agency. Some consideration should be given to using standard forms, particularly investigative reports, evidence forms, and chain-of-custody cards. Finally, it should be remembered that problems will emerge often in a situation involving so many persons from several agencies. Recurrent problems should not be allowed to destroy the unit's potential effectiveness. Agencies participating in a major case squad should participate in an investigation with the intention of successfully closing a case.

Major case squads offer the potential to improve the delivery of police services and squads can provide a workable solution to serious crime incidents across jurisdictional boundaries. At the same time, they can improve information flow on cases, and reduce expensive equipment and personnel costs. Lastly, major case squads are usually characterized by high morale, occasionally an important factor in the solving of difficult crimes.

On the other hand, lack of expertise or conflicting interagency values can reduce a unit's effectiveness. These problems, however, should not prevent law enforcement agencies from performing their primary responsibility of protecting the public. Multi-agency major case squads are not a panacea for the problems of reduced budgets and limited resources. They constitute a means to draw upon a valuable resource, the skills and knowledge of dedicated law enforcement professionals.

Preparing the Case for Prosecution

Communication between the prosecutor and investigators is essential in the preparation of a criminal case. It is the prosecutor's job to present the evidence in court, but it is the investigator who actually gathered the evidence and prepared the case jacket. The investigator becomes the primary source of information for the prosecutor on the case. Prosecutors will often ask questions about physical evidence, the circumstances under which statements and confessions were obtained, and how well a potential witness will testify on the stand. The investigator must be prepared to answer or to get answers to these and other questions asked by the prosecutor.

Organization of the Case

The evidence in a criminal case must be organized and presented to the jury in such a manner that it demonstrates the defendant's guilt. Normally, the best way to present a case is chronologically, that is, in the order in which the events occurred. The information gathered will consist of witness statements, police reports, transcripts of interviews with suspects, and laboratory reports. All evidence should be gathered, indexed, and placed in folders for easy access by the prosecutor. Case jackets are often several hundred or even thousands of pages in length.

The Law Enforcement Officer as a Witness

Peace officers sometimes incorrectly think that when an arrest is made in a case their work in the investigation is complete. In reality, the tedious task of repeatedly reviewing files has just begun. Officers must remember that the state's obligation in a criminal trial is to prove a defendant's guilt beyond a reasonable doubt. In order to demonstrate a defendant's guilt, it is necessary to provide the trier of fact with all the admissible relevant evidence. Much of this evidence will be presented orally on the witness stand. Without careful preparation, months or even years of hard work processing evidence, running down leads, and interviewing witnesses and suspects can go to waste. It is incumbent on investigators to be prepared to offer whatever information they can as testimony.

One of the ironies of criminal investigations is that skillful investigators often have limited experience testifying on the stand. The reality in the criminal justice system today is that well-prepared cases will more than likely be settled by a negotiated plea of guilty. The fact that they have done a good job of putting a case together will mean that may seldom be called upon to testify. A good investigator should never forget, however, that every aspect of an investigation can become an issue at trial. The incredible scrutiny of the police investigation of the O.J. Simpson case is perhaps one of the most graphic examples of what criminal investigators can anticipate from well-prepared defense attorneys. For that reason, an investigator must be able to present testimony to a jury in a clear and convincing manner.

Trial Procedure

The trial may be thought of as a form of combat in which the goal is to convince a trier of fact of a defendant's guilt beyond a reasonable doubt. The concept of trial by jury has evolved over several hundred years of Anglo-American jurisprudence. The Sixth Amendment to the United States Constitution guarantees every defendant in a criminal case the right to a jury trial. The jury trial is the capstone of the criminal justice system. It is the standard against which the actions of the investigator are measured. If the defendant exercises his right to a jury trial, the process will begin with the selection of jurors. Usually 12 jurors are selected with two alternate jurors if the trial is expected to be lengthy.

Prosecution's Opening Statements

In the opening statement, the prosecutor acquaints the jury with the nature of the charges against the defendant and provides some description of the evidence that will be presented to support the charges. At this point, the prosecutor presents an outline of the case he plans to prove.

Defense's Opening Statements

As in the prosecution's opening statements, the defense also tells the jury what he plans to prove. Under the Anglo-American system of justice, the state is required to prove the defendant's guilt be proven beyond a reasonable doubt in a criminal case. Thus, the defendant need not prove his innocence; rather, the defense attorney must only plant a reasonable doubt in the mind of one juror to get a hung jury or, better yet, from the defense's point of view, to cause the jury as a group to have a doubt about the defendant's guilt and gain an acquittal. The attorney for the defense will prepare what he thinks will most likely cause the jury to question the defendant's guilt. Richard "Racehorse" Haines, one of the most famous defense attorneys in the United States today, described his approach to preparing a defense in this way:

> Say you sue me because you say my dog bit you. Well, now, this is my defense: my dog doesn't bite. And second, in the alternative, my dog was tied up that night. And third, I don't believe you really got bit. And fourth (here he broke into a sly grin) . . . I don't have a dog. (Cartwright, 1980, p. 137)

Prosecution's Case-in-Chief

In the state's case-in-chief, the prosecution presents all evidence available to convince the jury of the defendant's guilt. Evidence includes real or physical and testimonial evidence as well as exhibits that might aid the jury in reaching a decision. As in any formal legal proceeding, admission of evidence is governed by the rules of evidence.

Defense's Case-in-Chief

In the defense's case-in-chief, evidence that casts doubt on the defendant's guilt is offered. Common defenses are mistaken identity, entrapment, duress, and insanity. Occasionally novel defenses, such as delayed stress syndrome or pre-menstrual syndrome, may be offered. Although these defenses are seldom completely effective in causing the defendant to be acquitted, they may result in the jury finding the person guilty of a lesser charge.

Defense's Closing Arguments

At this stage of the trial, the defense attempts to create a reasonable doubt in the mind of at least one juror. One of the most common defense strategies at this point is to emphasize the heavy responsibility the state has to prove guilt beyond a reasonable doubt and the seriousness of a guilty verdict. Defense attorneys often refer to the possibility of making a mistake that will have devastating consequences for the defendant.

Prosecution's Closing Arguments

In the closing arguments, the prosecutor summarizes the evidence and offers theories on how the evidence should be viewed as it reflects on the defendant's guilt. This is the state's last opportunity to convince the trier of fact that the defendant should be found guilty.

After both sides have summed up their cases, the judge charges the jury. In this stage, the judge explains the relevant statutory law to the trier of fact, the jury. At that point, it is up to them to determine if the defendant is guilty, innocent, or if there is a reasonable doubt about the defendant's guilt. They do this by comparing the evidence to which they have been exposed with the law they are allowed to consider.

Testifying on the Witness Stand

Testifying on the witness stand can be one of the most frightening experiences of a law enforcement officer's career, especially if the officer does not take the time to adequately prepare. Ironically, some of the most experienced investigators may have limited experience on the stand because so many of their cases culminate with a negotiated guilty plea. Careful preparation and attention to detail can prevent many of the potential mistakes that can be made on the stand.

Order of Examination of Witnesses

Direct Examination

On direct examination, the proponent of the witness' testimony asks the witness to take the witness stand to tell the trier of fact what he knows. Normally, on direct examination the witness will be asked provide a narrative account of whatever relevant evidence he may possess. Prosecutors should meet with witnesses in a pre-trial conference to review the questions they will be asked. Witnesses should be encouraged to answer questions in a straightforward manner and to respond only to the question presented to them.

Cross-Examination

When testifying, investigators generally encounter one of two types of cross-examination. One approach is to attempt to overwhelm, confuse, and intimidate the investigator by asking questions that require detailed answers in rapid-fire manner. The goal of this type of cross-examination is to upset and anger the witness, and thereby cause him to answer in a hasty or angry manner. In this type of cross-examination, the witness can expect to be cut off in the middle of answering or will be forced into a "yes" or "no" answer to a complex question. The attorney can be expected to change the line of questioning quickly in order to further confuse a witness investigator.

When encountering this type of cross-examination, the witness should keep some points in mind. First, the witness will probably have the opportunity to give a complete answer to the question during redirect examination. Therefore, do not become openly angry when cut off while attempting to answer a question. The investigator should listen closely to the question and answer only after he has a truthful and accurate answer. Do not become angry at the contemptuous, mocking, or tainting tone used by the attorney when he poses questions.

The other, and in many ways more effective, manner of cross-examination is referred to as the friendly approach. When witnesses take the stand, they anticipate aggressive, even ferocious, cross-examination. To their surprise they may be examined by an apparently low-key, easy-going attorney. The goal of this type of cross-examination is to lull the witness into a relaxed state. The attorney may begin by asking questions that do not seem to relate directly to the case. The attorney may even complement the investigator on some aspect of the case, only to bear down in another area in an attempt to lead the jury to the conclusion that other parts of the investigation were not as complete.

As mentioned earlier, the witness should listen to the question and attempt to determine where the questions are leading. The investigator should not answer hastily or in anger. As always, the answer must be truthful.

The key for a successful performance on the witness stand is preparation. In all cases, the investigator should review every aspect of the case in order to determine how his testimony relates to the state's entire case.

Before taking the stand, investigators should review the entire case, paying particular attention to their reports. Investigators should try to picture the scene, the objects there, and the distances between them. Be prepared to give exact distances only if they are known; otherwise, make it clear that the distances given are estimates.

Never try to memorize a testimony. Testimony delivered in this manner sounds artificial and is not convincing to the jury. Memorized testimony may be delivered in a complete, albeit unnatural, manner; however, on cross-examination the witness will be unable to respond to rapid-fire or complex questions with a previously prepared response.

It is important to listen carefully to all the questions asked and to understand the question before answering. The jury is expecting a thoughtful, honest answer. The investigator must take the time to think through an accurate response, but not take too long to answer because the response may appear unnatural and, possibly, dishonest. Each question should be answered loudly enough for everyone in the courtroom, but particularly the jurors, to hear.

Witnesses should answer only questions asked of them. Avoid volunteering information. By adding additional, unrequested information, the witness may appear to have a personal interest in convicting the defendant. If the investigator does not answer a question correctly, he should provide the correct answer immediately. The witness should avoid statements such as "that's all the conversation" or "nothing else happened." Statements of this type restrict the opportunity to introduce other information that the witness may remember at a later time.

Above all else, the investigator must remember to tell the truth. Every material fact should be admitted, even if it might harm the prosecution's case. Investigators should never lose their tempers on the stand. Professional law enforcement officers are there in court as witnesses for the state and should not allow aggressive cross-examination by a defense attorney to shake their composure on the stand. Juries are allowed to consider the appearance and demeanor of all witnesses, including peace officers.

It is essential to remain courteous and calm in the face of intense cross-examination by an aggressive defense lawyer. If cross-examination becomes intense, the officer should not look at the prosecutor's table as if waiting for help. This conversation is between the officer and the attorney conducting the cross-examination. If the attorney asks an improper question, the prosecutor will object at that point. A witness is required to answer all questions asked unless the trial judge rules otherwise.

Redirect Examination

On redirect examination, the proponent of the witness' testimony will seek to "rehabilitate" the testimony that may have been impeached on cross-examination. This is often done by providing the witness the opportunity to answer a question completely or to provide another perspective on an issue raised by the defense.

Re-Cross-Examination

On re-cross-examination, the opposing attorney can ask questions regarding issues raised during redirect examination. Once again, the attorney will attempt to impeach the witness regarding what was said on redirect.

Anticipation Defense Attacks on the Prosecution's Case

Attacking the Thoroughness of the Investigation

One of the most common approaches to attacking the state's case is to point out apparent oversights or errors in the investigative process. Advances in criminal investigative techniques have occurred in an uninterrupted streams for more than 100 years. These advances have provided the investigator with an impressive array of tools with which to build a case. They also provide defense attorneys with a means to attack the adequacy of the investigation. For example, police are repeatedly told how to protect crime scenes and to process evidence.

The defense attorney may attack the completeness of the investigation by asking why the investigators did not take certain steps. This is done in an effort to create the impression the investigation was slipshod. The attorney hopes that this line of questioning will lead to the impression that police stampeded into a "rush to judgment." That is, once the police identified the first available suspect, they proceeded to build a case on him. In the process, they ignored any other evidence that might exonerate the defendant. Common defense attacks include pointing to where investigators did not look for evidence, such as fingerprints, or where they did not gather samples from all the blood stains at an assault scene. The defense may also question why some tests were not conducted. The defense may also attack the test procedures, such as DNA analysis.

Pretrial Conference

It is standard for the prosecutor to meet with witnesses prior the trial to review their testimony and to get a firsthand look at the witness in an effort to gauge his or her effectiveness on the witness stand. During cross-examination, the defense may inquire into conversation between the witness and the prosecutor. The purpose of these questions is to suggest to the jury that the witness was coached to provide certain responses. The defense may be particularly inclined to use this type of questioning if the witness has seemingly memorized her testimony.

Looking for Inconsistencies in Witness Testimony

A competent defense attorney will file the appropriate discovery motions before the trial. Once prosecution documents are in the hands of defense attorneys, they will pour over witness statements, police reports, laboratory reports, and any other information they acquire in the hope of finding inconsistencies in the case. Inconsistencies may relate to times, statements, or any other aspect of the case. The goal is to find anything that may be used to plant the seed of reasonable doubt in the minds of the jurors, or at least in the minds of a few jurors.

Conclusion

The criminal trial is the capstone of the American criminal justice system. In order to convict, the state must demonstrate the defendant's guilt beyond a reasonable doubt. Criminal investigators are charged with the responsibility of gathering evidence and organizing it in order for the prosecutor to present it in court. The investigator must be prepared to assist the prosecutor as the expert who has gathered the facts in the case and to provide testimony if called upon to do so.

Acknowledgments

Much of the information in the section on fugitive investigation was obtained in interviews with Deputy United States Marshals and FBI agents whose duties include planning and conducting fugitive investigations.

References

Buchanan, Edna. *The Corpse Had a Familiar Face*. New York: Berkeley Books, 1987.

California v. Greenwood, 486 U.S. 35 (1988).

Cartwright, Gary. *Blood Will Tell: The Murder Trials of T. Cullen Davis*. New York: Pocket Books, 1980.

Sanders, William B. *Detective Work: A Study of Criminal Investigations*. New York: The Free Press, Macmillan Publishing, 1977.

14. Criminal Investigations in the Twenty-First Century

Tut, Tut, my dear sir, you must really pay attention to these details.

Sherlock Holmes, *The Adventure of Black Peter*, Sir Arthur Conan Doyle

Law enforcement is a dynamic and challenging profession. In the criminal investigation component of law enforcement, investigators are called upon to deal with a wide variety of people and situations. How investigators handle these situations often has an impact on the outcome of a case and, subsequently, how the public perceives the police. Several areas of the investigator's role may determine the long-term success of law enforcement. These areas are how the police deal with news media, the presentation of evidence in court, and the effect of community policing on the delivery of police services, particularly on investigative work.

Media Relations

While working with the news media, constitutional requirements placed on the police investigator often create contradictions and accompanying problems. On the one hand, the First Amendment states in part:

Congress shall make no law . . . abridging the freedom of speech or freedom of the press.

On the other hand, the Sixth Amendment states in part:

In all criminal prosecutions, the accused shall enjoy the right to a speedy and public trial, by an impartial jury of the state and district the crime shall have been committed . . .

The interpretation of these two conflicting requirements has led to a great deal of tension between the police and the media. Reporters interpret the First Amendment to mean the public and, therefore the media, have an absolute right to know everything about any event that is of interest to them. Police investigators are concerned about maintaining the integrity of an investigation, which is usually done by maintaining secrecy about a case under investigation. The investigator may be concerned with protecting the privacy of victims and witnesses, at least initially before the case goes to court. Investigators must also withhold information about the actual events of the crime to provide them with a means to check suspect statements or actions when a suspect is located. Edna Buchanan, Pulitzer prize-winning reporter for the *Miami Herald*, has long argued that the police and the media can both benefit from a friendlier yet professional relationship by sharing information. While both sides have valid arguments to support their positions, the answer to developing a workable relationship between the police and the media lies in establishing and adhering to an agreed-upon set of guidelines and policies.

Media Policies

In general, a police media relations policy should be based on the principle that the relationship between the police and media should be positive and professional. The position of the public information officer (PIO) should be created and the duties of this position clearly delineated. The person who serves as the PIO should be an experienced police officer, ideally one with investigative experience, who is familiar with all agency policies and procedures. The policy should identify what kinds of information can and should be released, and how it is to be released.

Duties of the Public Information Officer (PIO)

The PIO should be responsible for several duties, including gathering and releasing information to the media. The PIO may also be the person who is designated to make all statements to the media. The person serving in this position must have a good working relationship with all media representatives in the print and electronic media. In small departments, the chief may perform this role; in larger departments the chief may delegate the duty to a subordinate who reports directly to the chief.

Information that Can Be Released to the Media

Investigators are often unclear about what information should actually be released to the media. The following is a list informational items that can be released:

- The name of persons arrested, their ages, gender, residence, employment, and marital status
- The crime or crimes for which the person was arrested, charged, or if information was filed or an indictment was returned
- The name of the investigating agency
- The amount of bail, if any
- A brief description of the crime, including the time and date, and if anyone was arrested
- If force was involved in the arrest
- The age and gender of the victim (The victim's address should not be included.)
- This press release should note if the suspect is still at large and if considered dangerous (The release may also include names of other known suspects or vehicles the suspect may be using.)

Information that Should Not Be Included in a News Release

The names and addresses of victims of violent crimes, particularly, rape, and other sexual assaults should never be released. The press release must never contain the names of juvenile suspects or confidential informants. When considering whether to release names, investigators must be extremely careful to ensure that the next of kin have been notified in cases of death of serious physical injury.

The press release must not contain opinions about a defendant's guilt or innocence, and opinions about the quality of evidence must not be included. The release must not include comments about the character or lifestyle of any of the parties involved in the investigation. No reference should be made to any of the defendant's statements, including admissions, confessions, or alibis.

Talking to Media Representatives

When dealing with the media, particularly the electronic media, the PIO should follow some basic rules:

- As with an interrogation, or preparing to testify, the PIO must take the time to prepare. There is no excuse for not learning everything about a case before going before the camera or microphone.
- Listen to the question and be sure it is understood before answering. If the question is unclear, ask the questioner to rephrase it.
- Do not use police jargon, such as referring to individuals as subjects, and by all means avoid the use of profanity. At the same time try to be definite when possible, avoid phrases such as "I guess so."
- Do not be afraid to say you do not know the answer to a question. Say so. Do not make up an answer or provide a speculative answer.
- When talking to the media, do not lose your temper. Maintain composure in the face of intense questioning by reporters.

The PIO should be friendly, but professional. The image projected by the officer will have a profound impact on public attitudes toward law enforcement. Avoid the tendency to make jokes or to give a flippant response. Police officers can become cynical and accustomed to seeing the underside of life and respond to that reality with "gallows humor" to cope with the stress. Never forget the audience does not share this perspective and will be shocked or offended by such statements by an officer.

Taking the Media Along on a Warrant Service

During the 1998–1999 session, the Supreme Court handed down a number of decisions, which will have an impact on how officers perform their jobs. In *Wilson v. Layne*, 119 S.Ct. 1692 (1999), the Court ruled that allowing the media to enter private premises during the execution of a warrant is a violation of the Fourth Amendment. This was a civil suit, in which the plaintiffs argued that they had maintained an expectation of privacy even though the police had a search warrant. The Supreme Court agreed with the plaintiffs that their expectation of privacy had been violated. Therefore, police can continue to photograph or videotape scenes where search or arrest warrants are served, but they cannot turn these tapes over to the media nor can they provide the media with tapes. The media can continue to videotape and broadcast tape that was obtained in an area where a person does not have an expectation of privacy.

Freedom of Information Act

The federal government and many states have a Freedom of Information Law. These laws require that agencies release any record they possess on a person when an appropriate request is made. They do not, however, require that information relating to ongoing investigation be released. Specifically, information may not be released if:

- Release would interfere with law enforcement operations, including investigation
- Release would deprive a defendant of a fair trial or provide an unfair advantage to a party to the litigation
- Release would be an unwarranted intrusion into a person's privacy
- Release might compromise the safety of an informant or witness
- Release might compromise an investigative technique
- Release might jeopardize the safety of an investigator or police officer

Tensions between the media's obligation to keep the public informed and the criminal defendant's right to a fair trial cannot be eliminated. The creation of a public information office within a law enforcement agency, and the development of policies and procedures to guide the release of information to the media can reduce some of the problems.

The Police and Crime: Community Policing and the Investigator

Police administrators have come to realize that the police, working alone, are not likely to have a long-term impact on crime in the community. The police have learned that they must work with residents of the community to preserve or restore the sense of safety in the home and on the street (Skolnick and Bayley, 1986). Criminal investigators can enhance the feeling of security by identifying and apprehending criminals who threaten society. By investigating crimes using every available legal technique, skilled investigators can help convict criminals. Investigators must also play a role in the implementation of community policing as part of a department and community-wide effort to control crime and disorder.

Crime has had a devastating impact on the quality of life for many communities over the past 30 years. Although statistics reveal that crime has declined over the past few years, there remains a strong perception that crime, especially violent crime, is at an all-time high. As a result, law enforcement administrators and academicians interested in improving law enforcement have searched for a model for delivering police services that addresses both crime and fear of crime in a more meaningful manner. The perceived lack of success of traditional police strategies, including criminal investigations, has caused many police administrators and community leaders to consider the use of a model of policing that relies on enhanced communication and increased cooperation between the police and the community. This new approach to policing has been called by number of names, including community oriented policing or problem oriented policing. Community oriented policing or problem oriented policing provides a framework within which the police and the community can work to solve problems of mutual concern.

Crime Control

Historically the control of crime has been viewed from two very diverse perspectives, crime attack strategies and root causes strategies. Proponents of the crime attack strategies view crime as the result of characteristics unique to a group of people who choose to commit crime. Because crime is viewed as the result of an individual's exercise of choice to commit a crime, then the appropriate government response is to identify, apprehend, convict, and punish the offender. Once offenders have been removed from society, crime should decline. Crime attack strategies for crime control include career criminal apprehension programs, major case squads, and aggressive patrol programs. Criminal investigators have traditionally played a major role in crime attack strategies.

Steady increases in reported crime experienced over the past 30 years has caused police, academics, and the public to question the effectiveness of traditional crime attack policing strategies. Such strategies, when not supported by the community, cannot be successful in the long term in curbing crime. Additionally, it has been argued, crime attack strategies do not respond to the causes of crime; therefore, there will continue to be a problem.

George Kelling and James Q. Wilson, in their well-known article, "Broken Windows," suggested that community deterioration, as exemplified by broken windows, indicates a lack of community concern and is a signal that a neighborhood is in decline. Broken windows are a signal to drug dealers, prostitutes, and others, including criminals, that the area is now open to crime and disorder. Wilson and Kelling argue that the police should concern themselves with maintaining order and a sense of community in the neighborhood. Police should serve as community organizers to direct local efforts to repair the "broken windows" and to help maintain the community, and thereby address the root causes of crime. The belief that the police must work with the community to achieve mutually satisfactory solutions of problems of crime and disorder has evolved into the concept of community oriented policing. Herman Goldstein developed the concept in his book, *Problem Oriented Policing*. Goldstein described the need for a new approach to policing in this way:

> Societies often require that the police deal with an incredibly broad range of troublesome situations. Handling these situations within the limitations that we place on policing should extend to and focus on the end product of policing—on the effectiveness and

fairness of the police in dealing with substantive problems that the public looks to the police to handle.

Serious in-depth exploration of these substantive problems opens many new doors for constructive change in policing. It often leads to new ideas for improving effectiveness, to ways to engaging both the police and the community more productively, and to dealing with conditions that have undermined efforts to improve the police in the past. Most importantly, it leads to a whole new perspective on policing. (Goldstein, 1990, p. 1–2)

Community policing has a number of definitions, often depending on the user's perspective (Manning, 1984). One of the most commonly accepted definitions is offered by Eck:

> *Problem oriented policing* is a department wide strategy aimed at solving persistent community problems. Police identify, analyze, and respond to the underlying circumstances that create incidents (Eck, 1987).

Eck's definition emphasizes the need for community oriented policing to focus on problem solving in the community. Its approach to delivering police service goes well beyond traditional community or public relations programs. Police, including investigators, are expected to become catalysts for community change by directing community resources toward solving underlying problems.

Characteristics of Community Oriented Policing

Community or problem oriented policing seeks to overcome the limitations on traditional policing as practiced in the past. To be successful, problem-solving policing requires substantial structural changes in police departments. More importantly, however, police officers need to adopt a new attitude toward policing. As such, problem oriented policing has a number of unique characteristics.

First, problem oriented policing is proactive rather than reactive. Police are expected to move from the practice of waiting for problems to arise and then responding to a proactive concern for preventing problems before they become more serious. Problem oriented policing relies on concepts such as developing more sources of information, identifying a variety of solutions to problems, and a concern for more accurate measures of police effectiveness. These are tasks that have traditionally been part of the investigator's job.

Unlike traditional policing, however, problem oriented policing is not limited to information obtained from traditional sources of information, such as victims, witnesses, and suspects. It relies, instead, on developing any information that may be useful in defining and, ultimately, solving a community problem. Furthermore, problem oriented policing does not rely totally on the criminal justice process to resolve a problem. In using this model, officers are encouraged to consider and use whatever legitimate means are available to reach a resolution of a problem. Investigators obviously have considerable experience in gathering and analyzing information. This approach requires making some changes in how information is collated and disseminated, but clearly investigators can play a major role in the problem solving process, particularly in the scanning and analysis stages.

Issues Involved in Becoming Involved in Community Policing

Executive Support for Community Policing

A community oriented policing program cannot succeed without the unqualified support of the agency head, either the chief or the sheriff. The chief must become the champion of the program, constantly encouraging agency personnel to become involved and make the program succeed. Without command level support, the program is likely to be seen as another in a long line of fads that were expected to "revolutionize" policing.

Involvement of Agency Personnel

One of the assumptions upon which community oriented policing is based is the expectation of expanded decision making by patrol officers, investigators, and sergeants. Patrol officers, detectives, and sergeants will be expected to work with the public to identify and solve problems. They will be expected to exercise greater professional judgment and initiative in the performance of their jobs. Concomitantly, the supervisors or sergeants will change their roles, from control agents responsible for maintaining compliance with agency policy to facilitators. These changes require a substantial shift in supervisory practices and training. This transition is not necessarily easy, particularly in organizations with strong traditions of quasi-military supervision.

Another issue that must be dealt with is the impact that community policing will have on mid-level managers, the lieutenants and captains. Expanding the decision making responsibility of patrol officers, detectives, and supervisors is a move toward "flattening" the organization, that is, it can reduce the responsibilities and authority of mid-level managers. A change of this type may be threatening to administrators who occupy mid-level management positions. They could, in turn, respond by passively or overtly reacting negatively to a new program. The role of mid-level managers as facilitators must be made clear to lieutenants and captains before community policing is implemented.

Identifying the Public

The term *public*, when used by police officers, usually means anyone other than police officers. Program directors must identify the constituency to whom the program is to be directed. In some communities, the population is so homogeneous that there may, in fact, be a general "public." In most communities, however, there will usually be number of "publics" that are competing with each other for police services. Police administrators must decide which group is most in need of a community-policing program. Without defining a manageable area, program resources may be spread too thinly. Criminal investigators, with their detailed knowledge of the community and its residents, can be valuable in the process of identifying the various constituencies the police department must deal with.

Training

The literature on policing is rich with examples of police officers developing a wide variety of solutions to the problems they face. Community oriented policing can build on that tradition of problem solving. Training in community oriented policing focuses on the SARA model. SARA stands for Scanning, Analysis, Response, and Assessment. Each item is crucial to the success of the problem-solving model.

- *Scanning.* Define the problem and decide, often along with the public, whether it needs a response.
- *Analysis.* Gather information from a number of sources in order to determine the nature and extent of the problem.
- *Response.* Develop and implement the response created to the problem defined in the scanning and analysis phases.
- *Assessment.* Evaluate the impact and effectiveness of the response. If the problem has been adequately defined and the officer selected the appropriate response, then the problem should be reduced, and ideally eliminated, although rarely does a social problem disappear.

Investigators can adapt the SARA problem-solving model to the task of investigating crimes and to assist with the implementation of community policing. They have both training and experience in problem solving and everyday they are faced with a host of issues that require solutions.

Staffing

As with almost all police programs, community policing is a labor-intensive activity. It is crucial to get the right people involved in the program. Theorists in community oriented policing argue that this form of policing should become the standard approach to delivering police service. Experts in community policing are concerned that, at least initially, problem oriented policing requires skills that some officers do not currently possess and that will take time to develop.

Theorists also express concern based on a belief that the public has come to expect a police response to most calls for service. For the immediate future at least, administrators may begin to use community policing as a special program within the department. For example, a decision may be made to target a specific problem for community oriented policing program. While that program is underway, it will be necessary to have other patrol officers continue to answer calls for service.

Patrol officers and investigators who are responding to calls for service or following up on investigations may resent the perception that preferential treatment is being given to Community Oriented Police (COPS) officers. They may also feel that they are being required to carry more than their share of the workload. However, as the problem solving model produces result in terms of improved communication with the public and increased cooperation from the community, the value of the community oriented policing will reduce the tensions within the department.

Community oriented policing is based on the theory that as problems of crime and disorder are solved or reduced to a more manageable level, then calls for service should decline. If the theory is correct, then community oriented policing can become the standard approach to providing police services to the public.

With an understanding of community policing comes an understanding of the benefits of this model and the role the investigator can play. One of the most obvious benefits is the information developed in the course of conducting an investigation. That information will be of value at all steps in the SARA model, particularly the scanning and analysis phase.

Investigators are responsible for gathering and analyzing information. The same skills used by an investigator in gathering information can be applied to the scanning and analysis phases of the SARA model. Problem-solving is at the heart of the investigative process. Investigators, in pursuing the goal of finding the truth, often discover a great deal about the community and its residents. It is reasonable to encourage investigators to use that information to help find solutions to the problems facing the community.

Looking to the Future

It is not possible to predict the future with any certainty. It is useful, however, to look to the future in order to formulate reasoned responses to demands for police protection for the remainder of this decade and into the next century.

One of the inescapable realities of law enforcement is that peace officers see the underside of life on a daily basis. For that reason, law enforcement officers tend to be pessimistic and cynical. In a time when national news magazines feature stories entitled "War on Drugs: Why We're Losing" and it seems that we can look forward to new records for homicides each year, it is sometimes difficult to be optimistic. However, advances in investigative techniques provide a basis for optimism.

Crime Trends

After almost three decades of uninterrupted increases, reported crime has declined since 1991. That trend seems to be continuing through 1996, with one major difference, that is, violent crime involving young men. This group has a rate of victimization much higher than the national average. Criminologists are not able to explain the overall decrease with confidence. One suggestion is that the number of youths in their crime-prone years has declined, and therefore there are simply fewer people to commit crimes on the street at this time.

Another explanation for declining rates of reported crime may be that the practice of aggressive law enforcement and subsequent prosecution and incarceration may be incapacitating more serious offenders. These criminals are not able to prey on society, at least while they are incarcerated. The United States now has approximately one and a half million people incarcerated on an average day.

Whatever the explanation(s), the reduction in crime will, in reality, only bring crime back within levels that may be somewhat more manageable, thereby allowing the criminal justice system the opportunity to "catch up." Scholars are not optimistic about a continued decline in crime. Dr. Alfred Blumstein of Carnegie Mellon University predicts a dramatic increase in juvenile crime around the year 2000.

Community Oriented Policing

Another, more hopeful, explanation for the reduction in reported crime may lie in the early successes of community oriented and problem oriented policing. The decline may also be the result of efforts in many communities to stabilize neighborhoods and to provide area residents, particularly young residents, with alternative options to criminal activity.

Improved Cooperation within Law Enforcement and Other Criminal Justice Agencies

The commission of crime is often not a localized event. Crime networks are both national and international today. Agencies at the local, state, and federal levels must work together toward the goal of solving crimes and reducing the opportunity for criminals to continue in a criminal enterprise. The demonstrated successes of major case squads and multi-agency drug task forces provide modes for future agency cooperation.

Advances in Technology

Technology will continue to have a profound effect on criminal investigations as well as the entire criminal justice system. The use of DNA evidence will become as routine as fingerprints are today. In the years to come, geneticists may well be able to positively identify individuals by their genetic code.

Behavioral Sciences

Continued research into the practices of criminals by behavioral scientists is providing insights into how and why some people commit crimes. This information may lead to the increased ability to predict where and when criminals may strike in the future. It will lead to the ability to link offenders to other crimes through identifying the criminal's *modus operandi* using systems such as Violent Criminal Apprehension Program (VICAP).

Behavioral scientists are also learning how to detect signs of deception given off by criminals during interviews and interrogations. More effective interviewing and interrogation techniques are evolving as insights are gained into the criminal mind. Behavioral scientists are learning how to structure interviews and how and when to ask the appropriate questions.

Computers and Information Technology

Criminal investigation is, in large part, the continuous process of gathering, analyzing, and organizing huge amounts of information. The computer has made it possible to process that information much more rapidly and effectively. At its simplest, word processors have reduced the difficulties of report writing. Many departments are already "paperless," in that reports are called in, thus relieving the officer of the major time-consuming task of hand writing reports. It is possible to organize cases much more quickly using "multimedia" programs. Witness statements, laboratory reports, and investigative summaries can all be computerized. The use of CD-ROM may well reduce the need to accumulate and maintain huge, cumbersome, and often ineffective filing and record systems.

Several software packages that are now commercially available can be employed to handle the vast amounts of information developed in major cases such as homicides. These advances make it possible to release investigators from clerical tasks so that they can spend more time actually investigating cases.

Databases

Several states and the federal government already maintain extensive automated record keeping systems, such as the Automated Fingerprint Identification System (AFIS) and the Automated Latent Print System (ALPS), which provide immediate access to millions of fingerprints. In time, most, if not all, states will participate in these systems, which will be networked and thereby provide tremendous means to identify and track criminal offenders.

The Drug Fire program developed by the FBI provides a database on the characteristics of shell casings. The system can increase the value of evidence recovered at crime scenes where spent shell casings are recovered. In time, the Drug Fire system will be expanded to include information on bullets recovered at shooting scenes.

Scientific Evidence

The O.J. Simpson case has increased the public's awareness of how important scientific evidence can be in a criminal prosecution. Other advances will impact on the medico-legal aspects of criminal investigation.

Managing Criminal Investigations

Studies conducted in the 1970s and 1980s demonstrated that criminal investigation is a process that can be managed like any other process. It will become increasingly necessary to use the limited investigative resources available to the local, state, and federal governments in a systematic manner. The current generation of police administrators recognize the limits of the system and work to maximize their success by using what they have available. At the same time, they remain aware of new investigative techniques and technologies that increase the opportunities to aid investigators in achieving their primary goal of finding the truth.

A New Attitude Toward the Profession

In the 1960s and early 1970s law enforcement administrators and academics involved in the study of law enforcement were hopeful that law enforcement would achieve recognition as a profession along the lines of older established professions, such as the clergy, medicine, and law. Law enforcement, and particularly criminal investigations, seems to be moving toward recognition as a profession. Professional status is based, in large part, on the extent to which an occupation possesses certain basic characteristics, including:

- Creation of a full-time occupation
- Possessing a body of general systematic knowledge taught in an established training model
- Creation of professional associations
- Formulation and adherence to a code of ethics

Every day practicing professionals in the field of criminal investigation can be expected to exercise judgment based on the body of knowledge associated with the profession of law enforcement and criminal investigation. Those decisions will be made within the limits established in the law enforcement code of ethics. When looking to the future, it may be helpful to remember the analogy of the glass of water, whether it is better to think of it as half-full or half-empty. By reflecting on where law enforcement was 25 years ago and where it is today, it is possible to see the enormous improvements that have been made in the training, education, and application of technology in law enforcement. The Supreme Court is composed of justices who are inclined to allow law enforcement officers to exercise professional judgment undreamed of two decades ago. It is the obligation of the next generation of criminal investigators to build on the foundation built by their predecessors in the field.

Finally, perhaps the greatest cause for optimism in law enforcement and criminal investigation is the continuing infusion of talented, energetic young men and women into the field. They have acquired the body of professional knowledge in an academic setting, just as professionals in older recognized fields, such as medicine, law, and the clergy, have done for years. These young people will have the responsibility of protecting the lives and property of the residents of this country well into the next century. They are equal to the task.

References

Bayley, David H. *Police For The Future*. New York: Oxford University Press, 1994.

Buchanan, Edna. *The Corpse Had a Familiar Face*. New York: Berkeley Books, 1987.

Eck, Robert, and Spellmen, William. "Problem Solving Policing in Newport News." In: *Critical Issues in Policing*, Dunham, Roger G., and Alpert, Geoffey P., eds. Prospect Heights, Ohio: Waveland Press, 1993, p. 451–465.

Goldstein, Herman. *Problem Oriented Policing*. New York: McGraw Hill, 1990.

Hanlon v. Berger, 119 S.Ct. 1706 (1999).

Manning, Peter. "Community Based Policing." *American Journal of Police* 3:205–227, 1984.

Skolnick, Gerome, and Bayley, David H. *The New Blue: Police Innovation in Six American Cities*. New York: The Free Press, 1986.

Trojanowicz, Robert, and Bucqueroux, Bonnie. *Community Policing: A Contemporary Perspective*. Cincinnati, Ohio: Anderson Publishing, 1990.

Wilson, J.Q., and Kelling, G. "Broken Windows." *Atlantic Magazine* 249(March):29–38, 1982.

Wilson v. Layne, 119 S.Ct. 1692 (1999).

Appendix

Expanding the Patrol Officer's Role in Criminal Investigation and Assignment of Cases

Many Patrol Officers find criminal investigation to be a challenging and interesting component of the job. In some departments, the Patrol Officer's job may be restricted to identifying and securing the crime scene, while in others, Patrol Officers may be given considerable responsibility for conducting a detailed preliminary investigation. In small departments, the agency may conduct the entire investigation from the initial call to prosecution of the case. A question usually arises regarding how much a Patrol Officer should be responsible for and when an investigation should be handled by detectives. Well-run agencies have written comprehensive policies to guide officers and supervisors in determining how a case should be managed. The following is an example of one such policy.

Patrol Investigations Policy

The purpose of this policy is to outline the procedures for patrol personnel when handling patrol investigations and when it is necessary for them to contact a supervisor or personnel from other divisions of the department or agencies.

I. Supervisor Notification

A. Whenever certain incidents are investigated by a Patrol Officer, a Patrol Sergeant will be notified. The Sergeant will respond to the scene of the investigation, if needed, and will determine if the Watch Commander should be notified. Patrol Sergeants will use sound judgment in determining whether or not they should respond the scene of an investigation and/or contact the Watch Commander. Those incidents that require notification of a sergeant are as follows:

1. Child molestation
2. Union activities or strikes
3. Major fires, requiring a police response
4. Traffic crashes that require roads being closed
5. Sexual battery
6. Child abuse
7. Extortion
8. Any incident involving three or more units

B. Whenever certain incidents are investigated by a Patrol Officer, a Patrol Sergeant will respond to the scene and notify the Watch Commander. The Patrol Sergeant will, when appropriate, be responsible for passing necessary information to the Communications Watch Supervisor and requesting a detective from the most appropriate unit when necessary. Those incidents that require that a Sergeant to respond the scene are as follows:

1. An abduction that appears to be bona fide
2. A drowning
3. A sexual battery with serious injury to the victim
4. Aggravated child abuse
5. An officer calling for help
6. A bomb threat
7. A robbery of a business, or involving serious injury to a victim
8. An aircraft accident
9. A railroad accident
10. Whenever a major highway is blocked, or is to be closed
11. When a search warrant is served by a Patrol Officer
12. Arson with serious injury
13. An industrial accident with major property damage or serious injury
14. A hazardous material incident
15. A boating accident with a seriously injured or missing person
16. Traffic crashes with life-threatening injuries
17. Any traffic crash involving a police department vehicle
18. Unnatural deaths
19. Any battery with a life-threatening injury
20. Missing person cases that require an immediate search for the victim
21. Any dispute involving police department employees (on or off duty), including reserve officers and other law enforcement personnel
22. Food/product tampering
23. Any other serious or noteworthy incident that due to its nature requires the presence of a supervisor

C. In addition to a Patrol Sergeant, a Patrol Watch Commander will respond to the scene of certain incidents. It will be the Watch Commander's or his or her designee's responsibility to advise the Communications Watch Supervisor of the situation. Those incidents that require that a Watch Commander to respond to the scene are as follows:

1. All Special Weapons and Tactics team (SWAT) call outs involving hostage or barricaded subject situations
2. Any discharge of a firearm by police (except as a part of training, or disposing of injured animals)
3. Any accident involving death
4. Any escape of a prisoner involving a manhunt
5. Any explosion
6. A bomb threat if a device is located
7. A strike or union activity involving large-scale unrest, an unruly crowd, or serious injury
8. Any call involving the disorder, injury, or arrest of a law enforcement officer or government official

9. Traffic crashes involving the disorder, injury, or arrest of a law enforcement officer or government official
10. Termination of a police pursuit
11. A railroad accident involving serious injury or death
12. Any large-scale civil disorder
13. An aircraft accident with serious injury or death
14. Any incident likely to attract media attention

D. A summary of significant incidents (e.g., major crimes, accidents, and arrests, and other important activities) that occur on each watch will be documented on the Patrol Watch Commander's Daily Recap of Noteworthy Incidents Report. Watch Commanders will ensure that Noteworthy Incident Reports are submitted at the end of their shifts to the Chief of Patrol. The information on these reports is compiled and distributed through the chain of command of the Department of Operations and to the following:
1. The Deputy Chief
2. The Organized Crime Section
3. The Intelligence Section
4. The Community Affairs Division
5. The Planning and Research Division
6. All Zone Watch Commanders

II. Patrol Investigations

A. Patrol Officers conduct the only investigation of a major portion of the criminal offenses that are committed. In those cases where Patrol Officers conduct the sole investigation of an offense, they must be particularly diligent in:
1. Conducting a thorough investigation
2. Following up on all possible leads
3. Checking all sources of information

B. Uniformed Patrol Officers will be responsible for the preliminary investigations of all cases, with the exception of homicides, cases that are unusually serious or complex in nature, or cases involving covert and undercover activities. In such cases, the appropriate detective will respond and conduct the investigation.

C. Preliminary investigations of all offenses require the officer to be thorough. Officers will attempt to determine the following information:
1. Are there sufficient data to complete the General Offense or Incident Report?
2. When a report is written, include the who, what, when, where, why, how, and elements of the crime(s), recording the facts of the incident fully and accurately

D. Officers will, as part of the investigation:
1. Observe all condition, events, and remarks
2. Interview the complainant, victim(s), and witnesses
3. Conduct a neighborhood canvass to locate and identify witnesses
4. Secure the crime scene and protect the evidence for processing by evidence technicians or the crime lab
5. Arrange for the collection of evidence, if necessary

6. Attempt to identify, locate, and interview the suspect(s)
7. Determine if probable cause exists for an arrest of any suspect(s) and if so
   a. Effect the arrest and
      (1) Advise the suspect(s) of his (her/their) rights and interview him (her/them)
      (2) Transport the suspect(s) to be interviewed by a detective, if appropriate
      (3) Transport the suspect(s) to the Pre-Trial Detention Facility or to the Juvenile Detention Center (if the suspect is a juvenile, have the juvenile photographed and fingerprinted consistent with state statutes and agency policy)
   b. File the case with the State Attorney's Office or, in misdemeanor cases (if no arrest is made at the scene), direct the victim to the State Attorney's Office if the suspect is an adult, or to Division of Youth Services if the suspect is a juvenile
E. Officers will give victims and witnesses the following forms when applicable:
   1. A Case Information Card
   2. A "Directory of Help for Crime Victims" card
   3. A "When You Are a Victim of Domestic Violence" pamphlet
   4. A State Attorney's Information Card if the suspect is an adult or Citizens Information Card—Juvenile Offender if the suspect is a juvenile
F. Officers often receive information linking potential suspects to their cases. This suspect information should not be listed in the suspect section of the General Offense/Incident or Supplement Report unless there is probable cause for the arrest of the suspect. The information on suspects where probable cause has not yet been established should be listed in the narrative section of the report.

III. Follow-up Investigations

A. The follow-up investigation of a case is determined by the type of offense being reported. Offenses may fall into one of three categories for follow-up. The categories are listed here:

Category A Crimes: Misdemeanors

Patrol officers will have primary responsibility for follow-up investigations in the following types of cases:

- Misdemeanor assaults, including domestic violence cases
- Misdemeanor stealing
- Property damage
- Misdemeanor drug possession cases

Patrol officers may also investigate all other misdemeanors that are not part of a pattern of criminal activity and will not require extensive follow-up investigation.

In Category A crimes, the patrol supervisor shall have the authority to determine how the case should be assigned.

Category B Crimes: Misdemeanors and Felonies

Patrol officers will have primary responsibility for follow-up investigations in the following types of cases.

- Assaults, including domestic violence in which the victim does not appear to have sustained life threatening injuries
- Robberies with losses of less than $1,000
- Burglary
- Residential burglary with losses of less than $2,000
- Commercial burglary with losses of less than $2,000
- Stealing
- Stealing with losses of less than $2,000
- Motor vehicle theft
- Drug cases that result from vehicle stops or searches incident to arrest

In Category B crimes, the patrol supervisor shall have the authority to determine how the case should be assigned.

Patrol officers who have made an arrest in a robbery, burglary, or felony stealing case shall contact a detective from the appropriate section to determine if a detective should assist with the interview of the suspect. Patrol officers may request the assistance of a detective in an interview when the officer feels assistance may result in developing additional information that will be of use in solving other cases.

Category C Crimes: Felonies

Detectives will be responsible for follow-up investigations of all criminal homicides including the following:

- 1st degree murder
- 2nd degree murder
- Voluntary manslaughter
- Involuntary manslaughter
- All suspicious death cases including suicide
- Sexual assaults including
- Rape/Sodomy
- Child Molestation
- Felony assaults that are likely to result in death
- Felony assaults involving a serious habitual offender, either as a suspect or a victim
- Robberies including
- Bank robbery
- Robbery in which a felony assault occurred
- Burglary including
- Burglaries both residential and commercial with losses of more than $2,000
- Drug cases

The Drug Section will be responsible for any ongoing investigations and investigations that involve undercover police officers and/or confidential informants.

Before assigning a case to a Patrol Officer for follow-up, the patrol supervisor will review the case to determine if follow-up is justified. The supervisor will triage the case using the following criteria:

- Cases, which cannot be solved, will be forwarded to the MCI section for review and probably closure.

· Cases which cannot be solved with little effort and require little time will be assigned according to the Category A, B, and C classification system.

· Cases, which will require extensive resources to solve, will be forwarded to the detective section for screening to determine if follow up is appropriate. Serious crimes in this category will receive additional review.

If the case is assigned to a Patrol Officer, the supervisor will determine if the Patrol Officer has the training, experience, and resources needed to complete the assignment.

B. Category A assignment procedures are as follows:

1. Unless a detective initiates the original investigation, the Patrol Division and M.C.I. office have total investigative responsibility for any and all follow-up of these cases

2. Upon completion of the preliminary investigation, the officer's supervisor will review all reports, screen each case, and, based on solvability factors, determine if the case it to be followed up, cleared, suspended, or unfounded

3. Solvability factors and the degree of seriousness will determine if a case is to be followed up and the resources to be used in the effort. Solvability factors include, but are not limited to:

   a. Information that may lead to the suspect(s), such as addresses (even those of relatives or associates), phone numbers, license tag numbers, etc.

   b. A suspect's vehicle description

   c. The ability of the victim(s) or witness(es) to identify or describe the suspect(s)

NOTE: Certain types of incidents will be cleared after screening by the M.C.I. officer.

4. If solvability factors are present and patrol follow-up is required, the originating officer shall:

   a. Mark "yes" for "Patrol Investigation Continuing" on the General Offense/Incident Report

   b. In the left-hand margin of the report, write "M.C.I.-PATROL FOLLOW-UP"

   c. Initiate a follow-up investigation by investigating any item of information that may assist in clearing the case

   d. Upon conducting a thorough investigation that results in case clearance, complete a Supplement Report with the final case status. For Category A offenses, the final case status is due by the thirtieth calendar day from the date the original report was written and the case was assigned. The Supplement Report shall include the following information:

       (1) The details of the investigation, (i.e., re-interviewing victims, efforts made to locate the suspects, etc.)

       (2) State Attorney's Office information (i.e., SAO case number and division, Assistant State Attorney's name, and the date contacted)

       (3) The words "ATTENTION MCI OFFICE" in the left-hand margin of the report

       (4) All other pertinent information

5. If there are no solvability factors, officers will mark "No" for "Patrol Investigation Continuing" and indicate at the end of the narrative section of the report, "Patrol Efforts Suspended"

NOTE: If further information is developed by the victim or officer, the case may be opened again at a later time for further investigation and assigned to the appropriate officer. Cases turned in as "suspended" that appear to be solvable will also be returned for further investigation.

C. M.C.I. office follow-up procedures are as follows:
   1. The M.C.I. office will be staffed by a full-time Patrol Officer. The M.C.I. will follow up all misdemeanor, Category A, patrol-initiated M.C.I. investigations in which the victim has been referred to the State Attorney's Office or the Juvenile Offender was referred to the Division of Youth Services (DYS) [except domestic violence cases, drug cases, or any other incident in which the officer's supervisor determines patrol should follow up. See Section (3) below]. The State Attorney Information Card-Juvenile Offender should be routed to the M.C.I. Office, and the victim should be given a State Attorney's Information card or a Citizens Information Card-Juvenile Offender. The following procedures will apply:
      a. The reporting officer shall write the words, "ATTENTION M.C.I. OFFICE" in the left-hand margin of the General Offense/Incident Report
      b. The completed report will be submitted to the officer's supervisor for approval
      c. The supervisor accepting the report will ensure the words "ATTEN-TION M.C.I. OFFICE" are printed in the left-hand margin of the report and check for accuracy, legibility, and completeness. The print shop will make a copy of all reports designated to be routed to the M.C.I. office
   2. Copies of reports marked for Patrol follow-up will also be made by records personnel and placed in the designated collection box for M.C.I. reports. Personnel assigned to the M.C.I. unit will retrieve all reports marked for M.C.I. ("M.C.I.-Patrol Follow-up" or "Attention-MCI office") on a daily basis for filing and follow-up. If the report is marked for patrol follow-up, M.C.I. unit personnel will place a stamp on the report (for assignment purposes) that will indicate the date assigned, due date, sergeant assigned, and zone number. The report will then be placed in the respective sergeant's box. The assigned sergeant will ensure that the MCI follow-up case is assigned when the investigation is conducted. Examples of incidents *requiring* patrol follow-up (if solvability factors exist) are as follows:
      a. Burglary to an auto
      b. Burglary in which the suspect and the victim know each other
      c. Domestic violence cases
      d. Drug cases
   3. Once it is determined that the MCI officer will follow up the investigation, he or she will be assigned with the following tasks:

a. Retrieve copies of MCI reports daily from the collection box located in the print shop

b. File all MCI reports using the CCR number and date of the report

c. If 10 days after reporting the incident, a State Attorney Card or Juvenile Offender Card is not received in the MCI office, the MCI officer will clear the case using the appropriate clearance status

d. If the State Attorney Information Card or Juvenile Offender Card is returned to the MCI office within 10 days, indicating the victim has pursued prosecution, the M.C.I. officer will:

   (1) Complete a Supplement Report indicating the appropriate clearance status,

   (2) If the State Attorney decides to issue a capias or to upgrade the charges/offense, the case will be reassigned to patrol for proper follow-up, or

   (3) If the State Attorney Information Card indicates that the case was referred to County Court, the card will be placed in a suspense file pending final disposition. The M.C.I. officer will contact the State Attorney's Office at least every 30 days in an effort to obtain a final disposition of the case. By its own guidelines, the State Attorney's Office will have a maximum of 120 days to dispose of the case. Once a final disposition is obtained, the M.C.I. officer will clear the case by initiating a Supplement Report utilizing the appropriate clearance codes.

e. Reports generated by telephone reporting desk that require M.C.I. follow-up shall have the words "ATTENTION M.C.I. OFFICE" written in the left-hand margin of the report (the print shop will make a copy for the MCI Unit):

   (1) Upon receipt of the report, the M.C.I. officer will mail the victim a State Attorney Information Card or Juvenile Offender Card, whichever is applicable, accompanied with instructions on how to seek prosecution.

   (2) The M.C.I. officer will allow 15 days for the return of the State Attorney Information Card or Juvenile Offender Card. If the State Attorney Information Card or Juvenile Offender Card is not returned within the 15-day time period, the M.C.I. officer will clear the case by initiating a Supplement Report and using the appropriate clearance status.

   (3) If the State Attorney Information Card or Juvenile Offender Card is returned to the M.C.I. office within the 15-day period, the M.C.I. officer will clear the case using the appropriate clearance status, assign the case for patrol follow-up (i.e., arrest warrant issued, offence/charges upgraded by the State Attorney's Office), or place the card in a suspense file for further M.C.I. office follow-up.

D. Category A case status procedures require:

  1. Cases to be cleared by arrest, suspended, exceptionally cleared, or unfounded at the time of the original investigation or through a follow-up investigation

2. Cases to be cleared by arrest if an arrest is made for the offense (adult or juvenile)
3. Cases to be exceptionally cleared if the identity of the offender is known, his or her exact location is known, enough information exists to support an arrest, and the offender can be taken into custody. However, one of the following prevents an arrest:
   a. The State Attorney's Office declines to prosecute the offender, even though sufficient information exists to support an arrest and prosecution (the State Attorney's Office must be contacted in all felony cases).

NOTE: When a decision is made by the State Attorney's Office that constitutes exceptionally clearing a case, the State Attorney's name and the date he or she was contacted will be listed in the narrative of the report.

   b. The case is a felony and the victim refuses to cooperate in the prosecution or cannot be located and the State Attorney's Office declines to prosecute.
   c. The State Attorney's Office advises that the offender will be prosecuted on another violation with secondary offenses dropped or the case will be referred to another agency (i.e., Citizen Dispute, Family Violence).

NOTE: If the offender is a juvenile, the case is minor, and the officer prefers to handle the case orally or by written notice to the parents, the case can be exceptionally cleared or diverted for other action with approval of a supervisor.

   d. The offender is deceased.
4. Cases shall be suspended if:
   a. The follow-up investigation has been unsuccessful in producing sufficient information regarding the suspect(s),
   b. An arrest, warrant, or summons was issued for the arrest of a suspect but not yet served, or
   c. The S.A.O. declines to prosecute due to a lack of evidence, or there is a lack of information to support an arrest.
5. Cases shall be unfounded when an officer's investigation reveals that the offense never actually occurred.
6. The case status information shall be documented on the General Offense/Incident or Supplement Reports.
7. Supplement Reports are submitted by officers who have been assigned to the M.C.I. unit. M.C.I. unit personnel will collect these supplemental reports form the print shop and clear the case based on the final case status indicated on the report.

NOTE: By following the procedures outlined regarding M.C.I. follow-up investigations, sergeants no longer need to make copies of reports as long as the M.C.I. investigation form is clearly marked in the left-hand margin of the report with either "Attention-MCI Office" or MCI-Patrol Follow-up."

E. Category B assignment procedures are as follows:
  1. The Detective Division has primary responsibility for follow-up investigations of Category B offenses.
  2. If a Patrol Division officer initiates an investigation with solvability factors that would indicate the case can be cleared by a Patrol follow-up investigation, the officer shall mark "Yes" for "Patrol Investigation Continuing" on the General Offense/Incident Report.
     a. The Patrol Officer has investigative responsibility for this case through the end of the *fifth calendar day*.
     b. On category B cases, prior to the end of the *fifth calendar day*, a Supplement Report detailing the results of the Patrol Officer's investigation shall be submitted by the Patrol Officer assigned to the case.
  3. Although the Patrol Officer has assumed investigative responsibility for following up the case, a Detective will be assigned to the case after the fifth calendar day if it is not cleared by patrol. During the five-day period, the detective will forward all inquiries regarding the investigation to the Patrol Officer conducting the investigation and will be available to provide assistance to the Patrol Officer if needed.
F. Category B case status procedures require:
  1. The original investigating Patrol Officer to provide one of the following case clearance statuses on the Supplement Report:
     a. Unfounded
     b. Suspended (only for those cases for which a warrant of capias was issued but not served)
     c. Patrol efforts suspended or forwarded to the Detective Division for further investigation
     d. Cleared (either exceptionally or by arrest)

NOTE: Officers are reminded that interrogations of arrested suspects by detectives are required in certain Category B offenses.

  2. Officers within the department who wish to pursue cases beyond the five-day time limit must first consult with the detective assigned the case and coordinate all activities (i.e., interview, interrogations, filing, search warrants, etc.) through the detective. Extensions beyond the original five-day period will be granted on case-by-case basis by a Patrol Supervisor who will ensure the case is coordinated with the detective assigned the case.
G. Category C assignment procedures are as follows:
  1. The Detective Division has total responsibility for follow-up on all cases in this category.
  2. All investigative work beyond the preliminary investigation shall be coordinated with the detective assigned to the case.
  3. Any new information relevant to a case should be submitted on a Supplement Report.
H. Patrol Officers will consult the individual Operational Orders for each of the offenses in this category and follow the procedures outlined within those orders.

1. Patrol Officers will mark "No" for "Patrol Investigation Continuing" on the General Offense/Incident Report.
2. Patrol Officers cannot clear or suspend the *final* case status for Category C offenses.
3. Patrol Officers will, once they have completed their investigation, indicate at the end of the narrative section of their report "Patrol Efforts Suspended."

I. Patrol Officers are not restricted from making arrests for Category C offenses based upon their preliminary investigations *provided*:
   1. Probable cause exists for arrest.
   2. A detective has not yet assumed responsibility for the investigation.
   3. A detective is called to interview the suspect prior to booking.

J. Follow-up investigations made by Patrol Officers shall be coordinated with the appropriate unit of the Detective Division.

IV. Felony Filing

A. Felony S.A.O. filing procedures require the investigating officer to file the case within either of the following:
   1. Seventy-two hours (excluding weekends and holidays) [the time period will vary from state to state] for those felony suspects who were arrested on either an arrest warrant or on probable cause as outlined in Operational Orders. Officers are not required to file on arrests made with a capias.
   2. Thirty-six hours (excluding weekends and holidays) to obtain an arrest warrant or capias for those felony suspects who are still at large.

B. Officers will not advise the victim of a felony to contact the S.A.O.
   1. The S.A.O., once the case has been filed, may choose to have the victim speak with an investigator from the S.A.O. prior to issuing a capias or warrant.
   2. The Officer should contact the victim of the felony after he or she has filed the information with the S.A.O., and the victim knows the status of the case.

C. If the victim of a felony does not wish to prosecute the suspect(s), the case may not be cleared until the officer provides the information to the S.A.O., and the S.A.O. declines to proceed with prosecution. If this is done by telephone, the call shall be properly documented with the Assistant State Attorney's name, date, and time called in the narrative of the Supplement Report.

V. Misdemeanor Filing

A. Misdemeanor S.A.O. filing procedures require the investigating officer to:
   1. Direct the victim to the S.A.O. within five working days or to HRS, juvenile detention center if the suspect is a juvenile.
   2. Explain to the victim that no further action will be taken against the suspect(s) until the victim appears personally before the S.A.O. or the juvenile authorities appear at DYS, whichever is applicable.

B. If the officer has not received the S.A.O. Information Card or the Juvenile Card within 10days, he or she shall determine if the victim has appeared, document the results in a Supplement Report, and clear the case using the appropriate clearance status.

VI. M.C.I. Case Management

A. The MCI Office maintains records and monitors all reports marked "MCI-PATROL FOLLOW-UP" (follow-up investigations conducted by Patrol Officers).

B. The MCI Office also forwards to the Patrol Division those cases from either Tele-Serv or the Detective Division that require further investigation by the Patrol Division.

1. All administratively assigned cases will be given to the appropriate zone sergeants, who will assign them to the appropriate beat officer.

2. In cases reported to the telephone reporting desk involving a vehicle where the tag number or vehicle identification number is known (e.g., gas drive-offs), telephone reporting desk personnel will conduct a vehicle registration check and indicate the registered owner(s) in the narrative of the report. The M.C.I. Officer will then forward the report to the appropriate zone sergeant of the area where the suspect may reside for follow-up, rather than the area where the offense occurred.

3. The zone sergeant will place the officer's name and ID number in the appropriate space on the attached, Primary Incident Report (P.I.R.). The P.I.R. sheet will be returned immediately to the M.C.I. office for proper record keeping.

4. The officer assigned to the investigation will be responsible for ensuring that the completed M.C.I. package is returned to the M.C.I. office.

5. The M.C.I. office will be responsible for maintaining records of all administratively assigned and patrol-initiated investigations.

C. Supervisors are responsible for:

1. Retrieving cases assigned by the M.C.I. unit from their respective boxes and ensuring proper assignment and follow-up are done.

2. Monitoring the progress of their officers' follow-up investigations.

3. Ensuring cooperation and coordination between different officers, watches, zones, and divisions.

D. Some cases may require officers to assist the original investigating officer by conducting a follow-up investigation. This shall be coordinated through both officers' supervisors, who will ensure full cooperation in accordance with the investigation's needs.

1. The original investigating officer will complete an interdepartmental correspondence and attach copies of all reports written thus far in the investigation. The officer will then forward this package with instructions to the officer providing the assistance.

2. Officers providing follow-up assistance will fully cooperate with the needs of the investigation and submit a Supplement Report with documentation of the actions taken, results, etc. The MCI package will be returned to the original investigating officer with copies of any new reports.

E. The original investigating officer is responsible for the final case status and for submitting the completed MCI packet through the chain of command.

F. Officers shall not conduct follow-up investigations within one hour of any shift change unless:
1. They have the approval of their supervisor, or
2. An arrest will be made in the case.

VII. Civil Cases

A. Officers are often summoned to incidents where an investigation reveals that there is no evidence of any criminal intent or that any crime has occurred. Once it has been determined that the incident is solely a civil matter, officers shall advise the complainant of the civil status and complete a General Offense/Incident Report for the following circumstances:
1. Accidental deaths
2. Serious injuries that are the result of an accident, not involving culpable negligence
3. Lost property where
   a. Serial numbers are available
   b. The item is
      (1) Valued at $1,500 or more, or
      (2) One of a kind and may be identified by its distinct markings or by photographs.

B. Incidents where the victim of a property crime does not wish to seek prosecution against any suspect shall be considered a civil matter, and the complainant shall be referred to the Civil Court Division.

VIII. Detective Call Out

A. A Homicide Detective will be called to the scene on all:
1. Unnatural deaths
2. Accidental deaths
3. Sudden and unexplained deaths
   a. If a Homicide Detective is investigating the death, he or she will be responsible for calling out the Medical Examiner, and
   b. In those instances where a detective is not conducting a follow-up investigation, the investigating officer will contact the Medical Examiner's Office by contacting the NCIC
4. Battery cases when the trauma to the victim is life threatening
5. Suspected drowning cases where the victim's body has not been recovered (except in boating accidents in which the Florida Marine Patrol is conducting the investigation)
6. Cases of abduction or kidnapping of any public figure or corporate official
7. Cases of abduction or kidnapping not fabricated from domestic quarrels and when the victim is still missing at the time the incident is reported
8. Cases of abduction or kidnapping in which the suspect(s) is not known to the victim, family, or friends, and the victim is still missing at the time the incident is reported

9. Cases in which an officer is shot or otherwise sustains a life-threatening injury inflicted by criminal means

10. Case in which an officer shoots or otherwise inflicts a life-threatening injury upon another person

B. A Detective from the Child Abuse Unit will be called out on aggravated child abuse cases in which:

1. Injuries are such that death is likely or great bodily harm has occurred, and/or

2. A suspect has been arrested in connection with the incident.

NOTE: If the incident occurs after 4:30 p.m. or on a weekend or holiday, a Homicide Detective shall be called out to conduct an investigation.

C. A Sex Crime Detective will be called out on a sexual battery case when:

1. An arrest is made

2. The victim receives great bodily harm

3. There is a burglary in connection with the incident

4. The incident appears to be a part of a pattern or series of similar crimes

D. A Robbery Detective will be called out on a bona fide robbery 24 hours a day when:

1. There is a surveillance camera activation

2. The robbery is to a financial institution

3. An abduction is involved in the robbery

4. A suspect is in custody

E. An on-duty (0800-2400) Robbery Detective will be notified of a robbery when:

1. The victim has been seriously injured

2. A business has been robbed

3. The loss is $1,000 or more

4. The suspect has been identified

F. A Traffic Homicide Detective will be called out in traffic crash cases involving:

1. Death or life-threatening injuries

2. Hit-and-run traffic crashes involving death or life-threatening injuries

G. A Detective from the Intelligence Unit shall be called out on the following incidents:

1. Any incident involving suspected or actual terrorist activity

2. Incidents involving extremist, militant, or subversive groups (i.e., anti-abortion groups, Ku Klux Klan, The Outlaw Motorcycle Gang, antinuclear groups, Satanic groups, youth gang activity, etc.)

3. Any racial/civil disorder

4. Any racial, religious, or ethnic (R.R.E.) bias incident

5. Any other incident in which the presence of an intelligence investigator may be needed and authorization is obtained from a Sergeant or higher authority

H. On all felony juvenile Serious Habitual Offender (SHO) arrests, a member of the Juvenile Intervention Team, in addition to a detective from the most appropriate unit, will interview the juvenile SHO suspect. This applies for normal operating hours for a call out during non-operating hours for detectives.

NOTE: In incidents not covered in the above articles, if an officer believes that a detective can substantially aid in the initial investigation, a supervisor may authorize a call out from the appropriate detective unit.

IX. Arrests

A. A detective will be notified so that the suspect can be interviewed before being placed in the Pre-Trial Detention Facility when an arrest is made for:

1. Robbery
2. Homicide
3. Burglary (this does not include arrests for burglary to an auto or cases in which the victim and suspect know each other, such as an ex-spouse or boyfriend/girlfriend)
4. Sexual battery
5. All other sexually related crimes
6. Auto theft, when the suspect is cooperative and
   a. Evidence indicates the operation of an auto theft ring or "chop shop"
   b. There are multiple (three or more) stolen vehicle recoveries at the same location
   c. The suspect may have substantial information involving other auto thefts
7. True cases of abduction/kidnapping not resulting from a domestic dispute or quarrel
8. Forgery
9. Drug arrests involving felony amounts of an controlled substance and a vehicle is involved
10. Drug arrests involving trafficking amounts of a controlled substance whether or not a vehicle is not involved

B. In all cases involving counterfeit money, officers will request that the Detective Dispatcher notify the U.S. Secret Service. The U.S. Secret Service is available seven days a week, 24 hours a day.

C. When a suspect is transported to polices offices for the purpose of being interviewed by a detective, the transporting officer may be requested to remain with the suspect for security reasons. Examples of situations that may dictate that the officer remain with the suspect are as follows:

1. An arrest involving multiple prisoners
2. When the arrest occurs on the evening or midnight shift and the detective is alone in the office.

D. When a vehicle is impounded with a hold for investigations, a supervisor must approve the hold. The supervisor approving the hold is responsible for determining if a detective is needed at the scene. A hold will not be placed on a vehicle unless a detective is conducting a follow-up investigation of the offense.

X. Boating Accidents

A. The Marine Patrol will be notified of all boating accidents involving injury, death, or damages in excess of $500.

B. Depending on the circumstances of the accident and personnel availability, the Marine Patrol may or may not respond to the scene.

C. NCIC will notify the Marine Patrol of the accident. The investigating officer will inform NCIC of:
1. The extent of damages
2. The severity of any injuries
3. Any obstruction to navigation as a result of the accident.

XI. Other Call Outs

A. Requests for needed support services will be made as follows:
1. If the Medical Examiner is needed, officers will notify a Supervisor.
   a. The Supervisor will request homicide detectives to respond the scene
   b. The homicide detective will notify the NCIC dispatcher, who will call the Medical Examiner

NOTE: When homicide detectives do not respond to the scene, officers will obtain permission from their supervisor prior to calling the Medical Examiner.

2. Wrecker services will be requested via the NCIC dispatcher.
3. Department of Transportation assistance will be requested via the NCIC dispatcher.
4. Streets and Highways Department and public utility companies will be requested via the NCIC dispatcher.
5. Other non-emergency services should be requested via the NCIC dispatcher.

B. Notifications for Fire/Rescue, Evidence Technicians, supervisor, etc. will be made via the Zone Dispatcher. Notifications or requests for detective will be made through the Detective Dispatcher.
C. The Police Information Officer will notify the news media of any congestion or road closures due to crashes. No information as to victims or injuries should be given at this time.
D. An Evidence Technician will be called to photograph every traffic crash or damage incident involving Sheriff's Office vehicles or personnel.
E. The City Insurance Adjuster will be
1. Requested to respond to traffic crashes involving city-owned or -leased vehicles or property, including vehicles owned or leased by the Sheriff's Office, only when there is personal injury involved.

NOTE: Officers are not required to notify the City Insurance Adjuster when the vehicle is owned or leased by either the local utility authority, the local transportation authority, or the county school board.

2. Notified in cases of damage to property by an officer (e.g., kicking in a door on service of a search warrant, damaging a vehicle during a search, etc.) only when there is a personal injury involved.
F. The U.S. Secret Service will be notified in all cases that involve counterfeit money (see IX.B. of this order).

Chief of Police

Glossary

Abandonment: Giving something up without limitation as to any particular person or purpose.

Actus reus: The guilty act; a wrongful deed taken in furtherance of the criminal intent of the guilty mind. When the *actus reus* and the *mens rea* are present, a crime has occurred.

Admissibility: All items of evidence are admissible as long as they are both relevant and material, subject to certain other restrictions.

Admission: A statement or conduct made out of court by someone who is involved in the case that is inconsistent with the position he or she is currently taking or defending at trial.

Autopsy: The dissection of a body to determine the cause of death.

Burden of proof: It is the state's obligation to prove the defendant's guilt.

Burglary: The breaking and entering of an inhabitable structure with the intent to commit a crime.

Chain of custody: Evidence must be presented to a jury in substantially the same condition it was found.

Circumstantial evidence: Indirect evidence; secondary facts by which a principal fact may be rationally inferred.

Community oriented policing: A department-wide strategy aimed at solving persistent community problems. Police identify, analyze, and respond to the underlying circumstances that create incidents. Also referred to as **problem oriented policing**.

Confession: A statement admitting or acknowledging all the facts necessary for conviction of the crime at issue.

Corroborate: To strengthen or add to the weight of credibility by additional facts or evidence.

Corroborative evidence: Evidence that supports other direct or circumstantial evidence by showing reliability of sources.

Crime: An intentional act or omission in violation of criminal law (statutory or case law), committed without defense or justification, and sanctioned by the state as a felony or misdemeanor.

Criminal investigation: The process of legally gathering evidence of a crime that has been or is being committed.

Cumulative evidence: Additional evidence on issues that have already been proven by direct or circumstantial evidence.

Curtilage: The ground and buildings that are for the exclusive use of the person living there, including residential yards, fenced areas, garages, and outbuildings close to the house.

Defense: That which is offered and alleged by the party proceeded against, in an action or suit, as a reason in law or the fact why the plaintiff should not recover or establish what he or she seeks.

Direct evidence: Evidence that directly proves a fact in issue.

Documentary evidence (sometimes referred to as **writings**): Evidence in writing (checks, ransom notes, robbery notes, and suicide notes).

Entrapment defense: A person cannot be lured into the commission of a crime by police and then be prosecuted for it.

Evidence: Any species of proof, or probative matter, legally presented at the trial of an issue for the purpose of inducing belief in the minds of the court or jury as to their contention.

Felony: A serious crime punishable by more than one-year incarceration or imprisonment in a state or federal penitentiary.

Hearsay: A statement, other than one made by the declarant while testifying at the trial or hearing, offered in evidence, to prove the truth of the matter asserted.

Homicide: The killing of a human by a human.

Infancy: The period to reaching the age of legal majority.

Insanity: As a legal term, a mental disorder that affects the defendant's ability to exercise free will.

Interrogation: An interview in which the investigator is seeking to obtain information from someone who has been identified as a suspect in a crime.

Investigative detention: A peace officer has the authority to stop and briefly detain persons when the officer has a reasonable suspicion that the person has committed or is about to commit a crime.

Involuntary manslaughter: Criminally negligent homicide.

Judicial notice: Evidence of facts that are common knowledge.

Larceny: A trespassory taking and carrying away (asportation) of the personal property of another with the intention of depriving the owner of its use.

Malice: (1) The absence of all elements of justification, excuse, or recognized mitigation, and (2) the presence of either (a) an actual intent to cause the particular harm that is produced or harm of some general nature, or (b) the wanton or willful doing of an act with the awareness of a plain or strong likelihood that such harm may result.

Mens rea: A guilty mind; a guilty or wrongful purpose; a criminal intent. Guilty knowledge or willfulness. The intent to commit a crime.

Miranda rights: All suspects have the right to (1) remain silent, (2) be told that anything they say can be used in court, (3) have the advice of an attorney before and during the interrogation, and (4) have an attorney appointed by the court to represent them if they cannot afford one.

Misdemeanor: A crime punishable by less than a year of incarceration or imprisonment in a county or city jail.

Modus operandi (method of operation): The means by which a criminal commits a particular type of crime.

Motive: A need or desire that causes a person to act.

Munchausen syndrome by proxy (MSBP): A phenomenon in which a mother harms her child in order to receive attention from various medical and other professional personnel.

Murder: The unlawful killing of a human by a human with malice.

Plain view seizure: Police can seize anything immediately recognized as evidence if it is in plain view.

Preponderance of evidence: Evidence that is of greater weight or more convincing than the evidence that is offered in opposition to it; that is, evidence that as a whole shows that the fact sought to be proved is more probable than not.

Presumption: A rule of law that enables the party, in whose favor the presumption operates, to take the case to the jury without even presenting evidence of that fact.

Presumption of innocence: The government has the burden of proving every element of a crime beyond a reasonable doubt, and the defendant has no burden to prove his innocence.

Privileges: Rules of law that prevent the use of some evidence that would otherwise be admissible.

Proactive criminal investigation: A type of criminal investigation that emphasizes intelligence gathering and covert investigative techniques that target ongoing criminal activities, such as drug dealing, prostitution, and other types of organized criminal activities.

Probable cause: Where the facts and circumstances within the knowledge of the arresting officers are sufficient in themselves to warrant a person of reasonable caution to believe that an offense has been or is being committed.

Problem oriented policing: A department-wide strategy aimed at solving persistent community problems. Police identify, analyze, and respond to the underlying circumstances that create incidents. Also referred to as **community oriented policing**.

Proof beyond a reasonable doubt: Proof that leaves you firmly convinced of the defendant's guilt.

Proof: The effect of evidence; the establishment of a fact by evidence. Any fact or circumstance that leads the mind to the affirmative or negative of any proposition.

Rape: Unlawful sexual intercourse with a female by force or against her will.

Reactive investigations: Begin after a crime has been reported to the police. There are three types: "walk through," the "whodunit," and the "where are they" investigations.

Real evidence: Often referred to as physical evidence; consists of tangible objects that the jury can see.

Reasonable suspicion: That amount of evidence needed to justify an investigative detention.

Rigor mortis: The stiffening of muscles in the body, brought about by chemical changes that occurs after death.

Robbery: Stealing by force.

Search: A governmental intrusion into an area where a person has a reasonable expectation of privacy.

Self-defense: The right of every person to defend himself or herself against death or injury.

Solvability factors: Checklist of items of evidence that both patrol officers and supervisors can use to ensure the preliminary investigation is complete.

Stealing: A taking and a carrying away of the personal property of another with the intent to steal.

Sudden infant death syndrome (SIDS): The sudden death of an infant under one year old that remains unexplained after the performance of a complete postmortem investigation, including an autopsy, an examination of the scene of death, and a review of the case history.

Suspicion: More than no proof, but there is not enough evidence to justify any type of governmental intrusion into any area where someone has an expectation of privacy.

Testimonial evidence: Oral testimony provided by witnesses to a crime.

Totality of circumstances test: A test used extensively to determine the constitutionality of aspects of search and seizure. It emphasizes all the facts and circumstances in a situation, rather than a single factor.

Trier of fact: Refers to the eprson (the judge in a bench trial) or body of people (the jury in a jury trial) who has the exclusive obligation to make findings of fact in a legal proceeding.

Voluntary manslaughter: Unlawful homicide committed without malice aforethought.

Walk-through investigations: The suspect is already known to the police, and in many cases the suspect is in custody.

Where-are-they investigations (also referred to as **fugitive investigations**): The suspect has been identified, and it is the investigator's task to locate him or her.

Whodunit investigations: No suspect has been immediately identified.

Index

weight of evidence, 48
Criminals, government should not make
    deals with, 17
CSA (Controlled Substances Act), 262–63
Cumulative evidence, 50
Cupp v. Murphy, 190–91
Custody
    chain of, 89–90
    suspects in, 155–56
Cutting and piercing instruments, suicide
    by, 196–97
Cyanoacrylate (super glue fuming), 101–2

D

Databases, 311
Date rapes, 216
DEA (Drug Enforcement Agency), 66, 136
Death investigations, 177–206
Debris, inspection of, 253
Deceased's eyes, observing, 181–82
Deception
    arguments against use of, 16–20
        do not harm innocent, 18–20
        government should not make deals
            with criminals, 17
        government should not tempt weak, 18
        lying is immoral, 16–17
        truth telling is moral, 16–17
    is acceptable when used to accomplish
        good end, 15
    is acceptable when used to obtain convic-
        tion, 15–16
    using in criminal investigation, 13–14
    verbal and physical signs of, 165–66
Declarations, dying, 55
Defense attacks on prosecution's case,
    anticipation, 298–99
Defense wounds, 191
Defenses, 6–10
    anticipating, 9
    committed without defense of justifica-
        tion, 6–9
        entrapment, 8
        infancy, 6
        insanity, 6–7
        involuntary intoxication, 7–8
        self-defense, 9
    as felonies, 10
    as misdemeanors, 10
    sanctioned by state, 9
    in sexual assault cases, 215–16
Defense's case-in-chief, 295–96
Defense's closing arguments, 296
Defense's opening statements, 295
Deoxyribonucleic Acid (DNA), 109–10, 186

Depressants, 268–69
Detention, investigative, 43, 118, 134
Devices, timing, 256
Dickerson, Minnesota v., 44–45
Dickerson v. United States, 158–59
Direct evidence, 50
Dive team organization, 112–13
Dives, planning, 113–14
DNA (Deoxyribonucleic Acid), 109–10, 186
Doctrines
    Minnesota v. Dickerson and plain feel,
        44–45
    open fields, 46
Documentary evidence, 49
Doubt, proof beyond reasonable, 30–31
Dress and appearance, 162
Drowning, suicide by, 196
    case study, 196
Drug courier profile, 134–35
Drug Enforcement Agency (DEA), 66, 136
Drug investigations, 261–83
    drugs of abuse, 262–69
    proactive investigations, 261–62
Drug possession cases, 279–81
Drug-related crimes, investigating, 269–82
    briefing other officers, 277
    buy money, 277–78
    controlled buys of drugs, 269–71
    discussing stories with informants,
        278–79
    do's and don'ts of dealing with infor-
        mants, 271–74
    drug possession cases, 279–81
    entrapment, 271
    intercepting and recording conversations,
        274–77
    possession with intent to distribute,
        281–82
    searching informants, 277
    undercover officers, 279
Drugfire, 104–5
Drugs
    of abuse, 262–69
        cannabis, 263–65
        Comprehensive Drug Abuse Preven-
            tion and Control Act of 1970,
            262–63
        depressants, 268–69
        hallucinogens, 267–68
        narcotics, 263–65
        stimulants, 266–67
    controlled buys of, 269–71
    suicide by, 196
Due process, 151–52
Dying declarations, 55